Children's Literature
Volume 28

The editors gratefully acknowledge support from Hollins University.

Volume 28

Annual of
The Modern Language Association
Division on Children's Literature
and The Children's Literature
Association

Yale University Press

New Haven and London

2000

Children's Literature

Manuscripts submitted should conform to the style in this issue. An original on non-erasable bond with two copies, a self-addressed envelope, and return postage are requested. Yale University Press does not accept dot-matrix printouts, and it requires double-spacing throughout text and notes. Unjustified margins are required. Writers of accepted manuscripts should be prepared to submit final versions of their essays on computer disk in Word 97 or Rich Text Format.

Volumes 1–7 of *Children's Literature* can be obtained directly from John C. Wandell, The Children's Literature Foundation, P.O. Box 370, Windham Center, Conn. 06280. Volumes 8–26 can be obtained from Yale University Press, P.O. Box 209040, New Haven, Conn. 06520-9040, or from Yale University Press, 23 Pond Street, Hampstead, London NW3 2PN, England.

Editorial correspondence should be addressed to The Editors, *Children's Literature,* Hollins University, P.O. Box 9677, Roanoke, Virginia 24020 or to child.lit@hollins.edu

Set in Baskerville type by Tseng Information Systems, Inc., Durham, N.C.
Printed in the United States of America by Vail-Ballou Press, Binghamton, N.Y.

Library of Congress catalog card number: 79-66588
ISBN: 0-300-08234-7 (cloth), 0-300-08235-5 (paper); ISSN 0092-8208

A catalogue record for this book is available from the British Library.

The paper in this book meets the guidelines for permanence and durability of the Committee on Production Guidelines for Book Longevity of the Council on Library Resources.

10   9   8   7   6   5   4   3   2   1

PN
1009
.A1
C514
V.28

Contents

In Memoriam

Reviews

From the Editors

Volume 28, appearing at the close of both a century and a millennium, marks the end of another era as well. It is the first volume to have been planned after the death of its founder, Francelia Butler, and the editors would like to dedicate it to her memory. As most readers of *Children's Literature* know, Francelia was a pioneer in the field of children's literature. Not only did she found this journal nearly thirty years ago but she was also instrumental in founding the organization it represents, the Children's Literature Association. Through these institutions, as well as her teaching, scholarship, and the National Endowment for the Humanities institutes she hosted at the University of Connecticut, Francelia touched hundreds, even thousands, of lives, including those of many contributors to this volume.

Each of us editors was influenced by her directly. Elizabeth Keyser was a participant in Francelia's first NEH institute for the study of children's literature in 1982, as were advisory board member Jan Alberghene and contributors Gillian Adams and Steve Canham. Elizabeth vividly remembers how, after the institute's opening reception, she and Gillian were spirited away to Francelia's gingerbread house for an impromptu supper. Fifteen years later Elizabeth again visited Mansfield Hollow where Francelia, despite a grueling round of chemotherapy, had organized a birthday party for Cynthia Wells, the Yale University Press editor of *Children's Literature,* and Eric Dawson, director of the Peace Games, which Francelia founded. Julie Pfeiffer and book review editor Chris Doyle, like contributor Anne Phillips, were graduate students at the University of Connecticut during Francelia's last days there, and they co-edited the last volume of *Children's Literature* to be produced at UConn. Former book review editor John Cech, author of a poem dedicated to Francelia that appears in these pages, belongs to an earlier generation of her students. Editor-in-Chief Richard Dillard knew Francelia when they were both graduate students at the University of Virginia, and we are delighted to publish his essay, which, among other things, recalls the beginning of her academic career. In a very real sense, Francelia has brought all of us—board members, consultants, editors, and contributors—together, for which we are extremely grateful.

In recent years, Francelia turned her still-prodigious energy to battles (and we use the word advisedly) on two fronts. One was personal. As many readers know, Francelia lived far longer than anyone expected her to, given the virulent nature of her disease; time and again her cancer went into remission, seemingly because she willed it to do so. What kept her alive (to the astonishment of her medical advisors) was undoubtedly her larger battle, which, as Eric Dawson describes in "Francelia's Dream," was for nothing less visionary than world peace. Were Francelia still alive, she would be delighted by the articles in this volume that touch on or deal directly with the subject of peace education, from Peter Hollindale's discussion of the Quaker Anna Sewell's "plain speaking," to Penny Mahon's article on early peace educators ("Things by Their Right Name"), to Phyllis Bixler's account of the Lion and the Lamb Peace Center. But were Francelia with us as this volume goes to press, she would doubtless be appalled at the continuing violence in such places as Yugoslavia and East Timor. Francelia's vision of a world at peace, to which she dedicated the last years of her life, seems sadly more remote, though more desirable, than ever. She would not have despaired, however; nor, if we honor her legacy, should we.

In order to commemorate the end of the twentieth century, especially the past three decades, which, thanks in large part to Francelia's efforts, have been so rich for children's literature scholarship, we have asked Perry Nodelman, author of the influential *The Pleasures of Children's Literature* and *Words About Pictures,* to share with us his ruminations on the distinctive characteristics of children's literature (it is interesting to compare these with the thoughts of James Pettit Andrews, who, as Andrea Immel discusses in the "Varia" section, attempted to characterize children's literature at the end of his own century, the eighteenth). Then we asked two equally well-known scholars as well as members of our editorial board, Roderick McGillis and Margaret Higonnet, to respond to Perry's essay (a term that accurately describes its tentative nature). In addition to Rod and Margaret, we asked Tom Travisano, an advocate for the new, or newly defined, field of childhood studies, to comment on Perry's work. Then we gave Perry the opportunity to respond to his respondents. We hope that the resulting forum on the multiple pleasures of the genre will, as Perry hoped, provide insight or at least stimulate the kind of thinking that, as Margaret Higonnet believes of children's literature, leads to growth. But we also hope that the forum will itself provide some immediate pleasures, not the least of which may be the opportunity to hear scholars converse without pretension in their own distinctive voices. As Rod McGillis says in his opening paragraph, "let me say at the outset that I shall drop the scholarly convention of citation by surname and refer to my partner in conversation as Perry." He goes on to praise Perry's "circumspect" use of "specialized vocabulary," his willingness to write "in a language that does not foreground its specialized discourse." Contributors to the forum have been concerned to speak as plainly as possible and, if skeptical about the possibility of "right" names, at least careful to find appropriate and accessible terms for difficult concepts.

Our forum is followed by an essay that, like several of the books reviewed in this volume (such as the two on fairies in Victorian culture and Anne Higonnet's *Pictures of Innocence*), represents the intersection of children's literature and childhood studies identified by Tom Travisano. Kenneth Kidd's fascinating study of boyology at the beginning and ending of the twentieth century reveals how consistent have been our efforts to identify, celebrate, and preserve a unique boys' culture while ensuring that we prepare boys for responsible participation in our own. In fact, the theory and practice of boyology, as Kidd describes it, seem to have afforded some of the pleasure that Perry Nodelman attributes to children's literature — a tension between an innocent hedonism (experienced nostalgically and vicariously by adults) and its sacrifice on the altar of a gratifying superior knowledge. Readers will also be able to link the century-old tradition of boyology to the emerging discipline of childhood studies. Perhaps Kidd's provocative essay can enable proponents of the one to avoid the many pitfalls of the other.

Marilynn Olson, in her essay on the Golliwogg phenomenon, is also concerned with culture at the turn of the century, but whereas Kidd discusses early twentieth-century science and social science, Olson deals with developments in the visual and performing arts, and whereas he stresses continuity, she emphasizes how our sensibility in regard to such matters as race, gender, and colonialism has changed. Unlike Kidd, Olson focuses on specific works of children's literature, but she too is interested in the power of children's books to both reflect and shape adult culture. In fact, on reading Olson's essay in conjunction with Joseph Stanton's on Maurice Sendak (a contested case among forum contributors), it is tempting to see Sendak, with his immense popularity, commercialization, and links to other artistic media, as the Florence Upton of his generation. But, as Stanton indicates, Sendak's books, especially the later ones, lack the persistent lightheartedness that characterized the Uptons' Golliwogg and dolls. And unlike the adult readers who reveled in the Golliwogg, many of Sendak's adult readers have been more disturbed than delighted.

Peter Hollindale and Hamida Bosmajian reexamine individual works published a century apart. Hollindale, in a revisionist reading of *Black Beauty,* convincingly argues for its artistry as well as for its effectiveness as propaganda. As his title, "Plain Speaking," indicates, he is especially attentive to Sewell's language. Its precision, which he attributes to her Quaker heritage, also characterizes the antiwar tales of Anna Barbauld and John Aikin, published at the turn of the previous century. In these tales, as Penny Mahon demonstrates in her "Varia" essay, plain speaking becomes a means of exposing the vainglorious nature of war. The need for plain speaking, for calling "things by their right name," or at least by names that do not obfuscate and obscure, persists and perhaps has never been greater than in dealing with the Holocaust. Yet how does one present this subject accurately to children and young adults? Hamida Bosmajian explains how Doris Orgel in *The Devil in Vienna* accomplishes this feat while managing to spare young readers the full horror of her own nightmare experience. Indirection and elision enable Orgel to communicate as much of the truth as her young audience, and perhaps she herself, can bear.

Peace, pleasure, and plain speaking, then, are among the themes of volume 28. They were all valued by the founder of *Children's Literature* (who was famous for not pulling any punches), and she did much to ensure that they would prevail. As we prepare to move into the next century and millennium without her, we trust that her efforts will not have been in vain.

Elizabeth Lennox Keyser and Julie Pfeiffer

Articles

FORUM

Pleasure and Genre: Speculations on the Characteristics of Children's Fiction

Perry Nodelman

I like to read children's books. They gave me pleasure as a child, and it was the fact that they continued to give me pleasure as an adult that led me to focus my attention as a literary scholar on them. The assumption I begin with is that my pleasure might be a valuable source of insight. Understanding more about it might help me to determine which qualities make children's books different from others—a distinct kind of writing, a genre.

On the face of it, the children's books that particularly give me pleasure—older texts such as Beatrix Potter's *The Tale of Peter Rabbit,* Maurice Sendak's *Where the Wild Things Are,* and E. B. White's *Charlotte's Web,* newer ones such as Francesca Lia Block's *Weetzie Bat* or the picture books of Chris Raschka or the novels of the Canadian writer Brian Doyle—are quite different from each other. But they do have two things in common. First, they share the characteristics most usually identified with texts written for children, the ones I list in a chapter on this subject in my book *Pleasures of Children's Literature.* At least in comparison to many adult literary texts, they are short, simple, often didactic in intention, and clearly positive in their outlook on life— optimistic, with happy endings. But second, as the extensive critical discussion of many of these texts implies, their apparent simplicity contains depths, often surprisingly pessimistic qualifications of the apparent optimism, dangerously and delightfully counterproductive

Children's Literature 28, eds. Elizabeth Lennox Keyser and Julie Pfeiffer (Yale University Press, © 2000 Hollins University).

possibilities that oppose and undermine the apparent messages. These texts can be easily and effortlessly heard or read, but once read, they continue to develop significance, importance, complexity, to echo ever outward and inward. These are texts that resonate.

I like them, I believe, *because* they resonate—because they seem so simple and yet allow for so much thought. There's something magical about texts so apparently straightforward being so non-straightforward. I find more obviously complex texts much less magical.

These texts resonate so magically, I think, because they are trying to be optimistic and didactic at once. That's inherently self-contradictory; it leads to ambivalence, subtlety—resonance.

The nature of the contradiction becomes more apparent in a consideration of texts for children that are less obviously ambivalent. Many children's books (books that I tend to enjoy less) are either more purely didactic or more purely optimistic, preachy tomes about trains that stay on the track and teenagers who learn to cope with bullies or wish-fulfillment fantasies about children who defeat evil villains and save the world. Such books represent two opposite ways in which adults like to address children, based, I think, on different ways of thinking about how children differ from adults. The didactic stance implies that children are weak or fallible or somehow mistaken—in need of instruction in how to be better people, that is, more like adults. The wish-fulfillment stance implies that children are not only just fine as they already are but that what they wish for in their child-like, egocentric way is exactly what they need to imagine and ought to be. (I hasten to point out that the wish-fulfillment stance is, in its way, just as didactic as the other. It represents a way in which some adults like to imagine childhood and, I suspect therefore, would like children to imagine themselves. As a result, these books also work to teach children—albeit for a different purpose and in different and more subtle ways.)

These two opposing attitudes float free in our culture and in our minds—two contradictory ways we all tend to think about children, often at the same time. The texts I most enjoy try to do both these things at once. As didactic fables, they want to urge children to stop being childish and learn to be better and different. As wish-fulfillment fantasies, they want children to stay exactly as they so wonderfully are. They happily inform us that Peter Rabbit or Max of the Wild Things matures by being triumphantly wild and childlike, that Anne of Green Gables or Weetzie Bat can grow up without actually changing at all. Their ambivalence results from these pulls in opposite directions.

Nor is the ambivalence about idealizing childhood and condemning its inadequacies the only pull there is. There are others. Consider, for instance, a quality I suggested in *Pleasures* might be characteristic: that many texts for children are focalized specifically through the minds of child characters or begin, at least, by describing a world in ways that writers assume a child might understand. Even third-person narrators tend to speak of little more than what their protagonists can perceive and therefore show us little more than how their protagonists view and understand the world they move through. Usually, that understanding is an innocent one, based on our assumption that children lack the knowledge that comes with experience. But intriguingly, innocence—lack of knowledge—seems inevitably to imply its opposite. It does so, necessarily, differently for young, inexperienced readers than for me—but I think I can make a case that it does so in some way for both inexperienced readers and jaded sophisticates, so that the pleasures I obtain from these books may be not so different from the pleasures experienced by younger readers.

For myself, part of the pleasure of reading children's books comes from knowing more and better than the focalized characters do. I enjoy the opening of *Charlotte's Web* in part because I see through Fern's wonderfully complete ignorance of the world's complexities and of the implications of life on a farm. I know that in ridding the world of injustice, as her father says, she is committing herself to a position that, if followed through logically, would deprive her family of its income and herself of her happiness. I gain a similar pleasure from knowing more than Harriet does about the behavior of the people she spies on in *Harriet the Spy*, and, perhaps in a more sentimental vein, from admiring Anne of Green Gables's blithe ignorance of the ways in which her enthusiastic imaginings might conflict with more conventional adult standards. For me, the innocence of the point of view inevitably implies a wider realm of knowledge that I can compare the innocence with. I can then see with a youthful protagonist and also against that protagonist—and be, therefore, pleasurably pulled in two opposite directions. And in a really good book, I never have to conclude, as I do in overly obvious didactic fables, that ignorance is absolutely dangerous, or else, as I do in overly obvious wish-fulfillment stories, that ignorance is absolute and total bliss. I am left perennially pulled, in a state of wonderfully engaging and, for me, wonderfully pleasurable tension.

By definition, the inexperienced child readers who might more logically be viewed as the intended audience of these texts do not possess such a degree of knowledge and therefore cannot possibly have the same double relation with a childlike narrative point of view. They might, nevertheless, experience the doubleness, sequentially rather than simultaneously, as they make their way through a children's book.

Almost every children's story that starts by describing its protagonist's childlike point of view seems to come to a triumphant climax at the moment when the child sees past the innocence, acknowledges it as ignorance, and becomes more mature. In both *The Tale of Peter Rabbit* and *Where the Wild Things Are,* for instance, a movement into a pleasurably self-involved wish-fulfilling fantasy based on a relatively ignorant idea of what is possible leads the child protagonist to a moment of awareness that disperses the fantasy and leads him back to his family, presumably more mature and wiser. Thus, what at first appears merely pleasurably innocent turns out to be dangerously ignorant in relation to a wisdom achieved later. These books allow child readers to enjoy their identification with an innocent point of view only at the expense of being forced eventually to acknowledge its limitations.

And yet, surely, much of the pleasure for a reader resides in the earlier passages that allow the innocent point of view to be indulged. Most children's books end quickly, shortly after the point at which wisdom is gained, for the activities of the wise are simply less interesting to contemplate than those of the unwise.

I might even suggest that the moment at which innocence is transcended might be merely ritualistic—an obligatory but pro forma bow to didacticism placed there only to allow the imagination to be indulged, not really intended to be taken seriously or, even when intended to be so, not always taken seriously by imaginative young readers, who might put up with it simply for the sake of the fun that precedes it. But in fact, I suspect, readers of most ages mirror my own wonderfully ambivalent response—they want to enjoy the pleasures of innocence and want also to be told of the dangers of innocence and see them lead to innocence's demise.

The most pleasurable books for me create exactly that precarious but infinitely sustainable balance. Their climactic moments celebrate maturity but do so in a way that causes me to question the completeness of its wisdom. Consider, for instance, Stevenson's *Treasure Island:* Jim Hawkins assures us at the end that his adventure has taught him to hate adventures, a move that makes him seem like a sour-minded and self-centered boob to readers who have loved to hear about the adventures and also know how rich they have made him. His maturity seems so stupid that it makes his earlier innocence seem wise, so that innocence and wisdom deliciously undermine each other. There remains a pull in opposite directions, between the pleasure of not knowing and the mastery of finding out how much you didn't know.

Furthermore, every child who reads will read the story of innocence joyfully indulged and then sensibly transcended again and again as he or she progresses through childhood. Even if the child does not possess a sophisticated adult's repertoire of wisdom, he or she will quickly learn that the innocence that allows child protagonists their adventures will always in each text come to be seen as limiting ignorance. I suspect, therefore, that many child readers read children's books as I do, in the consciousness of how the pleasure of their innocent point of view might be being balanced and qualified by the pleasures of a deeper knowledge to come and also with a sense that the deeper knowledge, which surfaces only toward the end of the story, is also going to be undercut by the innocent pleasures in the next book.[1]

It's possible, then, that readers of all ages can respond to young protagonists getting into trouble owing to their trust in their own limited wisdom both by enjoying the wonderful chaos and self-indulgence of the trouble and by standing back, realizing how stupidly the characters are behaving, and feeling superior to them. Witness the way many of us respond to Curious George or The Stupids or even Anne of Green Gables, Harriet, Jim Hawkins, or Kevin Henkes's Chrysanthemum. Readers are happy to have a story confirm their own superior wisdom by having George or Anne or Chrysanthemum realize the errors of their ways—and yet, also, offer ways to see through or beyond the imagination-destroying and excitement-controlling limitations of that wisdom, and lust after just one more story about a wonderfully self-indulgent and self-trusting innocent who gets into more delightful trouble so that they can both celebrate the trouble and condemn it.

Why is this double pull so pleasurable? In terms of questions of knowledge in particular, of what we do and don't know as readers, I think it's in part because it's a sort of hiding game—as in some versions of Zen Buddhism, which imagine that the world we call real and the selves we call real within it are all merely various ways in which the infinite presence has hidden itself from itself, so that it—that is, we—can have the pleasure of finding itself—not-we—again. There is no purpose in this but the pleasure of the process. In the books I enjoy, the knowledge that transcends innocence is hidden from the narrator—but hidden in ways that allow astute readers to find it, to know more than the narrative itself is claiming to tell. And then, the joys of freedom and possibility and innocence that undercut mature knowledge are hidden from a newly wise narration—but hidden in ways that allow astute readers to remember it, to know more than the narrative now theoretically wants us to understand and commit ourselves to. And because the game is double, because innocence undercuts newly achieved wisdom just as much as the wisdom undercuts the innocence it theoretically supersedes, there is really no move forward or backward, no final wisdom to be achieved—no purpose in the game but the pleasure of the never-ending process.

There is, I think, another aspect to the pleasure: the way it allows us to indulge repeatedly in a ritual reenactment of the move from childhood to maturity, innocence to knowledge. In real life, for each of us, that happens only once. But in each book about Curious George, George gets into trouble and learns, in theory, not to be so curious. In almost every chapter of *Anne of Green Gables,* Anne gets into trouble and learns not to be so enthusiastic and unrestrained. And in children's book after children's book, characters get into trouble and learn wisdom from it, only to be superseded by the next character moving beyond innocence in the next book.

There are a number of Jungian interpretations of children's novels that identify various characters as the protagonist's shadow or anima, and describe how the story replicates an individual's move toward psychic integration. Such interpretations usually make the assumption that the fictional representation of this psychic voyage somehow takes readers along the same path, through chaos toward mental health. If they do, though, why would a reader who has gone through the process once and become an integrated whole as a result of it ever again need or want to read a similar book that replicated the experience? The answer might be the pleasure of the repetition. In the reading of children's fiction, the one-directional move from innocence to wisdom, ignorance to knowledge, youth to age and inevitably death is replaced by endless recurrence. Age succeeds youth only to be magically succeeded by youth once more. As we begin to read a children's book, each of us, young or old, can view the world as a child yet again, become, in imagination at least, a child yet again. And also, as we move toward the end of a children's book each of us, old or young, can grow wise and learn more than children know. As long as we continue to read these books, we can be ever again young and innocent, ever again older and wiser.

That ought to be impossible—which suggests another pleasurable aspect of children's books. They tend to deny impossibility. Indeed, I might almost commit myself to the position that the main subject of children's fiction is just that: impossible things happening. Rabbits talk and dress like humans, and spiders spell words in their webs. Forests grow in bedrooms and there are fairies at the bottom of the garden. The impossible happens even when the stories seem to take place in more obviously realistic worlds and are not so clearly fantastic. Young girls survive childhoods full of abuse with their cheerful good spirits intact and convert entire townships to their optimistic ways of perceiving things. Young boys almost single-handedly defeat entire crews of pirates. Other children successfully and even fairly easily survive in the wilds or in concentration camps or find ways of forging friendships with those who have declared undying enmity toward them.

The most important aspect of these impossibilities is that they *are* impossible or at best highly improbable, at least in the world we actually inhabit outside the confines of the texts, and that in the texts they nevertheless do happen. I love it when the world of a fiction allows more, and different, and more interesting possibilities than the world I know I'm actually stuck with.

I know I am not alone in this. A young reader of my fantasy novel *The Same Place but Different* wrote to ask if anything like what the novel describes ever happened to me—if I'd actually ever met any of the Strangers, the pernicious creatures from British fairy lore the novel describes. He suspected it hadn't, but he was hoping, fervently hoping. He wanted, he said, something like that to happen to him.

I don't. Although I love to imagine it happening, I would probably have a heart attack right on the spot if it actually did happen. It would be awful if a Stranger actually strolled into my life, just awful. Unlike my character Johnny Nesbit, I wouldn't know what to do. I'd probably end up whining or hiding in a dark closet until somebody else dealt with the problem and saved me and the rest of the universe. One of the reasons I like books of all sorts is that they allow me to enjoy experiences I would *not* enjoy in reality. All things considered, I think I like reality the way it is, like it enough to accept its occasional boring patches and its awful habit of letting bad things happen to good people. And I think I like impossible fictions because I know always exactly how impossible they are.

But their impossibility is not the only thing I like about them. I know that because I've gone through periods in my life when I've concentrated on reading other kinds of impossible fictions, science fiction or fantasy intended for adults, but eventually, always, I stop. I get bored. And I haven't yet got bored enough with children's fiction to stop reading it. So I have to ask why? What's the difference?

The difference reveals a second important aspect of my love of the impossible. I love it best when it happens in the context of a firmly established possible, and when the narrative in which it occurs takes a decidedly matter-of-fact attitude toward it. Thus, I particularly love *Charlotte's Web* because the story of the talking and writing spider emerges fairly seamlessly from a realistic story about life on a farm. I particularly love *Where the Wild Things Are* because an extraordinary forest grows inside a perfectly ordinary bedroom and the narrator doesn't seem at all surprised by it. I particularly love the ways in which the surrealistic details in various picture books by Anthony Browne are utterly unaccounted for—so much a part of the world of the narrative, apparently, that the narrator doesn't need to account for them or even mention them as being especially noteworthy aspects of the scene in front of us.

I do, of course, enjoy fantasies such as Ursula K. Le Guin's Earthsea books, which take place entirely in an alternate universe and thus deprive me of the pleasure of encountering impossibilities in the midst of a recognizable reality. But I don't enjoy them as much as books that include fantasy elements in real settings—and I tend not to see them as characteristic of children's fiction, which tends more toward Peter Pans and Treasure Seekers than it does to Earthseas.

My taste for the impossible appearing in a context of the familiar seems to be one more version of the knowledge game I talked about earlier. As I said, I like the impossible because I can recognize it as exactly that. So when a narrator matter-of-factly tells me that something impossible has just happened, I know I am being outrageously lied to—but lied to by someone who doesn't seem to know he or she is lying, or if he or she does, is quite fervently unwilling to admit it. Consider this opening sentence of a Grimm tale: "There were once a mouse, a bird, and a sausage that decided to set up housekeeping together."[2] It's wonderful to consider the possible existence of such a strange household; it would be less wonderful if I didn't know the true character of mice, birds, and sausages and therefore imagined that it might actually happen. Meanwhile, however, I'm wrong. In the world of the story, the impossible is not impossible. I know that sausages can't talk, but this particular sausage, the story tells me, just did.

The mouse, the bird, and the sausage are indeed living out their domestic drama before my eyes. I know that of course they can't be. I am reading that of course they are. So here I am again, being pleasurably pulled in two opposite directions by competing forms of knowledge, one based on innocence of the laws of real possibility, one based on an experienced acceptance of them.

It seems clear, then, that questions of competing forms of knowledge are central to children's literature—not all that surprising, since its very existence is predicated on distinguishing children from adults primarily on the basis of their innocence—what they don't yet know. But the pull in two opposite directions appears to be fundamental to all sorts of pleasure. Sexual pleasure tends to consist equally of the pleasure of delayed orgasm and the pleasure of the orgasm itself, so that the overriding pleasure results from the intermingling of the two, the pull between them. Fictional plots often offer a form of exactly this same tension—the pleasurable suspense of delayed knowledge and the pleasurable release of knowledge finally revealed. Will the sausage survive its predatory house mates? I want to know, I need to know, I don't want to know quite yet.

Most fiction, in books, in movies, and on television, offers some form of this tension. But children's fiction offers it in particularly intense forms for one other important reason—and one final source of particular pleasure for me. The children's fiction I most enjoy tends to exprss itself most often in terms of describing meetings and intermingling of things that are seen, by us and by the narrator and the characters, as belonging in different or even opposite categories. This fiction tends to misrepresent the complexities of the world we live in by organizing its spectrum of subtle variations into sets of fairly rigid binary oppositions that intersect in the same place or even within the same character.

In *Pleasures of Children's Literature* I list common binaries that relate to two basic ones—home and away. I suggest that homes tend to represent safety and boredom, places away from home danger and excitement; that homes tend to represent communal connection and suffocation, away individual freedom and isolation, and so on. Here, I'm less concerned with the meanings attached to these binaries than I am with the plots that engender them. The books I most enjoy tend to be about two clearly defined opposites confronting each other. In them, for instance, the present confronts the past, as a character goes back in time. Or perhaps the future meets the present, as characters in children's science fiction often confront less technological worlds than the futuristic ones they are used to. Or animal characteristics meet human characteristics in the body of one character. Or the inanimate intersects with the animate in the body of one doll come to life, or small people such as Stuart Little interact with big ones. Or, and in general, fantasy intersects with and exists within the world of reality, as in *Weetzie Bat.*

All these kinds of stories seem to have three common and necessary features.

The first is that there must be clear oppositions. This is not a subtle mixture of past and present, animal and human, good and bad, black and white turned subtly gray. The oppositions are clearly separated out. (This may be one of the reasons that children's literature can be seen as simple—it tends to work in terms of binary oppositions far more obviously than does much serious adult literature.)

The second is that the oppositions do intersect and interact but never actually and finally blend. A wildly luxuriant forest may grow in Max's sparse bedroom, but it's clearly a separate and opposite thing, and it's obviously gone by the time the book ends. The magic is not that two apparently opposite things become one larger, more subtle thing, as might happen in an adult story, but rather that two opposite things have intersected for a time, maybe done a dance with each other, but remained finally separate. There's an interesting scene in Janet Lunn's time fantasy *The Root Cellar* in which a character provides a Thanksgiving dinner by moving into different Thanksgivings across the decades and stealing a dish from each, so that all times intersect in one meal. But then the meal is over, the past recedes into the past, and the present remains itself and separate.

The third quality is that the oppositions tend to be represented by specific places—actual physical locations. Children's fiction often is focused on the nature of places—not just home but places like Green Gables or Treasure Island or Mr. MacGregor's garden or where the wild things are or Farmer Zuckerman's barn or Weetzie Bat's magical Los Angeles or the various old houses where characters in time fantasies find themselves in the past. And each of these places is associated with a set of values and concerns that exist significantly in opposition to another place that represents different concerns.

In *Children's Literature Comes of Age,* Maria Nikolajeva borrows a term from Bakhtin: *chronotope.* It refers to a specific combination of time and place. Nikolajeva says that it is "a genre category, that is, specific forms of chronotope are unique for particular genres. . . . As Bakhtin shows, every literary mode, epoch, genre and even writer can be defined on the basis of the way in which they organize time and space" (121–22). If that's true, I might well argue that the chronotope of children's fiction tends to be oppositionally double: spaces or places that are defined as opposite but intersect with each other in ways that imply interactions but finally preserve the sense of separateness. Nikolajeva herself speaks of E. Nesbit, a writer I much enjoy, in exactly these terms: "The absurd idea of letting magical figures and objects appear in modern London, and the inability of modern humans to make use of magic are thoughts which appealed to Nesbit, and this is what all of her children's books are based on" (161).

Why might children's fiction be operating in this way? I think it might go back to the dynamics of the situation that most basically defines children's literature: adults writing books for children. All such literature emerges from one shared and very basic assumption: that children are different enough from adults to need a special literature of their own and enough like each other that adult writers can actually provide texts that will appeal to large numbers of children as a group, with, presumably, group characteristics. In other words, all children's literature is written across what must inevitably be perceived to be a gap, written for and often about a group to which the writer does not belong.[3] Thus, the concept that allows children's literature to exist at all is in itself binary and oppositional. It requires an adult writer different from and in many ways opposite to the child reader implied (and perhaps especially, as I suggested earlier, in terms of knowledge). It requires that the adult intermingle with the childlike but remain finally separate from it. It seems possible, then, that all the other binary oppositions of children's fiction represent replications of this basic one — repetitions of the primal scene of a text's engendering, as it were.

And I think it could be argued that they are. Treasure Island, where the wild things are, Mr. MacGregor's garden clearly represent versions of childhood as utopia—places where you get what you childishly want and, by getting it, learn not to want it so much anymore. A voyage to them is almost literally a repetition of the act whereby an adult travels into the presumably childlike imagination that engenders children's books. (Note also how a focus on places allows this to happen. The lost time of childhood can be visited when it's metamorphosed into a place, because, whereas times pass, places can exist simultaneously.) That's particularly true in time fantasies, in which the old houses redolent of past time seem almost literal representations of a past gone and then reentered. Characters who represent blends of animal and human or toy and human, situations that mix miniatures with giants, all seem like variant forms of the same central oppositional view. Parts of them are childlike, parts adultlike. (Note, again, how literalizing metaphors allow magical interminglings. The child I once was myself is a memory buried in the past, but Peter Rabbit or the Indian in the cupboard is here and now and visitable.) And in all cases, the ambivalence of adults toward childhood, the sense that it represents a more deficient and yet superior way of seeing and being than adulthood, operates to create and maintain tensions—the pulls I spoke of earlier as giving me so much pleasure.

Indeed, the children's books I enjoy most remind me of the optical illusions often reproduced in books about the psychology of perception. Look once at the picture and it's the profile of an old woman's face; look again and it's a young woman's body. Look once at another picture and it's a vase; look again and it's two people staring at each other. But it's always one or the other; it's never possible to see both the old and the young woman at once or even to see some combination of the two. We see the old woman and know of the young woman only because she was there the last time we looked—and yet, the next time, there she is again. That's magical.

Furthermore, I suspect it's the maintenance of that tension, the old woman or the young woman but never the two combined, that leads to what strikes me as one final important source of my pleasure in children's fiction: its obsession with variational forms. Children's books tend to be constructed in terms of episodes that can be read as rejugglings of the same or similar components. They tend to occur in series in which the individual books represent variations of each other and tend, in any case, to be enough alike that often books by different authors can be read as reworkings of the same material: consider time fantasies, for instance, which represent an ingenious range of possibilities of using the same device and that nevertheless tend almost always to have significant thematic and structural similarities. Variational form seems most significantly to be a question of delaying closure or of avoiding its implications. The same story or a similar one can and must be retold many times, lest the happy ending triumph over the now-perceived-to-be unhappy beginning and end up claiming to show what happiness is once and for all—and in the process, presumably, kill childhood and the childlike forever. Variational form offers the pleasure of being not grown up and then growing up again and again.

And in doing so, I think, it suggests why the pleasures I've outlined need not be guilty ones. Ideological theorists—Fredric Jameson, for instance—speak of literary texts as places where contradictions are staged in such a way that their contradictory nature ceases to be obvious.[4] In this way, ideologies protect those subject to them from knowledge of their deficiencies and thus maintain themselves and their power over us. The children's texts I read with pleasure clearly represent contradictory versions of childhood, as wisely innocent or stupidly ignorant. But in these texts, these views are staged in ways that *don't* mask the contradictions or allow resolution. They work, therefore, to keep readers of all ages aware, freer from the pressures of ideology than other kinds of texts might leave them. The subjectivity they construct is always ambivalent and subtle, always conscious of ambivalences and subtleties—always both childlike and aware of the limitations of childlikeness.

I realize that the construction of such a complex and aware subjectivity in actual children might distress some adults, who'd prefer their children simpler and more one-sided and more malleable. Since it's the subjectivity that I tend to understand as what I am when I am being my best self and the kind of subjectivity I admire most in others of all ages, I can only celebrate it and wish all children had access to it.

Notes

1. This also means that children's literature might be equipping children who read it a lot with a peculiar sense of being both in childhood and somehow beyond it, outside it, superior to it—a sort of divided consciousness that allows them both to identify with childlike characters and be separate from them. This suggests some weirdness in terms of the ways in which texts construct childhood as something children are both involved in and detached from, part of and superior to—a weirdness I intend to explore further as I develop my thoughts on these matters.

2. "The Mouse, the Bird, and the Sausage" is usually found as number 23 in English translations of the collected tales of the Brothers Grimm. None of the translations of *Kinder- und Hausmarchen* in my possession have this exact wording for the opening sentence. I seem to have made it up by myself somewhere along the way.

3. Writers do, of course, claim that they belong to the group—that they write for a child hidden within them or the child they once were, or something like that. But what's significant about these formulations is that the child—a being still conceived as being separate from the adult who harbors it—*is* hidden within. Indeed, it's interesting how often therapeutic procedures far removed from literary concerns insist on thinking of childhood in terms of this hidden other within us. Our ideas about childhood tend always, it seems, to express otherness and difference and separation and the need to bridge the gulf.

4. "The aesthetic act is itself ideological, and the production of aesthetic or narrative form is to be seen as an ideological act in its own right, with the function of inventing imaginary or formal 'solutions' to unresolvable social contradictions" (79).

Works Cited

Banks, Lynn Reid. *The Indian in the Cupboard.* New York: Doubleday, 1981.

Block, Francesca Lia. *Weetzie Bat.* New York: HarperCollins, 1989.

Fitzhugh, Louise. *Harriet the Spy.* New York: Harper & Row, 1964.

Henkes, Kevin. *Crysanthemum.* New York: Greenwillow, 1991.

Jameson, Fredric. *The Political Unconscious: Narrative as a Socially Symbolic Act.* Ithaca: Cornell University Press, 1981.

Le Guin, Ursula K. *A Wizard of Earthsea.* New York: Parnassus, 1968.

Lunn, Janet. *The Root Cellar.* Toronto: Lester and Orpen Denys, 1981.

Montgomery, L. M. *Anne of Green Gables.* 1908. Toronto: Seal-McClelland and Stewart/ Bantam, 1981.

Nesbit, E. *The Story of the Treasure Seekers.* 1899. Harmondsworth, Middlesex: Penguin Puffin, 1958.

Nikolajeva, Maria. *Children's Literature Comes of Age: Toward a New Aesthetic.* New York and London: Garland, 1996.

Nodelman, Perry. *The Pleasures of Children's Literature.* 2d ed. White Plains, N.Y.: Longman, 1996.

———. *The Same Place but Different.* Toronto: Groundwood, 1993; New York: Simon and Schuster, 1995.

Potter, Beatrix. *The Tale of Peter Rabbit.* London: Frederick Warne, 1902.

Rey, H. R. *Curious George.* Boston: Houghton Mifflin, 1941.

Sendak, Maurice. *Where the Wild Things Are.* New York: Harper & Row, 1963.

Stevenson, Robert Louis. *Treasure Island.* 1883. London: Collins, 1953.

White, E. B. *Charlotte's Web.* 1952. New York: Trophy-Harper & Row, 1973.

The Pleasure of the Process: Same Place but Different

Roderick McGillis

> *Our ideas about childhood tend always, it seems, to express otherness and difference and separation and the need to bridge the gulf. . . .*
>
> *There is really no move forward or backward, no final wisdom to be achieved—no purpose in the game but the pleasure of the never-ending process.*
>
> —Perry Nodelman

I take my epigraphs from Nodelman's "Pleasure and Genre: Speculations on the Characteristics of Children's Fiction" (see the preceding essay). This essay provides the occasion for my own, which is not so much a response to Perry's as a continuation of an ongoing conversation. And let me say at the outset that I shall drop the scholarly convention of citation by surname and refer to my partner in conversation as Perry. I take it that much of the pleasure that reading books of any kind gives is the pleasure of conversation. It takes at least two to converse, and to converse implies not only more than one voice but also more than one point of view. To adapt a saying from an old friend, I note that without points of view there is no learning. And so I can begin by asserting that I learn from Perry and that my understanding of children's literature and its pleasures differs somewhat from his. Somewhat. I think we set out, however, with a similar sense of this literature's potential appeal to all readers.

Perry would, I suspect, sympathize with U. C. Knoepflmacher's assessment of the "subversive touches" in Thackery's *The Rose and the Ring:* "they kindle a pleasurable alertness that makes the reader—and especially the juvenile reader who enjoys detecting sham and trickery—an eager accomplice of a winking author" (107–8). I'd like to think that "pleasurable alertness" could aptly describe any reader's response to any literature, but the pleasure that Wordsworth describes as a "grand elementary principle" (140) is necessarily different from alert pleasure in that the latter results from attention and learning, whereas the former derives from immediacy and self-satisfaction. Pleasure, like

Children's Literature 28, eds. Elizabeth Lennox Keyser and Julie Pfeiffer (Yale University Press, © 2000 Hollins University).

anything else, is something we learn, and we can learn to enjoy it as an immediate sensation and also as a cerebral exercise. I'll invent a distinction to help me along here: elemental pleasure and alert pleasure. One we experience from infancy whenever anything satisfies our desire (especially for bodily pleasure), the other we have once we learn that our pleasure necessarily depends on something outside ourselves, something other than ourselves.

If we turn to the process of reading and the pleasures of the text, we can conclude that reading delivers or at least has the potential to deliver both elemental pleasure and alert pleasure. The first of these pleasures may result when we assume that reading has no other purpose than to keep us perennially playing the same game, never moving forward or backward, never achieving any "final wisdom." The pleasure is in the play, not necessarily a thoughtless play, but one that takes the game as important in and of itself and not what the game might indicate about the politics of interaction and not where the game comes from, who invented it, who sets the rules, and so on. The second of these pleasures results from the consciousness that the game pits the self against an other, whoever or whatever that other may be. Just as the first pleasure implies a reader and a text, two players in a game that may privilege one over the other depending on the attitude of the players, the second implies a plurality of readers and a text that speaks with many voices.

But let me be more concrete than I am above. The very notion of pleasure at the millennium's end is troubling. We remember Wilde's "new hedonism" from the last fin de siècle and we might equate this with an elemental pleasure, reading for the pleasure of the game, satisfying our needs and desires. On the other hand, the millennium seems to ask for serious thinking beyond the self. Thoughts of the future inevitably have a greater weight as an end draws nigh. How does pleasure fit with millennial concerns? Indeed, do the pleasures of reading even matter in the context of an uncertain future for the book? My answer: more than ever. We need readers alert to the pleasures of nuance and subtlety and even manipulation. We need readers alert to otherness, not necessarily to "bridge the gulf" but, more important, to recognize and tolerate the difference and to resist the urge to sameness. When Perry says, "But in fact, I suspect, readers of most ages mirror my own wonderfully ambivalent response," or when he says that he suspects "that many child readers read children's books as I do," I hear a desire to homogenize reading.

The interpretive instinct seems naturally to seek to convince others that the interpreter's way of reading is correct, valuable, and shared by others. Our efforts at interpretation are important because they mirror the ways in which we deal with things outside ourselves that impinge on us, reflect us back to ourselves, and thus challenge our assumptions. Interpreting is, in effect, dealing with an other. Whatever is other, outside ourselves (even as we are outside our own selves) is ultimately unknowable. Psychoanalysis has taught us that we inhabit a place that is, by definition, beyond our complete understanding. And theory these past couple of decades has taught us that texts too are beyond our complete understanding.

And yet some things and some aspects of textuality are not beyond our understanding, even if our understanding is never complete. We read and we encourage our children to read because we cling to the belief that by reading we and they will somehow become more complete human beings—whatever this means. Intuitively the push and pull of ambiguous meaning that Perry describes will be evident to readers young and older. Reading, whether we think of this as a game or as serious training for life, is that which brings us together into communities. But, as I hope this paragraph's drift makes clear, bringing together, bridging the gulf, enriching ourselves as human beings— such grand schemes have a sinister aspect. I refer to the urge to gather in, to essentialize, to infer that a particular view fits all. The particular-view-fits-all assumption is the one I grew up with; it is the one I find challenged by voices from the diaspora and by subaltern voices. This challenge is bracing and educational and healthy. Interpretation expands in response to this challenge.

I too enjoy the transformation of Max's bedroom into an exotic forest in Sendak's *Where the Wild Things Are;* I am especially moved by Sendak's homage here (as elsewhere in his work) to George MacDonald. But I have also learned to ask why this transformation occurs and what it may signify. Recent readings of Sendak's book take up the implications of this transformation from the apparently civilized bedroom to the more primitive forest. Adult readers have begun to question the implications of Max's cute colonialist activity in his night world, and I suppose an important issue for those of us involved with children and children's books is whether we should encourage our children to question the book in a similar manner. (Recent studies of *Where the Wild Things Are* that consider the colonial aspects of the books include John Clement Ball, "Max's Colonial Fantasy: Rereading

Sendak's *Where the Wild Things Are*" and Jennifer Shaddock, "*Where the Wild Things Are:* Sendak's Journey into the Heart of Darkness.") I have students each year who strongly indicate that to ask children to explore stories in this way is to ruin any pleasure they might take from merely reading for the plot, for the fun. Murdering to dissect remains a notion devoutly clasped by some readers.

Readers who wish to lose themselves in a book desire an immediate pleasure. My guess is that anyone who reads can experience this pleasure; it is available to anyone who learns to read. Alert pleasure, on the other hand, arises when we read to learn (see McGillis). Reading to learn means reading self-consciously, taking on our own authorial status. Such reading is something we need to practice, and when we first set out to undertake such reading we need guides. This is what people such as Perry and me are: guides to reading. But the notion of reading I am calling on here signifies something more than reading the letter, even more than reading literature. Literature, like everything else situated outside us and potentially impinging on us, is just there. Children's books are no different in this respect; they exist silently but temptingly flashing their colors to catch our attention. What we learn when we place these books in an institutional context is not these books, but rather ways of reading them. These ways are myriad, and we all know their labels, which range from formalist to childist reading. In short, I doubt that books for the young differ to any significant degree from books for the not-young. In saying this, I refer to narrative arrangements and choices of existents. Even a book by Dick Bruna, plotless and devoid of the intricacies we might associate with adult literature, offers a semiotic field in which the reader may play. Diction and subject matter may vary, but books for children produced within a culture must use the language and conventions of that culture. And without miring myself in the complexity of just what *culture* means, I think we can agree that children share much of the language adults use and necessarily live in that adult culture too. And of course the books published for children may aspire to reflect a specific child culture, but their producers do not inhabit that same culture in any pure way.

But I am beginning to drift from my course. I repeat, we teach criticism, not literature. This is something I learned long ago from Northrop Frye (for example, *Anatomy* 11), and the force of Frye's lesson is amply evident in recent studies of children's literature by writers such as John Stephens, Maria Nikolajeva, and Perry himself. Stephens and Nikolajeva set out to provide their readers with an enabling dis-course. *Canon, existents, chronotope, dialogism, focalisation,* and so on are terms these critics and others use to aid readers in their exploration and understanding of books. Such terms may apply to books written for readers both young and older than young. One of the attractions of Perry's writing is that its use of a specialized vocabulary is circumspect; Perry writes in a language that does not foreground its specialized dis-course—which is not to say that he does not have one. Such terms as *pleasure, genre, texts, ambivalence, focalized, protagonist, climactic moments, binary oppositions,* and from Nikolajeva (by way of Bakhtin) *chronotope* are sprinkled throughout the prose in Perry's essay. Many of the terms derive from an approach to literature that is essentially intrinsic, and they reflect a desire to conceive of "textuality" as endlessly recurrent and inward. The text can take us in, and texts for children have a spe-cial ability to take us in to a space in which the paradoxical coexistence of innocence and experience is nicely balanced. When we read a chil-dren's book, "each of us, young or old, can view the world as a child yet again, become, in imagination at least, a child yet again."

The difficulty I have with this privileging of the child is, in part, the burden of Jacqueline Rose's well-known study of children's fiction and more recently Karen Lesnik-Oberstein's *Children's Literature: Criti-cism and the Fictional Child.* At the very least Perry's "view the world as a child" begs the questions: What child? Whose child? But the more serious implication in this notion of viewing the world as a child is the sense it carries of a privileged space, a space within children's books where readers can cavort like Pooh and his friends in a Hundred Acre Wood of the mind, above the smoke and stir of the dim spot that is the real world where impossible things do not happen. The word *magic* often appears in discussions of children's books that wish to articu-late this sense of a retreat from the culture wars or from the field of ideological manipulations. Perry's argument, of course, is more subtle than this. For him, children's books more than other genres of litera-ture plunk the reader down front and center before contradiction, the contradiction of not knowing and knowing, of being child and adult at the same time.

The contradictions of children's literature have the effect, Perry ar-gues, of defeating "resolution." I suspect this means they participate in the never-ending figuration that deconstruction finds so attractive and so unavoidable. In fact, children's books (or at least the best of them) are so expressive of free play that they "work . . . to keep readers of all ages aware, freer from the pressures of ideology than other kinds of texts might leave them." This is the conclusion Perry reaches. And it is a very attractive conclusion. I wish it were so. Free from the pressures of ideology: this is a condition each of us might aspire to. We enter the world of children's books and come away kindled with alertness so that we burn with a hard gemlike flame that removes the crust of ideology that adheres to all of us. Well, perhap "removes" is not the most accurate word here. We are relieved, for at least the time of our inhabiting the world of the book, from strong ideological pull. Would it were so.

The catch is: the assertion that children's books are somehow expressive of a contradiction that counters a simple ideological position is itself ideologically loaded. Just as the child in the late eighteenth and early nineteenth centuries took on the values that a vision of pastoral once held, and just as literature at about the same time took on the values that the church's vision of spirituality once held, so now children's literature takes on the values once found in the canon of Western literature. The tradition of a certain neo-Platonism coming through Sidney and Pope and Coleridge and Arnold and Eliot and on into the prominent modes of Anglo-American criticism through mid-century finds its latest expression in this version of children's literature. This tradition calls to me with a profound attraction.

What troubles me in this attractive expression of a continuing tradition of liberal humanist thought is its apparent exclusivity. Much of the literature for children these days (and I don't think things have changed all that much) concerns itself with pressing social as well as psychological issues: sexual preference, gender roles, race and racism, labor and the job market, individual rights under the law, abusive situations in the family and elsewhere, the history of inhumanity and injustice, the exploitation of the ecosystem. Not all books express ambivalence when they take up such subjects. Not all books conceive of childhood the same way. Not all books deliver the same pleasures. Even the manner in which we experience pleasure differs from person to person, from group to group. Contact zones, diasporic experiences, hybridity, queerness, racialization, and other sociopolitical concerns manifest themselves in books for the young. In teaching children's literature, we can address such issues and guide young readers into the politics of reading. The literature will survive with or without us, but if we believe at all in the pleasures of alertness we will encourage those we teach to be alert both to the ways of reading and to the range of readings available. Let our libraries, our syllabi, and our interests be crowded with a literature that reflects a racial and cultural multiplicity. Let us teach the conflicts. Let us acknowledge, or better yet recognize, difference. Let us acknowledge the ideological underpinning of the books we read and the positions we take when we read. Who knows, maybe by continuing to confront contradictions within ourselves and within the texts we read, we may ease ourselves just a little from the pressures of ideology.

Works Cited

Ball, John Clement. "Max's Colonial Fantasy: Rereading Sendak's *Where the Wild Things Are*." *Ariel* 28 (1997): 167–79.

Frye, Northrop. *Anatomy of Criticism: Four Essays*. 1957. New York: Atheneum, 1966.

Knoepflmacher, U. C. *Ventures into Childhood: Victorians, Fairy Tales, and Femininity*. Chicago and London: University of Chicago Press, 1998.

Lesnik-Oberstein, Karen. *Children's Literature: Criticism and the Fictional Child*. Oxford: Oxford University Press, 1994.

McGillis, Roderick. "Learning to Read, Reading to Learn: Or Engaging in Critical Pedagogy." *Children's Literature Association Quarterly* 22 (fall 1997): 126–32.

Nikolajeva, Maria. *Children's Literature Comes of Age*. New York: Garland, 1996.

Rose, Jacqueline. *The Case of Peter Pan: Or the Impossibility of Children's Fiction*. London: Macmillan, 1984.

Sendak, Maurice. *Where the Wild Things Are*. New York: Harper, 1963.

Shaddock, Jennifer. "*Where the Wild Things Are:* Sendak's Journey into the Heart of Darkness." *Children's Literature Association Quarterly* 22 (winter 1997–98): 155–59.

Stephens, John. *Language and Ideology in Children's Fiction*. London and New York: Longman, 1992.

Wordsworth, William. "Preface to *Lyrical Ballads (1850)*." In *The Prose Works of William Wordsworth*, Ed. W. J. B. Owen and Jane Worthington Smyser. Oxford: Clarendon, 1974. 1:113–59.

Of Dialectic and Divided Consciousness: Intersections Between Children's Literature and Childhood Studies

Thomas Travisano

Through the medium of a disarmingly casual style, Perry Nodelman's "Pleasure and Genre: Speculations on the Characteristics of Children's Fiction" boldly lays out a range of important lines of inquiry for the study of children's literature. This essay will take up two of the most intriguing of these lines of inquiry with an eye toward the points of intersection they suggest between the now-established field of children's literature and the newly emerging field of childhood studies. Briefly defined, childhood studies is a multidisciplinary field that concerns itself with the nature of childhood experience and with ways cultures construct and have constructed childhood. It thus explores, among many other considerations, the diverse ways that writers and other creative artists represent and have represented childhood. Hence, participants in the field of childhood studies might approach with equal curiosity and analytical care stories aimed primarily at an audience of children, such as Kipling's *Just So Stories, Jungle Book,* and *Puck of Pooks Hill,* or a novel such as Dickens's *Great Expectations,* a text that aims primarily at an adult audience as it explores the development of Pip, its youthful narrator, who starts as a child staring at his parents' headstones in a remote country churchyard and ends as a romantic yet life-hardened young man-about-London who, after many troubles and disillusionments, is finally entering into full adulthood.

In a speculative note, Nodelman opens the initial line of inquiry I propose to follow. Here he suggests that "children's literature might be equipping children who read it a lot with a peculiar sense of being both in childhood and somehow beyond it, outside it, and superior to it—a sort of divided consciousness that allows them both to identify with childlike characters and to be separate from them." For Nodelman, this "suggests some weirdness in terms of the way in which texts construct childhood as something children are both involved in and detached from, part of and superior to—a weirdness I intend to explore further as I develop my thoughts on these matters." Nodelman

Children's Literature 28, eds. Elizabeth Lennox Keyser and Julie Pfeiffer (Yale University Press, © 2000 Hollins University).

reveals great intuitive insight when he suggests that an emergent awareness of a divided consciousness for the child reader immersed in children's literature is one of its most fascinating and important effects. But I wonder if he is equally correct when he suggests that this tendency to foster a divided consciousness reveals "some weirdness in terms of the way in which texts construct childhood." Arguably, there is nothing at all weird about this effect of making a reader aware of a divide in consciousness and thereby fostering in that reader a sense of identification and a sense of separation from both modes of consciousness. Arguably, one's recognition (knowing or not) of a divide in consciousness is one of the most pervasive, and perhaps even one of the most fundamental, effects of reading literature in any genre.

What Nodelman calls "divided consciousness" resembles in certain respects the "double-consciousness" that W. E. B. Du Bois defined for black Americans a century ago in the opening chapter of *The Souls of Black Folk*. Du Bois asserts that "the Negro" is forced to live in "a world which yields him no true self-consciousness, but only lets him see himself through the revelation of the other world. It is a peculiar sensation, this double-consciousness, this sense of always looking at one's self through the eyes of others, of measuring one's soul by the tape of a world that looks on in amused contempt and pity" (364). For Du Bois, double-consciousness is a product of the ways a minority is perceived by a more powerful majority, and thus the black individual of the turn of the last century found it hard to perceive his or her mature self through his or her own eyes. Thus, "the history of the American Negro is the history of this strife, — this longing to attain self-conscious manhood, to merge his double self into a better and truer self" (365). Hence, for Du Bois, double-consciousness is a product of the sense of otherness that black Americans are made to feel because of the ways that they are viewed by white Americans. The black individual's consciousness is doubled, and "self-conscious manhood" denied, because of the insistence and intrusiveness of external perceptions and judgments, which compel one to look "at one's self through the eyes of others."

Though what Nodelman calls "divided consciousness" bears some resemblance to Du Bois's famous formulation, it differs in one decisive respect. "Double-consciousness" reflects a sense of otherness produced by external social forces. "Divided consciousness," by contrast, reflects the awareness of a division that exists *within* the self, and this may be experienced by either a child or an adult. Each inhabits one side of this cognitive divide, and each has reason to feel curiosity about, and perhaps a kind of yearning to reach for or re-cover, the consciousness of the other. Although this division may be—and is—socially constructed or socially reinforced in all sorts of ways across a diverse range of cultures, the perception of a divided con-sciousness seems to have its origins in features that are not wholly de-termined by culture. That is, it starts in the necessary gap in knowl-edge and experience separating adult and child, but it also reflects increasingly measurable differences in both groups' cognitive devel-opment and brain function. Piaget long ago outlined a series of cogni-tive stages through which the developing child must pass en route to a fully operational adult consciousness. And although recent research in the field of cognitive development suggests that Piaget's categories may be too rigid and too culturally determined, further studies are also beginning to show that the gradual development of the human brain and nervous system as the child ages produces measurable dif-ferences in specific aspects of cognition. Thus Robert Kail argues that the measurable increases in brain processing speed as the child grows into adulthood function as a "fundamental mechanism of cognitive development" effecting changes in perception and mental processing that are "due, at least in part, to underlying biological factors" such as the steady growth and development of the child's brain and nervous system.

Current measurements of the differences between adult conscious-ness and the consciousness of the child remain crude and partial. Moreover, they define these differences as points on a continuum of development rather than sides of a single line of division. Thus, three-year-olds process differently from nine-year-olds, and the nineteen-year-old eldest daughter in a family of five may think more like an adult than she does like her younger siblings. Still, for the purposes of the present discussion, the metaphor of a divided consciousness re-mains apt and useful. And whatever the age at which one draws a divid-ing line between child and adult consciousness, it remains true that on a daily basis, throughout in every nation on the earth, children must communicate with parents, teachers, and other adult preceptors, and these preceptors must communicate with children, across a divide in consciousness.

This communication across a divide that is partly cultural but also partly hard-wired into our cognitive development is a principal con-cern of childhood studies. Nodelman seems to anticipate this when he observes that children's literature "emerges from one shared and very basic assumption: that children are different enough from adults to need a special literature of their own and enough like each other that adult writers can actually provide texts that will appeal to large numbers of children as a group, with, presumably, group character- istics. In other words, all children's literature is written across what must inevitably be perceived to be a gap, written for and often about a group to which the writer does not belong." What Nodelman seems ultimately to suggest is that children's literature helps a child to par- tially and temporarily peer across this divide, while remaining, at the same time, fully herself. Arguably, this effect allows one, whether child or adult, to peer into the mind of the other. And this peering across a divide is not a condition unique to children's literature but a more general condition of literary reading, though in adult literatures these divides in consciousness may be more various and are often socially determined by such factors as time period, locale, social class, cultural conditioning, race, or gender. For a child—let's posit a nine-year-old, since a reader of this age might be drawn toward most or all of the texts cited by Nodelman—the consciousness of the adult may be seen as the other. This other mode of consciousness is one the child confronts daily, if indirectly, through the words and actions of parents, teachers, aunts, uncles, adult family friends, media personalities, and so forth. Nodelman suggests that the child may also glean insight into the func- tioning of this adult consciousness, in intimate relation to her own, as she devours children's books written by adult authors. (I'm thinking now of my own nine-year-old daughter, who, after years of being read to, has recently emerged as a reader so voracious that she rarely has time for meals.) Still, the child cannot directly experience this adult consciousness, even if she understands that she will one day come to think this way herself.

Of course, for the adult, the process functions in reverse, but with a subtle difference. For now the child's consciousness represents the other, something that exists outside the self, represented perhaps by the children that may intimately surround one. But in this case it also lives on in shadow form inside the self in the shape of a partially re- membered mode of thinking and experiencing. As Nodelman astutely points out, "Writers do, of course, claim that they belong to the group [children]—that they write for a child hidden within them or the child they once were, or something like that. But what's significant about these formulations is that the child—a being still conceived as being separate from the adult who harbors it — *is* hidden within. Indeed, it's interesting how often therapeutic procedures far removed from literary concerns insist on thinking of childhood in terms of this hidden other within us. Our ideas about childhood tend always, it seems, to express otherness and difference and separation and the need to bridge the gulf." Just as children who read *Charlotte's Web* or *Where the Wild Things Are* can derive from these books an anticipatory intuition of the way an adult perceives and thinks — and thereby cross, albeit partially and vicariously, the divide separating adult from child consciousness — so adults who continue to read children's fiction attentively and imaginatively are accepting an invitation to cross this same divide, but in the other direction. In the process they reenter, if only partially and vicariously, a mode of understanding that they once had lived fully but that they now can only recover imaginatively.

Childhood studies would draw attention not only to this phenomenon of a divide in consciousness and to the ways cultures construct responses to it (partly, in Western culture at least, by writing children's literature) but also to a vast body of fiction and poetry written by adults for a primary audience of adults that attempts to cross this divide and thereby to imaginatively reenter the world of childhood. The fiction of Dickens, Proust, Welty, Salinger, and Faulkner, and the poetry of Wordsworth, Coleridge, Whitman, Lowell, Bishop, Jarrell, Plath, Roethke, Berryman, and Dylan Thomas, among many others, cross this divide in ways so various and so revealing that childhood studies must surely come to terms with them. What I would like to suggest for the present, however, is that the divide in consciousness tentatively defined in Nodelman's essay is likely to emerge as a fruitful point of intersection and further discussion by the complementary fields of children's literature and childhood studies.

The second line of inquiry I would like to take up — if only briefly because of space limitations — grows out of Nodelman's observation that in the field of children's fiction, "the books I most enjoy tend to be about two clearly defined opposites confronting each other." As Nodelman astutely suggests, in many of the best examples of children's fiction, "there remains a pull in opposite directions, between the pleasures of not knowing and the mastery of finding out how much you didn't know." He connects this pull to an important and oft-overlooked characteristic of the reading experience: "There is, I think, another aspect to the pleasure: the way it allows us to indulge repeatedly in a ritual reenactment of the move from childhood to maturity, innocence to knowledge. In real life, for each of us, that happens only once." As a younger or older reader experiences and reexperiences certain classic texts of children's fiction, "age succeeds youth only to be magically succeeded by youth once more." Again I would like to suggest that these contradictory pulls are not necessarily unique to children's literature. Such a phenomenon was described, more than fifty years ago, in a long-lost lecture on poetic structure by a distinguished poet, critic, and author of chilren's fiction in an essay that I recently had the good fortune to rediscover and publish. I am speaking of "Levels and Opposites: Structure and Poetry," delivered at Princeton University by Randall Jarrell in 1942 and first published in the *Georgia Review.*

Robert Lowell would later remark in an eloquent posthumous tribute to Jarrell that this intimate friend's key subject was his "lost, raw childhood, only recapturable in memory and imagination. Above all, childhood! . . . For Jarrell this was the divine glimpse, lifelong to be lived with, painfully and tenderly relived, transformed, matured— man with and against woman, child with and against adult" (96). Jarrell's attempts to explore the world of his lost childhood led him to create fine translations of four famous stories by the Brothers Grimm and to write four original books of children's fiction: *The Gingerbread Rabbit, The Bat Poet, The Animal Family,* and *Fly by Night* (the first illustrated by Garth Williams, the rest by Maurice Sendak). In his extensive criticism, Jarrell frequently advocates the writings of Kipling and Grimm, the partly child-centered poetry of Wordsworth, Rilke, Frost, Bishop, and Lowell, and such "unread books" as Christina Stead's novel *The Man Who Loved Children.* It's just possible that Jarrell's preoccupation with the divide between child consciousness and adult consciousness helped him to develop a dialectical notion of literary structure that chimes remarkably well with the principles of form and meaning that Nodelman articulates for children's fiction. Thus, in this lecture, which Jarrell composed as a twenty-eight-year-old instructor at the University of Texas and never published, he perceives that "a successful poem starts from one position and ends at a very different one, often a contradictory or opposite one; yet there has been no break in the unity of the poem. This unity is generated by the tension set up between strongly differing forces, by the struggle of opposites" (699). For Jarrell, the structure of a good poem is never unitary or static but always involves a dynamic struggle between conflicting or contradictory ideas. Thus, "we ought to realize how much of poetry, how much of its essential structure, is dialectical" (700). What Nodelman is suggesting as a possibly unique characteristic of children's fiction may now emerge, if Jarrell was right those many years ago, as a pervasive characteristic of the experience of literature. In any case, for Jarrell as for Nodelman, we experience literature not as the achievement of a unitary meaning but as an evolving dialectical action.

The dialectical principles active in literary structures connect in important ways with our earlier theme: that literature concerns itself, on a persistent basis, with divides in consciousness. Nodelman, as we have seen, acknowledges that "the books I most enjoy tend to be about two clearly defined opposites confronting each other." Some of these divides are as sharply drawn, and as clearly definable, as that between the consciousness of the child and the consciousness of the adult, the divide that sparks the action of so many children's books. But some divides, both in adult literature and in children's literature, may be so subtle as to be almost invisible, and the reader experiences them unconsciously. Thus the Brothers Grimm confront us with a divide between folk culture and literate culture that their own researches and transcriptions serve partly, though never wholly, to bridge. American readers of Shakespeare confront divides in time period, language, and cultural background. White readers of Zora Neale Hurston or Toni Morrison confront such a divide in racial terms, as do black readers of Faulkner or Flannery O'Connor. Richard Wright, a black male author whose politics and aesthetics clashed with Hurston's at many points, condemned her fiction in the strongest terms, and thereby helped to thrust her work, for decades, into undeserved obscurity. Wright, as a reader, was unable to cross the divide he confronted in her work. Ultimately, even if a reader shares the author's age, race, gender, time period, or locale, there will always be a divide between the author's experience and imagination and the reader's, as well as the inevitable divide between the world a reader re-creates from printed words (and sometimes illustrations) and the physical world and passing moment one presently inhabits. In a work of children's literature of continuing merit, a dialectic confrontation between the claims of childhood and the opposing claims of adulthood may be ever-present, and a tug-of-war across the divide in consciousness between author and reader may act itself out on every page, pulling the child forward into adulthood and pulling the adult back into a world of child-experience that the adult may pride himself on having grown beyond. But this child consciousness nevertheless exercises a powerful undertow of backward yearning and nostalgia, as well as curiosity about the forces that helped to shape the present self. It is just such points of intersection between the consciousness of the adult and that different, curiously familiar, yet maddeningly unattainable experience of the child that childhood studies proposes to consider.

Works Cited

Du Bois, W. E. B. "The Souls of Black Folk." In *Writings,* edited by Nathan Irrin Huggins. New York: Library of America, 1986.

Jarrell, Randall. "Levels and Opposites: Structure in Poetry." *The Georgia Review* (Winter 1996): 697–713.

Kail, Robert. "Nature and Consequences of Developmental Change in Speed of Processing." *Swiss Journal of Psychology.* 23 (Winter 1996): 102–22.

Lowell, Robert. "Randall Jarrell." In *Collected Prose,* edited by Robert Giroux. New York: Farrar, Straus, and Giroux, 1987.

A Pride of Pleasures

Margaret R. Higonnet

At the end of the eighteenth century, modern aesthetics was born with the publication of Kant's *Critique of Judgment*. The term *aesthetic,* referring to the pleasure derived from works of art, was critical to the concept that verbal arts should be distinguished from more practical, utilitarian, or purposive kinds of verbal practice. Whereas *literature* before had referred to many kinds of texts, including sermons and scientific texts, post-Kantian theorists have tended to limit the term to texts defined by (aesthetic) "purposiveness without purpose" (a leitmotif in Kant). To cite one of Kant's formalist visual examples: the pleasure inspired by the design of a tatoo may be separated from our assessment of its visual and physical impact on the body. Over the past two centuries, the pleasure of texts (not to mention tatoos) has continued to hold our attention, perhaps especially in the domain of children's literature, in part because the Romantics cultivated an image of childhood as a realm protected from adult purposiveness by the golden aura of innocent play. But the evident importance of didacticism in children's literature of the period also made it suspect, subject to debate: children's literature had a purpose and therefore could not be considered aesthetic.

Perry Nodelman's talk about children's literature concentrates on the pleasures of narrative, as he himself experiences them and as children (we speculate) may experience them. Although his own, confessedly adult, pleasure is his starting point, the purpose of his argument is to define children's literature.

Undoubtedly he is right that the key feature of children's literature, as commonly understood, is the situation of "adults writing books for children." These authors, he suggests, write across a gap in "experience," "knowledge," and "wisdom."[1] From this thesis flow many of his other arguments: that the pleasures of reading children's literature derive from the interplay of binaries, for example. Writing across difference may indeed lead to the reinscription of differences.

But a number of the themes and narrative structures to which No-

Children's Literature 28, eds. Elizabeth Lennox Keyser and Julie Pfeiffer (Yale University Press, © 2000 Hollins University).

delman is drawn in books for the young seem to me equally prevalent in adult culture—not surprisingly so, given the initial premise. Fantasy, as he acknowledges, has an enthusiastic adult following, whether the variant is *Star Wars* or *Paradise Lost*. Precisely the mix of the fantastic with a realistic mode intensifies the psychological power of E. T. A. Hoffmann's novellas, such as *The Sandman*. This generically unstable mode was a characteristic offspring of the Romantic era, the period when children's literature began to come into its own.

Nodelman suggestively links narratives of adventure that lead to chastening conclusions, which he interprets as stories of the passage from "innocence" to "experience" or "wisdom," with the narrative pattern of home-away-home, in which a chastened childlike protagonist returns to familial security with a new awareness of the dangers of ignorance. *The Tale of Peter Rabbit* typifies this pattern. Although common in books for children, narratives of maturation are also common in books for adults.[2] The *Bildungsroman,* another great Romantic invention, is one of the foundation blocks of the nineteenth-century novel. Similarly, the circle of a departure leading eventually to a return marks much of literature through time; consider the *Odyssey*.

Part of what fascinates Nodelman, however, is a psychological interplay or equilibrium between innocence and experience that seems to drive us to return to the same or similar texts. Tellingly, he confesses that the "activities of the wise" are less pleasurable or interesting than those of the unwise; we do not read, in short, in order to learn to avoid dangers or mistakes. The point is important: texts that look didactic often function in the opposite direction, opening a window onto risk-taking, defiance, anger, overeating, and other activities that we normally inhibit. Freud, commenting on our fascination with certain kinds of themes, suggests that reading itself puts us in a protected position: from the safety of an armchair, we can follow a protagonist into danger and even death, gaining imaginatively an experience that we could not literally gain without great cost. This is one explanation for the popularity of the *Trivialroman* or of soap operas on television. It has particular pertinence to child readers—less powerful, less mobile, less autonomous than adults but not necessarily less rebellious.

Paradoxically, one of the greatest Romantic writers for children, William Blake, in his much-loved *Songs of Innocence* and *Songs of Experience,* deconstructed such categories as "innocence" (equated by Nodelman in passing with ignorance) and "experience" (equated by Nodelman with wisdom). Indeed Blake, one suspects, is one of the authors Nodelman had in mind when he described his attraction to the simplicity that covers resonant depths that he attributes to texts for children, for poems such as "London" or "The Sick Rose" or "The Tyger," in spite of their brevity, continue to unfold their depths to readers of all ages.

A corollary of Nodelman's reflections is the hypothesis that children's texts embed two levels of reading, one adapted to a child's experiences and inscribed in a childlike protagonist, another adapted to adults' more sophisticated understanding and sense of difference from a child protagonist. In a note he adds that "children's literature might be equipping children who read it a lot with a peculiar sense of being both in childhood and somehow beyond it, outside it, and superior to it—a sort of divided consciousness that allows them both to identify with childlike characters and be separate from them."

Nodelman's somewhat romantic thesis offers me a springboard for further reflections. I agree completely with the claim that children's literature can offer a density and a richness in interpretative levels that many critics concerned only with adult literature often overlook. But criticism in the field is now so fertile that I am not sure we need to argue this point.

I depart from what I take to be Nodelman's thesis in two directions. First, I worry about attributing to children's literature the capacity to shape a child's divided consciousness. This is not because I think reflectiveness or reflexiveness is hazardous. It seems more likely to me that *all* encounters (including, of course, textual encounters) are capable of inspiring double vision: the displacement of a singular self that is the foundation of all visual and psychological perspective. Children seem to be capable of such self-division very early, although their appreciation of contradictions and their pleasure in paradox may not become apparent to adults until their verbal skills are developed.

My evidence is a simple anecdote, drawn from reading Helen Bannerman's *Story of Little Black Mingo* to my daughter when she was almost two. In this tale, Mingo, who has been kidnapped by a crocodile, is rescued by a mongoose whom she has pulled out of the water. Once he lands on the crocodile's island and sees a pile of eggs (the crocodile babies whose birthday was to be celebrated by the consumption of Mingo), the little mongoose eats up the eggs, then sails off in a pot with Mingo. The father crocodile, on his return to the island, flies into a rage: Bannerman shows him stamping on the sand and weeping enormous crocodile tears. My daughter, studying this picture, commented sympathetically but firmly: "The papa crocodile is crying. All the same, [the eggs] had to be eaten." In short, she could see the distress of the parent but recognized the happy narrative inevitability of the mongoose's hunger leading to Mingo's liberation.

I would go further and argue that every home-away-home narrative engages a double vision, a set of contradictory desires for risk and detachment as well as for security and attachment. Indeed, Nodelman makes this argument himself. This double vision, I think, is further at work in the picturebook's interplay between image and text. Both of these dialectics are effectively deployed in a story such as *Annie and the Wild Animals* by Jan Brett. In the margins, along with many other forest animals, Taffy, the missing cat whose loss Annie mourns, can be seen climbing into a hollow tree, making a nest, and nursing newborn kittens—whom she will eventually bring home. The child who reads the visual "text" knows more than Annie, indeed more than the narrator, whose words an adult might read aloud. As critics, we tend to privilege verbal narratives, but we need to keep in mind as well the different powers of visual narrative—to which, of course, Perry Nodelman has devoted a superb book. Visual narratives are more immediately accessible to preverbal and preliterate children. The power of the margin in this instance is available to the small child, the least powerful member of our society.

Moreover, I am ready to risk being accused of indulging in nostalgia or sentimentality by arguing that texts for children at their best invite many different kinds of knowing, in which the ostensibly more sophisticated knowledge is not necessarily the greater. For Nodelman, pleasure initially seems to be linked to superiority, or the pride that Thomas Hobbes called "sudden glory." Thus, as an adult, he enjoys "knowing more and better than the focalized characters do." Pride provokes pleasure. Quickly, however, he slides toward an oscillation between "innocence" and "wisdom" reminiscent of Schiller's *Letters on Aesthetic Education,* which argue that aesthetic maturity and freedom arise through the *Spieltrieb,* or transcendent play between rival drives. Once again, we find our critical models are Kantian, Romantic. Nodelman sums up his dialectic: "There is no purpose in this but the pleasure of the process."

Must we construct binaries? The fine apprehension of emotional tones and of complex relations of power may complement rather than displace rational analysis, economic assessment, or socialization within institutions. This is the argument that Dickens makes in *Hard*

Times, which can be read either as a realist novel or as a sentimental one—or both. I am always suspicious of hierarchies of knowledge,
such as the claim that language is the medium of knowledge—as if
dancers or painters could not know or express in their own way the
nature of being. Rather than relying on binaries, I find it useful to
think of our many senses collaborating in the construction of our
world, and I am fascinated by experimental authors (I think of Bruno
Munari and Eric Carle) whose books help small children explore
shape and texture as media for narrative, as well as words and images.

The second direction in which I would like to take the topic of pleasure, then, is the multiplicity of pleasures that children's literature af-
fords. There is no disputing the pleasure of narrative. But it is accompanied by many others—a pride not of lions but of pleasures.

Children's literature accompanies the transition from preverbal to
verbal childhood. It accompanies us through the rest of our lives, a
point that Nodelman makes forcefully. If we focus on the moment of
language acquisition, we can see why puns, homonyms, rhymes, nonsense terms, metaphors, or even catachreses cause such delight. The
child who is bilingual seizes instantly on possibilities of play offered by
each language: thus (again at about two or two and a half) my daughter came home one day bothered by the problem of translation of this
kind of play: "Maman, *soleil* et *courir,* ça ne rime pas" ("Mummy, *sun*
and *run* don't rhyme"). Linguistic purists are outraged by the passion
of bilingual children for macaronic confusion; clever books can capi-
talize on such confusions, however, as a mangled French version of
"Humpty Dumpty" (un petit d'un petit) demonstrates. Perhaps bilin-
gualism could be taken as a paradigm for children's abilities to juggle
different perspectives and values.

Whole books can be constructed out of nonsense rhymes. Delightful acts of aggression against conventional language and fairy tales
have been committed by writers such as Roald Dahl in his *Revolting
Rhymes* or the Ahlbergs in *The Jolly Postman.* To take a French example:
Philippe Dumas in *Les avatars de Benjamin* literalizes and visualizes
dead metaphors such as "slow as a snail" or "eats like a pig." [3] To be
sure, Dumas's book closes with little Benjamin having decided to become an elephant, emblem of wisdom. Standing naked in front of a
mirror, he hopes his "trunk" ("trompe") will grow (44). One may well
conclude that this final line is a wink for adults only, following the two-
level structure discerned by Nodelman in so much children's literature. But perhaps not. A child of my acquaintance told his mother one

day that he liked his penis so much he wished he had two. Whether or not we agree with Freud that the eroticism of small children is polymorphous, we may perhaps conclude that children know a good deal more about their bodies and their pleasures than many adults would like.[4]

Great books exfoliate: they reveal pleasures behind or beside other pleasures. Everyone, I suppose, loves *Goodnight Moon,* since it is a book that newborns tend to receive in triplicate. But not everyone notices that among the many pleasures offered by this book—with its hidden recurrent mouse, its resonant rhymes, its rhythm of objects singled out for separate contemplation followed by their collection in the cozy unity of a bedroom—is its density of allusion. Yes, of course: the three little bears, sitting in chairs. But also the mittens from the nursery rhyme. And *The Runaway Bunny,* the earlier book by Margaret Wise Brown, from which the ancestral fisher-bunny on the wall comes. I insist on the element of allusion because it is this kind of intertextuality that many critics would not expect to find in children's literature, in part because they believe that children are not sophisticated enough to recognize it, in part because they believe that adult literature is distinguished from that for children precisely by its density of allusion.

Aristotle argued in his *Poetics* that imitation, *mimesis,* was one of the pleasures fundamental to drama and ultimately to human nature. Imitation and repetition: twins, mirrors, rhymes are but some of the playful repetitions at work in texts for children, as well as for adults. Moral symmetries like "the helper helped" figure not only in the story of Mingo but throughout the Grimms' tales. The practice of repetition is part of the process of learning, of mastery, through which we all pass on our way to adulthood. These, I scarcely need add, are in a sense formal structures of learning that are prenarrative.

Perhaps one way of defining the direction in which I deviate here is to suggest that whereas narrative and argument move along a "syntagmatic axis," to use a term from Roman Jakobson, the pleasures of character, vocabulary, color, and so forth organize their riches along a "paradigmatic axis." If narrative pleasures are linear, other pleasures are more spatial. And if the "sexual pleasure . . . of delayed orgasm" followed by orgasm seems to be the model of many (masculinist) theories of narrative, for instance, that of Peter Brooks, other (perhaps more feminine) pleasures lie in the folds of irony and thickets of verbal texture.

Jakobson suggests that there are many different kinds of communication, among them "phatic" communication (355), by which he means the self-referential checking of channels of communication—knocking a microphone ("Testing, testing") or the early-morning chatter of birds, although how he knew what birds are testing, I do not know. Coleridge too talks about this phatic pleasure, reflecting on the texture and nonlinear movement of poetry, which he compares to the sinuous slither of a snake that passes along a path, embellishing and even impeding by deviation the otherwise purposive forward movement of statement.[5] Coleridge, of course, was a reader of Kant, and Nodelman is a reader of Coleridge. But in Coleridge's passage I would like to deflect our attention from the ends to the means.

These additional pleasures of the nonlinear and nonnarrative are what I want to foreground. They can be located in the lists of deep-sea creatures that fill the pages of Jules Verne's *Twenty Thousand Leagues Under the Sea*. They can be relished in the inventive excess of animal metaphors that Philippe Dumas lines up in his book about Benjamin. They proliferate in the complexity of peritextual features that we find in Anno. The success of *The Jolly Postman* lies in part in its intertextual interstices, the secrets within its envelopes; the Ahlbergs engage the reader interactively, with a fresh strategy of allusion for each allusion. I would point not only to the pleasure in acquiring language but to that in probing character, in recognizing familiar tones captured in dialogue, in atuning all one's senses. Whereas most narrative tends to drive toward closure, other aspects of verbal art expand within the reader's mind, producing not a pride in superiority but a pride in growth. These, too, are the pleasures of those who read children's books.

Notes

1. In the Victorian era, there are many examples of literature written by children for their siblings: the Brontës or Jane Austen, for example. The striking differences between those imaginative worlds and the worlds usually defined by books for children would bear further investigation.

2. I leave aside the question whether Peter matures; he certainly gets sick, which for some readers may come to the same thing. To apply the term *innocence* or even *ignorance* to Peter, however, is problematic; warned in advance, the little rascal gets into trouble from which somehow he must extricate himself. That exercise in autonomy seems to be the point.

3. Philippe Dumas, *Les avatars de Benjamin*. See also Dumas and Boris Moissard, *Contes à l'envers*.

4. For a study of the Romantic invention of childhood "innocence" and our modern difficulties in negotiating this invention, see Anne Higonnet, *Pictures of Innocence*.

5. In Coleridge's phrase, "the pleasurable activity of mind excited by the attractions of the journey itself. Like the motion of a serpent . . . at every step he pauses and half recedes" (2:356).

Works Cited

Ahlberg, Janet, and Allan Ahlberg. *The Jolly Postman or Other People's Letters*. London: Heinemann, 1986; Boston: Little, Brown, 1986.

Anno, Mitsumasa. *Anno's Medieval World*. 1979. Adapted from the translation by Ursula Synge. New York: Philomel, 1980.

Brett, Jan. *Annie and the Wild Animals*. Boston: Houghton Mifflin, 1985.

Brooks, Peter. *Body Works: Objects of Desire in Modern Narrative*. Cambridge: Harvard University Press, 1993.

———. *Reading for the Plot: Design and Intention in Narrative*. New York: Knopf, 1984.

Brown, Margaret Wise. *The Runaway Bunny*. Pictures by Clement G. Hurd. New York: Harper and Row, 1942 (renewed); pictures redrawn 1972.

Carle, Eric. *La petite chenille qui faisait des trous*. Paris: Fernand Nathan, 1972.

Coleridge, Samuel Taylor. Chapter 14 of *Biographia Literaria*. In *Norton Anthology of English Literature*. 3d ed. New York: Norton, 1974, 2:356.

Dumas, Philippe. *Les avatars de Benjamin*. Paris: Ecole des Loisirs, 1980.

Dumas, Philippe, et Boris Moissard. *Contes à l'envers*. Paris: Ecole des Loisirs, 1977.

Higonnet, Anne. *Pictures of Innocence: The History and Crisis of Ideal Childhood*. London: Thames and Hudson, 1998.

Jakobson, Roman. "Concluding Statement: Linguistics and Poetics." In *Style in Language*. Ed. Thomas A. Sebeok. Cambridge: M.I.T. Press, 1960. Pp. 350–77.

Munari, Bruno. *I Prelibri*. Milano: Danese, 1980.

Wordsworth, William. "Ode: Intimations of Immortality." In *Norton Anthology of English Literature*. 3d ed. New York: Norton, 1974, 2:175–81.

The Urge to Sameness

Perry Nodelman

What most struck me on first reading Rod McGillis's response to "Pleasure and Genre" was not something he says but something I said myself. Rod quite rightly chastises me for describing how texts of children's fiction invite us to "view the world as a child." Surely, I told myself, as I read these words, I hadn't actually said that? A frantic search through my own piece soon revealed the horrid truth: the offending words were there. I had, indeed, done exactly what I spend much of my professional life getting angry at others about.[1] I had based my reading of children's books on a generalization about children.

I hasten to say that I didn't really mean it—not in the way that Rod takes it. I was talking not about some existing "child" who might represent the behavior of a body of actual living children but about an intellectual construct, the concept of a child as unlike and opposite to adults because of a presumed innocence, a divergence from adult forms of thought. It is the perceptions of that imaginary child that I see adult and child readers sharing as they make their way through a text of children's fiction. That adults can experience it—for that matter, that adults writers are the ones who imagine it in the first place—suggests how detachable from the perceptual habits of living children I believe this construct to be.

Indeed, the major thrust of Tom Travisano's comments is to focus on my saying that and to suggest I am wrong about it—to make the case that there is in fact a generalizable childhood accurately represented by texts and existing in the world outside them. Such an essentialized childhood might indeed influence children as a self-fulfilling prophesy, a result of adults who believe it to be true acting as if it were true. But I remain committed to the position that this or any conception of childhood as a generalizable state distinct from other generalized states of being human exists primarily in human thought and language and is not, as Tom and the cognitive psychologists he quotes would have it, "hard-wired into our cognitive development." I'll say more about that later.

Children's Literature 28, eds. Elizabeth Lennox Keyser and Julie Pfeiffer (Yale University Press, © 2000 Hollins University).

Meanwhile, though, I can't be too hard on Tom and the psychologists when my sentence about viewing as a child replicates their behavior—when I myself so easily slipped into the very behavior I was in the process of separating myself from. Similarly, Rod is right to notice that my suspicion "that many child readers read as I do" implies a desire to homogenize reading, an urge to sameness. I meant to say something a little different, and I didn't say it clearly enough: not that actual readers inherently or even ideally share my reading strategies but that texts of children's fiction tend to set up conditions that invite readers to make sense of them in the ways I describe. This behavior might more accurately be ascribed to what reader-response theorists identify as "implied readers" than to real ones and represent ways in which the texts indicate and invite certain forms of meaning-making from those competent to interact with them as expected. I don't doubt that many readers do not act as expected, nor does it much bother me that they don't.[2] I do, though, suspect that many readers do in fact do what texts invite—that for good or ill, and despite personal differences, many of us do learn the competencies that allow us at least some degree of understanding of what writers and speakers want us to understand. Indeed, discussing what it is that texts seem to intend to do—determining how they might manipulate readers for or against their better interests—would hardly be worth doing if we believed that it never actually worked and that the texts did in fact always communicate entirely different things to different readers.

Rod knows that, of course. If he didn't, he wouldn't be concerned about whether we need to make children aware of the colonialist implications of *Where the Wild Things Are.* For that matter, he wouldn't need to make readers of this volume aware of what he understands to be the implications of my argument in "Pleasure and Genre." The possibility that children would become unwitting colonialists from their readings of Sendak, or critics unrepentant homogenizers from reading my article, implies Rod's own faith that a lot of people do read like each other and will, in fact, understand from texts what the texts seem to be wanting them to understand. It represents another version of the urge to sameness.

As I think about it, I find myself speculating that this urge is inherent in the very project of language. We would not have words, or texts of children's literature and criticism made up of words, if we did not wish others to see what we see and understand what we understand—to share our own experience. Furthermore, it's in the nature of language to misrepresent exactly to the degree that it implies samenesses in different experiences: consider, for instance, the wide range of differing shades and hues that might be represented (or mistakenly confused for each other) through the use of the single word *red*. Those who look at a range of differing colors and agree they're all seeing red might well be losing sight of the variations in their individual perceptions.

It's for this sort of reason that I find myself unwilling to go along with Tom Travisano's acceptance of the conclusions of cognitive psychologists. No matter how careful and objective their procedures, they can't study the special thought processes of children without having already decided that "children" is indeed a category of individuals distinct from other human beings, worthy of study exactly in terms of exploring ways in which it is distinct, so that the conclusion about categorical difference is already built into the original untested assumption that the category significantly and accurately represents reality. In other words: cognitive psychologists invest too much unexamined faith in the urge to sameness inherent in the linguistic and cultural categories such as "child" that they take for granted. The danger of their doing so is clear in the history of bad "science" that emerged in earlier times from a similar untested acceptance of the biological reality of linguistic and cultural categories such as "Aryan" and "Semitic." There might someday be evidence untainted by cultural assumptions that a special sort of childlike thinking is hard-wired into humanity, but I'm not holding my breath.

There is a further urge to sameness, I think, in childhood studies as Tom conceives of it. I'm prepared to accept the possibility that psychological or sociological studies of childhood might enrich our understanding of children's literature—but not necessarily by allowing for a unified view of the nature of childhood. Cardinal Newman's utopian vision of different academic disciplines all offering compatible insights into one unified truth is no longer true, if indeed it ever was true. The assumptions of psychology or anthropology or literary study offer different, competing versions of the meanings of the same phenomena. A perception of all of them might well foreground the limitations of the ways each of them purports to be comprehensive in its understanding of something so complex as being young and human. But it would need to resist the urge to elide their differences in a misguided faith that total and unified understanding is possible.

Margaret Higonnet, meanwhile, might be accused of an opposite urge to sameness, since her story about one unique child supports an assertion about what "children," in general, apparently, seem to be capable of. I share Margaret's conviction that we'll always be further ahead imagining what children are capable of than focusing, as the cognitive psychologists always seem to do, on what they might not be capable of. But the urge to imagine a sameness in children seems almost unavoidable in adults who choose to discuss children's literature.

And that, I think, is the major point of the project I've embarked on here. Children's literature exists simply because adults do imagine a sameness in the audience it's designed for, a set of shared characteristics that makes children enough like each other and similarly unlike adults to require special texts. My purpose is to explore the implications of that assumption in terms of how it creates distinctive characteristics in the texts it engenders. In other words: I want to figure out the similarities that result from the urge to sameness implied in the mere existence of something written by adults and called children's literature.

A major feature of my argument is a focus on the binary opposition between child and adult that the primal scene of adults writing for creatures conceived as being unlike themselves suggests and reinforces. Margaret questions that assumption—but does so, it seems to me, in revealingly utopian terms, asking "Must we construct binaries?" and going on to say, "Rather than relying on binaries, I find it useful to think of our many senses collaborating in the construction of our world." I sense a desire here that binaries *not* be so obvious a feature of texts written for children. I think I share that desire—it's pleasing to imagine less binary ways of thinking and texts that express them. But I am, nevertheless, convinced that the urge to sameness inherent in the linguistic category "child" and its inevitable opposition to the category "adult" mean that binaries do operate significantly in most children's literature most of the time, and that it's in our interest as scholars and in the interest of children to understand that better.

One reason for that is expressed by Rod's last sentence, which I heartily agree with: understanding the ways in which texts urge us to share the inevitably limiting worlds they construct, and helping children to understand them also, can only work to free us all from manipulation by them. Dropping a very significant *r* from one of my sentences, Rod imagines that my statement that the texts I admire work to keep us "*freer* from the pressures of ideology" actually suggested some impossible utopian condition of being *"free"* of ideology. I share Rod's belief that, as thinking beings, we exist only and always in language, only and always, therefore, in the context of an urge to sameness, only and always in ideology.

I did, nevertheless, want to explore how the particular "sameness" I perceive in a significant number of children's books might be a source of pleasure—and how the specific pleasure in question might lead to an awareness of how the implied reader of these texts might be led to be more thoughtful about impositions of ideological sameness. I wanted—I still want—to eat my cake and have it, too, to both be aware of the dangers inherent in texts and still celebrate their ability to please. My project began with the perception that, despite my lengthy record of publications performing exactly the kind of ideologically aware analysis that Rod recommends, I still take pleasure in the very texts my work characterizes as repressive. My theory of how these texts manipulate the readers they imply into relatively healthy forms of awareness is an evolving attempt to allow myself and others both ideological consciousness *and* pleasure.

And I do want us to be free to enjoy them. I'm troubled by the Calvinist suspicion of what pleases that I hear in Rod's statement that "the very notion of pleasure at the millennium's end is troubling." I'm equally troubled by the urge to sameness inherent in the suggestion that any reading of *Where the Wild Things Are* that enjoys it without taking note of its colonialist leanings is a deficient reading, a reading not quite guilty enough—that all reading must always be similarly aware of what Rod calls difference.

I'm especially troubled because Rod is not alone in expressing these attitudes. In her president's address to the American Studies Association in 1998, Janet Radway could hardly surprise anyone familiar with the current world of literary scholarship by calling for a refiguring of her discipline so that it would focus not on unified and exclusionary ideas of the American but on exactly the kinds of difference that interest Rod, that allow and include a variety of different points of view, and that therefore reveal the "intricate interdependencies" in culture and in texts of a range of matters such as nationalism, race, culture, ethnicity, identity, sex, and gender. But in a footnote about her own work, Radway seriously undermines her celebration of difference by saying, "I place my own work within the traditional, 'Americanist,' highly spatialized paradigm of culture that I believe the new work on race, ethnicity, sexuality, and gender explicitly challenges. . . . My thoughts in this address are now prompted by an engagement with the work of others that challenges this fundamental presupposition." Her work is now unacceptable, she claims, exactly because it is different from the work that would celebrate difference by always and inevitably insisting on it—by making each and every voice express the same unified support of difference rather than allowing a range of different voices to intersect in their saying of different things. This dangerously repressive and currently popular urge to sameness threatens to homogenize literary scholarship just as thoroughly as the positions it purports to move beyond.

For that reason, I'm delighted that Margaret, Rod, and Tom have been willing to enunciate their differences with my own positions, and I particularly applaud Margaret's invitation to me and others to explore a variety of pleasures offered by texts of children's literature in addition to the one I've been devoting my attentions to. As Margaret describes them and I understand them, these pleasures aren't necessarily restricted to texts written for children, which is why I haven't devoted much thought to them yet. But if I'm right in assuming that the basic situation of an adult writing for children affects all aspects of the texts produced, then these pleasures, too, must emerge differently in children's literature than elsewhere. I plan to be thinking further about that—and also about the relations between pleasure and ideology that Rod foregrounds for me, and about the relations between depictions of childhood in texts for children and texts for adults that Tom raises. My ideas can only grow richer by intertwining and becoming interdependent with these different viewpoints.

Notes

1. See, for instance, the chapter "Common Assumptions About Childhood" in my book *The Pleasures of Children's Literature*, or ask any of my war-torn students.

2. I have to admit it *does* bother me a little. I tend to see understanding texts as not much different from understanding anything else. We all have different experiences of and tastes in, say, sofas, and different ways of thinking about them and using them. And any one of us is free to understand, say, a sofa, as a urinal, and use it accordingly—but we might be a happier community if we all agreed to pay enough attention to intended meanings to realize when other objects weren't intended as urinals and therefore we could share dry places to sit. In other words: literature is a communal activity, reading and writing about reading are social transactions based on convictions about the possibility that information is shareable—and it often is.

Work Cited

Radway, Janet. "What's in a Name? Presidential Address to the American Studies Association, 20 November, 1998." Available at http://muse.jhu.edu/demo/american_quarterly/v051/51.1radway.html.

Boyology in the Twentieth Century

Kenneth Kidd

No earthly object is so attractive as a well-built, growing boy.
— H. W. Gibson

"Is your son physical, aggressive, difficult to manage at home and at school?" asks John Merrow in a 1998 edition of his NPR program *The Merrow Report,* available on audiocassette as *Will Boys Be Boys?* If so, join the club. Merrow's guest, the therapist and author Michael Gurian, explains: "Males tend to be testosterone driven. You and I when we were fifteen years old got seven surges of testosterone per day," and "testosterone is not a nurturing hormone; testosterone is a hormone that wants sex." Those seven surges, in tandem with "hard wiring" in the brain, clearly distinguish boys from girls, claims Gurian in the interview, and we need a "massive reeducation," even a "boy's movement," to redirect our attention to the specific features and challenges of boyhood.

Such a movement, in fact, seems to be underway. The feature article of the May 11, 1998, issue of *Newsweek,* titled "Boys Will Be Boys," chronicles the recent interest in boyhood, evidenced by new academic research and parent support groups and by a rash of boy-rearing and self-help manuals, notably Gurian's *The Wonder of Boys: What Parents, Mentors and Educators Can Do to Shape Boys into Exceptional Men* (1996) and William Pollack's *Real Boys: Rescuing Our Sons from the Myths of Boyhood* (1998). Apparently based in Boston, this boys' movement imitates the mythopoetic men's movement and asserts itself against the recent attention to girls. The rhetoric of crisis is at once sexist and indebted to feminism. Boys are allegedly just as at risk as girls, the argument runs, but we've ignored the warning signs. We've misunderstood biology, and in our haste to redress sexism we've ignored the physiology and culture of boys.

Some of the evidence is quite alarming; boys are statistically more likely to drop out of high school and college, to commit petty and violent acts of crime, to attempt suicide, and to be diagnosed with at-

Children's Literature 28, eds. Elizabeth Lennox Keyser and Julie Pfeiffer (Yale University Press, © 2000 Hollins University).

tention deficit disorder and learning disabilities. There is cause for concern, and works such as *The Wonder of Boys* and *Real Boys* usefully interrogate attitudes that naturalize such problems as the inevitable stuff of boyhood. Even so, these works redefine gender as biological sex and presume biology as destiny. They ignore axes of definition and displacement such as race and class, arguing that social imprinting is mere "soft wiring," negligible in comparison to the hard wiring of biology. The consensus seems to be that attention to class and race, as well as the wrong kind of attention to sex difference, is precisely what has caused the current crisis. At the same time, these texts posit something called "boy culture" that seems part hard wiring, part soft wiring, at once inviolate and the site of intervention.

What *Newsweek* calls "a hot new field of inquiry: the study of boys" (Kantrowitz and Kalb 55) seems instead a revisitation of early twentieth-century "boyology." *The Wonder of Boys* and *Real Boys* look a great deal like the boy-rearing handbooks published in the first two decades of this century. Like their predecessors, who were closely associated with character-building agencies such as the Boy Scouts of America and the YMCA, Gurian and Pollack address a popular audience and claim expertise in the field, but they rewrite the tenets of boy work in the privatizing and custodial language of middle-class therapeutic culture. Although character has a residual life in these new books, the modern boy worker is usually a clinical psychologist. The master narrative, however, is the same: boys are misunderstood and in crisis, and they are different from (more important than) girls.

Gurian is thus particularly critical of feminism, which in tandem with progressive social movements has distorted "the simple information our ancestors have always known—that boys and girls have been wired differently for millions of years and need special, gender-specific attention" (*Wonder,* xiv). He doesn't see his account as troubling for girls. "We ended up with two daughters," he chuckles in the *Merrow Report,* and "what's nice about having two daughters is that nobody can accuse me in their right mind of being anti-female; certainly a father of two daughters is hopefully not going to do anything that's anti-female." But in *The Wonder of Boys* the first "gender myth" Gurian attacks is that girls "have life much worse than boys" (xvii). For Gurian, gender is a dirty word (even a myth) used in the plot against boys; he prefers "biology" and "nature" as proof of irreconcilable differences between the sexes. Our culture's faith in a child's social conditioning indicates "our arrogant belief that it's possible for human beings to create society that is not driven primarily by nature" (28). Gurian longs for real boys, not the wooden creatures of social theory. No wonder *The Wonder of Boys* opens with the moving words of Geppetto: "Pinocchio! Oh Pinocchio! / You're a boy! / A real boy!"

Pollack also advises that we turn our attention from Ophelia to her neglected brothers, because "Hamlet fared little better than Ophelia" (6). Pollack is the co-director of the Center for Men at McLean Hospital-Harvard Medical School, where he also holds a professorship. One of his colleagues is Carol Gilligan, whose recent research on separation anxiety in four-year-old boys has energized the boy's movement. Pollack thanks Gilligan in his acknowledgments, noting— unlike Gurian—that boys have much in common with girls and that scholars of masculinity owe much to women's studies. Although Pollack's book represents a kinder, smarter brand of boy study than Gurian's, it too pits boy against girl. Discussing Nancy Chodorow's research on mother-child identification, Pollack contends that since boys have trouble establishing a masculine self against that maternal bond, it follows that "being a boy or being masculine is not so much based on the positive identification with father but on the negation of the male child's tie to mother." In other words, *"Being a boy becomes defined in the negative: not being a girl"* (28, italics in original). Here Pollack acknowledges that gender identity is binary but also reverses in psychological terms the social reality asserted by feminists: culturally speaking, being a girl is typically defined in the negative, as not being a boy. Pollack's formulation has a sociological reality effect: he implies that boys are invisible and unreal, the victims of a stable and positive girlhood. Real boys, he explains, hide "behind a mask" while girls live in plain sight.

These primers routinely invoke boy books and male coming-of-age narratives. *Pinocchio* and *Hamlet* share the limelight with assorted folktales, films such as *Stand by Me* and *The Lion King*, and of course *The Adventures of Huckleberry Finn*. "If Huck Finn or Tom Sawyer were alive today," Gurian remarks in the *Newsweek* piece, "we'd say they had ADD or a conduct disorder" (56). As the American ur-text of boyhood, *Huckleberry Finn* is particularly popular, showing up also in *The Little Boy Book* (1986) by Sheila Moore and Roon Frost and in Michael Ruhlman's study of single-sex education, *Boys Themselves* (1996). *Huckleberry Finn,* of course, helped consolidate the trope of the "real boy" popularized by the Bad Boy genre some years before, a trope still pervasive in the literature of boyhood and, as *Real Boys* indicates, in the literature on boy-rearing. Thomas Bailey Aldrich's *The Story of a Bad Boy* (1869), typically credited as the inaugural Bad Boy tale, claims to sketch "a real human boy, such as you may meet anywhere in New England," quite distinct from that "impossible boy in a storybook" of the didactic persuasion (2). In 1862 Henry Ward Beecher colorfully noted that the "real lives of boys are yet to be written" and that tales of impossibly good boys "resemble a real boy's life about as much as a chicken picked and larded, upon a spit, and ready for delicious eating, resembles a free fowl in the fields" (73–74).

Although journals such as *Children's Literature* typically address texts written specifically for children—or cross-written for adults and children—I'd like to broaden the term *boy book* to include the primers I've been discussing. Writing primarily (if not exclusively) for adults, Pollack and Gurian appropriate the boy book and adapt it to new ends, just as child readers appropriate and adapt ostensibly adult writing. Such revision is easy with the boy book, because it has always been understood as a cross-written genre; Twain and Aldrich were clearly writing for adult as well as child readers, and many Bad Boy books are basically memoirs in thin disguise. The classic boy book is a tale of rural or small-town life, usually studied as a subgenre of realism (Trensky), as autobiography (Jacobson), and as male homosocial quest narrative (Fiedler, Boone). It has also been assessed as part of the "body-machine complex" of fin de siècle America (Seltzer) and as antimodern fantasy or antebellum nostalgia (Rodgers, Brown, Lowry). The boy-rearing book of yesteryear and today is also "realistic," autobiographical, and homosocial in emphasis. It too is nostalgic for halcyon days, anxious about urban culture, and ambivalent in its depiction of boyhood as a world apart.

Like the literary boy book, the boy-rearing book spatializes boyhood, marking off its psychic interiority in familiar physical and temporal terms. To borrow from some classic boy books, boyhood is a "court," a "kingdom," a "whilom," an "epoch," even in Hannibal or other specific towns—a world of harmless pranks and dreamy reverie just slightly removed from the world of adults. By using such mythic language, boy book authors do not have to account for the actual spaces of boyhood, some less idyllic than others. The boy-rearing book also uses such language to evade the pressures of local setting and to suggest a gap in need of judicious bridging. Whereas Aldrich and Twain celebrate the boy-adult divide, the boyologists argue that boys require space but shouldn't be left unsupervised. Men are the natural interlocuters; in fact, the authors of such books are almost always men. Only men can claim access to the authentic and otherwise inaccessible world of boyhood, intervene when necessary, and make that world available to the public, translating its vernacular into self-help parlance.

Simultaneously, however, this spatialization implies that boyhood is a universal experience, to the disadvantage not only of girls but also of boys other than those whose smiling Caucasian faces adorn the covers of W. H. Gibson's *Boyology or Boy Analysis* (1916) as well as *Real Boys* and *The Wonder of Boys*. Pinocchio and Huck Finn surface in such works because they are innocent white boys who are also gently delinquent. Universality is claimed not only for boyhood innocence but also for the "boy problem," a staple of middle-class self-help and children's fiction alike.

The Boy Problem

The term *boyology,* an allusion to biology, was given sustained expression in 1916 by Henry William Gibson in his *Boyology or Boy Analysis.* Gibson's book originated in a series of lectures to YMCA groups, mothers' meetings, parent-teacher associations, and women's clubs. Dedicated to his mother, *Boyology* is a practical handbook for parents, teachers, and character builders, devoid of "technical or scientific terms," written for lay readers "short in psychology, physiology, pedagogy, and sociology, but who are long in common sense and 'heartology'" (x). Divided into thirteen chapters, the text outlines the characteristics of boyhood, provides helpful tables and charts, and offers tips on boy management. We learn, for example, that the "slanguage" of the typical fifteen-year-old boy includes expressions such as "Oh lu lu!," "Glory be!," "Do you feel like fruit? have an onion!," and "Rats, go to grass!" (48–49). A YMCA leader and authority on camping, Scouting, and church work, with twenty-six years of "actual contact" with boys, Gibson hopes that *Boyology* will secure the "inalienable rights of boyhood" and foster "genuine sympathy" for "the struggles of youth" (ix).

The only thing remotely innovative about *Boyology,* however, is its title, and even that was less novel in 1916 than it now sounds. Gibson's text is a standard example of the American primers of boyhood published during the first two decades of the twentieth century. It serves more as an epitome of the genre than an original contribution to "boy analysis." *Boyology* was a familiar term that Gibson and others used in their lectures and institutional work. Boyology gave boy work a philosophy, codifying a cluster of ideas about boyhood and the national character that also inspired church youth work, organized camping, and character-building agencies such as the YMCA, Boys' Brigade, Order of the Knights of King Arthur, Sons of Daniel Boone, Order of the American Boy, Woodcraft Indians, Big Brothers, and the Boy Scouts.[1] Modeled in part on urban child-saving efforts, these agencies directed their attention chiefly to white, middle-class boys. Most were organized from 1900 to 1920, decades that saw the publication of influential handbooks predating Gibson's, notably William Byron Forbush's *The Boy Problem* (1901), Granville Stanley Hall's two-volume *Adolescence: Its Psychology and Its Relations to Physiology, Anthropology, Sociology, Sex, Crime, Religion, and Education* (1904), and Baden-Powell's *Scouting for Boys* (1908), quickly embraced in the United States. *American Boy* magazine, sponsor of the Order of the American Boy, was founded in 1899 and achieved a circulation of 360,000 by 1929.[2]

Such texts and organizations were the legacy of at least half a century of meditation on boyhood. By the century's turn, the boy had become an important literary and social subject, appearing at the expense of the "vanished" native. According to its champions, boy culture was analogous both to earlier stages of civilization and to contemporaneous primitive societies. Typically bourgeois white men, boy workers saw themselves as ethnographers and role models. They concerned themselves chiefly with younger boys, aged eight to twelve, and adolescent boys, aged twelve to sixteen; Hall alone distinguished adolescence from boyhood, and even his work suggests more continuity than difference. As the historians of boyhood have shown, character building had nineteenth-century origins; boyology likewise was nascent in nineteenth-century social movements and genres, even if officially a twentieth-century phenomenon.

The works of Forbush and Gibson provide rough bookends for modernist, or classic, boyology, by which I mean the post-1900 spate of organization and publication. During this period, boy work emphasized group participation as the preferred mode of character building (Macleod xvii–xviii), and the sudden deluge of boy manuals reflects that emphasis on networking and collaboration. Forbush's *The Boy Problem*, with an introduction by G. Stanley Hall, was the most commercially successful of the handbooks (published first in Boston, by the way). Reprinted eight times between 1901 and 1913, it established the "boy problem" as the formulaic opening of and rationale for the genre. By the time Gibson's *Boyology* appeared, that problem had been addressed exhaustively. *Boyology* in fact concludes with an annotated "Six Foot Shelf" of 103 books and pamphlets "about boys or subjects analogous to boy life" (260), organized in categories like general parenting, advanced child study, sex instruction, vocational guidance, church work, and recreation. Representative titles suggest the aims and emphases of boyology: Kate Upson Clark, *Bringing up Boys* (1899), Nathan C. Fowler, Jr., *The Boy—How to Help Him Succeed* (1902), John E. Gunckel, *Boyville: A History of Fifteen Years' Work Among Newsboys* (1905), E. L. Moon, *The Contents of the Boy* (1909), Wilburn Merrill, M.D., *Winning the Boy* (1908), Hanford M. Burr, *Studies in Adolescent Boyhood* (1910), Albert M. Chesley, *Social Activities for Men and Boys* (1910), George Walter Fiske, *Boy Life and Self-Government* (1910), Joseph Addams Puffer, *The Boy and His Gang* (1912), Frank Orman Beck, *Marching Manward* (1913), and William McCormick's *Fishers of Boys* (1915).

Boyology was not a discrete discourse, and its contradictions and inconsistencies make generalizations difficult. It was asserted against, even as it borrowed shamelessly from, the domestic wisdom of women and the expertise of doctors, social workers, educators, and academic psychologists. Some of the most prominent boyologists were themselves doctors and educators, and were affiliated with the child study movement led by Hall, but they distanced themselves from that movement in their writings for the public. Although boyology had progressive as well as reactionary impulses, Gibson's title page announces its basic agenda, featuring a photograph of a smiling adolescent boy, with the caption "Boy-stuff is the only stuff in the world from which men can be made." Boyology was not an exclusively male domain, but its authoritative figures were men, by virtue of their adult character or residual boy-stuff.

Forbush and Gibson were the most visible spokesmen of boyology. A clergyman and physician, Forbush helped organize the Men of Tomorrow and the Order of the Knights of King Arthur in 1895 and became president of the American Child Institute.[3] Gibson authored a number of books on camping and church work and served as YMCA state secretary in Massachusetts and Rhode Island. Both describe the contributions of women to boyology as practical and anecdotal by nature and not by design, as pure "heartology" rather than the strategic presentation of ideas for the lay reader. Thus the boyologists could dismiss books by women with the very praise they lavished on their own volumes. Gibson calls Clark's *Bringing up Boys,* for instance, a book of "old fashioned, therefore, good common sense" and Christine Ter- hume Herrick's *My Boy and I* (1913) a "chronicle of incidents occurring in the home life of normal boys" (269–70). Like Gibson, these women had actual contact with boys, but unlike current researchers such as Gilligan, they could not claim authority in the field. They could only report from it. The common sense and episodic chronicles of women did not constitute expertise. Mothers were encouraged not to publish their own work but to join Forbush's institute, where they could attend lectures and purchase materials.

Like early 1900s boyology, the current boys' movement stars male popularizers who work closely with women but get most of the pub- licity. Gilligan may be at the intellectual center of the contemporary boys' movement, but I'd be surprised if she became its spokesperson. It too seems part of a backlash against women (and, more elliptically, against gay men); Gurian's comments are in perfect accord with the more masculinist wing of the men's movement. As I've noted, Pollack's work represents a less virulent strain—for instance, he challenges Gu- rian's remarks about confused mothers—but even *Real Boys* repeats more than it revises the truisms of classic boyology.

Boyology has to this day two major functions: to establish the bio- logical reality of boyhood and the boy problem and to translate that reality into a discernable culture, in and around which boy work could be conducted. Boyhood functions much like wildness or madness, in that its referents change in response to the changing patterns of be- havior that they are meant to signify. Even so, in classic and contem- porary studies alike, boyhood is imagined first as a biological state and then as a fashioned culture. These sequential terms have been fairly stable in the past century or so, even if their definitions have shifted. In *Boyology,* for instance, Gibson devotes Chapter 1 to physical charac- teristics, explaining that the boy is "like a little beast, and many things that make the difference between a man and a beast make no differ- ence with him. He is, though, a man in the making" (3). Gibson dwells on the boy's beastly nature before describing his civic and spiritual tendencies, which make manhood possible. The average boy, we learn, has around 1,700 square inches of skin, each of which contains "about 3,500 sweating tubes, or respiring pores" (10).[4] Chapter 1 of Gurian's *Wonder of Boys* is titled "Where It All Begins: The Biology of Boyhood," followed by Chapter 2, "The Culture Boys Create." Gurian doesn't portray the boy as beastly—such a description would undermine his attempt to ennoble the boy—and Gibson's vision of boy culture as a friendly gang would strike fear in the hearts of most contemporary readers. But the biology-culture sequence is sustained.

The next two sections of this essay adapt this sequence, suggesting its roots in evolutionary and social science. To some degree, boyologists recognize that culture is a form of intelligibility and that the biology-culture sequence often poses as fact-knowledge. Gibson and Gurian promise to transform biological facts into cultural capital, celebrating the mystery of boyhood to their own interpretive credit. The boy, writes Gibson in his foreword, "is the original sulphite, keeping everybody awake and interested when he appears upon the scene. He will ever be a new subject for discussion and analysis, and in need of friendly interpreters" (ix). Gurian hopes to topple myths with the apolitical facts, so that everyone can experience the wonder of boys. Boyhood is at once self-evident and in need of interpretation, a familiar but always novel subject.

Boyhood as Bio-Power

Appearing before the boy worker on the American scene was the boy himself, and in particular, the boy-savage, precursor to and playmate of the real boy. The trope of the boy-savage was reanimated and devilified by social science's revisions of evolutionary metaphor in the mid-to-late nineteenth century. As a set of claims about the individual and social body, boyology might be understood as an instance of what Foucault calls "bio-power," a post-Enlightenment merging of technologies regulating the species with those regulating the individual. Foucault doesn't single out evolutionary science for discussion, but he does identify "evolutive historicity" as the temporal mode of bio-power in *Discipline and Punish* (160). In *The History of Sexuality* Foucault further identifies the masturbating schoolboy as one of four modern subjects of surveillance and regulation. He makes clear that the biopolitical "right to life" shapes our understanding of the schoolboy and the forces that imperil him; by masturbating that boy "was in danger of compromising not so much his physical strength as his intellectual capacity, his moral fiber, and the obligation to preserve a healthy line of descent for his family and his social class" (121).

Foucault's schoolboy is essentially the American boy-savage, watched over by parents, teachers, Scout leaders, ministers, even the president. Three doctrines were crucial to the formation of modern biopolitical subjects, and particularly the boy: the doctrine of recapitulation; Herbert Spencer's theory of diversification, or progress from the homogeneous to the heterogeneous; and Jean Baptiste Lamarck's belief in the inheritance of acquired characteristics. The first, recapitulation, has received the most attention because of its extreme popularity and its overtly racist and sexist incarnations in literature and social science. Recapitulation's chief proponent was Ernst Haeckel, whose biogenetic law held that ontogeny recapitulates the adult stages of phylogeny. Recapitulation linked three biological disciplines: embryology, which traces ontogeny, and comparative anatomy and paleontology, which attend phylogeny.[5]

Recapitulation was not the only biopolitical narrative of what I call more generally ontogenetic-phylogenetic correspondence, but it was the most popular and easy to abuse. Popularizers converted this principle into a generic analogy, implying that Caucasian boys were temporarily equal to adult savages but would outgrow them. By the 1860s, the boy-savage association, underwritten by popular accounts of recapitulation, was axiomatic in American letters. Often cited as evidence is Charles Dudley Warner's breezy declaration in *Being a Boy* (1877) that "every boy who is good for anything is a natural savage," having "the primal, vigorous instincts and impulses of an African savage" (150). The savage became childlike, and the boy comfortably savage, such that Warner could sketch the "race of boys" (66).

Whereas recapitulation affirmed that each creature reenacted the development of its group, the second two evolutionary principles emphasized the "progress" of that development. Borrowing from Karl Ernst von Baer, Spencer reconciled recapitulation with the principle of diversification, writing in his essay "Progress: Its Law and Cause" (1857) that "from the earliest traceable cosmical changes down to the latest results of civilization, we shall find that the transformation of the homogeneous into the heterogeneous, is that in which Progress essentially consists" (40). He specifically notes resemblances between aboriginals and schoolboys: "the authority of the strongest makes itself felt among a body of savages as in a herd of animals, or a posse of schoolboys" (42). The differentiation of labor and production similarly occurs both in primitive cultures and "among groups of schoolboys" (50). Spencer's schoolboy is an instance of homogeneity but also the promise of diversification and Progress; boys may now be primitive, but they will evolve. In their manward march, boys recapitulate and surpass the savage, the feminine, the criminal poor, and the homogeneous, in its various social-sexual manifestations, becoming, to quote Theodore Roosevelt's "The American Boy" (1899), "thoroughly manly, thoroughly straight and upright" (164).

The third significant evolutionary principle, Lamarck's theory of the inheritance of acquired characteristics, was more closely affiliated with child-saving and forensic writing on "dangerous" populations than with boyology per se, but still it exercised some influence on boy work, particularly in the cities. Lamarck observed that, in some species, adaptations to environment become natural features in subsequent generations. Such an idea, of course, includes the threat of devolution as well as the promise of progress and was often used to condemn the immigrant poor. Even so, the Lamarckian strain of boy primitivism was potentially more ameliorative than the strictly recapitulationist account, which separated savage white boys from the real thing. The feral boy rather than the boy-savage is the motif of reformers, since children raised in wild or dicy environments could become productive citizens with makeovers or relocation.

These three evolutionary principles share an emphasis on boyhood as an indisputable reality, as a stage of life that follows the natural laws of evolution and that conjoins the macro and the micro. Boyhood became a synedoche for evolution and the Law of Progress, articulated and consolidated primarily along evolutionary and (later) literary-naturalistic lines. The force of this tradition can be felt in the modern insistence on the biology of boyhood, believed immune to narrative mismanagement. Our current culture prefers biochemical and genetic stories, and although they sometimes have strategic advantages (including their resistance to developmental narratives), we must monitor their claim to authority. In *The Wonder of Boys*, Gurian's confidence in brain science is uncomfortably reminiscent not only of phrenology but of the nineteenth-century faith in encephalization as the interpretive key to human nature.[6]

Like the literary boy books before them, the boy-rearing manuals of Gurian and Pollack claim universality for boyhood, representing it as a distinct world with its own features and laws. What Bill Brown calls the "chronotopic work of the boy's book" (173) is also the work of boyology more generally. Such spatialization, which tends temporally toward the mythic, is a standard feature of the biopolitical coordination of boyhood. The German educator Friedrich Wilhelm August Froebel, for instance, notes in *The Education of Man* (1826) that the boy "forms for himself his own world; for the feeling of his *own power* implies and soon demands also the possession of his *own space* and his *own material* belonging exclusively to him" (106, italics in original). Gurian adds that boys "tend to use up far more space than girls" (15). Girls play contentedly in small corners, while boys merit more room and presumably more private property. "So often the boy's brain cries out to us . . . : 'Give me more space!' " (*Wonder* 16).

In early twentieth-century boy books, as in the primers of boyology, the boy is an a priori positivity, a body actively engaged with the forces of history but rarely changed by them. For example, Rupert S. Holland's *Historic Boyhoods* (1909), with chapters on such figures as Christopher Columbus, Peter the Great, Daniel Boone, and Andrew Jackson (some of which first appeared in shorter form in *St. Nicholas*), implies that boyhood is more constant than variable, since these heroes allegedly shared fundamental character traits. The book's illustrations include a color picture of the archetypal snow fort, where boys reenact ancestral wars. In this book, the qualities of the boy, including innate savagery, anticipate future greatness, and multiplicity serves the interest of a familiar tale. Hartwell James's *The Boys of the Bible* (1905) likewise makes boyhood a constant by recasting biblical greats such as Isaac, Jacob, David, Absalom, and Jesus himself as "The Boy Who Obeyed," "The Farmer Boy," "The Shepherd Boy," "The Boy Who Would Be King," and "The Boy Jesus."[7]

More typically, boyhood is imagined in the archetypal singular. Dorothy Margaret Stuart's engaging *The Boy Through the Ages* (1926), first published in England, also uses the boy as a stable vantage point for historiography, tracing attitudes toward boys from cave-dwelling days to the middle of Queen Victoria's reign. "As the long pageant of boy-life through the ages passes before us," she rhapsodizes, "with its gay and sombre colours and shadows, and then narrows and recedes into the distance again, we see that the first great influence which moulded the minds of men and the lives of their sons was the love of learning" (281). Apparently the boy is a natural scholar. Ages and attitudes pass, but the "pageant of boylife" goes on. Most of these boyhood-of texts are single volumes, compilations in their own right, but some belong to a series. Francis Rolt-Wheeler's U.S. Service Series sought to inspire patriotism and a sense of history by dramatizing the boy-affiliated operations of federal agencies. My personal favorite, *The Boy with the U.S. Mail* (1916), is packed with photographs and thrilling tales, told in chapters such as "The Honor of the Postage Stamp" and "A Desperado Mail Carrier." "The handling and delivery of the U. S. Mail is alive with its own perils," Rolt-Wheeler warns in the preface; "Blizzards may howl and flood may rage, but 'The Mail Must Go Through.'"

In such texts, boyhood is imagined as a world at odds with (and partially imperiled by) dystopic worlds. In *The Boy Today* (1930), Mather Almon Abbott describes the boy as the victim of intellectualism, or "mental indigestion" (16), and of the "godless world," which includes "automobile world," the "bootlegging world," and of course the "hard-boiled world." But boyhood survives these predatory forces. With guidance, the boy today is the boy of yesterday and also of tomorrow. "Boyhood is fundamentally the same as boyhood has always been" (113). Boyhood is at once static and dynamic, inaccessible and supervised, singular and collective.

Social Pedagogy and the Culture Idea

The anthropological idea of culture, which found canonical expression in E. B. Tylor's *Primitive Culture* (1871), offered boyhood another, overlapping form of existence and intelligibility: as a culture or subculture, analogous to but independent of adult society. Boy-book writers had already suggested as much, and travel writers likened boy gangs to the heathen clans they encountered abroad. A less racist composite example is Bayard Taylor's travel narrative, *Boys of Other Countries: Stories for American Boys* (1876), which features five short stories about boys whom Taylor met overseas, including "The Little Post-Boy" of Sweden, with whom Taylor snuggles for survival during an icy night, and Hans, a German herd-boy about whom Taylor writes, in keeping with the spirit of the times: "Hans was not a bad boy: he was simply restless, impatient, and perhaps a little inclined to envy those in better circumstances" (124). He emphasizes the constancy of the boy and his enduring qualities: "I have found many instances among other races, and in other climates," he reports to his young readers, "of youthful courage, and self-reliance, and strength of character, some of which I propose to relate to you" (2). Taylor's collection is contemporaneous with Warner's *Being a Boy*, which takes the New England farm boy as its exemplary and exotic subject. The boy became both strange and familiar enough to merit his own culture, and the primers of boyology read much like travel narratives.

The boyologists also made creative use of a metaphor of recapitulation congruent with the culture idea: the culture epochs concept of the German philosopher Johann Friedrich Herbart. In the 1890s, American Herbartians used this concept to revitalize curriculum theory. The culture epochs concept extended culture into the domain of ontogenetic-phylogenetic relation; the parallelism between the development of the human race and the development of the individual suggested certain "epochs" in the child's mental life that required particular kinds of instruction and activity. These epochs dictated the very materials with which educators should work and the general emphasis of each grade level (see Kliebard 72–73). As with the concept of culture more generally, boy culture was not so much the sum of those stages, epochs, and materials but the promise and ostensible measure of their correspondence. As Christopher Herbert puts it in *Culture and Anomie*, "what gives [culture] ethnographic significance— what enables it to generate a method of research, a set of directed assumptions, problems, and procedures—is the presumption that this array of disparate-seeming elements of social life composes a significant *whole*, each factor of which is in some sense a corollary of, consubstantial with, implied by, immanent in, all the others" (5). The epochs concept implied precisely such wholeness and intelligibility and was inherently pedagogical and easily adapted. Froebel had already claimed that *"boyhood is the period in which instruction predominates"* (95, italics in original); boy workers had only to expand the field of instruction. Forbush's *The Boy Problem* is aptly subtitled *A Study in Social Pedagogy*, and social pedagogy and boyology quickly became synonymous. "For helping this age," writes Forbush, "social pedagogy, the combination of educative forces in a social direction, is a new and most important science" (26).

Forbush offers a synopsis of the "by-laws of boy-life," and the ways in which boys spontaneously organize, but stops just short of the culture idea. He is too invested in what he calls "instrumentalities" (management techniques) to endorse a more holistic concept, which might engender resistance to the intervention he advocates. But the epochs concept does inform a number of boyology primers, particularly George Walter Fiske's *Boy Life and Self-Government* (1910), revised from a series of lectures and published by the YMCA's Association Press. Fiske was a professor of practical theology in the Oberlin Theological Seminary, and *Boy Life* is quite practical and far less prescriptive than *The Boy Problem;* Fiske is even critical of some boy work organizations. But Fiske certainly has his own fantasy of boy culture to share, and he is just as eager to promote the proper instrumentalities. A quick detour through *Boy Life* suggests both the rhetorical appeal and the nonsense-logic of the epochs concept.

Boy Life opens with a diagnosis of "Jimmie, James and Jim," the tripartite self of the typical boy—respectively, the "rollicking savage," the "nice little man," and the "manly boyish fellow, frank of face and sound at heart," to whom the others give birth after much labor (12–13). These personas must surface at the appropriate time. "What if Jim comes too soon?" Fiske asks. Such prematurity will result in that most distasteful condition, "precocious little manhood" (15). Jimmie, James, and Jim escort us through Fiske's text, which emphasizes the birthright of boys to organize their own institutions. Fiske expresses reservations about using the term *government,* recognizing that it "has the usual inaccuracy of the figure synecdoche, the use of the part for the whole" (24), but embraces the equally figurative culture epochs concept. He cites the emerging literature of "social education" but locates citizenship firmly in a boy-driven pedagogy: "In all boy problems the boys themselves must first give us the cue; for after all, the Supreme Court of Boyville is the *heart of the boy*" (41, italics in original).

This concern with the sacred hearts of boys opens the third chapter, "Boy Life and Race Life," and inaugurates Fiske's Herbartian scheme. He cites recent authorities on the boy-savage parallel—Hall, James Mark Baldwin, and A. F. Chamberlain—to establish that "recapitulation is not merely a physical fact but *psychic and social as well,*" a fact "too great to be ignored by students and lovers of boys" (55, italics in original). Fiske cautions his readers that the theory has its limitations, and that boy lovers should not overlook "the modifying influence" of the boy's immediate environment (58). For Fiske, culture denotes that environment as well as past epochs. Fiske often speaks of "race culture," but he attributes the differences among boys to social factors, including urban distress, which hinder or accelerate recapitulation. Reviewing popular schemes of culture epochs, he provides a chart of Dr. Woods Hutchinson's five overlapping stages of "food getting," which correspond to stages of child development: Root and Grub, Hunting and Capture, Pastoral, Agricultural, and Shop and Commercial. The Hunting and Capture epoch, for instance, usually culminates in the seventh year; boys in this epoch fear strangers, practice methods of stalking, and are indifferent to pain and given to cruelty. They prefer games of stealth and assault, including Hide and Seek, Black Man, and Prisoner's Base (64). Boys in the next epoch develop both foresight and a passion for gardening (64).

Fiske's boy culture is political in theme and biopolitical in strategy; he divides the epochs into two larger categories: stages in the evolution of government (there are five) and stages of industrial evolution (four) (66–67). He then returns to the boy's instincts, reinterpreting them as the basis for an initially laissez-faire boyology. Don't interfere with recapitulation, he warns; allow the spontaneity of urge and emotion. Encourage the development of the will, but don't disrupt the transition in boy culture from primitive democracy through tyrannical feudalism to republican social democracy. If left alone, the boy's industrial instincts will likewise cycle through acquisitive, destructive, constructive, and cooperative phases, the last of which enables commerce and the growth of cities. Boy workers, notes Fiske, can learn much from a systematic study of "boy made societies" (115), the alleged basis of modern democracy. Unfortunately, the average boy's club or gang is short-lived and does not afford the boyologist a stable object of inquiry. If only, Fiske laments,

> in our study of boy life, we could discover a modern boy colony, with a distinct social life of its own, continuing through a series of years, isolated from cities and free from adult interference, how delighted we should be! Then we should be able to study boys in a true boy's world, and watch the activities of the unfettered boy will. Then we could discover how boys, untrammeled by adult notions and customs, would develop naturally such social and economic customs of their own as their needs required. Then, too, we might see clearly whether or not the influence of race habit would work out, and the modern boy really recapitulate the progress of the race. Such a self-governing boy world, if we could discover it, would also teach us many things about our subject of self-government in boy life. (118)

A close approximation conveniently supplies itself: the McDonogh School near Baltimore. Presumably a boarding school (the description is sketchy), the McDonogh School offers boys what similar institutions do not: lots of space, in the form of eight hundred acres of farm and forest, where boys and their cramped brains may roam at will. The teachers do not regulate their recreation, and over the years certain "customs and unwritten laws" (120) have evolved that echo the epochs of government and industry. As the grounds became more settled by the boys, more complex forms of land tenure and harvest emerged; unregulated use yielded to squatter rights, succeeded by private ownership and monopoly. A socialist political party even formed to protest capitalist travesties and promote land redistribution (of course it didn't survive). The McDonogh boys, concludes Fiske, "seem clearly to have proved the truth of the culture-epochs views along social, economic, and partly governmental lines" (142).[8]

Obviously the McDonogh School was designed for boys by adults, with specific means and to specific ends, and is hardly comparable to spontaneously organized boy peer groups. Fiske's step-by-step analysis of this boy colony illustrates how seductive the epochs concept could be. Fiske lives the contradiction of boyology, declaring the autonomy of boy culture while dictating its nature and nurture. The second half of *Boy Life* provides instructions for the supervision of boy republics, including manipulation of the "boy ballot" (210). Fiske contrasts his own practice with the "benevolent despotism" of boy work uninformed by scientific study and driven solely by charisma (206). He also appeals to missionary strategy: "Foreign missions are now conducted on the principle that each nation must be Christianized by natives. . . . China is to be saved by the Chinese. . . . Boys must be won and saved *by boys*" (200–201, italics in original). Or by men pretending to be boys. Even if "the adult should guide from the rear" (221), Fiske recommends the missionary position, having little use for alternative lifestyles: "How ludicrously pathetic are the little Amish boys, dressed in long pantaloons and old men's broad-rimmed hats, as soon as they get well out of the cradle" (42).

As Fiske's text demonstrates, the primers of boyology, whatever their anxieties and investments, construct a rhetoric of culture around the often contradictory axioms of boyhood. There is some consensus; boys are presumed to be primitive or savage to some degree and to spontaneously congregate, "for it is a law of nature," as Gibson explains in *Boyology*, "for bees to go in swarms, cattle in herds, birds in flocks, fishes in schools, and boys in gangs. . . . The most interesting thing to a boy is another boy" (82–83). And yet, boys also mimic adult social institutions such as the city and the republic, which are anything but homogeneous. Perhaps the homo-to-hetero master narrative makes both forms of culture possible, but in this and other respects boyology seems inconsistent at best. While arguing for the tripartite Jimmie, James, and Jim, Fiske urges readers "to find the truth in the strange *duality* of boyhood" (12, italics in original); Hanford Burr agrees in *Studies in Adolescent Boyhood* that "a kind of Jekyll and Hyde duality is very common, even though fond parents may shut their eyes to it" (12–13). Others take a less nuanced stance. "Boys are animals," Lilburn Merrill declares flatly in *Winning the Boy* (113). Some boyologists emphasize the receptiveness and curiosity of boys, whereas Gurian argues in *The Wonder of Boys* that they instinctively distrust the uncanny: "Aversion toward the strange is a deep-rooted instinct or emotion," and undirected "will make him a snob of the worst sort" (69). Boyology is less a set of coherent principles than a rhetoric of observation and intervention. "The sorting of boys is uncertain business at best," writes Fiske. "We are learning to let them classify themselves"—this after several hundred pages of careful sorting (201).

The culture idea has been particularly resilient in contemporary accounts of boyhood, sometimes challenged and sometimes taken at face value. Gary Alan Fine offers fresh insight in his engaging study of preadolescent Little League idiocultures, but E. Anthony Rotundo's chapter on boy culture in *American Manhood* (1993) repeats much of the received wisdom of the boyologists. Rotundo notes that the nineteenth-century self-made man was defined in contrast to the impulsive, aggressive boy, but he takes that boy as a positivity rather than a largely discursive creature. Nineteenth-century boy culture "was suprisingly free of adult intervention—it gave a youngster his first exhilarating taste of independence and made a lasting imprint on his character" (32). Rotundo seems not to recognize that such independence was likely more rhetoric than fact, and that character is carefully cultivated.

Even as he announces their freedom, Rotundo claims that the boys of yesteryear were "embedded in a feminine world," confined to home and forced to wear girls' clothes. Such practices ran counter to boy-savage instincts, which found an outlet in acts of casual violence. Boys thus formed a sadomasochistic subculture: "One of the bonds that held boy culture together was the pain that youngsters inflicted on each other" (35). Aggression and competition as well as playful cooperation abounded in this utopian zone. "Boys loved to compare themselves to animals," he notes, "and two animal similes seem apt here. If at times boys acted like a hostile pack of wolves that preyed on its own kind as well as other species, they behaved at other times like a litter of playful pups who enjoy romping" (45). Rotundo's boy culture is too derivative of Kipling and Baden-Powell. His discussion of adolescence shows the same vacillation between description and re-enactment of literary images. *American Manhood* is not only an analysis of boy culture but one of its more studied expressions.

Both *The Wonder of Boys* and *Real Boys* are extended exercises in the culture idea. Gurian is quick to emphasize his worldliness; born in the 1950s in Honolulu, he has lived in India, Wisconsin, Wyoming, Colorado, Israel, Turkey, and Spokane; his father worked on the Southern Ute reservation in northern New Mexico. Many chapters of *The Wonder of Boys* begin with an invocation of experiences abroad: "In eastern Brazil, among the Shavantee"; "There is an old Italian saying"; "It is a clear day. An old woman and a young woman wander to an already chosen place at the outskirts of their aboriginal village." The third chapter, "Boys Need a Tribe," advances Gurian's thesis that boys need a three-family tribe comprised of the nuclear family, the extended family, and the family of man. The boy's second birth into manhood is to be guided by fathers and male mentors who can revise the initiation rites of aboriginals; Gurian advocates everything but ritual fellatio and converts the classic folktale "Jack and the Beanstalk" into a story of quasi-sexualized initiation. The old man gives Jack the "magic seeds" he needs for his "initiatory Journey" (135). "When boys around us climb their beanstalks, they spend more time in the masculine realm" (137) and thus learn "A Sacred Male Role for the New Millennium" (250).

That sacred male role, as we might expect, is business as usual. Consider Gurian's warning in the *Will Boys Be Boys?* segment of *The Merrow Report* about the danger of pop culture icons as third-family members: "If Dennis Rodman is in my family, he's going to be a black sheep I would think. . . . If I'm trying to raise kids . . . and Dennis Rodman's in my family at the Thanksgiving dinner," that influence will be hard to combat. He then clarifies: "I'm picking Dennis Rodman out, you know; it could be anyone who's just kind of a crazy man setting the wildest, weird example." He admits, when pressed by Merrow, that it could just as easily be Mick Jagger. The lesson of *Guess Who's Coming to Dinner?* seems lost on Gurian.

Real Boys is politically more progressive but just as indebted to a rather selective form of ethnography and to the universalizing mythos of boyhood. Pollack draws from his clinical practice and his ongoing research project "Listening to Boys' Voices," conducted at Harvard Medical School. This project involves "studying hundreds of young and adolescent boys, observing them in various situations, conducting empirical testing, and talking with their parents" (xxi). In the introduction, Pollack returns us to the boy problem, writing that "Boys today are in serious trouble, including many who seem 'normal' and to be doing just fine" (xix). They hide behind the repressive Boy Code.

His rhetoric of crisis isn't consistent; in the beginning he stresses the severity of the boy problem but later praises the ingenious coping strategies of boys. Pollack questions the appropriateness of frontier myth, but he also adapts it: "I believe one of the reasons boys find the frontier so appealing is that they feel they are inhabiting a kind of emotional and physical frontier of their own" (348–49).

Pollack's real boys seem to exist outside of adult culture and even culture more generally; occasionally we hear about particular boys, but for the most part, listening to boys' voices means listening to Pollack tell us, selectively, about boys' voices. The boys seem almost phantasmic; Pollack must export and interpret their realism for us in the usual anthropological style. *Real Boys* is a compelling book, not only because of its insights and gentle tone but because of its utopian vision. It depends on a culture of boyhood familiar from the portraits of Tom, Huck, and other real boys—impossibly outside of and distinct from the elements that comprise and threaten said culture.

It may be that the culture idea is not simply an extension of bio-power but its most successful incarnation to date. In any case, it seems to unite the boy-rearing books of today and yesteryear. Distinguishing them is their program of intervention and their spin on the boy-savage trope. For Forbush and Gibson, boyology is a social movement, part grass-roots pedagogy and part institutional clout; for Gurian and Pollack, it is largely a private practice and a family affair. In *The Boy Problem* and *Boyology*, savagery is invoked not only because there was a clear distinction between racial others and the middle-class white boy, but also because savagery was often a less pejorative concept than we might assume, associated with self-reliance and entrepreneurial spirit. Although attitudes toward racial others ranged greatly, the boy-savage represented the positive virtues of savagery, safely contained in the middle-class home. In the works of Forbush and Gibson, boy work is a simple process of channeling boys' savagery into useful pursuits. In the more recent *The Wonder of Boys* and *Real Boys*, however, savagery is linked with dangerous external forces that threaten the family. Savagery is thus evacuated from middle-class boyhood and attributed to both society at large (the urban jungle) and specific populations (inner-city gangs).

A Womb of Their Own

Forbush and Gibson found it easy at the beginning of the century to praise the boy-savage and to suppress issues of class and race, and

Gurian and Pollack show the same disinclination to a truly multicultural boyology. The only example of such an approach that I've seen is Franklin Abbott's *Boyhood, Growing up Male: A Multicultural Anthology* (1993), which also resorts to the "real boys" trope. Women, however, have been more troubling for the boyologists, their centrality to the family impossible to ignore. If boyology is ostensibly men's work, it is also a domestic practice, defined in terms of the home front rather than the workplace. The boy takes his place in the working world only if he absorbs middle-class values at home. The character builders and boyologists acknowledged that women begin the training of boys and that Scouting and camping must imitate family structures. At the same time, they were jealous of the influence of women and argued (incoherently) that the early years of childhood are less consequential than the later conversion of boys into men, which they described as a rebirth.

The boy-rearing book typically demands the labor of women and other domestics but obscures the significance of that labor with both explicit dismissals and organic portraits of the boy outdoors. If boys are domesticated by women and then retrained by men, the logic runs, then the women's sphere is secondary in importance and reactive in nature. The boyologists can thus represent women as the original caretakers against whom they assert their own expertise, even as they insist that boyhood is somehow prior to all things maternal. The privatized family remains the province of the boy worker-practitioner, appointed to keep the boy at home literally and ideologically, and to downplay (if not belittle outright) the role of mothers.

Women challenging male expertise are treated harshly, especially in the boyology of the early century. In *Winning the Boy* (1908), for example, Lilburn Merrill lambastes a woman lecturer whose physiognomy and dress reveal "the mistake that had been made in creating her a woman" and whose views on boyhood are repugnant (35). He joins a long line of authorities who decry the monstrous issue of women, prefiguring the misogynistic Momism of Philip Wylie and company in the 1940s as well as intervening and more contemporary alarms about feminization.[9] If the mythopoetic men's movement has adjusted the rhetoric, it too perpetuates nutty narratives of feminization and sexual dysphoria. The ur-text is of course Robert Bly's *Iron John*, a primer for recovering archetypes such as the King, the Warrior, and the Wild Man. *Iron John* demonstrates the inefficacy of asserting what Jane Tompkins calls the "sentimental power" of women, since that power is precisely what's vilified and then regendered.

Bly's sexism is largely inspired by his focus on boyhood as a special stage of development. Echoing the recapitulationists, Bly asserts that "the boy is mythologically living through the past history of man" and that "the ancient practice of initiation [is] still very much alive in our genetic structure" (36). Bly's revision of *der Eisenhans* pits the boy against his domineering mother.[10] He writes that "every modern male has, lying at the bottom of his psyche, a large primitive being covered with hair down to his feet. Making contact with this Wild Man is the step the Eighties male or the Nineties male has yet to make" (6). We must free that man by stealing the key of autonomy from under our mother's pillow—"just where Freud said it would be" (11). "A mother's job is, after all, to civilize the boy, and so it is natural for her to keep the key." Even more disturbing is *King, Warrior, Magician, Lover: Rediscovering the Archetypes of the Mature Masculine,* by Robert Moore and Douglass Gillette, offered as an "owner's manual for the male psyche" (xii). Moore and Gillette distinguish Boy Psychology from Man Psychology using bizarre drawings of psychosocial pyramids. The successful Oedipal Child's "shadow self" is the auto- or homoerotic Mama's Boy, who compulsively masturbates, reads pornography, and avoids heterosexual sex and marriage.

Hungry for archetype, such primers posit boyhood as the developmental prelude to, and feminized betrayal of, the mature masculine. Boys, they claim, have been deprived of meaningful rituals and intimacy. We've seen how the boy-rearing books of Gurian and Pollack rely on that sense of homosocial deprivation; another example is Bernard Weiner's even more practical *Boy into Man: A Father's Guide to Initiation of Teenage Sons.* This handbook recounts the rebirth experiences of six adolescents forced by their fathers to spend a weekend in the wilderness of northern California. Ensconced in giant papier-mâché hands, the fathers "summoned" their sons from school to the campsite, where they spent their days baking bread, drumming, having their feet washed, and listening to the shaman's stories of "the King, the Prince, the Wildman and Coyote/Trickster" (40). On the front cover is a photograph of the men costumed as these characters. Before leaving home, the boys had to steal the key of autonomy from underneath their mothers' pillows. Despite their support, the mothers were discouraged from planning and barred from participating, though each wrote her son a special letter, and the ceremony included a brief speech from the masked "figure of Woman" (34).

My final example blurs the boundaries of primer and boy book and embodies the very worst of boyology past and present. Published by

Hyperion as a children's book, Bruce Brooks's *Boys Will Be* (1993) is a collection of essays cross-written for boys and those who work with them. *Boys Will Be* targets readers aged ten to fourteen, opining on a wide array of topics, including headgear, bullies, body odor, books, "Risky Pals," Arthur Ashe, and hockey. As Brooks explains in the "Non-exclusionary Introduction," sounding like Gibson and Gurian, it is "a book about boy stuff, written for boys to read, by a former boy who is now raising two boys of his own" (5). He then adds that "it is very likely that a federal judge can force me to write a precisely-equal-length book for girls" with articles about "the pros and cons of sparkle in lip gloss, or the twelve best ways of sucking up to teachers and making them think you are just the most devoted little helpful student in the whole wide world" (5). He implies that boys are blamed for society's woes and that girls should just stop griping until they'r' ready to share the blame.

Boys Will Be is a must-read for aspiring weekend warriors. Brooks's little truisms about boy stuff echo those of the character builders, whom he specifically mentions in the last chapter. Boys will one day discover the joys of sex and marriage, but "during a certain age boys enjoy the company of only boys. . . . This is the nature of life" (10). In that homogeneous "boy society" (14), language is not a means of communication but of signifying; boys are apparently trickster figures, as Shelley Fisher Fishkin has argued of Huck Finn. Echoing Leslie Fiedler, Brooks playfully uses such archetypes as the Good Boy (GB) and the Not-Quite-Bad Boy to distinguish his own son (a GB, of course) from "Risky Pals" or from the neighborhood riff-raff. He insists on the universality of fights and takes pride in his young son's scent: "Spencer's aroma was definitely an animal scent too, but one made by a more refined gland. It was musky but smart. It contained a mild wildness" that barely distinguishes the boy from the family dog (57). Brooks's wife wrinkles her nose, preferring the effeminate smell of baby products. After all, "girls never seem to give off a pungent natural aroma" (59).

Despite some engaging chapters, *Boys Will Be* is a nasty attack on girls, mothers, "clever social work theorists" (42), and misguided librarians (63). Brooks devotes an entire chapter to "Ten Things You Cannot Expect Your Mom to Come Close to Understanding." Ironically, he criticizes the boy workers for ignoring the needs of the boy. These men were wrong to assume the "innate savagery and deceitfulness of boys" (127). "The disrespect here is more than a matter of suspicion or distrust. It is a matter of ignoring what the boys themselves might want, because someone else always knows what's best for them" (128). Brooks's claim to authority is different from that of classic boyology only in his revision of the boy-savage trope; he too asserts a sexist boy culture whose realism he renders in a playful, writerly vein. The book betrays his caveat that "Becoming a man means more than endlessly living out a fantasy of boyhood" (119). Here again, civilization is women's work before it becomes the noble calling of men, in the familiar form of the boy book.

Boys Will Be appeared three years before Gurian's *The Wonder of Boys,* and it is far more disturbing because of its hyperbole and its status as a children's book. Unlike Gurian, Brooks is speaking directly to child readers, using and mocking the language of feminism. At times Brooks seems even to trope the conventions of boyology, recognizing that his book is part primer, but those moments quickly yield to the standard misogyny. Brooks's sentiments are neither natural nor benevolent; they depend on hateful cliché, and never more so than in their boasts of realism and novelty.

Conclusion

The racist and sexist impulses of boyology make it tempting to identify boyhood itself as a form of white male privilege, at once invisible and hypervisible. Although it has clearly functioned as ideological cover for some unfortunate attitudes, I do not want to vilify boyhood any more than I hope to recover its innocence. I've been harder on boyology, largely to counter its rhetoric of realism and altruism. Most of us, however, take interest in the education and management of boys, and perhaps there's such a thing as responsible boyology. How do we indulge our own boyologist inclinations without resorting to the images and practices that I've identified? Perhaps the first step is to acknowledge that the discourse of boyhood is already fashioned out of both a biopolitical essentialism and a strong commitment to the culture idea. It is easy to criticize particular ideological positions along the biology-culture or nature-nurture divide; a greater challenge is to historicize those positions and to account for the ways in which they coexist, whether in harmony or in contradiction (or both).

Boyology prospers because it accommodates shifts in rhetoric, redefinitions of biology and culture. The details are negotiable. Boyology is invested less in those seven daily surges of testosterone, for

example, or in the Root and Grub stage of boy culture, than in the
larger aims of boy work. Or as Gurian and Pollack put it in their re-
spective subtitles, in *What Parents, Mentors and Educators Can Do to Shape
Boys into Exceptional Men* and in *Rescuing Our Sons from the Myths of Boyhood*.[11] Boyology is not simply a story of biology and culture but also
an evolving professional enterprise, one not altogether different from
literary authorship.

Boyology was understood even by its earliest practitioners as both
theory and social pedagogy, and in this essay I've tried not only to describe and criticize boyology but to transform it into a useful scholarly
project. In her book *Home Fronts,* Lora Romero points out that feminism as a social and interpretive practice is fashioned from the very
codes of domesticity that it allegedly rejects. Boyology the critical discourse is likewise indebted to and inseparable from boyology the literary and social practice. Drawing from the engaging scholarship on
girl culture that has recently appeared, we might further argue that
boyology has shaped the lives of boys much as domestic ideology has
shaped the lives of girls. Boys, like girls, were confined to the domestic
sphere at least during childhood, and boyology and domestic ideology
may be not only analogous but discursively interdependent. Boyology
is arguably also a form of gender-role socialization and surveillance.

The differences between boyology and domestic ideology are as instructive as the continuities. As yet there is no "girlology," only assertions of "girl power" by pop groups such as the Spice Girls. The
bestsellers of Mary Pipher, Peggy Orenstein, and others were not interpreted in the national press as constituting a girl's movement or
a "hot new field of study." As a modern subject, the girl has been
less self-evident than the boy, more "sentimental" and abstract—imagined more as a "question" than a "problem."[12] In response, some critics have overemphasized the girl's "sentimental power."[13] In any case,
studies of domesticity and girlhood may help expose boyology as hazardous to everyone, including the boys about and for whom it claims
to speak.

Notes

1. For more on character building in its assorted forms, see Macleod, Jeal, Rosenthal,
and Seltzer.
2. *American Boy* was published in Detroit by William C. Sprague. In its inaugural issue
(November 1899), Sprague offered the following rationale for his new project: "This
paper is for boys—American boys, the brightest and best boys on the face of the earth.

It is not a family paper, tho' men and women with boys' hearts will read it. It is not a child's paper, of which we all know there are enough already" (Reck viii). *American Boy* was designed instead for "the wide-awake, aspiring American boy who is just turning the corner into manhood" (Reck viii). In 1929 it purchased the ailing *Youth's Companion*, which boosted its circulation. It began to fail during the Depression and finally folded in 1941.

3. Forbush was a disciple of Hall and of the YMCA's dynamic leader, Luther Gulick, who was co-founder with his wife Charlotte of the Camp Fire Girls.

4. Gibson also explains the physiological benefits of assorted sports, disparaging the "anemic boy prodigy" and the bookworm with "soft hands, tender feet, and tough rump from too much sitting" (18).

5. For an intriguing account of this principle and its life in social science and popular culture, see Gould's *Ontogeny and Phylogeny*.

6. For instance, my favorite recapitulationist, John Johnson Jr., insists in "The Savagery of Boyhood" (1887) that emotional precocity results from "unhealthy development of the brain," which like the rest of our organism "is subject to the all-embracing law of animal existence, which declares the development of the individual to be an epitome of the development of his race" (799).

7. The 1916 edition features a lovely engraving of David and Goliath on the front cover and a list of popular boys' series published by Altemus Books, including The Grammar School Boys, The High School Boys Vacation Series, The Young Engineers, and The Submarine Boys Series.

8. In *The Education of Man* Froebel had already offered a similar sketch of the evolving boy colony, before the epochs concept was officially launched: "Again, what busy tumult among those older boys at the brook down yonder! They have built canals and sluices, bridges and sea-ports, dams and mills, each one intent only on his own work. Now the water is to be used to carry vessels from the higher to the lower level; but at each step of progress one trespasses on the limits of another realm, and each one equally claims his right as lord and maker, while he recognizes the claims of the others. What can serve here to mediate? Only *treaties,* and, like states, they bind themselves by strict treaties" (111, emphasis in original).

9. Wylie's *Generation of Vipers* (1942) seems to have inaugurated the critique of Momism, or overzealous mothering, linked to the alleged feminization of America's boys, followed by David M. Levy's *Maternal Overprotection* (1943) and Edward A. Strecker's *Their Mother's Sons: The Psychiatrist Examines an American Problem* (1946). More recent tirades along these lines are Wylie's follow-up book *Sons and Daughters of Mom* (1971) and Hans Sebald's *Momism: The Silent Disease of America* (1976). Sebald, a sociology professor, argues that "a boy is much more vulnerable to the effects of Momism than a girl" (14).

10. For an extended critique of Bly's misreading of this tale, see "Spreading Myths About Iron John," chapter 4 in Jack Zipes's *Fairy Tale as Myth, Myth as Fairy Tale.*

11. Gurian's latest contribution to this growing body of literature is *A Fine Young Man: What Parents, Mentors and Educators Can Do to Shape Adolescent Boys into Exceptional Men.* Several other works about boyhood are in progress, including Michael Thompson's *Raising Cain: Protecting the Emotional Life of Boys,* and a book by Barb Wallis-Smith on boys' fantasy play. Like Pollack, Thompson and Wallis-Smith are based in Boston. Wallis-Smith has apparently become something of a pro-boy activist, making and selling t-shirts that proclaim "Boys Are Good."

12. For discussion of the "girl question," which predated the "boy problem," see Claudia Nelson and Lynne Vallone's introduction to *The Girl's Own.* Some critics have reversed the usual rhetorical order, notably Sally Mitchell, who discusses boyhood as a developmental phase for the New Girl (137).

13. Foucault's perhaps too-persuasive *Discipline and Punish* has reinforced the association of men with brute force and women with less tangible influence. Men punish,

the story goes; women offer a kinder, gentler form of control. Boys are spanked (even if we call it discipline); girls are taught the moral lessons they must come to symbolize. One challenge facing scholars of girl culture is to avoid the assumption that since girls were removed from the public sphere, their presence is best understood as an indirect moral influence. Lynne Vallone's account of girl culture is useful along these lines, demonstrating how Foucauldian analysis can resist its own rhetorical power. Vallone complicates the punishment-discipline narrative, suggesting that some "disciplinary" forms of eighteenth-century girl culture set the stage for such body-centered institutions as the Magdalen Hospital for penitent prostitutes.

Works Cited

Abbott, Franklin, ed. *Boyhood, Growing up Male: A Multicultural Anthology.* Freedom, Calif.: Crossing, 1993.

Abbott, Mather Almon. *The Boy Today.* 3d ed. New York: Fleming H. Revell, 1930.

Aldrich, Thomas Bailey. *The Story of a Bad Boy.* 1869. Hanover, N.H.: The University Press of New England, 1990.

Beecher, Henry Ward. *Eyes and Ears.* Boston: 1862.

Bly, Robert. *Iron John: A Book About Men.* Reading, Mass.: Addison-Wesley, 1990.

Boone, Joseph Allen. "Male Independence and the American Quest Romance as Counter-Traditional Genre: Hidden Sexual Politics in the Male World of *Moby Dick, Huckleberry Finn, Billy Budd,* and *The Sea Wolf.*" In *Tradition Counter Tradition: Love and the Form of Fiction.* Chicago: University of Chicago Press. Pp. 227–77.

Brooks, Bruce. *Boys Will Be.* 1993. New York: Hyperion, 1995.

Brown, Bill. *The Material Unconscious: American Amusement, Stephen Crane, and the Economics of Play.* Cambridge: Harvard University Press, 1996.

Burr, Hanford. *Studies in Adolescent Boyhood.* 5th ed. 1910. New York: Association Press, 1918.

Fiedler, Leslie. *Love and Death in the American Novel.* New York: Dell, 1960.

Fine, Gary Alan. *With the Boys: Little League Baseball and Preadolescent Culture.* Chicago: University of Chicago Press, 1987.

Fishkin, Shelley Fisher. *Was Huck Black? Mark Twain and African-American Voices.* New York: Oxford University Press, 1993.

Fiske, George Walter. *Boy Life and Self-Government.* 1910. New York: Association Press, 1912.

Forbush, William Byron. *The Boy Problem: A Study in Social Pedagogy.* Boston: Pilgrim's Press, 1901.

Foucault, Michel. *Discipline and Punish: The Birth of the Prison.* Trans. Alan Sheridan. New York: Vintage, 1977.

———. *The History of Sexuality: An Introduction.* Vol. 1. Trans. Robert Hurley. 1976. New York: Vintage, 1980.

Froebel, Friedrich Wilhelm August. *The Education of Man.* 1826. New York: D. Appleton, 1902.

Gibson, H. W. *Boyology or Boy Analysis.* 1916. New York: Association Press, 1922.

Gould, Stephen Jay. *Ontogeny and Phylogeny.* Cambridge: Harvard University Press, 1977.

Gurian, Michael. *A Fine Young Man: What Parents, Mentors and Educators Can Do to Shape Adolescent Boys into Exceptional Men.* New York: Tarcher-Penguin Putnam, 1998.

———. *The Wonder of Boys: What Parents, Mentors and Educators Can Do to Shape Boys into Exceptional Men.* 1996. New York: Tarcher-Penguin Putnam, 1997.

Hall, Granville Stanley. *Adolescence: Its Psychology and Its Relations to Physiology, Anthropology, Sociology, Sex, Crime, Religion, and Education.* 2 vols. 1904. New York: D. Appleton, 1992.

Herbert, Christopher. *Culture and Anomie: Ethnographic Imagination in the Nineteenth Century.* Chicago: University of Chicago Press, 1991.

Holland, Rupert S. *Historic Boyhoods.* Philadelphia: George W. Jacobs, 1909.

Jacobson, Marcia. *Being a Boy Again: Autobiography and the American Boy Book.* Tuscaloosa: University of Alabama Press, 1994.

James, Hartwell. *The Boys of the Bible.* 1905. Philadelphia: Henry Altemus, 1916.

Jeal, Timothy. *The Boy-Man: The Life of Lord Baden-Powell.* New York: William Morrow, 1990.

Johnson, John Jr. "The Savagery of Boyhood." *Popular Science Monthly* 31 (1887): 796–800.

Kantrowitz, Barbara, and Claudia Kalb. "Boys Will Be Boys." *Newsweek* 11 May 1998: 55–60.

Kliebard, Herbert M. *Forging the American Curriculum: Essays in Curriculum History and Theory.* New York: Routledge, 1992.

Lowry, Richard S. "Domestic Interiors: Boyhood Nostalgia and Affective Labor in the Gilded Age." In *Inventing the Psychological: Toward a Cultural History of Emotional Life in America.* Ed. Joel Pfister and Nancy Schnog. New Haven: Yale University Press, 1997. Pp. 110–30.

Macleod, David I. *Building Character in the American Boy: The Boy Scouts, YMCA, and Their Forerunners, 1870–1920.* Madison: University of Wisconsin Press, 1983.

Merrill, Lilburn. *Winning the Boy.* New York: Fleming H. Revell, 1908.

Merrow, John. *Will Boys Be Boys? The Merrow Report.* Interview with Michael Gurian. National Public Radio. Originally broadcast from the UCLA Graduate School of Education and Information Studies. Audiocassette. 1998.

Mitchell, Sally. *The New Girl: Girls' Culture in England, 1880–1915.* New York: Columbia University Press, 1995.

Moore, Robert, and Douglass Gillette. *King, Warrior, Magician, Lover: Rediscovering the Archetypes of the Mature Masculine.* San Francisco: HarperCollins, 1990.

Moore, Sheila, and Roon Frost. *The Little Boy Book: A Guide to the First Eight Years.* 1986. New York: Ballantine, 1987.

Nelson, Claudia. *Boys Will Be Girls: The Feminine Ethic and British Children's Fiction, 1857–1917.* New Brunswick: Rutgers University Press, 1991.

Nelson, Claudia, and Lynne Vallone, eds. *The Girl's Own: Cultural Histories of the Anglo-American Girl, 1830–1915.* Athens: University of Georgia Press, 1994.

Orenstein, Peggy. *SchoolGirls: Young Women, Self-Esteem, and the Confidence Gap.* New York: Anchor-Doubleday, 1994.

Pipher, Mary. *Reviving Ophelia: Saving the Selves of Adolescent Girls.* New York: Ballantine, 1994.

Pollack, William. *Real Boys: Rescuing Our Sons from the Myths of Boyhood.* New York: Random House, 1998.

Reck, Franklin M. "*The American Boy* Magazine, 1899–1941." In *The American Boy Anthology.* Comp. Franklin M. Reck. New York: Thomas Y. Crowell, 1951. Pp. vii–xiv.

Rodgers, Daniel T. *The Work Ethic in Industrial America, 1850–1920.* Chicago: University of Chicago Press, 1974.

Rolt-Wheeler, Francis. *The Boy with the U.S. Mail.* Boston: Lothrop, Lee & Shepard, 1916.

Romero, Lora. *Home Fronts: Domesticity and Its Critics in the Antebellum United States.* Durham: Duke University Press, 1997.

Roosevelt, Theodore. "The American Boy." In *The Strenuous Life: Essays and Addresses.* New York: Century, 1899. Pp. 155–64.

Rosenthal, Michael. *The Character Factory: Baden-Powell and the Origins of the Boy Scout Movement.* New York: Pantheon, 1986.

Rotundo, E. Anthony. *American Manhood: Transformations in Masculinity from the Revolution to the Modern Era.* New York: Basic, 1993.

Ruhlman, Michael. *Boys Themselves: A Return to Single-Sex Education*. New York: Henry Holt, 1996.

Sebald, Hans. *Momism: The Silent Disease of America*. Chicago: Nelson Hall, 1976.

Seltzer, Mark. *Bodies and Machines*. New York: Routledge, 1992.

Spencer, Herbert. "Progress: Its Law and Cause." 1857. In *Herbert Spencer on Social Evolution: Selected Writings*. Ed. J. D. Y. Peel. Chicago: University of Chicago Press, 1972. Pp. 38–52.

Stuart, D. M. *The Boy Through the Ages*. New York: George H. Doran, 1926.

Taylor, Bayard. *Boys of Other Countries: Stories for American Boys*. New York: G. P. Putnam's Sons, 1876.

Tompkins, Jane. *Sensational Designs: The Cultural Work of American Fiction, 1790–1860*. New York: Oxford University Press, 1985.

Trensky, Anne. "The Bad Boy in Nineteenth-Century American Fiction." *Georgia Review* 27, no. 4 (winter 1973): 503–17.

Twain, Mark. *Adventures of Huckleberry Finn*. Ed. Walter Blair and Victor Fischer. Berkeley: University of California Press, 1985.

Tylor, Edward B. *Primitive Culture: Researches into the Development of Mythology*. 1871. 2 vols. New York: Putnam, 1920.

Vallone, Lynne. *Disciplines of Virtue: Girls' Culture in the Eighteenth and Nineteenth Centuries*. New Haven: Yale University Press, 1995.

Warner, Charles Dudley. *Being a Boy*. Boston: Houghton, Mifflin, 1897.

Weiner, Bernard. *Boy into Man: A Father's Guide to Initiation of Teenage Sons*. San Francisco: Transformation, 1992.

Zipes, Jack. *Fairy Tale as Myth, Myth as Fairy Tale*. Lexington: University of Kentucky Press, 1994.

Turn-of-the-Century Grotesque: The Uptons' Golliwogg and Dolls in Context

Marilynn Olson

The Golliwogg books, beginning with *The Adventures of Two Dutch Dolls — and a "Golliwogg"* (1895), were extremely popular annual Christmas offerings from Longmans, Green until 1909. Aware of the annual anticipation, reviewers sometimes expressed a "Here's another Golliwogg book, it must be Christmas" resignation about them, occasionally shaking their heads over why the Golliwogg had taken over nursery life in the way that it had. But in spite of this prominent position in turn-of-the-century English children's literature, present-day histories of children's literature pay surprisingly little heed to the Golliwogg books.[1] Given that the books had remarkable illustrations and influenced other works both technically and thematically, that they were the first English picture books with a black protagonist, that they had ubiquitous spin-off toys, greeting cards, games, dolls, and household items ("fortunes were made from the Golliwogg"),[2] and that the series inspired Claude Debussy's popular *Golliwogg's Cakewalk* and considerable affection from those who were raised in its era, this lack of critical attention is unfortunate. That the Golliwogg books are perceived as icons of racism as well helps to explain critical reticence, but failure to study the Golliwogg seriously distorts its era in children's literature, an era in which interchange between children's culture and the adult avant-garde was particularly marked. The notable popularity of the Golliwogg motif when seen in its context suggests that this particular series said something significant to thinking adults as well as to children, that in its day it embodied the "spirit of the age."

The series was originated by Florence K. Upton, then twenty-one years old, the talented daughter of a talented family of British emigrés to New York State. Like a number of young women of her era, she was motivated by the desire to support her family, since her father had died in 1889, leaving her mother to raise four children by giving voice lessons. Upton had already been illustrating for four years when she turned to the idea of picture books while on a visit to her rela-

Children's Literature 28, eds. Elizabeth Lennox Keyser and Julie Pfeiffer (Yale University Press, © 2000 Hollins University).

tives in London. She and her mother used the comfortable royalties
that resulted from the Golliwogg series to take her siblings to Paris so
that they could all receive art training, an enterprise that eventually
resulted in her painting career. After her training, Upton continued
to live and work in England, while the rest of the family returned to
the United States.[3]

Upton painted from models, and before painting she wired the figures (the wooden dolls are jointed and look much like artist's mannequins) into the ludicrous positions they assume in the stories (Norma
Davis's book *A Lark Ascends* includes photographs of Upton at work).[4]
Her mother, Bertha, then wrote the galloping verses that describe the
illustrations. That the books were produced in this fashion, with verses
following preexisting illustrations, points to an extremely close collaboration between the mother and daughter, although they sometimes were not in the same country. Presumably plot notes by Florence
must sometimes have accompanied the pictures, but the details of the
working relation have not been documented.[5]

The characters in the Upton series are the Golliwogg (a term Upton
invented), the model for which was a black ragdoll from her childhood
unearthed by a London aunt, and five Dutch (deutsch) wooden dolls
of varying sizes. The original ragdoll, an American toy purchased at
a fair with a leather face and rather stiff-looking body, had been mis-
treated (used as a throwing target) by the Upton children in Florence's
youth. He most closely resembles the Golliwogg of the first books—
that is, he has thin lips and a triangular nose that bring a later doll
hero, Raggedy Ann, to mind. The face of the Golliwogg evolved, eventually settling into gentler, more flexible features, but from the first
he had a more attractive body and proportions than the original toy.
Although Upton and others discussed his grotesque appearance, the
pictured figure has pleasing compactness and flexibility and has decorative clothes. Though the original ragdoll's clothing may have been
that of a minstrel, the dress of Upton's Golliwogg just as readily suggests the dress of the Bohemian artist, an allusion close to Upton's life.
The reference to the "artist head of Golliwogg" in the first book supports this suggestion (45).

The stories themselves, picaresque adventures, are contained in
oblong books of about sixty pages, which subsequently made them difficult to anthologize and thus more easily forgotten by children's literature historians, even though the Golliwogg books comically interpreted for the nursery market many of the groundbreaking events of

their time. After the first book, in which the characters meet in a toy shop on Christmas Eve, each begins with the Golliwogg enthusiastically instigating a new, usually topical, adventure that the dolls must help him with:

> "You look astonished, Peg, my girl,
> To note our summer goal,
> But just as sure as you stand there,
> We'll find the great North Pole!
>
> To reach it, you will have to climb
> O'er fields of ice and snow
> Where monstrous polar bears prowl round,
> And lonely rivers flow.
>
> Sarah and I have made our plans
> To build a lovely boat,
> *She* knows how strong it ought to be
> On Arctic seas to float."
>
> (*The Golliwogg's Polar Adventure*)

They travel by bicycle, electric auto, and balloon; discover the North Pole in 1900 (ahead of the explorers—and also Winnie the Pooh); have a "kodak" tour of Africa (ahead of Teddy Roosevelt's safari); and fight a war (unlike the Boer War, bloodless).[6] The series also includes a visit to Holland (a popular site of children's literature since *Hans Brinker* and a joke on "Dutch" dolls), a fox-hunt, the Golliwogg's impersonation of Santa in a flying swan sleigh, a circus, a seaside resort (rather satirically treated), and a robinsonnade.

All of the books involve whole-hearted, exhilarating participation, a variety of elaborate costumes, catastrophes in which everyone crashes in spectacular ways, and suspenseful rescues of whatever member of the loyal band has come to grief. The Golliwogg, a big thinker and go-getter, is also a thoughtful and considerate friend.[7] He is the accepted suitor of Sarah Jane, the second largest doll, who is a model of loyalty and competence. The other notable characters are the largest doll, Peg, who is sometimes malicious and always strong-minded, and dauntless Midget, who is so tiny that her inclusion in the group automatically makes it look out-of-proportion and odd. Meg and Weg are medium-sized dolls with less individual character (figure 1).

Although the books are not difficult to understand, they are unusual. In our urge to puzzle over or censure the series, it is easy to

Figure 1. *The Adventures of Two Dutch Dolls—and a "Golliwogg,"* p. 50.

forget that they were *always* very odd. Lively, sweet, and funny, they are a contribution to the grotesque in children's literature, a particularly strong nineteenth-century strain that includes elements of the Alice books as well as many other English and German classics.[8] And in embodying attributes generally associated with the grotesque, the books also combine fin de siècle ideas associated with two important artistic movements of the period. Jean Pierot's *The Decadent Imagination 1880–1900* (1981), for example, identifies some of the qualities that tie the Golliwogg books more closely to this adult context.[9] Pierot associates the decadents with "allegiance to the most spectacular aspects of modernity," such as Golliwogg's auto-go-carts, airships, bicycles, and

Figure 2. *The Golliwogg in War!* p. 18.

other topical inventions and pursuits. Pierot also describes the decadents as "avid for acquaintance with foreign customs"—clearly also true of the Golliwogg, as it is of characters in the nearly contemporary Oz books. And, of course, the decadents preferred the fantastic in art to naturalism.[10] In this series, however, it is not easy to distinguish between the forces of decadence and the forces that diametrically opposed it.

For example, the Golliwogg and the Dutch dolls, in their exotic qualities and their extremely animated manner, are also allied with artists who rejected the decadent label. Indeed, the most obvious quality of the series is its exaggerated energy. The Golliwogg's most characteristic mood is exuberance, and he is usually portrayed as working away at some task to accomplish his great aims (figure 2). Wilhelm Kayser's *The Grotesque in Art and Literature* mentions the relation of the commedia dell'arte to the grotesque, in that its nature cannot be assessed from its language "but only from the way in which it is acted

Figure 3. *The Adventures of Two Dutch Dolls—and a "Golliwogg,"* p. 14.

or, better still, from the movements performed by the actors."[11] But it should be noted that the Golliwogg's enthusiastic movements, unlike, say, those of E. W. Kemble's turn-of-the-century sketches of black children, are more purposeful than amusing, and the slapstick elements are not limited to the Golliwogg but are also characteristic of the (white) dolls. Because of their jointed structures and their impetuousness, the Dutch dolls are even more humorous than the Golliwogg, since his upholstered and fully clothed body looks more normally human, whereas many of their activities draw attention to their segmentation and literal woodenness (figure 3).

It should also be noted that the Golliwogg and the dolls always overcome the difficulties of their situation. The universe is not nihilistic, as it would be, for example, in a real clown routine. The friends race through adventures in which carnivores, mechanical devices, physical laws, social conventions, and their own sketchy plans threaten to defeat the company—but their spirit always triumphs. For example, when the Golliwogg falls down the chimney on Christmas Eve and remembers, belatedly, that he could have just used the door:

> But here a smile uplights his eyes
>   And dries his falling tears:
> "This still shall be the happiest day
>   We've had for many years—
>
> Come! leave this mess upon the floor,
>   Dear girls, we'll have our ride:
> I quite forgot the magic sleigh
>   Awaiting us outside!"
>   (*The Golliwogg's Christmas*)

In other words, in their slapstick fashion their adventures are silly and bizarre but not seriously alienating. The Golliwogg is considerably more capable than, say, Tristram Shandy of controlling the malevolence of physical objects and restoring harmony. His energy is both amusing and positive, and both energy and childlikeness were qualities that interested the avant-garde artists of the period.

In connection with the end of the nineteenth century, many scholars have commented on the widely held belief that European civilization was doomed and the European races degenerate.[12] In response to the belief that mainstream European art was decadent and failing and that vital energy must be found elsewhere, many changes in literature, music, and art were attempted, especially those that sought to go outside what artists perceived to be established European modes. We are all familiar with the introduction of African sculptural forms in early twentieth-century art, for example, although this phenomenon was not the first indicator of the movement. In view of the insistence of the avant-garde that authentic and vital forces were associated with African, Polynesian, and various peasant cultures, with children's drawings, and with other "primitive" sites, it is tempting to wonder whether the Golliwogg's extremely energetic style, inventiveness, and capacity for hard work reflect this sense that the future was coming from outside European culture, as many artists with a similar interest in throwing off conventionality believed. If the Golliwogg is partially an early creation of what Lemuel Johnson calls the "negrophilism" of the first two decades of the twentieth century, a time when "iconoclastic brilliance 'chose savage artists as its mentors'" (x), then the Golliwogg's racial identity, such as it is, would have been seen positively by these artists.

Turn-of-the-century children's literature is not ordinarily a place for finding enlightened racial attitudes. But when Greta Little calls the

Golliwogg a hero, she is stating the truth as it is found in the text of the Upton stories, where the Golliwogg is always seen as an admirable and serious character (287). The stories never belittle the character—indeed, they promote him as a role model. But we cannot help observing today, as the adults of that day probably would have observed without sharing our disapproval, that the doll possesses a minstrel show version of African features.[13] What the character's *appearance* actually conveyed to its child audience is a mystery. We do know that Florence Upton herself perceived a contrast between illustration and text, citing children's enthusiasm for the character as proof of their superior ability to perceive truth beyond appearances. Edith Lyttelton's *Florence Upton, Painter* (1926) notes that Upton wrote to some American friends in 1902, "another [reviewer] says that I know my public, but for the life of him he cannot understand why it is that 'anything so hideous should please and even fascinate children.' Ah, Gay, the Golliwogg *is* ugly, but he has a good heart, and he is a dear fellow, and are not children way ahead of adults in reading character? They see his beautiful personality. What are *looks* to them?" (12). Under these circumstances, one might ask whether Upton was intentionally taking a toy that might not be viewed with admiration—for racial as well as other reasons—and mischievously or edifyingly proving the opposite in the admirable character, high respectability, and dependable intelligence of her hero.[14]

In truth, however, the Golliwogg is appealing in appearance to many people (the grumpy critic apart), and, in fact, children's picture books do not succeed when the protagonist does not appeal visually to children. Moreover, the toy versions of the Golliwogg (with which the Uptons had no connection) immediately became extremely popular and, like the slightly later teddy bear, a doll that was given to boys as well as girls. Indeed, there is some reason to believe that Upton was simply wrong about children's need to read character in order to see the doll positively. For example, Lyttelton also records Upton's 1917 comments on a portrait sitting in which she attempted to occupy the child sitter by bringing the girl a (requested) Golliwogg doll. Upton's journal notes: "I have never seen a child in such a passion of love as she was for the time being with that Golliwogg—it was extraordinary. She had to keep on biting her lips to keep from smiling. Sometimes she pressed him to her with almost quivering passion saying under her breath 'Oh, you *darling*.' It was a revelation to me" (14). Surely there was a great deal of variation in reception of and perceptions about this doll, and Upton's (or any Anglo-American adult's) initial impression of the Golliwogg's ugliness may have been based on the image's degrading past, or it may have reflected a preference for associating childhood with pastoral or sentimental surroundings. But Upton apparently failed to see that the Golliwogg might be associated with black *people,* which makes her commentary hard to interpret in a time when such lack of awareness is not possible. In view of the interest of the avant-garde in non-European sources of inspiration, however, the Golliwogg's ubiquity, popularity, energy, and blackness seem to constitute a childhood site encouraging an idea—negrophilism—that had not yet surfaced in adult cultural productions.

Although the qualities of simplified and ideal form that the Fauves (1906) and various other turn-of-the-century painters took from so-called primitive art were congruent with some of the ideas that they had already developed internally, the notion of non-European art as *iconoclastic* was undoubtedly an important idea that achieved expression in the years just after the inauguration of the Uptons' series. When Debussy created his *Golliwogg's Cakewalk* (1908), for example, he was not only referring to a popular contemporary children's book and using some pre-jazz rhythms, but he was also using the cakewalk as a send-up of Wagner's *Tristan.*[15] His groundbreaking dissonances and parody of a much-admired composer—while using non-European and nonadult sources—make the piece a nosegay of modern trends also present in the series from which he took his title.

The iconoclastic aspects of the Golliwogg books were present in the very first volume. When Peggy and Sarah Jane awaken in a toy store, they resolve to use the midnight hours to advantage. Seeing a dressed doll, they are suddenly aware of their sartorial deficiency, and Peggy sends Sarah up a nearby flagpole to fetch a flag (figure 4):

> Then up the pole with trembling limbs,
> Poor Sarah Jane did mount;
>> She dared not lag,
>> But seized the flag,
> Ere you could twenty count.
>
> Big Peggy gazed with deep concern,
> And mouth wide open too;
>> Her only care
>> That she might wear
> A gown of brilliant hue.

Figure 4. *The Adventures of Two Dutch Dolls—and a "Golliwogg,"* p. 7.

The flag in question is an American flag, and they make from it a red-and-white striped dress for Peggy and a starry blue dress for Sarah, both flimsy and revealing. The remaining three Dutch dolls—Meg, Weg, and Midget—often do not wear dresses at all.

There are at least two iconoclastic, carnivalesque details here. First, the dolls are defacing a national symbol in an era that could not have been more aware of flag etiquette than America was at the time.[16] The flag dresses continue through the series, although making and wearing costumes for expeditions is a regular feature of the outings. Moreover, it is unusual to be using *naked* female characters. The overthrow of social decorum in each case is never mentioned in the series. Rather like Mary Poppins, the dolls are oblivious to these conventions. Indeed, although the dolls and the Golliwogg sometimes aspire to fash-

Figure 5. *The Golliwogg at the Sea-side,* p. 7.

ion success, they always judge by whether their costumes are stylish or not, overlooking the fact that their personal appearance never conforms to any available norm. They are *always* pleased with themselves.

Since the dolls are free from any kind of worry about propriety or comeliness, there are fantastic jokes attached to clothing that has no function but decoration. Why, for example, do some dolls prepare furry polar expedition outfits to go to the pole, while others are apparently completely comfortable while wearing only hats? Then, too, the startling nakedness of the dolls is exacerbated by the fact that the Dutch dolls are obviously intended to be dressed when played with. They have paint and a more finished look, for example, halfway down their arms and legs, showing where the limbs would project from sleeves and under skirts and how the joints and bare segments would ordinarily be concealed. We bring to the dolls' strangely inhuman bodies something like the wonder with which we confront the Tin Woodman of Oz: a kind of uneasiness at their mechanical, but living, natures (figure 5).

A third area of iconoclastic innovation is that the Golliwogg and
Sarah Jane are sweethearts, a point that has to be considered in connection with assessments of racism (and the great popularity of the
series in places where racial tolerance was not pronounced). Indeed,
the relationship between the Golliwogg and all the girls is one of gal-
lantry. Their mutual affection can be seen in the verses that end the
Christmas book, for example, in which the Golliwogg has tried to substitute for the Santa he didn't believe in "for little Sarah's sake." Dis-
covering that there really is a Santa, after he had tried to arrange
Christmas all by himself, he needs encouragement:

> "Now for a kiss!" cries Sarah Jane,
> "A kiss apiece, you know;
> For who deserves it more than you,
> *Under the mistletoe!*
>
> There never was, nor e'er will be
> Another day like this!
> So, let's record it with a vow,
> And seal it with a kiss!"
>
> They clasp him fondly in their arms,
> This modest, gentle knight—
> —And so we'll let the curtain fall
> Wishing them sweet "Good Night."
> (62)

The rather grown-up relation between the Golliwogg and Sarah Jane
is one of the reasons that little children could model themselves on
the series, but not one of the kinds of transgression that they would be
likely to recognize—which is also the case with jokes about President
Roosevelt and militarism. This dual-audience transgressive appeal is
also applicable to an additional aspect of the series tied to the artistic
context.

One of the ways in which the grotesque can be expressed in literature or art is in the reduction of human beings to the doll-like:
Lucy Lane Clifford's "Wooden Tony" or Hoffmann's *Nutcracker* are examples. Puppets and commedia dell'arte masks are related to this
effect, as they are to other aspects of the grotesque. The simplified
made-up faces of participants in minstrel shows also fit this profile,
in addition to giving it a different slant. Doll-like humans, harlequins,
and masks represented an extremely important aspect of turn-of-the-

Figure 6. Paul Klee: *Senecio* (1922). Oeffentliche Kunstsammlung Basel, Martin Bühler, photographer.

Figure 7. *The Adventures of Two Dutch Dolls—and a "Golliwogg,"* p. 35.

century art, literature, and music, an era that produced a large number of works around these motifs.[17]

Examples abound. Klee's *Senecio* (1922) is presumably an ideal—that is, nonnaturalistic—way of looking at a human face rather than a realistic portrait of Peggy. But it *looks* like Peggy (figures 6, 7). Joseph-Emile Muller in his *Klee: Figures and Masks* says of the piece that "at first sight *Senecio* is scarcely more than an impassive, harmless doll's head. But soon one feels the fire in those eyes which seem to roll in their sockets. The tenderness of the yellow and pink seems to possess an ambiguous meaning" (n.p.)—an ambiguity significant to grotesque work and an ambiguity that the Upton series suggests. Klee himself said, "The legend which describes my drawing as infantile . . . must stem from those linear combinations in which I attempted to show a man [as] an object, while preserving the total purity of line" (n.p.). Here the human being as doll and the iconoclastic artist as childlike combine.

Modigliani, also an admirer of African masks who made a number of masks himself in 1911 and 1912, painted people so that they appear doll-like or masked, as noted by his critics and interpreters.[18] Human beings are treated in a similar way in the work of Erich Heckel or Paula Modersohn-Becker in Germany.[19] And one of Picasso's early experimental works (*Nude Against Red Ground,* 1906) also demonstrates this idea. In this painting, executed in the same period in which he was drawing harlequins and in which the Upton books were still being writ-

Figure 8. Pablo Picasso: *Nu sur fond rouge* (1906). Paris, musée national de l'Orangerie, collection Jean Walter et Paul Guillaume. R.M.N.-Picasso.

ten, one can see that the girl is apparently in the process of being turned into a segmented doll (figure 8).[20] Picasso's portrait of Gertrude Stein uses a similar technique; he simplifies her face into a rigid mask, an approach that removes her from ordinary fluid humanity.[21] In short, the resemblance of dolls and doll-like masks to artists' mannequins had special significance in this era; it is reasonable to suppose that artists must have seen the Golliwogg books as signifying clusters of ideas that we no longer bring to them.

It is interesting, however, that there is probably a break here between adult and child ideas of the "doll-like." The adult views the doll as less than human in potential, an object, and the doll-like as someone possibly petrified by the condition of society. The iconoclasm inherent in drawing people as dolls comes from making evident this sad truth and from the new techniques used to convey the idea: thus, although this approach can be playful, it is not really happy. Children, however, are more apt to perceive doll play as providing freedom from the constraints of their lives. In other words, doll lives, because they are controlled by a child's imagination, have the potential to be better (and more grown-up) than child lives. For children, then, the dolls in the Upton series enjoy liberation from convention and social constraints, as well as from fear of injury because of their wood and rag construction, and they have the imaginative freedom associated with doll play. They have a better time than the rest of us.[22] It is a specific freedom from propriety, however—not being clothed—that further allies the Dutch dolls with the avant-garde of the early twentieth century.

The iconoclasm involved in using naked female dolls in the series must also be placed in this wider context. The naked woman, often associated with the exotic primitive or with prostitution or the harem, was a staple of nineteenth-century high and popular art (Frascina 59–62, 122–23). Many of the modern pieces associated with the Fauves or Picasso were iconoclastic reworkings of this kind of female nude, an attempt to look at the form—as well, sometimes, as the ideology that made the odalisque a popular subject—in a new way. Typically, the nakedness of the female body is an obvious focus of such pictures, but the qualities that make the body sensuous or erotic are eliminated. For example, speaking of Picasso's universally cited *Les Demoiselles d'Avignon* (1907), Francis Frascina says that in contrast to the rich conventional language of the nineteenth-century works of Ingres and Bouguereau, "the signifiers in *Les Demoiselles* (figure 9) appear 'crude', 'dissonant', 'ugly', 'ambivalent.'" He speaks of their "mask-like faces" and "angular bodily forms" (122). In much the same way, I would argue, the Upton dolls are feminine and found in romantic situations but are devoid of sexual parts and sensual qualities.

One of the ideological motives for this iconoclasm on the part of avant-garde painters, as we can imagine, was a desire to unsettle the form and to unmask the social forces that made naked women, often "primitive" naked women, conventional artistic and popular cultural icons. Like les demoiselles, who are still striking the poses of the conventionally lovely, we see the Dutch dolls primp and adorn themselves, basking in the Golliwogg's respectful admiration. Independent of conventional ideals of appearance, the dolls manage their "angular bodily forms" with panache, a perky contrast, presumably, to what the Fauves later had in mind. But the child reader of the Golliwogg books is regularly exposed, as was the viewer of Fauve paintings, to the parts of the female body that in daily life would be kept hidden. In neither case did these parts have any sexual interest. Following Leslie Fiedler's discussion in *Freaks,* in which he called freak shows an opportunity for children, in particular, to be reassured about their own identities (I'm not a freak, they are), we might wonder whether children felt themselves allied to the dolls because of this aspect of their appearance.

Figure 9. Pablo Picasso: *Les Demoiselles d'Avignon* (June–July 1907). Oil on canvas, 8′
× 7′8″. The Museum of Modern Art, New York. Copyright © Estate of Pablo Picasso/
Artists Rights Society (ARS), New York. Acquired through the Lillie P. Bliss Bequest.
Photograph © 2000 The Museum of Modern Art, New York.

Children, too, are sexual beings, beings who experience, perhaps, the
same level of romantic attachment as the dolls in the stories, but whose
attachments are officially denied as such.

New and old artistic approaches to the female form are still with
us, but our era is more likely than the Uptons' to note the gender in-
equality suggested by the fact that some of the Dutch dolls are naked,
whereas the Golliwogg is clothed (figure 10). The dolls constitute a
kind of harem, perhaps reminding us of Edward VII's social excesses.

Figure 10. *The Adventures of Two Dutch Dolls—and a "Golliwogg,"* p. 48.

He, too, was fond of fancy uniforms. And much of the time the Golliwogg has the important idea that sets the narrative off and the others
fall in behind. In the first book, however, the Golliwogg defined one
aspect of their relationship less conventionally. While being pelted in
the face with snowballs by the "steady aim of Sarah Jane," a maneuver
that Bertha Upton calls "very serious fun," Golliwogg retaliates (but
in a more sporting way):

> "Vengeance!" he cries, "I'll pay them out!
> If girls will play with boys,
>   There's got to be
>   Equality,
> So here's for equipoise!"

And then some monster balls he makes,
He does not spare the snow
And as each back
Receives a whack,
Like ninepins down they go.

(55)

Gentle knight or no, points for "steady aim," managerial skills, know-how, and dauntless courage are distributed among the principal figures in the group, with Midget constantly receiving commendation for her ardent spirit.[23]

We can examine nowadays both the Golliwogg's blackness and the dolls' gender position just as we might examine the iconography of the painters who sought to bring a new vision to the odalisque tradition. Although overthrowing older conventions, although often carrying idealistic political meanings, the now-grotesque naked females in the pictures (forms that are identified with the supposed sexual innocence of childhood as well) continue to imply that women and children are still being understood in conventional ways.[24] Jill Lloyd discusses the German painter Max Pechstein's murals (and by extension the work of other members of the Brücke) in terms useful for the discussion of such nudes:

> The association of women and children with [the Brücke] concept of the primitive, which we shall find constantly recurring in the studio, bather and street scenes, relates to the sexual and racial politics of social Darwinism, which regarded both women and native communities as "children" occupying a lower rung on the evolutionary ladder. For *die Brücke* these associations had positive rather than negative connotations, suggesting a life force and an intuitive, "natural" alternative to the rationalizing and calculating "masculine" temper of their times. But this touches the ambivalent and problematic heart of their primitivism: for the "attack" on bourgeois codes and practices inverted rather than truly subverted existing evolutionary criteria, and thus *reproduced* many of the ruling prejudices of their times in a new and "positive" guise. (47, emphasis in original)

There is reason, in other words, for the anxiety we feel when faced with this interesting series.

We are also aware, as the musicians and artists of that day were not, that turn-of-the-century admiration of the primitive was based on a substantial ignorance of the cultures out of which the "primitive" arti-facts came. "[T]he absence of an accessible iconography or history to these objects allowed them to be easily absorbed into modern artis-tic culture," as Gill Perry explains in "Primitivism and the Modern" (56). Artists identified the primitive with the more "authentic" view that they sought to achieve by throwing off European decadence, but, of course, this "primitivism" was a Eurocentric myth. They simply did not know much about the cultures that had produced the art they admired, and they were defining them in a way that we have doubts about, even if, in these terms, the Golliwogg is really an incongruous *Übermensch.* The avant-garde artists were of their time, as were the Up-tons. In a humble way, the Uptons *did* "dethrone . . . life and put art in its place," and the iconoclasm and wit of the Dutch dolls and the Golliwogg, their ability to be read as indicative of contemporary feel-ings about the human condition, contributed to their broad audience appeal. If we are now unable to read the Uptons without anxiety, the attempt to read them as the iconoclasts of their generation may have read them identifies our own shibboleths. More than one hundred years after the Golliwogg and Sarah Jane were invented, if they cannot help us "subdue the demonic aspects of the world" as Wolfgang Kayser thought that the grotesque should do, they may at least remind us to be conscious of the power of our own demons, as well as the cleansing power of human energy.

Notes

1. See Norma S. Davis's *A Lark Ascends* p. 105 f, for the fullest statement of this com-plaint, also reflected in Greta Little's *DLB* entry.
2. See Lyttelton's *Florence Upton, Painter* (1926): "The shops all made Golliwogg dolls and unfortunately, as Florence had neglected to patent him, she let drop a considerable fortune. One German manufacturer, who made little Golliwoggs with seal hair, is said to have netted thousands of pounds" (11).
3. Upton became a *societaire* of the New Salon in Paris, but her portraits and Dutch landscapes are realistic works. She was not an avant-garde painter, and, moreover, the Golliwogg came *before* she was exposed to either the Art Students League or studios in Paris. She used the Golliwogg money to get there.
4. The original toys still exist (in the Bethnal Green Museum). They were auctioned with some original artwork from the series in World War I to pay for an ambulance, which had the Golliwogg and Florence Upton's name on the side.
5. Florence Upton realized that this was an unusually close collaboration. Later em-ploying the same medium used by Conan Doyle, Upton continued to receive posthu-mous messages from her mother long after the series had ended. As in the case of Yeats, Upton's automatic writing was very useful to her.
6. Sarah Jane shoots a wooden soldier and immediately comes to her senses about the realities of war: "That instant, Sarah hears a cry, / She sees a soldier fall, / And

"Have I killed him dead!" she shrieks / Then bolts across the wall // And rushing o'er the level plain, / Fast fall the scalding tears; — / Remorseful little Sarah Jane, / Her breast is choked by fears!" The toy soldier's better-than-human construction allows him to be promptly repaired. The children of England were very enthusiastic about the Boer War. A reviewer recommended the Upton book as an antidote to "war fever," although it is unclear whether he did so because *The Golliwogg in War!* depicted Sarah Jane's remorse or because she (in response to the Golliwogg's determination to find an enemy to satisfy his martial urge) decides that toy soldiers, themselves, will do: "We always did detest / Those pigeon-chested, puffed-up men / In scarlet blouses drest . . . / Methinks examples such as these / Had best demolished be, / To make room for a nobler sort, / From all such follies free."

7. Among his most notable admirers were Sir Kenneth Clark and Thomas Osborne, founder of the Osborne Collection. Kenneth Clark said, "I identified myself with him completely, and have never quite ceased to do so" (7).

8. Among many others, Hoffman and Busch, Lear and Carroll, Dickens and Tenniel, Cruickshank and Grandeville, Doré and Browning had all been more or less amusing and more or less grotesque before this.

9. "By throwing themselves [the decadents] heart and soul into this desperate quest for the new, the rare, the strange, the refined, the quintessential in everything, or for the exceptional—terms that recur constantly in the writing of the time—they were to come eventually to feel that they had pushed literature to its furthest limits, that they had dethroned life and put art in its place, thereby, for a while at least, rendering it bearable" (10, 11).

10. A related motif Pierot also identifies with the fantastic stories of the decadents is that of anthropomorphized plant life (also important in Art Nouveau): "a vegetable kingdom that has ceased to be stationary, passive, and fragile, and has become . . . animated . . . and aggressive." The Uptons' use of this motif may have influenced the terrible vegetables in *Dorothy and the Wizard in Oz* (1908).

11. See Kayser's *Grotesque in Art and Literature*. Baudelaire in particular remarked on the quality of movement in Cruickshank, saying "the whole of this diminutive company rushes pell-mell through its thousand capers with indescribable high spirits, but without worrying too much if all their limbs are in their proper places": this remark could as easily describe Golliwogg and Co. Chesterton said that "energy and joy are the father and mother of the grotesque."

12. For example, Barbara Tuchman (*The Proud Tower*), Cecil Eby (*The Road to Armageddon*), and many more. Works mentioned in the text include Johnson, Frascina, Perry, Neubauer, Pierot, and Pavolini. Sometimes this belief is allied with those of Friedrich Nietzsche.

13. The Golliwogg, of course, does not look any more like an African human than Raggedy Ann looks like a non-African one. In both cases, their looks partly have to do with their construction out of sewing materials—button eyes and so on. Both are arresting and appealing as doll characters but would be frightening as living humans. But there is no external referent to make Raggedy Ann seem to be a *mocking* face, whereas the mask-like Golliwogg face summons up the whole minstrel tradition to anyone familiar with it. Davis attributes much of the notorious reputation acquired by the Golliwogg to the myriad spin-offs from the series, particularly Enid Blyton's Golly and other products and advertising uses to which a "golliwog" figure was put. What Davis calls the "Golliwog-with-one-g" is often racist, had nothing to do with the Uptons (who did not have the licensing rights or any control over how their character was used), and, of course, is often simply elided into the Golliwogg (with two g's) by children and adults who did not meet the Golliwogg before he became a household name. Eric Bligh also strongly differentiates between the beloved character of his youth and the crowd of unauthorized golliwogs. It should be noted, however, that five of the Golliwogg books

actually do include stereotypical nonwhite characters. That the Golliwogg should be treated *differently* by its creator is another oddity.

14. Upton's character is not easy to read. She and her mother did really shocking things, but no one seems to have reconciled the amount of *conscious* mischief the mother-daughter team was perpetrating with Florence's otherwise fragile and serious personality. I would note, however, that their non-Golliwogg picture book *The Vege-Man's Revenge* (1897) involves a youthful heroine who is buried alive and then (after she sprouts) chopped up and eaten by vengeful vegetables. That this plot is extremely peculiar in a children's story seems to me to be self-evident. No one could do such a book without noticing what she was doing.

After lampooning Roosevelt and his "hunter-man" activities in the opening pages of *Golliwogg in the African Jungle,* Upton remarked in a letter to Longmans (Davis 95), "We ought to send Roosevelt a copy of the Jungle Book when he comes. But they say he has no sense of humor." This is the closest one can come, apparently, to the idea that Upton and her mother were *consciously* outrageous. Little children would be much less amused by a lampooning of the American president, presumably, than their parents would be.

15. René Peter in *Debussy Remembered* says that Debussy was very fond of reading children's books (139). The Wagner reference is first cited in the reminiscences of the first public performer of the *Cakewalk,* Harold Bauer (*Debussy Remembered* 157), who was informed on this point by the composer. The connection is also cited in Vallas's *Claude Debussy* 183.

16. As any reader of *St. Nicholas* can see, the 1880s and 1890s brought flag etiquette, military reviews, public salutes, and so on to the fore in American society. Americans were very aware of the build-up of the navy, the need for weaponry to guard ports, and similar concerns that probably originated with the German occupation of Paris in the 1870s but that led to the Spanish-American War. *The Youth's Companion* had mounted a campaign to put a flag in every schoolroom (and was active in establishing the "Pledge of Allegiance" as a ritual).

17. Gian-Paolo Biasin has an extensive list in *Montale, Debussy, and Modernism* 19. He also cites Jean Starobinski, *Portrait de l'artiste en saltimbanque.*

18. For example, Corrado Pavolini remarks, "there is a splendid figure of Guillaume (1916) elegant in a black felt hat, his cravat neatly tied and his chalky face like a cheap carnival papier-mâché mask under the false colours of electric light" (12).

19. For example, *Fränzi with Doll* or *Hude* (both 1910) by Erich Heckel, or *Seated Nude Girl with Flowers* (1907) by Paula Modersohn-Becker.

20. Jean Guichard-Meili states, "the treatment of the face and arms, the hardened line, the masque of a primitive idol, which is on the point of transforming the face of the model, anticipate the so-called 'negro' figures of 1907 and the famous *Demoiselles d'Avignon,* which are the introit to cubism" (n.p.).

21. Discussed in *Pablo Picasso: A Modern Master* by Richard Leslie, 23–27, and also in connection with *Nude Against Red Ground* in *Picasso: The Early Years 1881–1907* by Josep Paulau i Fabre, 469–72.

22. Kuznets observes (27) that Hitty, a later doll, similarly enjoys dollhood's advantages, in her case, lack of conscience.

23. The relation between the sexes is not so lopsided as it appears at first glance, in other words, but it is noncontemporary enough to give the reader of Kenneth Clark's autobiography pause to wonder exactly what modeling his relation with the other sex on the Golliwogg's example entailed.

24. To varying degrees, the idea of the "primitive" possessing power to overthrow bourgeois or decadent civilization is associated with Nietzsche. The Brücke group noted here "took their group name from *Thus Spake Zarathustra.* The metaphor of the bridge (die Brücke) is used by Zarathustra in the book to represent man's journey from absorption in a decadent culture to a state of freedom and 'overcoming'" (Harrison 66).

Works Cited

Bauer, Harold. "Harold Bauer." In Nichols. Pp. 156–58.

Biasin, Gian-Paolo. *Montale, Debussy, and Modernism*. Princeton: Princeton University Press, 1989.

Bligh, Eric. *Tooting Corner*. London: Secker and Warburg, 1946.

Clark, Kenneth. *Another Part of the Wood: A Self-Portrait*. London: John Murray, 1974.

Davis, Norma S. *A Lark Ascends: Florence Kate Upton, Artist and Illustrator*. Metuchen, N.J.: Scarecrow, 1992.

Fiedler, Leslie. *Freaks: Myths and Images of the Secret Self*. New York: Simon and Schuster, 1978.

Frascina, Francis. "Realism and Ideology: An Introduction to Semiotics and Cubism." In Harrison et al. Pp. 87–183.

Guichard-Meili, Jean. *Picasso: From Barcelona to the Pink Period*. New York: Tudor, 1967.

Harpham, Geoffrey Galt. *On the Grotesque: Strategies of Contradiction in Art and Literature*. Princeton: Princeton University Press, 1982.

Harrison, Charles. "Abstraction." In Harrison et al. Pp. 184–262.

Harrison, Charles, Francis Frascina, and Gill Perry. *Primitivism, Cubism, Abstraction: The Early Twentieth Century*. New Haven: Yale University Press, 1993.

Joachimides, Christos M., Norman Rosenthal, and Wieland Schmied, eds. *German Art in the Twentieth Century: Painting and Sculpture 1905–1985*. Munich: Prestel-Verlag, 1985.

Johnson, Lemuel A. *The Devil, the Gargoyle, and the Buffoon: The Negro as Metaphor in Western Literature*. 1969. Port Washington, N.Y.: Kennikat, 1971.

Kayser, Wolfgang. *The Grotesque in Art and Literature*. 1957. Trans. Ulrich Wisstein. Bloomington: Indiana University Press, 1963.

Kuznets, Lois. *When Toys Come Alive*. New Haven: Yale University Press, 1994.

Leslie, Richard. *Pablo Picasso: A Modern Master*. New York: Smithmark, 1996.

Little, Greta. "Bertha Upton and Florence K. Upton." *Dictionary of Literary Biography* 141. *British Children's Writers, 1880–1914*. Ed. Laura Zaidman. Detroit: Gale, 1994. Pp. 284–92.

Lloyd, Jill. *German Expressionism: Primitivism and Modernity*. New Haven: Yale University Press, 1991.

Lyttelton, Edith. *Florence Upton, Painter*. London: Longmans, Green, 1926.

Muller, Joseph-Emile. *Klee: Figures and Masks*. New York: Tudor, 1961.

Nichols, Roger. *Debussy Remembered*. London: Faber, 1992.

Paulau i Fabre, Josep. *Picasso: The Early Years 1881–1907*. Trans. Kenneth Lyons. Barcelona: La Poligrafa, 1996.

Pavolini, Corrado. Introduction. *Modigliani*. New York: New American Library, 1966.

Perry, Gill. "Primitivism and the 'Modern.' " In Harrison et al. Pp. 3–86.

Peter, René. "René Peter." In Nichols. Pp. 124–42.

Pierot, Jean. *The Decadent Imagination 1880–1900*. Trans. Derek Coltman. Chicago: University of Chicago Press, 1981.

Starobinski, Jean. *Portrait de l'artiste en saltimbanque*. Geneva: Skira, 1970.

Upton, Bertha, and Florence K. Upton. *The Adventures of Two Dutch Dolls — and a "Golliwogg."* London: Longmans, Green, 1895.

———. *The Golliwogg at the Sea-side*. London: Longmans, Green, 1898.

———. *The Golliwogg in War!* London: Longmans, Green, 1899.

———. *The Golliwogg's Christmas*. London: Longmans, Green, 1907.

———. *The Golliwogg's Polar Adventures*. London: Longmans, Green, 1900.

Vallas, Léon. *Claude Debussy: His Life and Works*. 1933. Trans. Maire and Grace O'Brien. New York: Dover, 1973.

Plain Speaking: Black Beauty *as a Quaker Text*

Peter Hollindale

In Part 4 of Swift's *Gulliver's Travels,* "A Voyage to the Houyhnhnms," Lemuel Gulliver describes the customary methods of treating horses in his own country, England, to the highly intelligent and rational horse who is now his master. He does so with his usual complacency and injudicious frankness: "I owned, that the Houyhnhnms among us, whom we called Horses, were the most generous and comely animal we had; that they excelled in strength and swiftness; and when they belonged to persons of quality, employed in traveling, racing, and drawing chariots, they were treated with much kindness and care, till they fell into diseases, or became foundered in the feet; but then they were sold, and used to all kinds of drudgery till they died; after which their skins were stripped and sold for what they were worth, and their bodies left to be devoured by dogs and birds of prey" (258–59). The noble Houyhnhnm is, not surprisingly, indignant when he hears the story of his species's degradation at the hands of Men, who are the brutish Yahoos in this land of rational equine oligarchy, and he wonders "how we dared to venture upon a Houyhnhnm's back."

> I answered, that our horses were trained up from three or four years old to the several uses we intended them for; that if any of them proved intolerably vicious, they were employed for carriages; that they were severely beaten while they were young for any mischievous tricks: that the males, designed for the common use of riding or draught, were generally castrated about two years after their birth, to take down their spirits, and make them more tame and gentle; that they were indeed sensible of rewards and punishments, but his Honour would please to consider, that they had not the least tincture of Reason any more than the Yahoos in this country. (259)

Point by point, Gulliver's account to the Houyhnhnm is in miniature the life story of one of fiction's most famous horses, Black Beauty, the eponymous hero of Anna Sewell's novel, published in 1877. Where the

Children's Literature 28, eds. Elizabeth Lennox Keyser and Julie Pfeiffer (Yale University Press, © 2000 Hollins University).

experiences are not Black Beauty's own, they are those of his friend, the mare Ginger.

Improbable as the parallel may seem between Swift's urbane and waspish eighteenth-century satire and an essentially simple nineteenth-century story written in the cause of animal welfare, there are similarities between the two. Foremost of these is the fictional tactic of admonitory role reversal. Instead of horses as seen by men, we are shown humankind as seen by horses. In each case the effect is to expose the callousness that is inherent in the very concept of ownership—the commodification of the living creature. In Sewell this depends for its avoidance or correction on the personal responsibility and intervention of humane individuals. Swift summarizes an accepted, economically governed process of abuse, and *Black Beauty* illustrates it through the flesh-and-blood experience of living horses. Swift's strategy is to empower the horse, Sewell's to dramatize its impotence, but the purposed reformative insight is the same. Of course, Swift's object is to puncture human arrogance and presumption, not to improve the lot of horses, but he still provides an analogous and prophetic text for Sewell's enterprise.

In particular, we should note the equivalent status of Reason in both writers. Swift's Houyhnhnms are embodiments of rational life and discourse, and in such company Gulliver is unwise to speak of English horses as having "not the least tincture of Reason." Likewise Black Beauty, whom we think of chiefly as a passive victim of human use and misuse, is also constituted by Sewell as the humble, unassuming voice of practical Reason, whose very simplicity gives the powerful quality of self-evidentness to his intuitions of rightness and justice in both equine and human affairs.

In its unlikely correspondence with Swift we can find some guidance to the status of *Black Beauty* as one of the world's best-selling novels and perhaps the most influential of all animal stories. The book's lasting popularity is often attributed to its innovative contribution to the cause of animal welfare. It survives, readers commonly suppose, because its original reformative compassion is expressed through an amateurish but engaging simplicity of episodic storytelling that appeals especially to the narrative tastes and ready sympathies of children.

The argument of this essay is that neither of these assumptions is correct. Although it is undeniable that *Black Beauty* is a lastingly influential propagandist text (and is still not obsolete in that role), it owes its status to literary qualities, not to revolutionary welfare insights. Considered as a tract, the book is not original at all. However different Swift's objectives may have been, *Gulliver's Travels* demonstrates that the leap of imagination needed to reposition the horse in human awareness was possible a hundred and fifty years earlier. John Locke, in *Some Thoughts Concerning Education* (1693), had expressed the link between treatments of animals and human beings that is intrinsic to Sewell's thinking: "they who delight in the Suffering and Destruction of inferior creatures, will not be apt to be very compassionate or benign to those of their own kind" (180). By the end of the eighteenth century there were already instructive stories for children, designed to civilize the growing child in the use of power over other creatures, such as Sarah Trimmer's *Fabulous Histories, Designed for the Instruction of Children, Respecting Their Treatment of Animals.* Such educative texts were often cast, like *Black Beauty,* in the form of animal autobiography. In the nineteenth century, before *Black Beauty* appeared, humane societies in both Britain and America were already actively promoting the better treatment of horses.

Among Anna Sewell's humanitarian predecessors were a number who, like Sewell, were Quakers. They were active in the antivivisection movement, and the Quaker Joseph Pease had persuaded Parliament to insert two clauses into an act designed to protect animals in the City of London and Westminster. In so doing, he had furthered the work of the Royal Society for the Prevention of Cruelty to Animals, the major animal welfare organization in Britain.

On the other hand, if *Black Beauty* is not original as propaganda, neither is it a simple propagandist story. The book's echo of Swift reveals the unobtrusive skill that enables Sewell to constitute her hero both as helpless victim of human injury and as naively rational commentator on human behavior. His observations embrace many aspects of conduct not impinging directly on horses. Freed from the preconceptions that usually surround it, *Black Beauty*'s stature as a classic plea for animal welfare is not diminished, but it emerges also as a more deeply imaginative, more carefully structured and more morally eclectic work than most verdicts on it have assumed. It is crucial to our understanding of the book that Anna Sewell was the product of a Quaker background and that *Black Beauty* is not properly intelligible as a literary work without some reference to Quaker language and ideas.

Although Quakerism is a complex phenomenon, subject to successive historical changes since its founding by George Fox and also to internal schism within particular societies at various times, certain general features can be regarded as constants of Quaker beliefs and practice. Among them are a pacific and humanitarian attitude to human behavior, a rational morality, and a clear and obdurate outspokenness in these causes. For a Quaker, to be pacific is not to be passive. The idea of "plainness" is essential to Quaker practice: plainness in its double senses of simplicity and candor.

Quaker "plainness" is often associated with visual austerity in the circumstances of everyday life. Famously—but also significantly—for many years the only prints permitted to adorn the walls of Quaker homes were of William Penn making his treaty with the Indians, the interior of a slave ship, and the building plans for Ackworth School (Punshon 131). The trio is significant because the first is an image of peaceable community with fellow creatures whom many non-Quakers would have felt did not merit it; the second is a reminder of cruelty and atrocity against other human beings; and the third is an affirmation of the power of education, Ackworth being the first Quaker boarding school. All these concerns are reaffirmed in the context and purpose of *Black Beauty*.

Certainly *Black Beauty* was designed to educate. I do not wish to deny the well-intentioned functionalism of Anna Sewell's motive in writing the book, or her success at the level of propaganda, but rather to argue that the novel breaks through the restrictive bounds of its benign utilitarianism to achieve a largely unnoticed complexity of language and narrative structure. It emerges as a much finer literary work than it is usually given credit for being.

Sewell's conscious purpose was "to induce kindness, sympathy, and an understanding treatment of horses," and the book's laconic style, its concentrated brevity of incident, its formation from self-contained chapters and episodes, though partly attributable to the ordeal of its composition during Sewell's protracted and debilitating final illness, were also astutely designed for its intended readership. *Black Beauty* was originally written not for children but for adults working with horses. Naturally they included very young adults indeed (like Joe Green in the book) who nowadays would still be at school but in Victorian England were already earning a living for themselves and their families. For working men and boys, with basic literacy but nothing more, and with little time for reading, the simple prose, short chapters, and instructively dramatic episodes made the book a pleasurable and effective teaching aid; and so it was for the children who quickly became its adopted audience. For half a century after its publi-

cation children read *Black Beauty* in a world where horses were a prominent and indispensable feature of both rural and urban life. Margaret
Blount, in a study published a century after *Black Beauty,* records its
effect on her as a child:

> It made me look, on my way to school, more intelligently at the
> coal carts that plodded all day between the station and the gas-
> works, at the plaque on the wall that said for many years "Please
> slacken bearing rein going up hill," and I watched the carters
> putting on the metal brake shoes and wondered—as a horse—
> what it was like going downhill with a heavy load behind. But be-
> yond these feelings was the one that if the horse were I, or anyone,
> and the story really about me, or people, then the school was the
> breaking-in stable and many people were led or driven through
> life with a series of owners and made to run, walk or trot without
> being able to argue about it. (253)

This is a tribute to the book's continuing success in alerting children to
the fate of horses, its main subject. But Blount also draws our attention
to the breadth of the book's humanitarian concerns. She draws her
analogy between horses and human beings because the book invites
her to. The simple anthropomorphism that is often regarded as a naive
limitation in Sewell's writing, the fact that Black Beauty is given a non-
mimetic speaking voice, is one of its great strengths. Its uniform linguistic plainness is the reason why it seems to Margery Fisher "almost
like a dialogue between horses and men" (46).

Plainness and simplicity, however, are not necessarily naive or amateurish qualities. Blount remembers the wall plaque asking drivers
to "slacken bearing rein going up hill." The existence of this plaque
would have been largely due to Sewell, because *Black Beauty* was instrumental in securing the modified use and eventual disappearance
of the bearing rein. The bearing rein is the book's central image of
cruelty to horses. It was a fashionable device that forced a horse to
carry its head higher by exerting pressure on the head and neck. In
consequence it made horses look artificially smart, at terrible cost
to their comfort and also their efficiency, because a horse prevented
from lowering its head could not use all its strength in drawing a load.
The cruel result was especially pronounced when a horse was going
uphill. Sewell's attack on this iniquitous fashion provides an excellent
example of the deft narrative organization and subtleties of prose that
are obscured by the book's ostensible simplicities.

The bearing rein makes carefully spaced appearances in the narrative and works as a gradually intensifying image through Black Beauty's experience of the suffering it causes. In chapter 11, when Black Beauty is still a prized, well-tended, and unblemished horse at Birtwick, his master, Mr. Douglas, meets a friend and equal, Captain Langley, who makes use of the bearing rein. Douglas's reproof to Langley is a model of Quaker admonition—rational, persuasive, courteous yet uncompromising—but it also carefully registers the social status of the two (they are "gentlemen" and equals, but not aristocratic) while subtly exposing the point of least resistance for persuasion to attack—in this case, a cunning compliment to Langley's military professionalism. Langley likes to see "my horses hold their heads up":

> "So do I," said Master, "as well as any man, but I don't like to see them *held up:* that takes all the shine out of it. Now you are a military man, Langley, and no doubt like to see your regiment look well on parade, 'Heads up,' and all that; but you would not take much credit for your drill, if all your men had their heads tied to a backboard! It might not be much harm on parade, except to worry and fatigue them, but how would it be in a bayonet charge against the enemy, when they want the free use of every muscle, and all their strength thrown forward? I would not give much for their chance of victory, and it is just the same with horses. . . . You may depend upon it, horses were intended to have their heads free, as free as men's are; and if we could act a little more according to common sense, and a good deal less according to fashion, we should find many things work easier." (41)

The stern and businesslike probity of Mr. Douglas's speech accords generally with Quaker attitudes toward the right use of language, but the passage is also a socially realistic man-to-man exchange, involving intelligent psychological calculation on Douglas's part (and on Sewell's as teacher): the appeal is simultaneously to respect for fellow creatures and to enlightened self-interest. The analogy with soldiers is a shrewd particular argument for Langley's benefit but also a vivid and telling image that furthers the book's general intertwining of human and animal welfare.

The bearing rein makes its next major appearance in chapter 22, when Black Beauty has been sold to the Earl of W—— at Earlshall Park, where the Earl's fashion-conscious wife insists on its use. This is Black Beauty's first direct endurance of it, intensifying his experience from that of mere observer, as he was in chapter 11. It causes him acute discomfort, but the episode concentrates on Ginger's rebellion (chapter 23), so that Black Beauty is positioned as part sufferer, part observer. Through this incident, moreover, the book's propagandist targeting is lifted socially from the professional and gentlemanly bourgeoisie to the aristocracy.

In the episode I specially wish to consider, chapter 46, the social range of the campaign against the bearing rein is completed when it is addressed to the ordinary working man. By this time Black Beauty has fallen on hard times ("sold, and used to all kinds of drudgery") and is pulling overloaded carts for a corn dealer and baker. His driver, Jakes, uses the bearing rein. (It is the fashion for carters as well as countesses.) The focus is now squarely on the horse's own suffering. In chapter 46 Black Beauty is trying unsuccessfully to draw a cart uphill, with the bearing rein in place, and being whipped for his failure.

At this point a nameless lady intervenes. It is tempting to think of the lady as Sewell herself, playing a walk-on part in her own narrative rather as the film director Alfred Hitchcock used to make surreptitious appearances in his own movies. At any rate, the lady's views are indistinguishable from Sewell's. When she first offers to help, "the man laughed." (As if a mere woman could help!) When she offers reasons why the bearing rein might be a practical hindrance, he agrees, "with a short laugh," to try "anything to please a lady, of course."

The experiment works, and the short paragraph describing it is a masterly prose reflection of Black Beauty's physical effort: clause by clause, it matches first of all the horse's strained, laborious initial pull; then the tension of maximum breath-sapping struggle ("I spared no strength"); next its slight easing into successful movement ("the load moved on"), followed by sustained but bearable labor and the relief of final well-earned pause: "Jakes took the reins—'Come on, Blackie.' I put down my head, and threw my whole weight against the collar; I spared no strength; the load moved on, and I pulled it steadily up the hill, and then stopped to take breath" (176). Jakes acknowledges the lady's vindication but says he cannot abandon the bearing rein entirely because "I should be the laughing-stock of all the carters." Even so, when she has gone, he resolves to "try her plan, uphill, at any rate." And why? Not just because it works (enlightened self-interest again) but because the lady's linguistic and social nuancing, like Mr. Douglas's earlier, has been both courteous and shrewd: "'That was a real lady, I'll be bound for it,' said Jakes to himself; 'she spoke just as polite as if I was a gentleman' " (177). Gender contempt has been neutralized by social compliment, an effect minutely registered in the changing threefold reference to laughter.

Yet the lady has not compromised her argument, which is the same as Mr. Douglas's to Captain Langley. The social language has changed to reflect the characters and situation, but the grave and plain reiteration of principle connects the two and confirms the deft artistic structuring:

> "Is it not better," she said, "to lead a good fashion, than to follow a bad one? A great many gentlemen do not use bearing reins now; our carriage horses have not worn them for fifteen years, and work with much less fatigue than those who have them; besides," she added in a very serious voice, "we have no right to distress any of God's creatures without a very good reason; we call them dumb animals, and so they are, for they cannot tell us how they feel, but they do not suffer less because they have no words. But I must not detain you now; I thank you for trying my plan." (177)

Such strong displays of courteous interference formed a hard example for the book's young readers, and no doubt many older ones. Alison Uttley, later a celebrated children's writer and herself a formidable character, read the book as a farm child in Derbyshire in the 1890s and recorded her reactions in her autobiography. They show the strength of the book's emotional appeal and the effect of its practical advice but also reveal its unnervingness as a model for personal action: "*Black Beauty* was a book which enthralled us, so that it was read aloud several times. I was deeply moved by this book, and implored my father to remove the blinkers from our horses' heads. [See *Black Beauty*, chapter 10.] He was adamant, and explained they would shy. I kept a lookout for horses with bearing-reins, and wondered if I dared speak to strangers about this. Luckily I was too bashful to be a reformer" (147). Luckily Anna Sewell, even in her long, grave illness, was not. Instead she wove her classic story around the Quaker attitudes expressed by an unnamed character in chapter 38: "My doctrine is this, that if we see cruelty or wrong that we have the power to stop, and do nothing, we make ourselves sharers in the guilt" (148).

Black Beauty does not, of course, work consistently at a high level of stylistic and narrative skill. The chapter recounting Jakes's encounter with the lady ends worthily but anticlimactically with a disconnected afterthought about the bad effects of ill-lit stables. Sewell can revert to the simple didactic handbook at a moment's notice. But the greater part of the book is both narratively skillful and imaginative, a work of instructive art. The bearing rein is in every sense an exemplary instance of this. It is for Sewell both a unique and a representative malpractice, standing as an image of human ill-treatment of horses; but it is also an image in the poetic sense, unifying and intensifying the seemingly episodic narrative. This gives special poignancy to the occasion of Anna Sewell's funeral, as reported by her biographer, Susan Chitty. The horse-drawn hearse drew up at the Sewell house, and Anna's mother, Mary Sewell, was heard to exclaim, "Oh, this will never do!," and was shortly seen in conversation with the undertaker's man. "A moment later a top-hatted figure was seen moving to the head of each horse in turn. He was removing the bearing-rein from all the horses in the train" (222).

Mary Sewell was herself a prolific and successful writer, though she was sixty before she began. If we are surprised to find such literary expertise in Anna Sewell's only book, written with didactic motives at the end of her life, this may be because we overlook not only her good education—Quakers were pioneers in valuing the education of girls and had a tradition of encouraging articulate and reformist writing by women—but her actively literary family background. Long before she wrote *Black Beauty*, Anna Sewell was her mother's household critic, and by all accounts a severe and outspoken one. She fulfilled what would now be the role of the publisher's reader and editor. Nor was Mary the only practicing writer in the Sewell clan. Anna's aunt by marriage, Anne Wright, wrote a number of educational nonfiction works for children, and her Aunt Maria (Mary's sister) progressed from retelling Bible stories to writing romantic novels. Oddly, just as Anna was finishing *Black Beauty*, her Aunt Maria published a novel that was also about a black horse, entitled *Jennet Cragg, the Quakeress*.

Given Anna Sewell's education and her literary background, it is hardly surprising to find on close reading that *Black Beauty*'s linear and episodic simplicity of narrative is deceptive. The book is carefully structured, and the unifying object of its structure is to reinforce that parallelism between horses and humankind that was intuitively perceived by Margaret Blount as a child. Of course the primary purpose of this integral analogy is to make people apply to horses the same principles of care and kindness that they should to other people, but its secondary intention, rooted in the humanitarianism of Quaker thought, is to remind people of their duties to themselves and to each other. The moral core of the book is chapter 37, "The Golden Rule," where Polly Barker voices the central precept: "you know we should do to other people as we should like they should do to us" (142).

Several examples will show how the book enforces this parallel, both in the main lines of narrative organization and in details. The story is conceived as a four-act drama. Part 1 is the story of Black Beauty's idyllic colthood, chiefly in the ownership of Squire Gordon at Birtwick Park. The only ill-treatment the horse endures in this period is accidental and due to the misguided kindness of young Joe Green after the horse's heroic gallop to summon the doctor to the squire's ailing wife. Part 2 traces a decline in the horse's fortunes. He is sold to an ostensibly good home, but one, as we have seen, where he is forced to endure the fashionable bearing rein. Before the end of Part 2, however, the horse has suffered far worse at the hands of a drunken servant and is sold on to casual and less caring ownership. There is a remorselessness about the events of Part 2. Black Beauty is virtually ruined by illustrative variants on the three major causes of equine suffering: fashion (causing horses as sentient beings to be treated as mere objects), thoughtlessness, and deliberate cruelty. All three are also important in Quaker doctrine directed against man's inhumanity to man.

Part 3 is wholly concerned with Black Beauty's life as a London cab-horse. This is an interval of relative happiness in the horse's fortunes. His owner, Jerry Barker, is thoughtful, knowledgeable, and kind; so are his family. Black Beauty has slipped in status from gentleman's horse to working horse, and Part 3 is a kind of proletarian equivalent of his earlier existence at sumptuous Birtwick Park, but place for place the horse's treatment is similarly benign. After the rapid downfall of Part 2 the horse's own experience is temporarily stabilized, so that he is spectator as much as actor and observes the human scene as carefully as the horse's. The parallels are clustered in this section. Moreover, this is the stage that shows the closest identification between the situations of horse and owner. Both Jerry and Black Beauty are comfortably housed; both are "good servants," hardworking and honest, motivated by principles of care and duty; both are clear-sighted spectators of human and animal behavior; both depend for their very survival on ability to work; and even their brief intervals of rest and pleasure are the same, as we see in their shared enjoyment of a day in the country in chapter 37, "The Golden Rule." Although it is not Black Beauty's most prosperous time, in a way Part 3 represents the novel's ideal point of moral equilibrium in relations between horse and human.

The stasis of Part 3, like that of Part 1, is closed by human illness. A key character (Mrs. Gordon at Birtwick, and now Jerry) is sick, so a human household must move to a kinder climate (the Gordons overseas, the Barkers from London to the country), and the horse must be sold. Part 4 then provides a short but dramatic finale, distilling in four brief chapters a reversal of Parts 1 and 2. Black Beauty descends into his worst state yet, followed by a dramatic rescue and the restoration of the opening pastoral idyll. Recognized by Joe Green, once the well-intentioned ignorant boy who harmed him, Black Beauty's recovered fortunes are epitomized by the recovery of his original name. Renamed by successive owners, he has never lost his "good name" in the other sense, and now he publicly retrieves it.

Even this brief outline may demonstrate that the episodic chapter-based narrative is contained within a more sophisticated unifying structure and also that Black Beauty's downfall is discontinuous, intercut with wider animal and human fates which he mediates to readers as ingenuous observer. The most obvious parallel is with another horse, Ginger. Unlike Black Beauty, Ginger has been ill-treated as a young filly. She represents the obverse of Black Beauty's fate, and nothing more clearly exemplifies the underestimated structural finesse of the novel than chapters 7 and 8, in which Ginger tells her story to Black Beauty at Birtwick. The brief preceding chapter, "Liberty," can be read as a redundant eventless episode, arbitrarily introduced as a mini-sermon on yet more desirable experiences for horses. Once we come to Ginger's story in the next two chapters, it is clear that this is not so. Chapter 6 completes the unified story of Black Beauty's youthful good luck, which point by point is then contrasted with Ginger's early memories. Ginger has not enjoyed the formative and necessary pleasure of early freedom: "it was dreadful to be shut up in a stall day after day instead of having my liberty" (23). Other contrasts are just as carefully pointed. Black Beauty was ill-treated by a cruel boy (chapter 1) but the boy was quickly and harshly dealt with; boys threw stones unchecked at Ginger, and so caused her to regard them as enemies. Black Beauty was gently broken in, Ginger harshly so. Just as Ginger's memories form a systematic sad reprise of Black Beauty's luckier early life, so they are predictions of future ordeals that Black Beauty will eventually undergo. Ginger has already suffered the bearing rein, which Black Beauty will meet at Earlshall, and she has already been kept by a good master who employed a bad groom, just as Black Beauty will be in chapters 30 and 31, "A Thief" and "A Humbug." Not only do these chapters give Sewell a pretext for educative contrasts and repetitions, but they are artistically pivotal in the structured narrative of Black Beauty's own decline.

The dual fates of the two horses, after their separation in chapter 27 at Earlshall, come together one last time in chapter 40, "Poor Ginger," where Ginger recounts the last stage of her contrasting story and is then seen dead. Without the Quaker perspective it is easy to misread this double narrative and see Ginger's fate just as a sadder version of Black Beauty's own. But Ginger's response to her ill-treatment has been violent and ill-tempered, for reasons that the modern reader is quick to excuse. Victorian Quakers did not excuse it. Sewell excites pity for Ginger and constructs her narrative to show in no uncertain terms how important it is to train young horses kindly and humanely. But pity does not entail indulgence. Black Beauty, when his turn comes to suffer, displays a quiet fortitude that contrasts with Ginger's rebellion. He is offered as a model, she as a suffering creature who should certainly rouse our pity, but also as a bad example. This is in tune with Quaker strictness. The contrasting fates of the two horses are structured with more complexity and more severity than modern sympathies can easily respond to, but they speak for the culture that produced the book.

In Sewell's thinking, what is true for horses is also true for human beings. When young Joe Green makes Black Beauty ill through well-intentioned ignorance, the groom John Manly's reaction uncompromisingly refuses to make allowances. Chapter 19, "Only Ignorance," is a sustained attack on the "Only." Ignorance, like thoughtlessness and irresponsible cruelty in the other instances that Manly cites, is not excusable, because Quaker humanitarianism is an absolute and overrides all mitigation for those who flout it. In ways such as this *Black Beauty* integrates good treatment of horses within a wider system of values and makes a many-sided case for education.

The structured parallel between horses and humans is most powerfully articulated through the succession of servant figures, mostly grooms and drivers, of whom Joe Green is one. As Black Beauty's fortunes decline, so do the status and quality of his carers. At Birtwick, John Manly, as his personified name suggests, is the ideal and measure by whom all the rest are judged. Black Beauty in his prime is tended by human duty in its prime. Manly's assistant, James Howard, still young like Black Beauty, has been properly trained (as Black Beauty has) and is almost as good as Manly. (Sewell repeatedly links the raising and training of colts with that of boys.) The inexperienced and younger Joe Green makes a near-fatal error but learns well—as we see at the end.

In Part 2, Mr. York at Earlshall is a lesser man than John: he is competent but pusillanimous and will not stand up for his horses. Reuben Smith (chapter 25) is a steeper fall from servant grace: a skillful and likeable man with the fatal flaw of drunkenness, disastrous in its consequences. The thief Filcher and the humbug Smirk are far worse grooms, reflecting the horse's worsening fate. In Part 3, Jerry Barker does not count in the succession, because he is Black Beauty's owner and is self-employed, but through his eyes and the horse's we see other cab-drivers, less well placed. They are mostly anonymous but include Seedy Sam (chapter 39), whose impoverished, enslaved existence and miserable death are skillfully placed to mirror Ginger's (chapter 40). Finally, in Part 4, the nadir is reached with the hideous Skinner (another personifying name) and a cruel unnamed cab-driver, before the horse's final deliverance through reunion with Joe Green. Step by step, human qualities, human status, and human fates match those of Black Beauty himself.

The constant parallels between horse life and human life, together with Black Beauty's role as a naive observer and his conversations with other horses, are Sewell's means to introduce into the book a fuller range of Quaker preoccupations. Even if she may have lapsed from membership of the Society of Friends, her moral consciousness did not stray far from them. Quaker pacifism is articulated through Black Beauty's friendship with Captain, his fellow cab-horse at Jerry Barker's. Captain has been a military horse and served in the Crimean War. More especially, he took part in the heroic but infamous Charge of the Light Brigade, the subject of Tennyson's celebratory poem, in which the British cavalry, because of a bungled order, charged straight into Russian gunfire and sustained huge losses. Three hundred sixty-two horses were killed in the charge. Captain is a survivor, and in chapter 34 his story is a powerful denunciation of what Wilfred Owen would later call "war, and the pity of war." Tennyson famously said of the brave cavalry, "Theirs not to reason why," but Sewell's horses *do* reason why, just as Quakers did. Black Beauty asks, "Do you know what they fought about?" Captain responds: "No," he said, "that is more than a horse can understand, but the enemy must have been awfully

wicked people, if it was right to go all that way over the sea on purpose
to kill them" (129). The horse's naive puzzlement is itself a sufficient
moral answer.

The evils of alcohol are another repeated preoccupation. It was Reuben Smith's drunkenness that ruined Black Beauty in chapter 25, but
this aspect of human behavior, like several others, is most prominent
in Part 3. In chapter 42, "The Election," Jerry Barker refuses to vote
for the party he would otherwise support because their candidate is
a brewer, and risks incurring anger as a result. (The election Sewell
refers to was the last in Britain before the introduction of the secret
ballot.) Moreover, Jerry refuses to use his cab to "bring up half-
drunken voters." Later, in chapter 44, Jerry acts as an unofficial missionary of the temperance movement, and it emerges somewhat im-
probably that Jerry is himself a reformed drinker. The damage that
drunken grooms and riders cause to horses enables Sewell to show
how drinkers also harm their families and themselves. Again the welfare of horses is integrated in a wider scheme of Quaker social values.

Positive social virtues such as thrift are also quietly voiced. John
Manly tells James Howard that "now of course I have top wages, and
can lay by for a rainy day or a sunny day as it may happen" (60), and
Jerry Barker gives as one reason for his avoidance of Sunday work that
"I have laid by more money in the Savings Bank than ever I did before" (137); later he roundly declares that a man who "does not pay his
debts" cannot be religious, and thus speaks for the strong Quaker link
between financial probity and religious devotion.

Although many of its concerns are still topical, it is difficult for modern readers to recognize the full imaginative achievement of *Black
Beauty* because in our day horses are a valued recreational luxury, and
even in the parts of the developed world where horsemeat is part of
the human diet it is rare to see evidence of equine suffering in public
places. Even for those indifferent to them, they are flesh and blood.
In mid-Victorian England things were utterly different. Horses were
ubiquitous, and a material necessity for both rural and urban life. They
were a commodity, an investment, a depreciating asset like a car, and
widely treated in the same unsentimental way.

Something of the standard attitude of the time can be seen in the
Journal of Beatrix Potter, written slightly more than four years after the
publication of *Black Beauty.* At fifteen Potter was already a considerable
natural scientist, accustomed to keeping live animals and dissecting

dead ones. Neither then nor at any time of her life was she a sentimentalist—quite the opposite—but not surprisingly she liked animals and took enormous interest in them. Her caustic comment on the disposal of a family horse is therefore indicative of the general attitudes that Anna Sewell faced: "Rufus = Prince, the chestnut horse is disposed of at last. Papa sent Reynolds to the Zoological Gardens to enquire the price of cat's meat: £2 for a very fat horse, 30/- for a middling one, thin ones not taken as the lions are particular. However, he is sold to a cab owner along the road for £15. He was bought a year ago for ninety. Papa says he never made a good bargain." And a few lines later in the same entry: "Convenient way of disposing of horses once practiced by someone Papa knew in the North of England. They turned one loose on the road, and sold the other for 7/6" (8–9).

This everyday financial commodification of the horse (which the young Beatrix takes for granted while deriving sardonic pleasure from the ludicrous human performance) suggests the national mentality that Anna Sewell's novel did so much to change. We should not underestimate the sympathetic precision with which she was able to occupy on our behalf the physical experience of horses. Nor should we belittle the modified anthropomorphism, the endemic analogy with human life, which she rightly perceived as her most powerful persuasive instrument.

For present-day readers the early impacts of modern technology especially reveal the book's alert imaginative force. Three times in *Black Beauty* Sewell draws our attention to the false equation between horses and engines, reminding us in the process that the historically recent arrival of mechanical engines had altered perceptions of horses for the worse. In chapter 9 Merrylegs complains that "Boys . . . think a horse or pony is like a steam engine or a thrashing-machine, and can go on as long and as fast as they please" (31). (He goes on to describe his vigorous methods of teaching them otherwise.) In chapter 29 Black Beauty objects to the town drivers and rail travelers who "seemed to think that a horse was something like a steam-engine, only smaller" (104). And in chapter 38 Black Beauty contrasts the gentleman who gives him a pat and a kind word with the "ninety-nine out of a hundred [who] would as soon think of patting the steam engine that drew the train" (147). Just how imaginative and how needfully prophetic these comparisons were can be seen from an official history of the Royal Society for the Prevention of Cruelty to Animals, published in 1924:

When railroads were first made it was suggested that horses would
no longer be required. . . . When motor-cars were introduced the
same cry was raised, but with each change the necessity for protecting horses has really increased, since they have, as it were,
fallen from their high estate and are now looked upon by the majority as a cheaper, and therefore an inferior, form of traction.
The price of a horse is less than that of a motor-car, and his driv-
ing needs less skill and knowledge; therefore, even though the
wretched animal is worked to death, his work will earn the cost
of his successor! In this way his treatment has become, in many
cases, worse. (Fairholme and Pain 239–40)

The RSPCA had been concerned about the welfare of horses for a
century, and even at this late date its anxieties continued on the very
grounds that Sewell had foreseen.

Whatever its influence and individual success, it would be wrong to
see *Black Beauty* as a central precursor of the modern story about animals. Susan Chitty claims (241) that "*Black Beauty* started a new category of book, the animal story." Margaret Blount, however, who calls
the book "the most famous and best-loved animal book of all time,"
also says it is "perhaps the last of the great moral tales, the last great
first person narrative in the Listen-to-my-life style" (249). It is Blount
who (in both statements) seems nearer to the mark. As we have seen,
there were many animal stories (and animal autobiographies) before
Black Beauty, and although the succeeding years have produced numerous similarly anthropomorphic tales, the greatness of the subsequent animal story has taken different directions. Two in particular are
dominant. One is the story that draws on the strengths of fable and
folktale to re-create the animal world as a competitive brotherhood—
a poetic antecedent of modern ecological science. The Uncle Remus
stories of Joel Chandler Harris and the Mowgli stories of Kipling's
Jungle Book are classic examples of this line. The other is the more intensely naturalistic story, perhaps taking its cue from early controver-
sies about whether animals can feel pain, which seeks more daringly to
occupy animal consciousness and in the process ask what "animal consciousness" can mean, and where it intersects with human consciousness. Jack London's *White Fang* and *The Call of the Wild* are great texts of
this kind, as are Henry Williamson's *Tarka the Otter* and Kipling's magnificent story "The White Seal." Both lines of development have enor-
mously enriched the twentieth-century children's book.

By comparison with them, *Black Beauty* is old-fashioned. Yet it retains its hold, not only for its propagandist strength but for its major and too-little-recognized qualities as a work of literature: its power of dramatic incident, its skillful blend of episodic and integrated narratives, its balancing of individual voices with a common moral idiom, and its lucid expression of values—rooted in Quaker tradition but still urgent nowadays for horses and people alike—with which child readers are still quick to sympathize.

Works Cited

Blount, Margaret. *Animal Land: The Creatures of Children's Fiction.* London: Hutchinson, 1974.

Chitty, Susan. *The Woman Who Wrote "Black Beauty": A Life of Anna Sewell.* London: Hodder and Stoughton, 1971.

Fairholme, Edward G., and Wellesley Pain. *A Century of Work for Animals: The History of the RSPCA 1824–1924.* London: John Murray, 1924.

Fisher, Margery. *Who's Who in Children's Books.* London: Weidenfeld and Nicolson, 1975.

Kipling, Rudyard. *The Jungle Books.* London: Macmillan, 1894 and 1895. Includes "The White Seal."

Locke, John. *Some Thoughts Concerning Education.* London, 1693. Ed. John W. and Jean S. Yolton. Oxford: Clarendon Press, 1989.

London, Jack. *The Call of the Wild.* New York: Macmillan, 1903.

———. *White Fang.* New York: Macmillan, 1906.

Potter, Beatrix. *The Journal of Beatrix Potter: From 1881 to 1897.* Ed. Leslie Linder. London: Frederick Warne, 1966.

Punshon, John. *Portrait in Grey: A Short History of the Quakers.* London: Quaker Home Service, 1984.

Sewell, Anna. *Black Beauty: His Grooms and Companions: The Autobiography of a Horse.* London: Jarrold and Sons, 1877. Oxford University Press (World's Classics) edition. Ed. Peter Hollindale. Oxford and New York: Oxford University Press, 1992.

Swift, Jonathan. *Gulliver's Travels.* London, 1726. London: Collins, 1952.

Trimmer, Sarah. *Fabulous Histories Designed for the Instruction of Children. Respecting Their Treatment of Animals.* London: T. Longman, 1786.

Uttley, Alison. *Ambush of Young Days.* London: Faber and Faber, 1937.

Williamson, Henry. *Tarka the Otter.* London: Faber and Faber, 1927.

Doris Orgel's The Devil in Vienna: From Trope into History

Hamida Bosmajian

Doris Orgel was reluctant to write *The Devil in Vienna*, a narrative she later considered "probably the central book of my career."[1] Born 1929 in Vienna, she was nine years old when Hitler's army crossed the border on March 11, 1938, and annexed Austria to the Third Reich in what was euphemistically called the *Anschluss*. She remembers how Hitler's official arrival licensed the public abuse of Vienna's Jews and, although this frightened her, she was not surprised because "it was not so different from the way I had imagined the world right along" (Nakamura 196). Her childhood reading had already introduced her to the notion that "being white meant being superior to other races, but that Jews, although being white, were inferior and to be despised" (196). As a child reader of the Wild West stories of Karl May, she would have been exposed to May's racism and anti-Semitism but also to the blood brotherhood ritual between Old Shatterhand and his Apache friend. In childlike imitation of such magic and with a touch of feminist revisionism, the Jewish girl Inge Dornenwald and the Hitler Youth girl Lieselotte Vessely bond themselves in blood sisterly love in *The Devil in Vienna* by drinking a few drops of each other's blood in cooking wine (1988, 31). Needless to say, this childish ritual, expressive of genuine affection and love, would have been an anathema to any National Socialist.

Doris Orgel's grandfather was jeered at and publicly humiliated by the Nazis who forced him and others to scrub off with toothbrushes anti-Nazi slogans on walls and sidewalks. Her father was dismissed from work because he was Jewish, and nine-year-old Doris was dismissed from her third-grade class along with seven Jewish classmates. The family managed to escape Vienna by August 1938, but only later did young Doris realize that "we got out by a hair's breadth." She does not think of her family and herself as "survivors" and feels that this word belongs to those who suffered imprisonment in concentration camps. Nevertheless, as is the case with most survivors, it took her

Children's Literature 28, eds. Elizabeth Lennox Keyser and Julie Pfeiffer (Yale University Press, © 2000 Hollins University).

a long time to shape her memories into a story that could be told. For many years, even in the company of other refugees, "we never mentioned anything about our lives before coming to America." The taunts and insults suffered in Nazi Vienna still burdened her and others with the silent shame they felt as children (Nakamura 204). Around 1960 Ursula Nordstrom of Harper and Row, who had already edited two of her books, asked: " 'When are you going to write about being a Jewish child in Vienna, and how you got out?' " (Nakamura 207). *The Devil in Vienna* was published eighteen years later. The diary of thirteen-year-old Inge Dornenwald, a composite of her older sister and herself, became for Orgel the mode that could contain her painful memories.

Inge's intelligence, imagination, and precociousness enable Orgel to accurately contextualize the narrative politically and historically, but the young reader will respond primarily to Inge's and Lieselotte's efforts to maintain their friendship in difficult times.[2] That same reader might also become aware of how Inge grows through her sense of being Jewish, how she suffers from anti-Semitism, and how she also knows that she is not the person described by the Nazis. The reader may also empathize with Lieselotte's struggle to maintain her personal and religious values and her friendship with Inge even though she is pressured to align herself as a Hitler Youth *Jungmädel* in the Federation of German Girls (BDM). The politically and historically astute reader, however, realizes that history will destroy that friendship and negate the implicit authorial desire that such a human relationship could transcend the vicissitudes of history. Although Orgel relates to the reader the essential events occurring between February 10 and March 30, 1938, the nightmare of history that began for Vienna's Jews during the early days of the *Anschluss* remains largely an authorial subtext that is, however, unmistakably the foundation of Inge's diary. Hitler, though never seen in person by Inge, is a real presence in Vienna, but, though Orgel never demonizes him, he will be for the young reader identified as the Devil in Vienna, a trope that spares the young reader the cruel reality of history. Orgel's narrative exhibits that special relation between text and subtext so characteristic of all narratives about Nazism, Judeophobia, and the Holocaust. In shaping her memory through the diary of a young girl, Orgel creates a narrative distance between herself and the memories that haunt her and that she spares the young reader through a story that can be told about the time when Hitler came to Vienna. Moreover, the genre "diary of a young girl" by definition places limitations on what can be narrated through that point of view.

Claudia Maria Toll has given extensive critical attention to *The Devil in Vienna* in her study of the primacy of aesthetic and literary values over pedagogic goals in youth literature about National Socialism. She argues that the narrative respects the young reader's maturity not only by avoiding a hortatory or instructive tone but also by offering a multilevel narrative perspective. As Inge Dornenwald writes about events occurring between February 10 and March 31, 1938, she also reflects on early childhood experiences, presents entire conversations in direct speech, and copies into her diary, without comment, Lieselotte's letters about her experiences in the Hitler Youth. The literary value of the work, argues Toll, is brought out by the fact that Orgel's narrative distinguishes itself from other youth narratives about this subject in that it problematizes the act of writing about Nazism and the persecution of the Jews. Inge has already grasped that language is ambivalent and multileveled and at times does not suffice to express the inexpressible (68):

> When confronted with true unbearableness, language fails. Although she never turns mute, Inge occasionally and consciously surrenders conceptual precision and resigns herself to casual discourse simply because she cannot express herself any better. But she still attempts to articulate, as when she writes: "Going home by myself, I had awful thoughts: Like that the hole they smashed in Herr Fried's store window is connected with the hole in the world I thought I was just making up as a way of writing how I felt on Saturday, and so that hole is just as real. This doesn't sound as though it makes sense, but it does to me." (Toll 72)

Toll concludes that what is for Inge at first a metaphor, describing her psychological reaction to trauma, becomes realized in the smashed window of Nazi aggression (72).

The narrative is titled *The Devil in Vienna,* not *The Story of a Friendship.* Inge's and Lieselotte's friendship can only be contained in a book (240), for, no matter how much the author focuses on the narrator, it is the political and historical context that defines Inge's life. Something has intruded into Vienna, something that will destroy the comfortable middle-class life of the Dornenwalds and the friendship between two girls. The intruder, who is never depicted directly, is foreshadowed through the metonymy of the devil, but Inge, who cannot bring her-

self to say "Hitler is in Vienna," stops using the metonymy as historical reality makes itself felt. It is Mitzi, the Dornenwalds' maid, who,
prone to the superstitions of folklore, utters for the last time the decisive trope on March 14: " 'Today comes the Devil to Vienna' " (133).
Orgel's subtext makes it clear tha⸱ such tropological thinking is ata-
vistic and prevents us from astute critical thought about the trauma
human beings inflict on other human beings in political and military
history. My discussion will focus on how the narrative moves from and
between trope and historical reality and how that context shapes Inge,
Lieselotte, and the world both girls inhabit. As children they both believed in the devil; as adolescents they experience how human evil begins to tear apart their friendship and their world. My discussion will
begin with Inge's use and rejection of "the devil," her rejection of the
temptations of Nazism, and her affirmation of herself as a Jewish girl.
I will then move to how Lieselotte tries to resist the tremendous pressures to become a politically coordinated (*gleichgeschaltet*) Hitler Youth
girl. The ground for the struggle of both girls is history, and the historical context will make their friendship impossible.

As Inge begins her diary on Thursday, February 11, the weekend of
her thirteenth birthday, she is home alone and experiences "writer's
block." She has been assigned to write on the topic "My Best Friend"
with her "real and true feelings" (5), but her best friend Lieselotte
moved three months earlier to Munich, where Herr Vessely, a fanati-
cal Nazi, was assigned to work for the party. Moreover, Inge must not
write about her true friend because the friendship has already been
forbidden by both sets of parents. Though Inge has received one letter
from Lieselotte, she experiences a deep fear: "I don't know whether
she got my letter, or why she didn't write me again, or whether she has
changed, or how. It's possible, it's even probable, she isn't my friend
anymore. I'm more scared of that than the Devil—in whom of course
I don't believe anymore" (10). Fear, Lieselotte, and the devil are thus
connected from the beginning.

The word *scared* always triggers the memory of the first time she felt
that emotion as a six-year-old in the forbidden underground viaduct
where she encountered the "devil" after hearing of him in legends
about St. Stephen's Cathedral. While still struggling with the alphabet,
she had written her first story about the mischief the devil wrought in
Vienna (10). The child Inge internalized the legendary image of the
devil as a repository for "badness," but the adolescent Inge senses that
losing Lieselotte to an anti-Semitic ideology is far more scary because

that loss means that Inge necessarily would be as Other to her best friend as the devil is to the culture in general.

She remembers how she entered the dark viaduct, heard a match struck, and knew she saw the devil because "his eyebrows seem to slant weirdly devilishly up." Her encounter in the darkness of the viaduct foreshadows not only the devil Hitler but also Nazi depictions of "the Jew." The "devil" invites her with a " 'Come here, little girl' " and then orders, " 'Look,' " as he exposes himself to her and she sees "a stick or something stuck straight out from his unbuttoned pants" (13). Inge knew at the time what that "something was and knew that he wanted her to touch it. As a thirteen-year-old she wonders why she still cannot use the appropriate word" (13). As a child, she ran in panic out of the viaduct, relieved to find Lieselotte and her brother, Heinz, outside. Heinz defuses Inge's fright: " 'Did old Kaugummi [chewing gum] Karl open his pants? Did he show you his Schwanz [tail]?" (14). Heinz, too, uses a trope for *penis,* but his somewhat coarse humor eases Inge's fright.

Though she eventually develops her first and much-approved crush on a family friend, Inge's early childhood memories establish a subtextual association between sexuality, seduction, and forbidden political power. In 1938, Inge will be encouraged by her grandfather to look at the anti-Semitic slogans on the walls and even the demonized and pornographic images of Jews in *der Stürmer,* for to be informed becomes a survival strategy. Nazism, however, was also seductive in its grasping *(erfassen)* and political alignment of youth through an emotional rush that, quite intentionally, supplemented youthful sexual energy. Inge's intimacy with Lieselotte the *Hitler Mädel* becomes a life-threatening intimacy that must be forbidden, but the lies and maneuvers both girls exercise as they plan their trysts resonate with the strategy of secret love. On her birthday, Inge panics over the prospect of losing Lieselotte; she watches the telephone, hoping that Lieselotte will call from Munich: "Then my mind went blank. As blank as the page before me, as the big empty desert must be. I felt I was in a desert too—hot, and my lips and throat were dry. And I thought, Lieselotte's different now, she doesn't care about me anymore, she doesn't want to know me" (70). Inge, as a Jewish girl, is by definition aligned with the Nazi caricature of "the Jew" as satanic seducer. It is unlikely that any of this becomes obvious to the young reader, but this subtext in part explains why it took Orgel such a long time to shape her memories

through the genre of a girl's story and at the same time retain the complexities of "fascinating fascism" (Sontag 1970, 80) and the authenticity of her personal pain.

In its next manifestation the trope of the devil in Vienna reveals
mythic power. Inge recalls how she and Lieselotte stood outside St.
Stephen's Cathedral and intimidated Mitzi by telling her the legend
of how the second steeple came to be shorter because the builder
contracted with the devil, who eventually manifested himself triumphantly as a "huge gigantic shape with a green vest and horns . . . seen
hovering over the shambles" (22–24). Frightened, Mitzi, the house-
maid, accepted the story as truth, but, as the three entered the cathedral, Inge wished she, too, could have dipped her hand into the holy
water. Had she been able to do so, she and Lieselotte might not have
succumbed to naughty and uncontrollable laughter when both saw a
pretentious woman scratching her behind. Inge still feels ashamed by
her behavior, still wonders "what possessed us" (26), and she exor-
cises these feelings by telling a story that projects her as someone who
has no recourse to names and rituals that may protect her from the
devil who "tickled the girl's funny bone (which people think is near
the elbow but is actually somewhere else, only the Devil knows where)"
(29). Seeing the woman scratch her buttocks and laughing at her again
relates that laughter to sexuality, but it also insinuates that, if Inge
were not Jewish and could have crossed herself with holy water, the
incident would not have occurred (27). Inge thus defines herself as
an outsider. It does not matter to her that Lieselotte also misbehaved
in a sacred place; Inge, the outsider, feels guilt, and the incident becomes her myth of origin of Otherness, a state that will become official
policy once the Nazis seize political control of Vienna and demonize
"the Jew as devil." By definition, Inge is in "league with the devil," the
father of lies, as she continues her friendship with Lieselotte in spite
of her parents' prohibition. Nevertheless, her "fall" not only leads her
to maturation but also eventually facilitates the rescue of the Dornenwald family.

Inge must overcome her attraction to Catholicism and to Nazis—
both generated by her need to belong—and accept herself as a Jewish girl in a dangerous time. When Inge was ten years old, Lieselotte
taught her the seductive tune and words of the "Horst Wessel Lied,"
the Nazi anthem, which followed the national anthem at every official
occasion in the Third Reich. Doris Orgel translates the first stanza:

Raise high the flag,
Close fast and firm the ranks,
SA, march on,
With calm and steadfast tread!
Our comrades who were shot in red-front reaction,
March in spirit side by side with us.

(48)

Inge remembers on February 12 how "the words sounded noble. And the melody stirred up feelings in me I didn't know I could have, such as wanting to march also and being sorry for the 'comrades who were shot in the red-front reaction,' whatever that was. I pictured their shirt fronts getting red with blood" (49). Again, Inge cannot explain these feelings that make her long to be swept up in the rush of unthinking communal alignment. Orgel projects ten-year-old Inge as hovering between childhood—her (mis)reading of "red-front reaction" as bloody shirt fronts—and the more critically thinking adolescent who, in 1938, is no longer "ignorant about world events" (48).

As Lieselotte teaches her the Nazi song, the child Inge fantasizes herself singing it in a crowd that welcomes Hitler, who singles her out because of her beautiful voice. When she tells him her name, he frowns and asks, " 'Isn't that a Jewish Name?' " Inge confirms her identity and offers proof with her Mogen David pendant. "Hitler clasps his hand to his forehead and exclaims, 'I have been wrong about the Jews!' And from then on he likes Jews and treats them like everybody else—because of me!" (49). In her daydream Inge is in control; she can proclaim her Jewishness in the crowd and convert Hitler into a philosemite. The "devil" has been reformed; the little girl is his redeemer.[3] The underlying pathos of this dream is the magical reasoning so typical of children in distress. In Inge's fantasy her excellent singing of a Nazi street fighters' song enables her to stop anti-Semitism with a single voice and thus make the world whole. When she later picks out the tune on her family's piano, her father and mother are outraged and severely limit her contact with Lieselotte. At this point Inge resolves: "As soon as they left, I sat down and wrote my heart out, how angry, disappointed and betrayed I felt. I remember I began, 'On this night I cease to be a child. Children do as their parents tell them. I won't, I can't, because they are wrong. I *will* stay best friends with Lieselotte'" (51). Inge moves to a new level of ethical and self-perception where, as a thinking and feeling person, she engages in the struggle to acknowledge differences rather than to subsume persons in metonymic definitions. She records and remembers the moment of her "fall" precisely, for it is at this point that she breaks with parental authority and begins the lying that divides her into the officially good daughter and the faithful "blood sisterly" friend of a young Nazi.

The most poignant moment of Inge's struggle as a writer occurs in her entry for Saturday, March 12, 1938, one day after the *Anschluss* of Austria. It is sabbath; her father and grandfather have been arrested by the Nazis and are forced to scrub the pavement of Vienna with toothbrushes while Nazis and bystanders jeer and taunt them: "Something happened today that tore a hole in the world, at least that's how it felt. I couldn't have imagined it yesterday. I will write it down very calmly, or the hole (which got patched back together) will open again, and I'll feel again as though it is swallowing me up" (120). Systematically, she narrates the facts of that day, as they were told to her and as she experienced them. Nobody can comfort her, not even her usually controlled mother, who sobs "so hard that the bed shook. I felt I was in a nightmare, falling, as though the bed with us in it was falling down the hole. At the same time I felt very angry, like shaking her and screaming, You be the mother, you comfort me!" (122). Inge's only defense is the act of writing, which enables her to order raw experience and emotion and to place that ordering between herself and events.

The immediacy of the diary and the fact that Inge is at home on the day Vienna's Jews were abused in the streets limit the means with which the events of the day can be communicated, but they also preserve Inge from internalizing "the hole in the world." The metaphor does not become "a hole in the heart" or a "hole in her being" as is frequently the case in memoirs of traumatized Holocaust survivors. Her writing, the support of her family (even as she rebels against them), and the fact that she experiences only what were the initial stages of persecution make it possible for her to remain relatively whole as a Jewish adolescent.

The disaster has come and torn the fragile assumptions of the Dornenwalds, the illusions of reprieve that made them delay applying for the quota numbers necessary to escape Austria. Highly conscious of her thirteen-year-old self at this historical moment, Inge had literally seen the writing on the walls in meter-high letters: "Jews, Go Croak" (*Juda Verrecke*) (29). She looked, and looked away, but her grandfather admonished her: " 'You should look. As hard as you need to, to know what you are seeing. Then you should write down what you saw. . . .

It's good to write down what you see, also how you feel about it. It helps you understand things better. And later it helps you to remember'" (89).

Though Inge writes in part because she needs to communicate her feelings for Lieselotte and her anger against her parents, it is the historical crisis that transcends the "dear diary" mode. During those weeks that crisis will transform the Dornenwalds' comfortable life into a life or death situation. Once the "devil" has been welcomed to Vienna, flight is the only option for survival; no compromises are possible. Inge must, therefore, replace personal desires and feelings with clear-headed thinking. The diary, given to her by her grandfather as a book with empty pages, becomes during that time a repository of events and the containment of a friendship that history has made impossible. As Inge says to Lieselotte during their farewell meeting: "'Our friendship is in a book now'" (240). On one hand it is an achievement; on the other it is an expression of mourning. Inge's last sentence to her friend is in reply to Lieselotte's "'I wish I could read it'": "'I wish you could, too. May be some day you will'" (240). The friendship is over because of the rupture history opened between the two girls. Inge knows this but retains the wish for that friendship, a desire that informs the entire text.

Inge copies into her diary Lieselotte's letters about her *Hitlermädel* experiences, making them part of her text. Moreover, by the time she copies them, she has read the letters so many times that she "almost knows them by heart" (151). Thus she internalizes what it means to be a young female Nazi, but in copying the letters without commentary into her diary, she retraces Lieselotte's experiences vicariously, confirms Lieselotte's loyalty by making her part of the text, and, at the same time, controls and maintains the friendship history denies her.

Lieselotte, too, has a symbol parallel to Inge's "hole in the world." Her world also suddenly fractures and makes her conscious that nothing is normal anymore. When her father belts her for having lied about avoiding a class in National Socialist Ideology and for continuing to befriend Inge, she describes to Inge how she once had a favorite cowbell: "It sounded like green meadows and cows coming back after grazing on clover all day. I rang it and rang it. Then Heinz wanted to ring it, and he grabbed it. I grabbed it back, and the clapper came out. So then it was mute. . . . I feel like that bell now" (172).

Whereas the narrative line concerning Inge is typical of ironic comedy where the hero escapes a society that cannot be redeemed, Lieselotte, if she is to preserve her personal and religious values, will experience an increasing tragic isolation even as she appears to be politically coordinated. After her first *Jungmädel* excursion her vision is bleak indeed:

> Looking down at the path, seeing all those dark-skirted, wind-jacketed, brown-capped girls marching by, was like seeing my whole future. I'll have to march with them, do everything they make you do; there is no way out. It made me want to die. In my religion that's an awful sin. And I can't confess it. . . . I just hope that God can forgive me directly [without confession and absolution] and that God helps me stay as I am. . . . On the outside I will be like them. . . . On the inside, God willing, I'll stay the me you know. (159–60)

Because Lieselotte has the appearance and personality that corresponded to the image of female leadership in the Federation of German Girls, her struggle will not be easy. During this decisive first outing, *Führerin* Irmgard recruits her enthusiastically, not only because Lieselotte's father is advancing in the ranks of the SA but also, though Orgel does not mention it, because Lieselotte belongs by definition to the *Kampfzeit*, the time of struggle, of the Austrian BDM, which, like all Nazi affiliations, was outlawed in Austria before the *Anschluss*.[4] After her family moves to Munich so that Herr Vessely can continue working in the SA, Lieselotte, in a fantasy parallel to Inge's singing the "Horst Wessel Lied," imagines that Inge will march with her in this first outing: "That would show them! Then they'd know what Quatsch [nonsense] that is, the stuff they say about the Jews" (152). As it is for Inge, the "nonsense" is everywhere. She describes the picture from Streicher's notorious book in which Jewish children are dismissed from school to the jeers of Aryan classmates.[5] Accepting anti-Semitic propaganda in order to be accepted by her peers is a constant temptation for Lieselotte and the sinister side to the theatrics and glamour of the "fascinating fascism" that attracts her. Lieselotte's struggle to resist Nazi definitions suggests again the authorial wish that such a friendship, even if one partner in it has to go into inner immigration, is indeed possible.

Lieselotte's hope that Irmgard, the much-admired *Jungmädel Führerin*, could not possibly be anti-Semitic is shattered by Irmgard herself. Among the *Jungmädel* Lieselotte can escape her domineering father, her passive mother, and her bullying brother. Irmgard is beautiful,

and many of the "girls have crushes on her." During the outing, Lieselotte's perceptions, too, are charged with preconscious erotic tension.
Irmgard tells her enthusiastically about the events planned for the
group, including a giant youth rally where Magda Goebbels, the most
beautiful woman in the Reich, may make an appearance. She also
promises that she will do everything to get Lieselotte into "Faith and
Beauty," a select group within the BDM where girls considered physi-
cally and ideologically perfect prepared themselves for their designated roles in National Socialism.[6] Lieselotte admits to Inge that she
felt "so flattered my whole head started buzzing," but she also wondered why her belly ached the whole time (155).

Enthusiastically Irmgard asks her if she is not proud to be living in
such exciting times and when she answers affirmatively Irmgard asks
her to carry the flag. In writing to Inge, Lieselotte must split her consciousness as she juxtaposes "swastika" with "Inge, if you had seen me
holding it, would you ever want to see me again?" At the time, however, she did not think of Inge. Instead, "I felt so strange, I felt as if
my own breath from my lungs was rushing into it [the flag], making it
billow like that, as if the flag were pulling me, instead of me carrying
it. . . . Can you possibly know what I mean?" (156). Lieselotte is not
conscious of Hitler's rhetoric regarding the flag, but the banner and
her relation to it exert their effect on her thirteen-year-old self. Hitler
wrote in *Mein Kampf*:

> *And what a symbol it really is!* Not only that the unique colors, which
> all of us so passionately love and which once won so much honor
> for the German people, attest our veneration for the past; they
> were also the best embodiment of the movement's will. As Na-
> tional Socialists, we see our program in our flag. In *red* we see
> the social idea of the movement, in *white* the nationalistic idea,
> in the *swastika* the struggle of the mission for the victory of the
> Aryan man, and, by the same token, the victory of the idea of cre-
> ative work, which as such always has been and always will be anti-
> Semitic. (496–97, emphasis in original)

By being offered the opportunity to carry the Hitler Youth version of
that flag, Lieselotte is called on to join and lead. Indeed, it appears
to her that her feeling of elation over being selected animates the
flag. Embodying the essence of the movement, the flag could not billow without the living person and, at the same time, as an emblem of
the miranda of power the flag empowers and pulls the adherent for-

ward into the movement's future. Orgel emphasizes this by having the troupe of girls start off the Hitler Youth anthem: "Unsere Fahne flattert uns voran" ("Our Flag Billows Before Us") as they are led by Lieselotte into the "new time" (156).[7] As yet the pressures on Lieselotte are relatively mild, but they are likely to increase, especially after Inge, her check and conscience, has disappeared from her life. Uniform and insignia, songs and propaganda, coupled with the need to be accepted by her peers, are pressures that threaten her promise to remain, if only in her deepest self, loyal to her young Jewish friend. When on her last day in school (March 22) Inge attends a Nazi-dominated school assembly, she is glad for her Jewishness, which excludes her from uttering Nazi propaganda, whereas Lieselotte has to rely on the "switch" in her mind that, she thinks, will enable her to turn the propaganda she utters into gibberish and thus save her from becoming a politically coordinated Nazi (207).

As flag and song inspire and inflate Lieselotte's ego during the outing, she matures, not, like Inge, through a "fall" but in her body's coming of age through the menarche. "White as a sheet" and with an acute bellyache, Lieselotte runs into the woods and stares at the inside of her underpants, where "the crotch was bright, bright red." Unable to comprehend at first what this signifies, she admires the stains "as if they were tulips." Then she worries that "I've hurt myself, I don't know how, I don't know where, but somewhere deep, too deep to ever heal. . . . Inge, can you imagine? I would never tell this to anyone else as long as I live" (157). It is not the discomfort of the menarche that has hurt her; rather, the deep wound that will never heal is her alignment with Nazism. It is a wound that makes her fleetingly consider suicide, even if that is against her religious values (159).

The blood of physical maturation becomes thus associated for Lieselotte with the ultimate blood sacrifice demanded by National Socialism of those willing to die for the *Führer,* as well as the bloody violence against all those the Nazis defined as the "other" or the enemy. Irmgard defuses Lieselotte's embarrassment and anxiety over the menarche by handing her a napkin and reassuring her matter-of-factly: "Just think, it happens to half the people in the whole world, every single month" (158). Lieselotte, whose mother tells her not to speak about the menarche so that her father and Heinz won't be offended by this "women's business" (161), is deeply grateful to Irmgard, who demonstrates the modern attitudes the Nazis advocated in these matters (158). Having trusted Irmgard with this intimate experience,

Lieselotte is encouraged to ask: " 'Irmgard, do you believe the things people say about the Jews?' " (159). With certainty the leader replies: " 'Sure! Don't you?' " and gleefully begins to sing "when Jewish blood spurts from our knives" while assuring Inge that girls do not carry knives, but Hitler Youths do, and " 'they are no toys' " (159). Though flippantly sung and casually commented on here by the *Führerin,* the blood imagery points to the murderous destiny the Nazis designed for the Jews of Europe.

Whatever joy and confidence Lieselotte experienced during the outing evaporates. She wants to escape into the woods and live on berries like a fairytale character, but she knows this is impossible and that her only option is her dismal vision of marching *gleichgeschaltet* (politically coordinated) into the future while trying to preserve her inner self with God's help alone, for she experiences herself as isolated from family, from peer group, and from Inge. Orgel has written for Lieselotte what is potentially a tragic story line about a girl conscious of her alienation in a mass movement.

Against her father's wishes, Lieselotte signs up for religious instruction rather than National Socialist ideology. When Herr Vessely is informed about how she lied and manipulated the system, he belts her three times. Lieselotte screams "like an animal" and vomits as her father not only destroys her world but rids her "of any good feeling I'd ever had for him" (170). Her "fall" is different from Inge's in that her confession and promises are inauthentic and ethically invalid because exacted during the infliction of physical violence and pain. For Inge the fall involves consciousness, guilt, and ethical conflict as her disobedience endangers the family. The brutality of Herr Vessely, however, though it makes Lieselotte mute, cannot force her to be ethically compliant or to have qualms over disobeying an abusive parent.

Inge reads Lieselotte's letters, written between November 9 and November 16, 1937, on March 15, 1938, the day Hitler addressed more than 200,000 enthusiastic Austrians in Vienna. Orgel artfully sublimates that celebratory day, which would truly have annulled Inge's fantasy of single-handedly rescuing the Jewish people. As a *Jungmädel,* Lieselotte has to strew flowers "for you know who" (143) in Hitler's triumph, a sight the friendship could not endure. Father Ludwig, Lieselotte's uncle, who refuses to flag the swastika at his church, is also in a minority, for the cardinal of Vienna—and Orgel does not comment on this—not only ordered all of Vienna's churches to flag the swastika but visited Hitler on March 15 to pledge the loyalty of Vienna's Catholics to the Nazi regime.

The lone symbolic gesture of a parish priest protesting the *Anschluss* and the friendship of two girls pledging undying "blood sisterly love" to each other are an authorial projection of a desire comparable to Inge's redemption fantasy, namely, that the personal can make a difference and that friendship with all its intimacies can survive the onslaught of a violent and death-driven political movement. Authorial desire that personal friendship can endure the violence of history is undercut, however, by events, particularly those of March 11–15, 1938. As one historian has stated, the Nazi takeover of Vienna on March 13 gave "the world an illustration of the *Blitzverfolgung* or lightning persecution" of the Jews that surpassed anything that had transpired so far in Germany (Berkley 259). Whatever seems outrageous in Orgel's narrative—such as Inge's father and grandfather being forced to scrub the streets—must be duplicated in scope and intensity many times in order to approximate historical reality.

For Hitler the triumphant return to cosmopolitan and multinational Vienna was a return to the place that had rejected him as an artist and turned him into an anti-Semite who admitted in *Mein Kampf:* "In this period there took shape within me a world picture and a philosophy which became the granite foundation of all my acts" (22). Vienna was thus a highly symbolic place for Hitler, who as a "down-and-outer" once stood awestruck "in front of the Opera" and who perceived the whole Ring Boulevard "like an enchantment out of *The Thousand-and-One-Nights*" (*Mein Kampf* 19) until the day his fantasies were realized when he addressed the masses in the Heldenplatz on March 15, 1938. Orgel spares young readers this triumph of a loser, spares them the enthusiasm of the Viennese, and spares them the sight of Lieselotte's participation in this event. She includes, however, enough historical information and examples of the harassment and humiliation of Jews to indicate that she is deeply familiar with the events that transpired in the few days covered in Inge's diary.

Inge records several events leading to the *Anschluss*. With the help of Germany, Austrian Nazis staged an unsuccessful putsch to gain control of the government in 1934. German policy after this focused on the possibility of achieving the *Anschluss* through an evolutionary process, facilitated especially by Franz von Papen, who was appointed ambassador to Vienna in 1936. The patience of German and Austrian Nazis ran short by 1937, the year the Vesselys moved to Munich because the Nazi Party was outlawed in Austria. Of the political events before March 11, 1938, Orgel includes Hitler's summoning of Chancellor Schuschnigg to Berchtesgaden to propose a nonmilitary annexation of Austria (Orgel 59) and demand the legalization of the Nazi Party as well as the release of all political prisoners. This "mountain top meeting," unlike the mountaintop meeting between Hanna and Franz Dornenwald as imagined by Inge (81), ended in an impasse. Schuschnigg returned to Austria and decided by March 6 to hold a plebiscite on March 13 for Austrian self-determination. Inge's family and friends, as well as the liberal teachers of Inge's humanistic gymnasium, welcomed this plan. On "black Friday," March 11, however, Hitler commissioned Göring to demand by telephone the resignation of Schuschnigg and the appointment of Nazi front man Seyss-Inquart to the office of chancellor. Inge records these events in detail (117–19) and includes a reference to Schuschnigg's moving resignation speech. But, as the family listens intently to the speech, Evi Fried, the only daughter of their Jewish neighbors, asks Inge to play. When Inge later hears that "the government has fallen" (119), she regresses into child-like literalness by imagining Austrian officials before an execution squad.

On March 12, under the pretense of "straightening out the chaos in Austria," Hitler arrived in Linz and in Braunau, his birthplace.[8] On March 14, Hitler made his triumphal entry into Vienna, an event that is a textual blank in *The Devil in Vienna* because Inge is at home and Lieselotte is a participant in Vienna's welcome of Hitler. It is a significant textual blank, a very conscious and ethically motivated authorial choice that denies Nazism its inflated theatrics, its "triumph of the will," and focuses instead on the beginnings of Nazi brutalities against the Jews, which, after the onset of "the final solution," were never to be recorded but were to be, according to the head of the SS, "a page of glory in our history which has never been written and is never to be written."[9]

On March 11, the day before all Viennese schools were closed to make youths available for pro-Nazi demonstrations (Botz 74), Inge and her classmates are translating Cicero: "As yet I have encountered no man who would not rather yield to Caesar's demands than fight" (115), a critique of Austria's attitudes and a tribute to Latin, a language loved by Orgel and her mother. As the students leave school, they see that the streets are crowded with Nazis (116). As a warm-up for the main event, the Reich Youth leader Baldur von Schirach had arrived in Vienna to address 40,000 "Hitler Youths and BDM girls who in disciplined and orderly fashion lined up before him . . . [as] . . . he announced that 'from today on the Austrian Jungvolk would cease to exist, there would be only one Hitler Youth' " (Botz 70). Most of them participated in Hitler's triumphal entry into Vienna and listened to his March 15 address in the Heldenplatz, where he declaimed: "as Führer and Reich Chancellor of Germany I announce to history that my homeland has become part of the German Reich." The masses responded with roaring applause, sustained "Sieg Heils," and the singing of the German national anthem and the "Horst Wessel Lied." It is in this context that Lieselotte must be imagined. The pressures to conform in such situations are tremendous. Hitler concluded his business in Vienna that afternoon by receiving Cardinal Innitzer, who pledged his wholehearted support followed by a pastoral letter instructing Catholics to vote for the *Anschluss* in the plebiscite. The Catholic Church's official position, then, makes Uncle Ludwig's stance very radical and rather unlikely as he facilitates the escape of the Dornenwalds and others by predating baptismal records.

Random and systematic violence against Europe's third-largest Jewish community began from the first days of Nazi rule; the Austrian police stood by:

> The most visible and wide-spread form that this lightning persecution took was street-cleaning actions. Jews, young and old, rich and poor, religious and non-religious, were ordered out into the streets to scrub pro-Schuschnigg slogans and symbols from the sidewalks and pavements. But the Nazis added several features to make the work more in keeping with their purposes. The water given to the Jews was often mixed with acid, which burned their fingers, and the implements they were given for this "cleansing" were often toothbrushes. Wealthy Jews were ordered to wear their best clothes.
>
> As the Jews bent over their work, storm troopers and Hitler Youth stood by to harass and humiliate them in every way possible. In Währing, one of Vienna's wealthier sections, Nazis, after ordering Jewish women to scrub streets in their fur coats, then stood over them and urinated on their heads. (Berkley 259)

When Inge's father and grandfather come home from this ordeal on March 12, she does not recognize them: "I thought they were two old beggars. . . . O.O. was stooped over like a ninety-year-old man. Vati's eyes were red and swollen, he could hardly see out of them. His hands shook. His mouth quivered when he spoke" (127). They, too, had used the toothbrushes and had buckets of ammonia thrown over them while the crowd "joked and jeered, and not one said a word against it" (128). Dornenwald also mentions the moral heroism of Chief Rabbi Dr. Taglicht, who, while scrubbing the street, said, "I am cleaning God's earth," a gesture of almost futile dignity, desperately remembered in the midst of rampaging abuse (Orgel 128; Berkley 260).

Orgel was no doubt familiar with a well-known photograph depicting a Jewish boy painting the word *Jud* on the foundation of a Jewish business as he is being supervised by a Nazi in Austrian attire and surrounded by jeering youths (Berkley opposite 275). When Inge walks home on March 18, she encounters just such a scene: "I saw a bunch of people standing outside a stationery store. A little boy with a skull-cap on was painting J E W on the window. A man in leather pants with a swastika armband on was making him do it. I only saw it for a second. I didn't need to look longer than that. It will always be there in my mind, and so will Herr Fried's store, smashed in, even when I am an old, old woman" (192).

Throughout the narrative, Orgel emphasizes the manner in which Inge sees anti-Semitic slogans scrawled on the walls: she looks at the threatening image and looks away, but the image stays imprinted (89). What she sees now distorts normal reality so that for a moment she is not sure what is real. When she arrives with Evi Fried on March 18 at Herr Fried's jewelry store to have the chain to her Mogen David necklace repaired, the trope of the "hole in the world," the deep wound inflicted on her when her father and grandfather were abused by the Nazis, concretizes itself in the shattered window of Fried's store, and her perception is momentarily disoriented in a world gone awry: "When we were nearly there, a car drove by, and the sun hit the windshield in such a way, it made a glare that hurt my eyes. I put my hand over my eyes. When I took my hand away, I thought my eyes were not working right—because the glass window of Herr Fried's jewelry store looked all zigzagged to me . . . it was smashed" (189–90). As the necklace, symbolic of her Jewish identity, is repaired, she relates the window to "the hole in the world I thought I was just making up as a way of writing how I felt on Saturday, and so that hole is just as real" (192). Metaphor has once more become historical reality.

The hole in the world, the abyss that destabilizes everything, makes life unbearable to Franz Dornenwald's business partner: " 'Ingelein, he killed himself. They sent his brother to Dachau. Max couldn't bear it. He thought he might be next' " (187). Orgel acknowledges with one

example the drastic increase in suicides after the *Anschluss,* especially
between March 11 and 18, the majority of whom were Jews (Botz 98–
105). How close Franz himself is to this act is revealed in his need for
comfort as he pulls Inge into his lap and tells her that his partner did
not have a daughter who would have kept him from such a desperate act. Inge, who has just come from a meeting with Lieselotte, feels
sick with guilt as she extricates herself from her father's embrace. Ten
days later, when she goes with her mother to the Yugoslavian consul-
ate to negotiate for visas, she sees a *Stürmer* headline: A HUNDRED JEW-
ISH SUICIDES DAILY NOT ENOUGH. THOUSANDS NEEDED. GOERING CALLS
FOR JEW-CLEANSED VIENNA (226). By that time it is clear to her that she
"cannot go on 'endangering our lives'" by having Lieselotte as a friend
(213).

The Dornenwalds cannot get a visa unless they present officials with
a baptismal record dated no later than 1936. They hope that Father
Ludwig will let them fill in the dates, but he insists that Herr and Frau
Dornenwald go through the ritual of baptism. Thus the priest's willingness to falsify the date on the certificate is undercut by his unwill-
ingness to spare the Dornenwalds the ritual. The enforced baptism,
enacted so many times throughout history, makes Inge glad that she
does not have to be present, because as a minor she will travel with
her parents: "I didn't want to be there when it happened" (234). Young
Inge can remain officially Jewish. In gratitude for the girls' friendship,
which facilitated the Dornenwalds' escape to Yugoslavia, Inge's parents allow them one final get-together. They go to the Prater, Vienna's
amusement park, and, when both are at the top of the Ferris wheel,
Inge has the impulse to release her blue balloon and Lieselotte follows suit. As they watch them sailing into the sky, Lieselotte allego-
rizes: "'They look like our friendship floating away.'" Inge, however,
neither needs nor can afford tropes: "'No, they're just balloons. They
just have helium in them, not blood'" (240). After describing how
Inge assures Lieselotte that their friendship will be in a book that she
might, some day, be able to read, Orgel leaves blank the moment when
the two friends actually part. At best, Lieselotte must live with a split
consciousness, hiding her real self in her innermost being. Inge, however, can achieve closure through her maturation. She has accepted
her Jewishness and no longer desires to be accepted by the community that ostracizes her. Finally, she has given closure to her friendship
by containing it in a diary. As a result, Inge is "not sad to be leaving
Vienna behind. Oh, sure, it's where I was born, and where my parents

were born—and if we were not getting out, it's also the place where we might die. I don't mean when we're old, I mean a lot sooner" (242).

The sparing of the child, the shielding of the child as character and reader, is accomplished first of all by Orgel's choice of genre, which places Inge's account of history within the relatively narrow context of her life. There is one other gap, however, that the diarist herself creates. Inge emphasizes repeatedly that she writes in order to record how she "really feels" about Lieselotte, but Inge never describes those feelings as history begins to deconstruct their friendship. She describes her behavior toward Lieselotte, her actions and reactions, but not the nature of her bond. The dichotomies "a Nazi girl's best friend is a Jewish girl" and "a Jewish girl's best friend is a Nazi girl" create a subtextual uneasiness throughout the narrative. Except for very overt conflicts such as parental prohibitions, the implications of that uneasiness remain unexplored. The central fiction of the narrative—the possibility that such a friendship could endure through atrocious history—is made plausible by the immediacy of a thirteen-year-old's narrative point of view. I suspect that it was also for Orgel a necessary fiction, a stay against the hopelessness and despair that overwhelmed Jewish families during those days and in the months that followed. Inge leaves Vienna before Lieselotte is consumed by Nazi history, by the ruthless dominance that tore a hole in the world and negated hope for the fragile bond of friendship.

Notes

1. All biographical information is taken from Doris Orgel's essay about herself in *Something About the Author.*

2. Although a few critics have expressed doubts as to Inge's interest in current events, one Jewish survivor of that time remembers: "We children had to be alert and informed, and read the daily news, and not just the sports pages" (Chaimowicz 292).

3. Such fantasies were even part of dreams remembered by victims of anti-Semitism. See Beradt, *The Third Reich of Dreams* 127–29. Beradt records the dream of a Jewish doctor who "cured Hitler . . . the only one in the Reich who was able to."

4. The members of Germany's Hitler Youth who joined before October 2, 1932, were considered "old fighters" and received a gold medal in 1934 in recognition. After the seizure of power in 1933, the Hitler Youth soon lost their militant aura and became politically coordinated as *Staatsjugend,* youth of the state. In Austria the time of struggle lasted, of course, until the *Anschluss.*

5. Julius Streicher endorsed the infamous picture book by Elwira Bauer, *"Trau keinem Fuchs auf grüner Heid und keinem Jud bei seinem Eid": Ein Bilderbuch für Gross und Klein.* This book includes Aryan children jeering as Jewish students are dismissed from school and, significantly, has on its final page a picture showing Jews being driven out of the country along a one-way street. The image on the back cover shows a grotesque caricature of a Jew behind the star of David. The slogan underneath that image reads: *Eine Lösung*

der Judenfrage, eine Erlösung der Menschen (A solution of the Jewish problem, a salvation of humanity). Satanic images abound in this picture book.

6. "Glaube und Schönheit," officially established by Baldur von Schirach, the Reich Youth Leader, in 1938, emphasized "feminine" education in domestic sciences and fashion design along with physical fitness and ideological correctness. Membership was not automatic and was for girls seventeen years or older. Orgel is probably correct in assuming that "Glaube und Schönheit" was discussed informally in 1937, but Lieselotte would not be eligible to join for at least four years.

7. The anthem was composed by Baldur von Schirach for the film version (1934) of the prototypical Nazi youth novel *Hitlerjunge Quex.* Its first stanza reads: "Our flag unfurls before us. / Moving into the future / Man for man. / We march for Hitler / Through night and need / With the flag of Youth for Freedom and bread. / Our flag unfurls before us, / Our flag is the new time / And our flag leads us into eternity! / Yes, our flag is more than death."

8. For historically summative accounts of Austria and the *Anschluss* consult Berkley, *Vienna and Its Jews;* Brooke-Shepherd, *The Anschluss;* Botz, *Wien vom "Anschluss" zum Krieg;* Chorherr, *1938—Anatomie eines Jahres;* Wagner and Tomkowitz, *Anschluss: The Week Hitler Seized Vienna.*

9. This famous quotation is from the speech given by Heinrich Himmler in October 1943 when he exhorted the SS, who were by then implementing the final solution, to remain "decent" in spite of the difficult orders they had to follow. History, for once, seems to have been just in that the "unwritten page of history" has been filled indeed!

Works Cited

Bauer, Elwira. *"Trau keinem Fuchs auf grüner Heid und keinem Jud bei seinem Eid": Ein Bilderbuch für Gross und Klein.* Nuremberg: Stürmer Verlag, 1936.

Beradt, Charlotte. *The Third Reich of Dreams.* Trans. Adriane Gottwald. Chicago: Quadrangle Books, 1968.

Berkley, George E. *Vienna and Its Jews: The Tragedy of Success, 1880–1980.* Cambridge: Abt Books, 1988.

Botz, Gerhard. *Wien vom Anschluss zum Krieg.* Vienna and Munich: Jugend und Volk Verlagsgesellschaft, 1978.

Brooke-Shepherd, Gordon. *The Anschluss.* New York: J. B. Lippincott, 1963.

Chaimowicz, Thomas. " 'Lacht nicht ich wasche Gottes Erde': Als Jude und Legitimist im Wien von 1938." In *1938—Anatomie eines Jahres.* Ed. Thomas Chorherr. Munich: Carl Ueberreuter, 1987.

Chorherr, Thomas, ed. *1938—Anatomie eines Jahres.* Munich: Carl Ueberreuter, 1987.

Hitler, Adolf. *Mein Kampf.* Trans. Ralph Manheim. Boston: Houghton Mifflin, 1962.

Nakamura, Joyce, ed. *Something About the Author.* Autobiography Series 19. New York: Gale Research, 1995.

Orgel, Doris. *The Devil in Vienna.* New York: Penguin, 1988.

Sontag, Susan. "Fascinating Fascism." In *Under the Sign of Saturn.* New York: Farrar, Straus & Giroux, 1972/80.

Toll, Claudia Maria. *Ästhetik im Abseits: Der pädagogische Gestus als Prinzip der Gestaltung von Kinderliteratur am Beispiel von Büchern zum Thema Nationalsozialismus.* Frankfurt am Main: Peter Lang, 1986.

Wagner, Dieter, and Gerhard Tomkowitz. *Anschluss: The Week Hitler Seized Vienna.* Trans. Geoffrey Strachan. New York: St. Martin's, 1971.

Maurice Sendak's Urban Landscapes

Joseph Stanton

My purpose is to consider several Maurice Sendak books in which images inspired by New York City play an important part. I will be considering several different sorts of dream Manhattans, primarily in the picture books *In the Night Kitchen* and *We Are All in the Dumps with Jack and Guy*, but my discussion must be grounded in the realistic Brooklyn implicit in Sendak's illustrated stories for *The Sign on Rosie's Door*. My thesis is that there is in much of Sendak's best work an exciting tension between the mundane particularities of everyday life on one hand and the theatrical glories of the fantasy life on the other. My emphasis on urban examples is, to some extent, an arbitrary limitation that will serve to keep this essay to a reasonable length, but the limitation also aims to make possible an examination of Sendak's tendency to use the two faces of New York City—the Brooklyn of his childhood and the Manhattan of his childhood and his adulthood—as symbolic sites. As we shall see, although Sendak tends to equate Brooklyn with the mundane and Manhattan with the phantasmagoric, the two boroughs of his imagination are complexly interrelated, and the here-and-now particular and the far-away exotic are intermixed in every one of his urban pictorial narratives.

It comes as no surprise that discussions of *The Sign on Rosie's Door* have been dominated by Sendak's very interesting autobiographical commentaries on the year he spent recording, in notes and drawings, the antics and romanticisms of a "really" real Rosie, who lived across the street from his parents' Brooklyn home. Sendak has frequently spoken and written of Rosie as his primal character—the "ferocious," romantic, stubborn, courageous, and secretly vulnerable child from which all his child protagonists have derived. But Sendak's own Brooklyn childhood was also primary to the urban attitudes evident in Rosie and the many characters who followed after her; furthermore, in Rosie's yearnings for Broadway stardom we can see Sendak's own ferocious romanticism about the magicalness of Manhattan, that fabled place of lighted towers, food, and movie palaces.

Children's Literature 28, eds. Elizabeth Lennox Keyser and Julie Pfeiffer (Yale University Press, © 2000 Hollins University).

The stories in *The Sign on Rosie's Door* demonstrate—in their deft, understated capturing of a theatrical yet needful child and of the energetic street life of children in one particular neighborhood—that Sendak is as much a writer as he is an artist. The unresolved nature of these stories is part of their gift of truth. To put it another way: although nothing terrible (or terribly important) happens in these stories, Rosie does have more than a little bit at stake. When the other kids go home, abandoning Rosie and breaking her hold on them so that our little star must sing "On the Sunny Side of the Street" to an empty backyard, Sendak lets us keep the sadness of it and does not resort to the sort of farcical resolution that concludes most of his picture books.

The stories in *The Sign on Rosie's Door* are told almost entirely through dialogue. The charm of the work derives from the amusing absurdity of what we hear the kids say in the midst of their make-believe play and from the seeming authenticity of each scene. Anyone who is still a child, or has overheard kids at play, or can reach back to memories of childhood can recognize that Sendak has astutely observed and recorded persuasive enactments of childhood. Sendak's unpretentious achievement in his little collection of Rosie stories is a significant contribution to the "here-and-now tradition" in American children's literature.[1]

The here-and-now tradition has been well explained by Leonard Marcus in his biography of Margaret Wise Brown. The "fairy tale wars" is the term Marcus uses to describe a crucial rivalry and difference of opinion that worked itself out in the children's literature industry as it developed and expanded from the 1920s through the 1940s. On one side of the rivalry were the proponents of fairytale fantasy led by Anne Carroll Moore of the New York Public Library; on the other side were the advocates of the here-and-now storybook—stories based on the mundane experiences of everyday urban life, with an emphasis on capturing the kinds of things kids actually say—led by Lucy Sprague Mitchell, director of the Bank Street School. Margaret Wise Brown became the laureate for the here-and-now camp, but its later practitioners included such people as Ruth Krauss, many of whose works were fundamental exercises in getting the words straight from the mouths of children.[2]

Ruth Krauss was, of course, the here-and-now practitioner with whom Sendak had most contact. Sendak's work on *A Hole Is to Dig* and some of Krauss's other works involved him in the here-and-now enterprise of constructing stories for kids by listening well. The here-and-now emphasis on urban life and on carefully observing and listening to children was clearly advantageous for Sendak. It gave him encouragement to find his stories on his Brooklyn street at a time when he was ready and able to engage in that sort of research. Whereas colleagues of Sendak's, notably Ezra Jack Keats, built careers around the rich material of ordinary lives on city streets, Sendak's embrace of the unadorned urban moment was not sustained. Sendak had no desire to choose between fairy tales and urban scenes. The strategy of several of his best books has been to intermix the fairytale fantastic with the urban-moment mundane to create new and unusual works; of special importance in this regard are the exhilarating and magical *In the Night Kitchen* and the stern and nightmarish *We Are All in the Dumps with Jack and Guy.*

Kenny's Window—published four years before *The Sign on Rosie's Door* and sixteen years before *In the Night Kitchen*—clearly indicates Sendak's obsession with fantasy and his interest in urban streets. The window through which Kenny dream-travels to hobnob with a talking four-footed rooster, who lives in a vaguely defined magical garden, is a window in a realistically depicted Brooklyn brownstone, very similar to the ones lived in by Rosie and, of course, by Sendak himself. In *Kenny's Window* the urban world of Kenny's street and Kenny's room predominates, at least visually, over Kenny's dream worlds. Even the Chagall-like visions of the flying rooster and the flying horse are suspended above the mundane architecture of Kenny's quite ordinary city street. The presentation of the fantastic within the context of the mundane that Sendak will so marvelously develop in *In the Night Kitchen* is implicit but largely unrealized in *Kenny's Window*. Though he wanted to envision subconscious dream material in this work—the book is dedicated, in part, to his analyst (Lanes 64)—he is not quite ready to unlatch the window that he was to so gloriously throw open in his mature works.

The year after *Kenny's Window* appeared, Sendak published an illustrated book with a more parable-like plot about running away from home and then being happy to return that anticipates the plot of *Where the Wild Things Are* in certain respects, but, as in *Kenny's Window,* there is no departure from the mundane urban streets. *Very Far Away* turns out to be a bare room in an empty basement, where Martin and his animal friends necessarily manufacture their notions of the exotically far away inside their heads. The reader sees little glimpses of these fanciful realms in cartoon balloons above the characters' heads, but the artist does not give us any visual escape from the urban here and now of Martin's neighborhood. At the end Martin happily returns home to find resolutions to his complaints.

The pictures in *Very Far Away* are more satisfying than those in *Kenny's Window,* but the biggest improvement is in the story. In fact, the story is a wonderful read-aloud piece that seems much more interesting without the pictures.[3] One striking and enjoyable discovery for attentive perusers of *Very Far Away* is the odd circumstance that the urban backdrop that appears to be Brooklyn on pages seventeen through twenty-one suddenly changes to what is obviously Greenwich Village from page twenty-three through the end of the book. Perhaps Sendak was working on this volume when he moved from his parents' home in Brooklyn to an apartment in Greenwich Village. Perhaps a book about running away from home struck a personal note concerning Sendak's desire for escape to the very far away known as Greenwich Village. This sort of little joke embedded in the details would be carried to extremes in his later books. Another amusing oddity in *Very Far Away* is a cameo appearance by Sendak himself, who rounds a corner walking his dog Jennie just as Martin emerges from the very-far-away basement.

Although a feeling for the details of modern urban life also lies at the heart of *In the Night Kitchen,* the here-and-now impulse is overwhelmed by a fairy tale–like fantasy that is bizarrely inhabited by many of the essential ingredients of Sendak's urban childhood. Mundane details of a Brooklyn kitchen are everywhere, and everywhere they are shaped to resemble a caricature of the New York City skyline. A manic fantasy prevails. The tension between the prosaic kitchen and the fabulous kingdom it has been made into is basic to the power of this tale. So intermingled are the beloved ordinary utensils and the dream-fantasy rendering of a Manhattan-fantasy facade that it is not possible to separate one from the other. The real streets of Sendak's earlier books are no more to be seen. Dream has swallowed the urban world whole.

Sendak has commented in several places on how *In the Night Kitchen* grew out of his delightful childhood memory of visits to Manhattan, his love of movies—especially Mickey Mouse cartoons and Busby Berkley musicals of the 1930s—and the eating-out occasions central to Manhattan visits (*Caldecott & Co.* 166–7, 174–6), but this fantasy picture poem was also heavily influenced by the fairy tales and nursery rhymes that Sendak had been extensively studying. The fictions and poems of the anonymous oral tradition we refer to as the works of "Mother Goose" are key influences on *In the Night Kitchen*. Sendak and others (Lanes 173–75; Cech 182–83) have discussed the echoes of Mother Goose rhymes in the alternating verse-prose dynamic of *In the Night Kitchen*, but an obvious and important oral-tradition influence has not been much noticed. Cech has spoken of Sendak's three bakers as parallel to gods of fate in certain myths (202–3), but a more mundane folkloric parallel can be found in the innumerable tales of witches and other gruesome figures who await the accidental arrival of children for cooking in their ovens. Such evil crones are often portrayed as laughing and jovial despite their evil ways, making them not all that different from the jolly Oliver-Hardy threesome. In some respects these three bakers cavort around their bowl of batter in a manner suggestive of the three witches in *Macbeth*. Despite the fairytale situation, *In the Night Kitchen* does not follow a fairytale plot. No witch or chubby chef gets shoved into the oven in the conclusion of this tale. Instead, the narrative, such as it is, follows the whimsical semi-nonsense pattern of a nursery rhyme. This text is poetic from first to last—one of the several masterpieces of picture poetry that the children's picture genre has given us. But the lack of a fairytale plot should not cause us to overlook the fairytale situation.

One of the explanations Sendak has given for his harmlessly demonic bakers and for the baking motif in general is that it is his "vendetta" against the Sunshine Bakery, which used to advertise, during the years Sendak was a child, that they "bake while you sleep." Sendak reports that his younger self found this notion distressing. How could they be so cruel as to do all this wonderful baking while poor little Maurice was sleeping and missing all this exciting action (*Caldecott & Co.* 174–75)?

One of the reasons that we should pay careful attention to this motivation is that there is another even more powerful one nested within the multiple meanings of this work. Sendak's vendetta has as its antagonist Death itself, subtly associated with the demise Mickey effortlessly averts. Sendak injects an element of fatality into his mysterious night bakery by use of the folkloric motif of the evil baker who cooks kids in the oven. The wit of this motif adds a sardonic undertone and an edge of real danger to this dream adventure. It also should not be overlooked that by adding little mustaches to the Sunshine Bakery bakers Sendak not only made them into Oliver-Hardy clones but also fused the benignly sunshine-bright advertising-logo bakers with the nightmarish image of Adolf Hitler, whose chambers for the extermination of Jews made him an embodiment in recent historical time of the oven-stoking wicked witch. The Hitler connection is a subtle undertone that Sendak himself may not have had consciously in mind as he developed the image, but it is a key ingredient in the work. Sendak's parents were both Jews who emigrated from Poland. It is hardly surprising that the Holocaust can be implicated in Sendak's books. The Nazi death camps are mentioned by most commentators on the nightmarish bakery of *We Are All in the Dumps,* but it could be argued that they are more crucial to consider as an underlying motif of *In the Night Kitchen.*

The jolly brightness of *In the Night Kitchen* stands in stark contrast to the circumstances of Sendak's life at the time he was writing it. His mother passed away, his father was diagnosed with a terminal illness, and Sendak himself suffered a serious heart attack. In a letter, Sendak explained the strength of character his hero is required to possess: "Mickey has to care about himself in every possible way, because I think he's in the land of the dead, for the most part. His parents are not to be found to help him. So then, with his nerviness, his sensibility, and his basic mind, he makes himself an airplane . . . he does something to sustain himself during his very suspenseful, strange, mystifying experience" (Deitch). The bravado of Mickey—who climbs out of an oven, makes and flies a plane over the "milky way," then dives down to the bottom of a bottle as tall as a three-story building—is a heroic response to the grim fact of mortality. During this magical adventure Mickey achieves several baptismal rebirths. Not only does he escape an oven, but he reemerges after two submersions: one in the batter and the other in an excess of milk. Sendak—who as a child was often sickly and on at least one occasion was not expected to live through the night—has constructed an unwavering superchild to triumph over the night. In addition to creating a picture-book masterpiece, he addresses his fears of death—the ultimate thing that goes bump (and thump, dump, clump, lump) in the night—when it must have seemed everyone around him was dying.

Despite the grim context in which Sendak was creating this picture book, it is quite possibly Sendak's most boisterous and cheerful book. Paradoxically the Manhattanesque dream kitchen is, despite the initial menace of the ovens and the (demon) bakers, a place where something of legendary wondrousness can be made. It is a place of positive production, the place where ferment leads to product. Sendak's night kitchen is the deep, dark, dangerous, hard-to-get-to place where imagination resides. The fusion of the urban and the folkloric lies at the heart of this work's odd magic. The mythos of Manhattan carries with it the double suggestion that the Big City is simultaneously a place that can kill and a place where great things can be cooked up.

How did Sendak manage to fold his ferocious folktale into a joyously magic Manhattan dream world? Winsor McCay's "Little Nemo in Dreamland" comic strips (circa 1907), which Sendak discovered just before creating *In the Night Kitchen,* helped him arrive at the method for this lovely urban madness (*Caldecott & Co.* 77–85). It is clear that many images in Sendak's picture book are directly derived from McCay: most often cited are the images of Nemo falling through dream space, of little Nemo flopped half out of bed (with the bed and Nemo parallel to the picture plane), and of an inexplicably gigantic Nemo climbing around a toy version of Manhattan. More important than the borrowing of imagery was the example of McCay's use of the child dreamer. McCay's straight-ahead and rapid presentation of absurd dream worlds was a liberating influence. McCay makes no apologies and offers no complex literary framing devices to explain how Nemo gets to his dream world; he offers no tornados in Kansas, no falls down rabbit holes. The dreams just happen to Nemo and last until he falls out of them. Sendak uses this simple formula to its best advantage.

If I am correct in my contention that Sendak manages to include some rather horrific allusions between the lines of *In the Night Kitchen,* one might ask how he decently accomplishes such things in a picture book for children. This is, of course, the same question that has hovered around all three of the books in his so-called trilogy. Taking seriously Sendak's tying of the three books together as a package will distract this discussion briefly from its urban theme, but a richer view of Sendak's success in his urban masterpiece, *In the Night Kitchen,* can be had if we briefly examine how he incorporated profound and menacing symbolism into delightfully comic and entertaining forms in all three works of his trilogy. A quick look at the layerings of meanings in *Where the Wild Things Are* and *Outside, Over There* can help us define the similar dynamic in *In the Night Kitchen.* A full discussion of the allegorical nature of Sendak's three most admired and most often debated original books can be found in Geraldine DeLuca's 1984 essay, but a few key points can be made here.

Where the Wild Things Are was the first and bore the brunt of public complaint, though it is the most mild-mannered of the three. *Outside, Over There* is perhaps the most severely ominous of the three, with its kidnapping of a baby by demonic goblins represented as shadowy hooded figures that seem to have been modeled after the murderous dwarf of the movie *Don't Look Now*—a horror film, based on a Daphne Du Maurier story, that came out in the mid-1970s, around the time Sendak would have been at work on *Outside, Over There.* The standard answer—along the lines that Sendak helps children of all ages face their fears—begs the question. The strategy Sendak uses to sail past the anxiety of most readers derives from his clear grasp of the basic dynamic of the cartoon tale. The example of the steady march through absurdity presented in Winsor McCay cartoons is not Sendak's only source for his use of a self-confident protagonist and a plot that is stylized farce. At the heart of these three Sendak masterworks is the movie cartoon as invented by Disney and developed further by others. Mickey Mouse is one prototype of the unflappable protagonist; Warner Brothers' Bugs Bunny is another. Max is in no more danger from the silly wild things than Bugs Bunny is from the gun-wielding Elmer Fudd.[4] Each of the trilogy's protagonists faces challenges, and the challenges become more and more formidable as the trilogy develops. Max's wild things only look dangerous. They are push-overs from the first moment of Max's resistance. Mickey, however, seems lost to us for a short time; he is entirely submerged in batter and thrust into the oven before he pokes through and begins to take charge of the situation. The urban demeanor of the night kitchen, though in many respects jazzy and fun, does not offer easy comfort to Mickey. Mickey's stalwart heroism is, in fact, underscored by his situation as a child alone in the city night. The third work in the trilogy, *Outside, Over There,* goes beyond the influence of the simple cartoon farce and shows the influence of Disney epics such as *Pinocchio,* which was Sendak's favorite Disney animated film (*Caldecott & Co.* 111–17). Comic antics do not carry either Ida or Pinocchio easily past their difficulties. In these two stories the protagonists fail rather completely before they finally rise to the occasion and triumph.

In addition to the masterful use of cartoon farce, Sendak adds delight and verve to his rendering of the dark adventures presented in his trilogy by the deft use of poetic form. A substantial commentary on Sendak's use of verse in his trilogy is available in Amy Sonheim's book. She comments on how Sendak uses formal verse to decorate and enliven the dark and dangerous moments in these books. For instance, the ordinary world of Mickey's going to sleep is narrated fairly prosaically, but the world of the dream bakers is charged with poetic intensity (105–10). The pattern here can be likened to the situation at the beginning of *Macbeth*, where the intensely poetic chantings of the three witches contrast sharply with the blank-verse conversation of Macbeth and Banquo. Both the farcical nature of the cartoon catastrophes and the formality of poetic language serve to bounce the protagonists blithely through the dark nights of Sendak's soul in his three big books.

Sendak's use of visual and verbal liveliness to delight and animate the work creates situations where it might be possible to be frightened the first time through any of these three books, but where most readers will find the works a happy romp in subsequent rereadings. As works of poetry, these books are intended primarily for rereading. (The first reading is simply a necessary warm-up procedure.) Any adult who has endlessly reread *Where the Wild Things Are* to a child can confirm the magicalness of the work's poetic effects.

The versions of New York City implicit in *The Sign on Rosie's Door* and *In the Night Kitchen* are largely artifacts of Sendak's childhood: a carefully observed Brooklyn on one hand and a dream Manhattan on the other. *We Are All in the Dumps with Jack and Guy* gives us nightmare renderings of both Brooklyn and Manhattan, but the dream world presented this time does not seem as thoroughly dreamed as the magic amalgam of Manhattan skyline and Brooklyn kitchen Sendak gave us in *In the Night Kitchen*. Despite its origin as the visualization of two almost nonsensical nursery rhymes, *We Are All in the Dumps* seems rather calculating and overfilled with visual explanation. While making slides of the book, I became exasperatedly aware of how redundant the pictures are. In several cases similar images follow one after the other to impose a prosaic and somewhat bulky storyline on the frail frame of the lovely, strange little Mother Goose rhymes. *In the Night Kitchen* is a masterful picture-poem whose hard-earned and pain-inspired lyricism carries us through a deeply felt reverie full of laughter and delight, but *We Are All in the Dumps* is a heavy-handed moral lecture that seems to come more from Sendak's head than from his heart.

The case in favor of admiring *We Are All in the Dumps* has, however, been well argued by Peter Neumeyer, who notices much of interest in this richly allusive and handsome book. Neumeyer catalogs the allusions to Blake's chimney sweeps, the fleeting fly-by appearance of Mozart as an angel, the sad demise of picture-book maker James Marshall, the photographs of street urchins by Jacob Riis, the AIDS epidemic, the starving children of an African drought, the note of thanks to Iona Opie for her help with the nursery rhymes, and multiple other little reflections, jibes, and jokes. Perhaps Neumeyer's most interesting identifications of allusions are the religious images—a Deposition, a Pietà, and a Resurrection that are presented as the "Poor Little Kid" transcends his near-demise. Neumeyer makes much of the beauty of the double-page spread in which the kid is taken down from the moon (in a deposition-like way).[5]

In *We Are All in the Dumps* Sendak gives us an image of a city of the 1990s in which the homeless huddle together inside cardboard boxes, and this also suggests in fascinating ways the impoverished London of Charles Dickens or of William Blake. Although this fable cobbles together several times and places, we are primarily located in New York City, but there is no love of the Big Apple evident in this book. Sendak, who no longer lives primarily in New York City, gives us here neither a marvelous Manhattan nor a beloved Brooklyn. Cameo appearances by Trump Tower and the Brooklyn Bridge do, however, confirm those habitats as the contexts for these mean streets.[6]

It is instructive to contrast the apathetic, shaven-headed waifs of *We Are All in the Dumps* with the prancing, full-of-fun, mischievous kids we witnessed in *The Sign on Rosie's Door*. Both sets of youngsters are seen in streets, but in the two cases the circumstances and attitudes of the children are very different. Rosie and friends are out in the street to play, and for Rosie all her play points toward future glory—her impossible but lovely dreams of someday being a Broadway star. By contrast, Jack and Guy and company just want to survive and keep the rats at bay. The "poor little kid" is a dreamless victim.

Obviously, there are allusions to the Holocaust implicit in the orphanage and the bakery to which the kittens and the poor little kid are taken by the villainous rats; however, the unexplained escape of the kid to the field of rye where Jack and Guy find him, as Sendak strains to shape his tale to the words of the nursery rhyme, seems, to me at least, to deflate the threat of this supposed Holocaust. There is no coherence to the kidnapping and no plausibility to the escape of the sickly child. The storage of the kittens on shelves could be suggestive of the way Jews were treated in the death camps, but it is not entirely clear how that allusion is supposed to work. For anyone who has dealt with kittens or children such open-shelved storage has scant plausibility. Why would a kitten stay on a shelf? No wonder the kid got away if this is the way the rats confine their prisoners. Sendak has often praised Randolph Caldecott's illustrations of nursery rhymes, and this book must be, in part, an effort to equal that master. But Caldecott's illustrations, as odd as they sometimes are, never lack inherent plausibility. Sendak's fantasy tries so hard to accommodate all the details of both nursery rhymes that he does not entirely succeed in keeping his plot under control.

The greatest peculiarity of this book, and the vehicle for Sendak's sermonizing, is the annoying, know-it-all moon he shoves into our faces. One of the most repetitive elements in the book visually, this celestial busybody is somewhat of an insult to the reader's intelligence. It is there in every frame dictating how we should react to each scene. This inescapable know-it-all is a representation of a stern adult conscience and seems the complementary opposite of the rebellious child that is the dominant figure in most of Sendak's best books. The moon's looking over the shoulder of the characters and its intervention as a deus ex machina to save the day and force Jack and Guy to participate in the rescue makes the supposed protagonists almost unnecessary. This moon is, however, central to some gorgeous picture-making. There is, for instance, considerable visual excitement to the moon's entry into the action. It is wonderful to see this fabulous globe-with-a-face pick up Jack and Guy in its mouth and transport them to the site of rescue, and there is magic to the moon's leap into the fray in the form of a gigantic cat (with a fascinating Cheshire-cat grin). But for all its graphic interest, the moon-cat's pomposity makes it a narrative liability.

The moon as observer of kids in the street constitutes a kind of return to the observation of kids Sendak gave us in *The Sign on Rosie's Door,* but the observer of Rosie and her friends was Sendak himself, a largely invisible presence watching only to appreciate and never to judge. Sendak's creation of the harshly judgmental moon-observer indicates a shift in attitude and sympathies of which Sendak himself may not be aware. Perhaps he no longer finds it easy to identify with children. (He has, perhaps, sent his inner child to its room.) Sendak's championing of the impoverished, the ill, and the abandoned is admirable, but the application of his remarkable talents to scold and to admonish seems less than their best use.[7]

Though the hectoring moral tone of Sendak's images for *We Are All in the Dumps* makes it less than his most delightful work, there is an operatic magnificence to this production—the result, perhaps, of his extensive theatrical work in recent years—that makes it a fascinating return by Sendak to the picture-book enactment of the urban here-and-now. In the here and now of the 1990s Rosie and her Brooklyn pals are starving and apathetic, there is no chicken soup with rice in sight, and the Manhattan dream world has become entirely nightmare.

No doubt the shift in Sendak's attitude toward Manhattan that takes place in the interim between *In the Night Kitchen* and *We Are All in the Dumps* is, at least in part, reflective of Sendak's personal shift of feelings toward life in the big city. The romance of Manhattan's bright glitter and relentless energy seems to have become less satisfying for him for a variety of reasons. Not long after the publication of *In the Night Kitchen* Sendak moved his primary residence to rural Connecticut for reasons of "health" and "solitude." Sendak's darker view of Manhattan in *We Are All in the Dumps* and his illustration work for a new edition of Herman Melville's *Pierre, or the Ambiguities* would seem to reflect a willingness on Sendak's part to acknowledge that Manhattan can be seen to have much in common with the dismal London of Blake or Dickens. That the magical Manhattan has not entirely receded for Sendak can be observed in his hilarious illustrations for Arthur Yorinks's *Miami Giant,* a delightfully silly revision of the King Kong story. But it is worth noting that the giants' bad experiences in Manhattan cause them to flee back to Miami. The closest they are said to come to a return to Broadway is a rumored move to suburban Long Island.

Sendak's illustrations for Melville's *Pierre, or the Ambiguities*—a brutally adult book for which Sendak's illustrations envision a cruel and claustrophobic nineteenth-century New York City—could be seen as the climatic descent of Sendak's bold, rebellious child into the despairs of darkest adulthood. In a review of Sendak's illustrations for *Pierre,* Jed Perl notes that "our memories of all Sendak's slyly exultant heroes and heroines are buried deep inside Pierre's wild-eyed, incredulous look in the book's last, awful illustration. . . . The kid has grown up and lost, and Sendak is right there by his side" (34).

It is, however, hard to believe that Sendak's rebellious child will accept permanent defeat. As Mickey rose again from the bread dough, as Max stared down all the monsters, and as Ida rescued her sister from the goblins, so can we expect the indomitable Sendak child to recover his or her audacity in future books. It will be interesting to see if the next phase in Sendak's work will emphasize his interest in the dark woods of the fairy tale that has been steadily increasing in his mature work or if his continuing preoccupation with urban scenes

will be carried further or if he will find new ways to merge his dangerous places. It seems unlikely, however, that Sendak will ever return to
the understated treatment of here-and-now lives of children on ordinary city streets. His mature works are all too grandly operatic to allow
room for a lovely little one-note singer like Rosie.

Notes

1. Lucy Sprague Mitchell's 1921 collection *Here and Now Story Book* surprises readers
by beginning with a long, polemical introduction by Mitchell, "What Language Means
to Young Children," which she pointedly addresses "to parents, teachers and writers."
Although Mitchell did not insist that a here-and-now tale had to be urban in focus,
Mitchell and her Bank Street colleagues were very attentive to the fact that the here
and now for their students was New York City. Furthermore, the predominantly city-
oriented nature of the tales in *Here and Now Story Book* suggests that Mitchell regarded
the city as the inevitable environment for most modern children. This assumption per-
vades much material for children that grew out of the progressive education movement.
Some of the preoccupations of the *Sesame Street* television series, for instance, could be
regarded as direct descendents of Mitchell's *Here and Now Story Book*.

2. Sendak greatly admired Margaret Wise Brown and included a tribute to one of her
books in his *Caldecott & Company* (125–27), a collection of essays and interviews. Among
the many Brown-derived motifs that can be observed in Sendak's work are his use of
sounds in ways that recall Brown's here-and-now "noisy books" (the "racket" Mickey
hears coming from the night kitchen is an obvious instance) and his deployment of the
moon in ways that recall *Goodnight Moon* and other moon-obsessed Brown books.

3. Because *Very Far Away* is more interesting as a literary piece than as an example of
Sendak's visual art, listening to it as presented by Tammy Grimes on her audio recording
of Sendak's work reveals the strength of the piece more clearly than an examination of
the book itself. Sendak's deft and suggestive text enables the reader to conjure visions of
"very far away" that the pictures, drawn in the understated style he sometimes employed
in the 1950s, cannot equal.

4. It should be noted that Charlie Chaplin was a big influence on the cartoons that
made their mark on Sendak, and, of course, Sendak was also directly influenced by the
farcical antics and transcendent grace of Chaplin's best sequences.

5. There is an interesting similarity between Sendak's Deposition image and a scene
of similar loveliness in Tomie dePaola's *Sing Pierrot, Sing*. Sendak probably borrowed the
image directly from Renaissance art, but the scene in dePaola's book might have alerted
him to the possibility.

6. Peter Neumeyer misidentifies the bridge as the Queensborough Bridge (34), most
likely because he is assuming that the derelict part of the city in the foreground would
be Queens, but it is important to my discussion to understand that Sendak has included
the Brooklyn Bridge, a symbol of his ongoing concern with Brooklyn, the borough of
his childhood days.

7. Another example of Sendak's impulse toward the didactic, adult point of view can
be found in a book he published in 1976 called *Some Swell Pup*, which is an extended lecture on the proper treatment of pets. In this pompous book a hooded dog figure acts as
an intervening know-it-all in a manner that resembles the behavior of the bossy moon
of *We Are All in the Dumps*. Although it could be pointed out that cautionary tales can be
found at every phase of Sendak's career, a look at his best-known early cautionary tale,
Pierre of the *Nutshell Library* boxed set of small volumes, reveals that, although Pierre
does eventually curb his cantankerousness enough to admit the value of "caring," the

emphasis in the story as a whole is on Pierre's insistent preference for preferring not to care. For the most part the emphasis in most of Sendak's early works, even when they are cautionary tales, is predominantly on the stubborn, rebellious energy of the child. Sendak's parable of the boy who allowed himself to be eaten by a lion because he "did not care" is returned to us in a new way with *We Are All in the Dumps*, which ferociously insists on compassion, but this time the ferocity is the province of the adult perspective.

Works Cited

Cech, John. *Angels and Wild Things: The Archetypal Poetics of Maurice Sendak*. University Park: Pennsylvania State University Press, 1995.
Commire, Anne, ed. "Sendak, Maurice." In *Something About the Author*, vol. 27. Detroit: Gale, 1982.
Deitch, Gene. Audio letter, 19 April 1984, Weston Woods Studios production archives, quoted by Cech (202).
DeLuca, Geraldine. "Exploring the Levels of Childhood: The Allegorical Sensibility of Maurice Sendak." *Children's Literature* 12 (1984): 3–24.
Don't Look Now. Dir. Nicolas Roeg, 1973 (based on a story by Daphne Du Maurier).
Grimes, Tammy. *Where the Wild Things Are, In the Night Kitchen, Outside Over There and Other Stories by Maurice Sendak Performed by Tammy Grimes* (audio cassette). New York: Caedmon, 1988.
Krauss, Margaret. *A Hole Is to Dig: A First Book of First Definitions*. New York: HarperCollins, 1952.
Lanes, Selma. *The Art of Maurice Sendak*. New York: Abrams, 1980.
Marcus, Leonard. *Margaret Wise Brown: Awakened by the Moon*. Boston: Beacon, 1992.
McCay, Winsor. *Little Nemo in the Palace of Ice and Further Adventures*. New York: Dover, 1976.
Melville, Herman. *Pierre, or the Ambiguities*. Ed. Hershel Parker, illus. Maurice Sendak. New York: HarperCollins, 1995.
Mitchell, Lucy Sprague. *Here and Now Story Book*. 1921. New York: Dutton, 1948.
Neumeyer, Peter. "We Are All in the Dumps with Jack and Guy: Two Nursery Rhymes with Pictures by Maurice Sendak," *Children's Literature in Education* 25, no. 1 (1994): 29–34.
Perl, Jud. "Where the Wild Things Are." *The New Republic*, 18 March 1966: 30–34.
Sendak, Maurice. *Caldecott and Co.: Notes on Books and Pictures*. New York: Farrar, Straus and Giroux, 1988.
———. *Hector Protector and As I Went Over the Water*. New York: Harper & Row, 1965.
———. *In the Night Kitchen*. New York: Harper & Row, 1970.
———. *Kenny's Window*. New York: Harper & Row, 1956.
———. *Nutshell Library*. New York: HarperCollins, 1962.
———. *Outside Over There*. New York: HarperCollins, 1981.
———. *Really Rosie*. Music: Carole King. New York: HarperCollins, 1975.
———. *The Sign on Rosie's Door*. New York: HarperCollins, 1960.
———. *Some Swell Pup, or Are You Sure You Want a Pup?* Written with Matthew Margolis. New York: Farrar, Straus & Giroux, 1976.
———. "Sources of Inspiration." In *The Zena Sutherland Lectures, 1983–1992*. Ed. Betsy Hearne. New York: Houghton Mifflin, 1993. Pp. 1–25.
———. *Very Far Away*. New York: Harper & Row, 1957.
———. *We Are All in the Dumps with Jack and Guy*. New York: HarperCollins, 1993.
———. *Where the Wild Things Are*. New York: HarperCollins, 1963.
Sonheim, Amy. *Maurice Sendak*. New York: Twayne, 1991.

Yorinks, Arthur. *The Miami Giant.* Illus. Maurice Sendak. New York: HarperCollins, 1995.

Other Works of Interest

Brown, Margaret Wise. *The Noisy Book.* Illus. Leonard Weisgard. New York: Harper & Row, 1939.

Cott, Jonathan. "Maurice Sendak: King of All Wild Things." In *Forever Young.* New York: Random House, 1977. Pp. 187–219.

Grimm, Wilhelm. *Dear Mili.* Trans. Ralph Manheim, illus. Maurice Sendak. New York: HarperCollins, 1988.

Grimm, Wilhelm, and Jacob Grimm. *The Juniper Tree and Other Tales from Grimm.* Trans. Lore Segal and Randall Jarrell, illus. Maurice Sendak. New York: Farrar, Straus & Giroux, 1973.

————. *King Grisly-Beard.* Trans. Edgar Taylor, illus. Maurice Sendak. New York: Farrar, Straus & Giroux, 1973.

Keats, Ezra Jack. *Whistle for Willie.* New York: Viking, 1964.

Nodelman, Perry. *Words About Pictures: The Narrative Art of Children's Picture Books.* Athens: University of Georgia Press, 1988.

Opie, Iona, and Peter Opie, eds. *The Oxford Dictionary of Nursery Rhymes.* Oxford: Clarendon, 1951.

Schwarcz, Joseph H., and Chava Schwarcz. "Sendak's Trilogy: A Concept of Childhood." In *The Picture Book Comes of Age.* Chicago: American Library Association, 1991. Pp. 194–205.

Sendak, Maurice. *Higglety Pigglety Pop! or There Must Be More to Life.* New York: Harper & Row, 1965.

————. *Seven Little Monsters.* New York: Harper & Row, 1976.

Varia

James Pettit Andrews's "Books" (1790): The First Critical Survey of English Children's Literature

Andrea Immel

Sarah Trimmer has always been regarded as the first major children's book critic because she wrote "Observations on the Changes Which Have Taken Place in Books for Children and Young Persons" in 1802. In this essay, which was the genre's first retrospective analysis, Trimmer showed how children's books had developed into a separate branch of literature during the eighteenth century.[1] It was the historical dimension of Trimmer's "Observations" that distinguished it from the thoughtful notices that Jabez Hirons and William Enfield wrote on new children's books for the *Monthly Review* during the 1780s and 1790s, a course of study with suggested readings such as Erasmus Darwin's *Plan for the Conduct of Female Education* (1797), or the wide-ranging discussion of children's reading in the Edgeworths' *Practical Education* (1797).[2] But it turns out that Trimmer's "Observations" was not the first critical history of children's books in English. There was an earlier attempt that has not been recognized for what it is: the brief but interesting essay "Books" buried in the 1790 "Addenda" of James Pettit Andrews's *Anecdotes, &c. Antient and Modern* (1789).[3] Andrews's text, with illustrations from each of the children's books he discussed, accompanies this commentary.

Andrews's "Books" was reprinted at least once during the nineteenth century, but I have not tried to trace its subsequent publication history. In 1819 the *European Magazine* ran a series called "Fragments. Being Thoughts, Observations, Reflections, and Criticisms, with Anecdotes and Characters Ancient & Modern," and the text of "Books" appeared there without attribution to Andrews as the twenty-ninth

Children's Literature 28, eds. Elizabeth Lennox Keyser and Julie Pfeiffer (Yale University Press, © 2000 Hollins University).

installment. The essay's reprint is not entirely unknown: in item 36 of their bibliography of Christopher Smart, Betty Rizzo and Robert Mahoney discuss "Books" because its author identified Smart as having edited the *Lilliputian Magazine* (1751–52) for John Newbery. Rizzo and Mahoney assumed that this was the essay's first appearance in print and made a shrewd guess that Stephen Jones, the *European*'s editor, might have been its author. The son of Giles Jones, one of Newbery's authors, Stephen was certainly in a position to have picked up information about that firm's practices and personnel, and he credited *Goody Two-Shoes* (1766) to his father in the *New Biographical Dictionary*. Earlier in his career, Stephen produced several well-received children's books including *The History of Tommy Playlove and Jacky Lovebook* (1783), *The Life and Adventures of a Fly* (1787), and *The Oracles* (ca. 1792), all published by Elizabeth Newbery. On the other hand, the essay contains a number of details that strongly suggest that its author was more likely to have been a man of Giles Jones's generation, not Stephen's. First, there is the author's style: phrases such as "a race of infants," "a well-known philanthropic bookseller," and "combat every malignant propensity" sound suspiciously old-fashioned for a piece written around 1819. More important is the essay's chronology, which does not square with a composition date as late as 1819. The author begins by describing the "whole juvenile library" of forty years ago: if he were writing in 1819, then his list of publications presumably would have consisted of titles from the late 1770s, by which time children's book publishing was established as a specialty within the book trade. Also significant is the fact that the rather motley selection of books he mentions date to the 1740s, about twenty years prior to Stephen Jones's birth, when fewer works especially for children were available. Finally, the author ends his analysis of the last forty years' progress around 1790: If he had been writing a survey of the genre's development in 1819, then why would he have neglected to discuss a single title published in the years between 1790 and 1819?

Stephen Jones may well have been better qualified to have written an essay like "Books" than its real author, James Pettit Andrews, who was a historian, an antiquarian of note, and an occasional contributor to the *Gentleman's Magazine*. He seems to have had no known connection with the children's book trade, either as an author or a reviewer and he had no surviving children.[4] If Andrews lacked any compelling professional or private interest in young people and their books, then why did he consider the subject worth an essay? I can only guess that Andrews, who represented himself in *Anecdotes'* allegorical frontispiece as an alchemist seated in his library before an enormous alembic distilling the essences of weighty volumes, had noticed that the number of books being written for children had increased dramatically during his lifetime. As a bookman, he must have regarded it as a fascinating new development, which he believed would initiate significant advances in modern education. What impressed him most was talented writers' increasing willingness to invent stories for children and the way the stories' quality had improved with each successive wave of authors. It has to be said that Andrews drew his conclusions from an extremely small sample of books—just five—so it is doubtful that he tried to establish how many children's books had actually been published between 1740 and 1790. But his remarks on the genre's development were remarkably perceptive, so perhaps he had a wider knowledge of children's books than can be inferred from "Books." First, he divided the fifty-year period under discussion into three stages, which correspond to those still used by children's books historians: the 1730s and 1740s, whose most innovative bookseller was Thomas Boreman in the Guildhall; the 1750s and 1760s, which were dominated by John Newbery in St. Paul's Church-yard; and the 1780s and 1790s, the era of John Marshall in Aldermary Church-yard. Second, the books Andrews selected as representative of each stage turn out to be titles still regarded as important.

Andrews considered the books from the first stage, which coincided with his boyhood, as noticeably inferior to what was on the booksellers' shelves at the time of writing "Books." He judged a good children's book by strictly utilitarian terms: reading a work should improve the child's "knowledge and practice of morality and humanity" (Andrews, "Books" 17). Because he was inclined to regard any text as a waste of time if it did not teach children to be more responsible adults than their parents, he was dubious about any fiction that incorporated marvelous, supernatural, or folkloric elements. So it is hardly surprising that he pronounced Mother Goose's fairy tales superfluous, even though Perrault's *contes* concluded with verse *moralités*—but perhaps Andrews assumed that the stanzas were tacked on to counter the usual objections against the genre (figure 1 A + B).[5] He was not much impressed with the available nonfiction either. In its third English edition by 1744, the abbé Lenglet du Fresnoy's *Geography of Children* presented young readers with great chunks of useful information to digest in catechistical form (figure 2), but Andrews thought it a

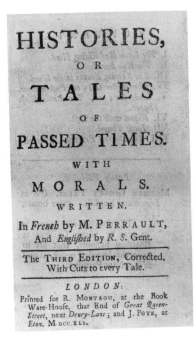

HISTORIES,

O R

T A L E S

O F

PASSED TIMES.

WITH

M O R A L S.

WRITTEN.

In *French* by M. PERRAULT,
And *Englished* by R. S. Gent.

The THIRD EDITION, Corrected.
With Cuts to every Tale.

L O N D O N:

Printed for R. MONTAGU, at the Book
Ware-House, that End of *Great Queen-
Street*, next *Drury-Lane*; and J. POTE, at
Eton. M.DCC.XLI.

Figure 1. Before the appearance of editions especially for children, boys and girls would have read Perrault's fairy tales in an octavo edition like this one. All illustrations reproduced from copies in the Cotsen Children's Library, Princeton University Library, unless otherwise noted.

"dry" and "uninviting" work (17).[6] He also criticized some "minute volumes" about Westminster Abbey and the Tower of London as neither especially informative nor moral because he recalled that their author had "intermixed spectre-stories with topical description" (17). He must be referring to Thomas Boreman's "gigantick histories," the series of tiny illustrated guidebooks to London's major tourist attractions published between 1739 and 1742: the second volume on the Tower of London does contain "spectre-stories" associated with two parts of the building. Children probably enjoyed the merry verse tale about the night the devil appeared on the Battery and "The Wolf in Sheep's Clothing; or the Villain Triumphant," the improbable true story of the Irishman Blood's unsuccessful attempt in 1673 to steal the crown from the Tower, which was probably freely adapted from the account in John Strype's 1720 expansion of Stow's *Survey of London and*

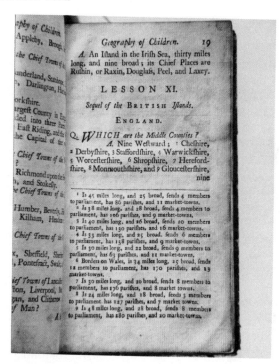

Figure 2. An especially dry and uninviting page from the third edition of Lenglet du Fresnoy's *Geography for Children* (1744). Cotsen Children's Library, Los Angeles.

Westminster (figure 3). Andrews's mention of Boreman's miniatures is especially interesting, because we know that he owned copies of most of them as a boy.[7] Thomas Boreman was one of the first to publish children's books by subscription, circulating a prospectus for a forthcoming title so that interested customers would make down payments for copies before publication. As was customary, Boreman drew up a list of the subscribers' names that was bound in the book when it appeared. The subscribers' lists reveal that Master Jemmy Pettit Andrews purchased both volumes on St. Paul's, the first volume on the Guildhall giants, and the second volumes of the sets on Westminster Abbey and the Tower of London (figure 4). So Andrews's analysis of children's books available during the 1740s may be based to some degree on the books he remembered reading when young.

Andrews's comments on the genre's next stage of development,

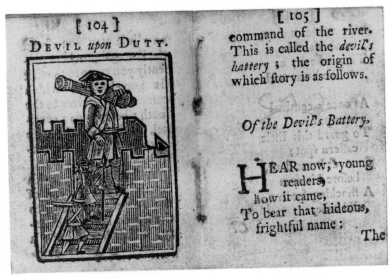

Figure 3. Andrews recalled having read this "spectre-story" about a soldier who met the devil on patrol one night in *The Curiosities of the Tower of London.*

which focused on the *Lilliputian Magazine,* one of John Newbery's best-known publications, were much more enthusiastic. Andrews's praise of the *Lilliputian Magazine* is significant given the volume's current reputation: children's books critics consider the *Magazine* important because it was the first of its kind, not because its contents were especially good; that it ceased publication after just three numbers is usually interpreted as proof that it somehow failed to find its audience.[8] Actually, the *Lilliputian Magazine*'s publishing history suggests that it was quite successful by the standards of its own times, which vary in several important ways from modern ones for periodicals. The *Lilliputian Magazine* had a second lease on life as a one-volume miscellany well into the 1780s, and individual pieces were reprinted in other publications issued by Newbery's successors, provincial and American booksellers.[9] So Andrews quite correctly regarded it as a contemporary classic, a work that helped raise the overall quality of children's books during this period, although he departed from contemporary opinion when he credited this achievement to the editor, Smart, rather than Newbery, his publisher.[10] Andrews warmly praised Smart for having "inculcated the best of principles" in his little readers but

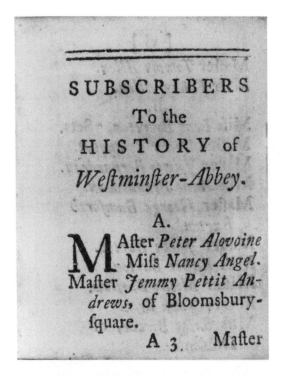

Figure 4. Andrews, who would have been about five at the time, is third on the sub-scribers' list for Boreman's *Description of Westminster Abbey,* volume 2 (1742).

criticized him for just one lapse of judgment: the inclusion of the mar-velous tale of Tommy Trip and Woglog the great giant (this was the first of several installments that appeared in several other Newbery books). Andrews rather humorlessly dismissed the giant as a mere "machine" introduced into the story to terrify little readers into good behavior (figure 5). But at a time when people regularly complained about servants threatening uncooperative children with bogeymen to make them mind, his objection reflected a genuine contemporary concern.[11] If the story is read straight (which is not easy, because its tone sounds tongue-in-cheek to us now), then the example of a boy who wanders out in the fields after dark and meets up with a truculent giant who would just as soon toss him into the river as eat him up could be taken as an indirect injunction to obey one's parents.[12] It would

Figure 5. Andrews objected to this scene from the *Lilliputian Magazine*, in which Tommy Trip and his dog Jowler prepare to make the giant Woglog drop his small victim.

have been interesting if Andrews had also discussed the fables of child empowerment featuring characters like Master Hiron, who serves as his boy-king's chief advisor, little Turvolo, who directs his country's troops during war, and the orphan Polly Meanwell, who wins the king's hand when she chooses death rather than confinement in his seraglio after he rescues her from an unprincipled pirate.

Mary Ann Kilner's *Jemima Placid; or The Advantages of Good-Nature* (1783) was the kind of children's story Andrews admired without reservation. He had no idea that Kilner was its author, because she and her sister-in-law Dorothy succeeded in keeping their identities from the public well into the nineteenth century: neither Trimmer nor the anonymous woman compiler of the *Juvenile Review* (1817) knew who had written the works they recommended to parents so highly. If reviewers in the *Monthly* and the *Critical* thought Mrs. Barbauld and Lady Fenn were transforming reading instruction with child-centered methods, Andrews grasped that John Marshall's authors, including the Kilners, were effecting a similar revolution in the teaching of manners and morals with their "histories in common life," a kind of fiction for young people pioneered by Sarah Fielding in *The Governess* (1749). His comments suggest that he must have agreed with Mary Ann Kilner's rationale for describing children as they are, as expressed in her preface to *Jemima Placid:* The children's writer should depict the "vexations" that are "a severe exercise to their patience," even though the material may strike an adult as trifling: these incidents are anything but inconsequential to little people, who are, after all, in the process of learning how to handle increasingly complex moral problems (Kilner v–vi). Allow children to see themselves in fiction—that is, ordinary boys and girls interacting with their families, friends, and servants— instead of allegorical personifications of character traits (figure 6). So Kilner's readers watched how the heroine Jemima said good-bye to her brothers, pets, and favorite spot in the garden without complaining even though she did not want to stay with relatives until her mother recovered from a serious illness. Children must have sympathized with Jemima as she tried to get along with her spoiled cousins, who couldn't be bothered to make her feel a part of the family during her long visit because they were too busy complaining that all their toys bored them silly, squabbling over whether the first to occupy the window seat was obliged to share it with the other, or insisting that they were not too ill to go to a dance after one of them threw up in the coach en route. Andrews was so confident that Kilner had tailored her material to the experience and understanding of her readers that he felt certain they would learn easily what their duties were but also be much more likely to apply what they read to their own circumstances. He announced, "Should they be as negligent of what is right, as many of their fathers were before them, they will be doubly faulty" (Andrews, "Books" 19).

To get a clearer sense of Andrews's contribution as a Georgian children's book historian and critic, we need to compare his survey with Trimmer's more wide-ranging "Observations," which considered topics as diverse as Locke's influence, the impact of circulating libraries on religious instruction after the Restoration, and non- or anti-Chris-

Figure 6. Andrews praised Kilner for discouraging children's "malignant propensities" by showing them what they were like when they misbehaved: here Jemima Placid's cousins quarrel about which toys they should take on a visit to a relative's house.

tian values in modern children's books. At first glance, Andrews the antiquarian would seem to have had very little in common with Trimmer, the era's foremost authority on children's books, as well as one of its leading figures in the movements providing education and charity to the lower classes.[13] Although Trimmer (1740–1810) outlived Andrews (ca. 1737–97) by thirteen years, they were in fact exact contemporaries who grew up during what Trimmer called the first period of "Infantine and Juvenile literature" (Trimmer 62). So it is perhaps not surprising that she divided up the genre's recent history into the same stages—stages dominated by many of the same people—as Andrews had. It is also interesting that they seem to have based their analysis of the genre's early development on their scattered memories of childhood reading, rather than on any kind of quantitative analysis of the number and type of books issued for young readers during those years. That their lists of children's books published during the 1740s and 1750s should diverge so widely is telling—the only book they both mentioned was Mother Goose, one neither much cared for —because it suggests that nursery libraries probably varied considerably from family to family this early. As different as their lists are, both Andrews and Trimmer emphasized new works written especially for children during the first half of the century such as Gay's *Fables,* the translation of Lenglet du Fresnoy's *Geographie,* Boreman's gigantick histories, Sarah Fielding's *Governess,* the *Lilliputian Magazine,* and Madame Le Prince de Beaumont's *Magasin des enfans,* rather than texts such as Aesop's *Fables* that had served for centuries as reading instruction's foundation. Even though they were not entirely satisfied with the books produced during the 1740s and 1750s, Andrew and Trimmer still saw this period as a crucial one in the transformation of children's books during their lifetimes, culminating in the late 1780s with the Kilners' realistic stories about contemporary children.

This much they agreed on. But when they had to predict what impact this new and separate literature for children might have on its readers, who were supposed to constitute an especially impressionable audience, Andrews and Trimmer ended up on opposite sides. He argued that the new genre's effects could only be beneficial, whereas Trimmer pointed out some of the troubling implications its existence posed. Andrews sounds like a meliorist in "Books," with his endorsement of the notion that the ubiquity of print during the late eighteenth century insured the progress of enlightenment and that children, as one segment of the reading public, would not be passed by. The more books they had to choose from, the more they would read, and the greater the likelihood that they would be improved by reading's "secret influence on the understanding." Of course, when he wrote "Books" during the late 1780s, there seemed every reason for unbounded optimism, what with authors of the caliber of Mrs. Barbauld, Lady Fenn, the Kilners, and Trimmer all writing for children and young people. So if Andrews was satisfied to show how the genre had reached its present state of excellence, he may have assumed that there was no going back: successive generations of children's writers would uphold the new standards and good books like *Jemima Placid* would drive inferior ones off the market. We cannot be sure that he subscribed uncritically to the idea, however, because we do not know what he made of the next wave, children's books published during the 1790s, the last decade of his life. When Trimmer looked back over

these years in the *Guardian's* books reviews, she was not especially san-
guine. She argued that although more books were being published for
children, more of them were of indifferent literary quality, ephemeral
appeal, or dubious morality. Some of the ones she found most objec-
tionable were translations from French and German such as Arnaud
Berquin's *The Children's Friend* (1788), the radical Helen Maria Williams's 1795 English version of Bernardin de Saint Pierre's *Paul et Virgi-
nie,* or George Brewer's *Life of Rolla* (1800), a retelling of Sheridan's *Piz-
zaro,* the hit of the 1799 theatrical season, based on a play by Kotzebue.
She noted that books like the ones just mentioned could very well reverse the advances that had been made, because there were more authors who were writing for money rather than for the audience's benefit, and the new books they produced frequently displaced better ones
on a family's library shelves. Finding copies of Fielding or the Kilners
at the booksellers' was not especially easy these days, she remarked.
She also pointed out that the increasing number and variety of books
had proved to be a very mixed blessing for parents, who rapidly discovered how bewildering and time-consuming it was to select appropriate books for their children without some kind of reliable guide or
review journal to help them evaluate children's books and works on
education as they appeared on the market.

In their analysis of the growing market for children's books, Andrews and Trimmer also touched on the related issue of the genre's
evolving canon and its implications for contemporary education.
Which books should every child know? Under what circumstances
could new texts be added to that group of fundamental works? And
when should a new book be allowed to supplant an old one? Trimmer feared that the flourishing of a separate literature for children
might threaten the Bible's primacy by reopening the subject of Scripture's role in early instruction, a vexed question since the Restoration. In *Some Thoughts Concerning Education* (1693), Locke had made
a case for introducing the Bible to children in nonsectarian abridgments (which, to the best of his knowledge, did not exist) in order
to avoid "that Confusion, which is usually produced by promiscuous
reading of the Scripture, as it lies now bound up in our Bibles" (Locke
302). A century later, there was quite a variety of Bibles especially
adapted for children's use, as well as entertaining fictions that were
supposed to reinforce Christian values when children were reading
primarily for their amusement. What should have been a most desirable trend, from Trimmer's perspective, had had unintended conse-

quences: the best new books struck some people as doing a better job than the Bible in teaching children the things necessary to be known—which did not necessarily include the truths of revealed religion. Trimmer's anxieties have usually been dismissed as anti-Jacobin paranoia by critics who have not established much of a contemporary frame of reference. In his discussion of children's reading, Andrews proved to be more open than Trimmer to the possibility of substituting modern for traditional texts, if the new ones proved to be superior to the old. As we have already seen, Andrews's enthusiasm for little moral histories such as Kilner's *Jemima Placid* stemmed partly from his conviction that children absorbed principles more readily from what they read with pleasure than from material assigned as a task, and he further explored this idea in another essay, "The Bible Should Not Be Used in Teaching to Read." He argued that boys tended to despise the Bible and rarely reread it because it was associated in their minds with having been "teazed, and buffeted, and flogged" during the first stages of formal instruction (Andrews, "Bible" 271). He did not go so far in either essay as to suggest that the new fiction for children ought to be substituted for the Bible as the more effective vehicle for teaching children ethical values or religious tenets. On the other hand, he does not specify the circumstances or age when children ought to be introduced to Scripture, nor does he suggest alternative methods of instruction that would be less likely to make reading from it such a distasteful exercise.[14] Andrews's frankly pragmatic remarks about the Bible and moral histories for children suggest that Trimmer had quite correctly perceived that some of her contemporaries' attitudes toward the Bible were changing in ways that could eventually undermine its importance in religious education.

Andrews' optimistic, liberal view of late Georgian children's books offers us more than an intriguing contrast to Trimmer's more complex and troubling one. His "Books" provides some much needed context for the genre's development, a phenomenon that has yet to be successfully integrated into eighteenth-century English social, cultural, and intellectual history. Indeed, there is enough new material in "Books" to encourage us to reformulate our historical paradigms, which are still informed by F. J. Harvey Darton's oppositions between didacticism and levity, chapbooks and classics, fairy tales and moral tales, now more than eighty years old. Andrews's perceptive analysis suggests that the genre's first critics were far more engaged in the contemporary debate about the impact of a rapidly changing print culture than twentieth-century literary historians have assumed. Andrews grasped that the question of what children read would assume greater significance in discussions about education as the market for children's books continued to expand, because more children would be exposed to a greater variety of hornbooks, catechisms, primers, Bibles, schoolbooks, and chapbooks than ever before. He also tried to evaluate the new genre's place within the contemporary world of letters and realized that the rise of a separate literature for children raised many of the same questions that the proliferation of any new genre had during the century.[15] Surely there are other essays like "Books" waiting to be recovered that would enrich our view of the genre's history and reception, if only we would go looking for them.

Books

> If the rising generation do not greatly excel their parents in the knowledge and practice of morality and humanity, they will loudly contradict every philosopher, every poet, and every divine, who has even glanced at the subject of education.

Forty years ago, an author would have been ridiculed, had he dedicated his talents to the service of a race of infants. The whole juvenile library consisted, then, in a dry, uninviting book, called 'Geography for Children,' and in a set of minute volumes which described Westminster Abbey and the Tower of London, and which, to the best of the Editor's remembrance, intermixed spectre-stories with topical descriptions. Mother Goose, also, added her tales, but from them neither instruction, nor moral, were to be gained.

The ingenious Christopher Smart was the first man of genius that thought the minds and morals of children deserved literary attention. In his Lilliputian Magazine, he inculcated the best of principles, but he thought it necessary, still, to make use of a species of machine, and 'Woglog the Great Giant' was introduced to amuse and to terrify, by turns, the young student.

Encouraged, probably, by the success of Mr. Smart, there now arose a new description of authors, under the patronage of a well-known philanthropic bookseller. These have exerted their utmost abilities to compose histories in common life, which may tempt the little reader to study, and, at the same time, may lead him in the paths of good-nature and virtue. They have succeeded, and

the library for the use of children, now abounds with productions,* which, although minute in size, and gaudy tinsel covers,
are not unworthy the inspection of persons far more advanced
in life and experience, than those for whose use they are des-
tined. Beside inculcating the best principles of religion and duty,
these writers combat every malignant propensity. They set infantine cruelty in the most odious light, and even condescend to
level their batteries against sloth, and dirtiness. Children bred up
in the constant study of such maxims, must, one may hope, retain
some part of them in their minds, and, should they be as negligent of what is right, as many of their fathers were before them,
they will be doubly faulty, as they have opportunities of improving their ideas, which never occurred to their ancestors.

Notes

1. The essay, which Trimmer subsequently revised, appeared in the *Guardian of Education*. Lance Salway reprinted it in *A Peculiar Gift*.

2. For a revisionist view of the Edgeworths as educational theorists, see Mitzi Myers's
"'Anecdotes from the Nursery'" in the *Princeton University Library Chronicle*.

3. I found this essay while reporting eighteenth-century imprints to the Eighteenth
Century Short Title Catalogue when a graduate student at the University of California
at Los Angeles.

4. For a brief biography of Andrews, see the *Dictionary of National Biography*. His contributions to the *Gentleman's Magazine* are listed in Kuist.

5. Andrews's better-known contemporary Edward Gibbon also mentioned fairy tales
as stories he read with fascination as a boy during the 1740s but that no longer delighted
him. If anything, Gibbon seems slightly apologetic for mentioning such things at all.
For two recent discussions of eighteenth-century attitudes toward the genre, see Adams,
"The 'contes de fées' of Madame d'Aulnoy," and Tucker, "Fairy Tales and Their Opponents."

6. Whatever its limitations as a school text, Lenglet du Fresnoy remained in print
at least until the end of the century: it was in its nineteenth edition in the 1780s. See
Sheridan's *Nicolas Lenglet du Fresnoy and the Literary Underworld of the Ancien Regime* for a
bibliography of the *Geography*'s French and English editions.

7. Andrews is the only contemporary to have mentioned Boreman's innovative children's books, to my knowledge. See Muir 60–61 for a discussion of Boreman's "gigantick
histories."

8. See p. 22 of Drotner's *English Children and Their Magazines*.

9. See the entry for the *Lilliputian Magazine* in my forthcoming *John Newbery and His
Successors* for an analysis of its contents and the most popular stories' continued circulation in unauthorized reprints.

10. On whose authority Andrews attributed the *Lilliputian Magazine* to Smart remains a mystery. If it seems peculiar that he neglects to mention Smart's publisher, who

*Among these may be pointed out 'The History of Jemima Placid,' which abounds with
interesting scenes.

was something of a man of letters in addition to being an innovative entrepreneur, we should keep in mind that Andrews may not have been aware that Newbery was involved with the production of the *Lilliputian Magazine*, which first appeared under Thomas Carnan's imprint. If Andrews was relying on his memory rather than working from an actual copy, he simply may not have remembered who published the book.

11. See pp. 52–53 of Myers's " 'Servants as They are now Educated.' "

12. There are a few nursery rhymes that try "to obtain peace by intimidation," as the Opies point out in their *Oxford Dictionary*. One such example is number 16: "Baby, baby, naughty baby, / Hush, you squalling thing, I say. / Peace this moment, peace, or maybe / Bonaparte will pass this way. / Baby, baby, he's a giant, / Tall and black as Rouen steeple, / And he breakfasts, dines, rely on't, / Every day on naughty people. . . ."

13. Mitzi Myers provides an overview of Trimmer's achievements in the introduction to *Revolutionary Reviewing*.

14. Andrews was not the only man to question the Bible's efficacy when used as elementary reading for children. His well-known contemporary Knox, the educator and compiler of the *Elegant Extracts* series of literary anthologies, thought picture Bibles were not especially good introductions to Scripture. See my discussion of Knox in "Some Picture Bibles and Their Illustration."

15. Although not much concerned with children as readers, chapter 4, "Readers and the Reading Public," in John Brewer's *The Pleasures of the Imagination* offers an excellent analysis of the transformation of print culture during the period.

Works Cited

Adams, D. J. "The 'contes de fées' of Madame d'Aulnoy: Reputation and Re-evaluation." *Bulletin* of the John Rylands University Library of Manchester 76, no. 3 (autumn 1994): 5–22.

Andrews, James Pettit. "The Bible Should Not Be Used in Teaching to Read." In *Anecdotes &c., Antient and Modern*. New edition, corrected and much enlarged. London: John Stockdale, 1790.

———. "Books." In the addenda to Andrews's *Anecdotes &c., Antient and Modern*.

Brewer, John. *The Pleasures of the Imagination: English Culture in the Eighteenth Century*. New York: Farrar Straus and Giroux, 1997.

Drotner, Kirsten. *English Children and Their Magazines, 1751–1945*. New Haven and London: Yale University Press, 1988.

Immel, Andrea. "Some Picture Bibles and Their Illustration." *Newsletter* of the Children's Books History Society 59 (November 1997): 20–22.

Johnson, Samuel. *Adventurer* 137. In *The Idler and the Adventurer*. Ed. W. J. Bate, John M. Bullitt, and L. F. Powell. Yale Edition of the Works of Samuel Johnson, vol. 2. New Haven and London: Yale University Press, 1963.

Jones, Stephen. *New Biographical Dictionary*. London: E. Newbery, 1794.

Kilner, Mary Ann. *Jemima Placid; or The Advantages of Good Nature*. London: John Marshall, 1783.

Kuist, James. *The Nichols Files to the Gentleman's Magazine*. Madison: University of Wisconsin Press, 1982.

Locke, John. *Some Thoughts Concerning Education*. In *Educational Writings*. Ed. James L. Axtell. Cambridge: Cambridge University Press, 1968.

Muir, Percy. *English Children's Books 1600–1800*. London: Batsford, 1985.

Myers, Mitzi. " 'Anecdotes from the Nursery' in Maria Edgeworth's *Practical Education* (1798): Learning from Children 'Abroad and at Home'." *Princeton University Library Chronicle* 60, no. 2 (winter 1999): 220–50.

———. *Revolutionary Reviewing: Sarah Trimmer's Guardian of Education: An Index*. Los Angeles: Department of Special Collections, University Research Library, University of California, 1990.

————. " 'Servants as They are now Educated': Women Writers and Georgian Pedagogy." *Essays in Literature* 16, no. 1 (spring 1989): 51–69.

Rizzo, Betty, and Robert Mahoney. *Christopher Smart: An Annotated Bibliography, 1743–1983*. New York and London: Garland, 1984.

Salway, Lance. *A Peculiar Gift: Nineteenth Century Writings on Books for Children*. Harmondsworth: Kestrel, 1976.

Sheridan, Geraldine. *Nicolas Lenglet du Fresnoy and the Literary Underworld of the Ancient Regime*. Oxford: Voltaire Foundation, 1989.

Trimmer, Sarah. "Some Observations on the Changes Which Have Taken Place in Books for Children and Young Persons." *Guardian of Education* 1 (May–June 1802).

Tucker, Nicolas. "Fairy Tales and Their Opponents: In Defense of Mrs. Trimmer." In *Opening the Nursery Door: Reading, Writing and Children 1600–1800*. Ed. Mary Hilton, Morag Styles, and Victor Watson. London and New York: Routledge, 1997.

"Things by Their Right Name": Peace Education in Evenings at Home

Penny Mahon

> *Learning to understand war and peace should be a necessary facet of children's education. . . . They need an education that affirms life and encourages new thinking about conflict, progress, and peacemaking. . . . Peace education has become a legitimate concern.*
>
> —Ruth Meyers

Peace education has a long history; commitment to "an education that affirms life and encourages new thinking about conflict, progress, and peacemaking" can be traced back as far as the end of the eighteenth century. In the Romantic period, peace education was shared by both men and women, although in Victorian and Edwardian society it tended to become gender-specific. The roots of peace education can be found in the collaborative text *Evenings at Home,* the work of two late eighteenth-century dissenters, siblings Anna Barbauld and John Aikin.

A concern for peace is one of several social and moral themes evident in children's literature in the late 1700s and early 1800s. One of the most sensitive was slavery, which Anna Barbauld, Amelia Opie, and the Taylor sisters all treated in their children's poetry.[1] Others, according to Margaret Cutt, included the relation between landlord and tenant, the treatment of animals, and the social divide between rich and poor.[2]

The moral issue of war, however, does not appear to have received modern critical attention. This is a surprising gap in current scholarship. Although recent critical texts have addressed the complex effects of competing ideologies on the literature of the Romantic period, no one has yet explored to any significant extent the way in which the dominant militarist ideology was challenged.[3]

I would argue that if militarism is the "process whereby military values, ideology and patterns of behaviour achieve a dominating influence over the political, social, economic and foreign affairs of the

Children's Literature 28, eds. Elizabeth Lennox Keyser and Julie Pfeiffer (Yale University Press, © 2000 Hollins University).

state,"[4] then it was a subject of recurrent concern for several writers of the Romantic period, and their work was a radical critique of militarist systems in general and of Pitt's Tory government in particular. Alan Richardson and Sonia Hofkosh argue that "writers now neglected were at one time thought close to the 'center,' and that their engagement with questions of empire made no small part of their contemporary claim to cultural centrality" (8). Issues of war and peace were embedded in the rhetoric of several Romantic writers whose work elicited positive critical response in their day. One such work was Anna Barbauld's antimilitarist and remarkably subversive essay *Sins of Government, Sins of the People* (1793). Her later poem "Eighteen Hundred and Eleven" (1812), on the other hand, provoked an abusively critical reaction.[5] The breadth of response from such prestigious journals as the *Analytical,* the *Monthly,* the *Quarterly,* and *Critical Reviews* highlights the extent of her reputation over a period of nearly twenty years and the duration of her engagement with the war-and-peace debate.

The prevalence and vigor of such a debate was hardly surprising. Although the eighteenth century had been by no means pacific, "the wars of the French Revolution and of Napoleon were qualitatively and quantitatively different from their immediate predecessors."[6] The differences involved the unique ideological basis of England's war with France, which continued with brief intervals from 1793 to 1815, the broad geographical scale of the conflict and the aggressive nationalism with which England pursued that conflict, the use of people's armies rather than mercenaries, and the suffering of huge numbers of French civilians. These factors placed enormous strains on Britain's economy, manpower, finances, and government (Emsley 4).

The details of the war-and-peace debate during the years of war with France have been ably documented by J. E. Cookson, who maintains that antiwar activity from 1793 to 1815 was directed almost exclusively by the rational dissenters, specifically the Unitarians. Their rational Christianity involved a firm belief in human perfectibility and their conviction that war was "an eradicable evil" (a belief not shared by the evangelicals).[7] These Friends of Peace, among whom were the Aikin siblings, were not an organization as such but a linked fellowship of people with similarly liberal religious and political views, anxious to extend religious and political freedoms and to protest against what they saw as a war interest within Anglican and Tory ranks.

Public opposition to the war was expressed primarily through the liberal press, in periodicals and pamphlets. Particularly in the early years, the official Fast Days, which were intended by the government to solicit victory from the Almighty, would often be used to preach antiwar sermons. Cookson cites nearly 250 "pamphlets, published sermons and other occasional works" (295), written between 1793 and 1815, by at least sixty different authors critical of England's war with France.

In this period, both literature for adults and the relatively new genre of children's literature disseminated an antiwar ideology. Three stories from the Aikins' *Evenings at Home* explicitly exemplify peace education and serve as vehicles for that theme: "Things by Their Right Name" by Anna Barbauld and "The Cost of a War" and "The Price of a Victory" by John Aikin. A broad and less overt antimilitarist ideology inheres in other stories from *Evenings at Home*, in certain history texts for children by Maria Hack and Thomas Morrell, and in work by Priscilla Wakefield.[8] These writers are unusual in having made children's literature the site of radical political concerns, and the Aikins ultimately provoked an extremely critical review of their work by the educator and children's writer Sarah Trimmer that displays the dramatic contrast between the Aikins' radical antimilitarist ideology and the implicitly militarist framework within which Trimmer and other conservatives were working.

Evenings at Home, a six-volume, 900-page collaborative venture, was begun in 1792 and completed in 1796, that is, during the initial years of England's war with France, when the government became increasingly anxious about subversive antiwar and antiestablishment factions. John Aikin's and Anna Barbauld's published opposition to the war spirit of the time points up their courage in confronting public sentiment with specifically antimilitarist stories in *Evenings at Home*.[9] Barbauld composed "Things by Their Right Name," which takes the form of a conversation between Charles and his father over the nature of meaning. Geoffrey Summerfield characterizes it as "a deft performance, [relating] to another key issue in the book, which rests on the knowledge that naming is crucial not only in matters of moral judgement, but also in the act of knowing anything" (108). In emphasizing the relation between language and meaning, the story echoes a theme already touched on in another story, "Traveller's Wonders." Probably by Aikin, "Traveller's Wonders" encourages greater empathy with foreign nations and customs by objectifying and re-visioning British customs. Aikin's concern is clear: "We daily call a great many things by their names, without ever enquiring into their nature and properties; so that, in reality, it is only the names, and not the things themselves, with which we are acquainted" (1:31). In her subtle exposure of the true meaning of war and battle as crime and murder, Barbauld reiterates Aikin's philosophical argument within a specific antimilitarist context.

"Things by Their Right Name" is a dynamic and readable piece whose three pages concisely and cleverly reveal the reality behind militarist discourse and anticipate George Orwell in his essay "Politics and the English Language."[10] The dialogue is a type of extended riddle: the young protagonist Charles Osborn demands that his father tell him a "pretty" story about "a bloody murder" (150), exhibiting a delight in violence that gives Barbauld's fictitious children a pleasantly convincing quality. The father begins his tale, but Charles constantly interrupts with criticisms: it should be midnight and the "bloody murder" should be committed by "ill-looking fellows." He can't understand why his father refuses to include classic ingredients like these. "Tall, personable men" who make no attempt to conceal themselves (151) commit a murder on a summer morning. Charles is suitably horrified that in the process a village is set on fire, but the fact that twenty thousand people are eventually murdered is too much for his credulity:

Charles: . . . What! They lay still, I suppose, and let these fellows cut their throats!

Father: No, truly—they resisted as long as they could.

Charles: How should these men kill twenty thousand people, pray?

Father: Why not? The murderers were thirty thousand.

Charles: O, now I have found you out! You mean a BATTLE.

Father: Indeed, I do. I do not know of any murders half so bloody. (152)

In this simple attempt to re-vision the act of war, the child reader is forced to concentrate on its victims rather than on its ideological justifications or its attractive heroes. Earlier authors such as Tobias Smollett, Samuel Johnson, and William Cowper had exposed the horrors of war, but never to such a young audience.[11] One of the earliest eighteenth-century texts to criticize war was Jonathan Swift's *Gulliver's Travels* (1726), and the chapbook abridgments quickly reached a child readership. But Barbauld's "Things by Their Right Name" is the first antiwar story written specifically for children, and it became a paradigm for others. Her technique is imitated—and carried to gruesome extremes—in later peace tracts and periodicals for children, although it can be argued that these peace tracts owe more to the tradition of colorfully violent chapbooks and broadsheets than to Barbauld's more restrained rationalist discourse.[12]

Further blurring of semantic boundaries occurs in a subsequent story by Aikin. In "Two Robbers," he compares Alexander the Great with a common Thracian robber. Aikin's purpose clearly is to equate war and murder as Barbauld had done in "Things by Their Right Name." In this instance, Aikin emphasizes the equivalence of the guilt incurred by those who prosecute war and those who commit murder. Alexander proudly asserts his claim to Fame's praise: "Ask Fame and she will tell you. Among the brave, I have been the bravest; among sovereigns, the noblest; among conquerors, the mightiest" (2:150). The robber, for his part, emphasizes their essential parity: "What is a conqueror? Have not you, too, gone about the earth like an evil genius, blasting the fair fruits of peace and industry;—plundering, ravaging, killing, without law, without justice, merely to gratify an insatiable lust for dominion?" (151). The robber in Aikin's story emerges as morally more admirable than the soldier: he regrets his evil actions while Alexander hesitates in acknowledging his:

> Robber: I believe neither you nor I shall ever repay to the world the mischiefs we have done it. . . .
>
> Alexander: . . . Are we then so much alike?—Alexander to a robber?—Let me reflect. (152)

Aikin's most overtly antiwar contributions to *Evenings at Home* are the two stories "The Price of a Victory," in volume 4, and "The Cost of a War," in volume 5. "The Price of a Victory" begins with a young boy named Oswald rejoicing over a recent victory.[13] His father carefully explains that although there is nothing wrong with wishing one's country well, particularly if "its prosperity can be promoted without injuring the rest of mankind" (4:51), a victory will often mask both dubious motive and grievous suffering. He warns his son that war affects not only those killed in battle but also the wounded and the bereaved, so that with ten thousand dead, there are "twenty thousand people made unhappy" while "eight to ten thousand more are lying in agony" (53–54). The father tells the story of Walter the weaver to illustrate his comments. A recruiting sergeant attracts Walter with fine tales about the splendors of military life and traps Walter into joining the army through drink. In his wretched military life, Walter suffers hideous injuries, lies amid the carnage of the battlefield, languishes in a crowded, unsanitary hospital, and journeys home an invalid. The price of the army's victory is Walter's life: he dies the following spring, his sweetheart soon after, and his destitute parents end their lives in the workhouse. Walter's own words express the futility of his life and his death: "I am told that peace has left the affairs of my country just as they were before" (60).

Aikin's second antiwar story, "The Cost of a War," deconstructs traditional concepts of the hero—as general, patriotic leader, and militant king—and replaces them with new pacific models. Aikin states his mission overtly in the opening paragraph: he hopes that the following story "may serve to abate something of the admiration with which historians are too apt to inspire us for great warriors and conquerors" (5:55). Aikin may have been naive in dismissing old favorite heroes, such as Achilles and Alexander the Great, in the face of the manifest taste for bloody exploits among England's buyers of chapbooks. Rationalists of his type did not appreciate what Geoffrey Summerfield calls "the grateful terror" of the old tales (39). But one respects his aspiration and his intent, despite his refusal to face the reception-based fact that fear is often the cause of a book's delight.

Early in "The Cost of a War," Aikin indirectly identifies the origins of the military hero and of militarist history in general in the works of the classical authors (5:62) whose warriors had strongly influenced the public's conception of valor and heroism. Aikin's critique is echoed by later peace writers, who aimed to revise the educational emphasis on classical literature because of its militarist discourse. For instance, the Reverend David Bogue, head of the Gosport Missionary Society, speaks in the *Herald of Peace* of the modern tendency to venerate classical at the expense of Christian virtues, especially in schools: "They teach the child to hate or despise every nation but his own; they represent war as the theatre of glory."[14] An anonymous letter in the same edition of the journal addresses "the prevalence of the War-spirit" in children, due to "the warlike tendencies of their . . . classical pursuits" (105–6). The military hero Aikin selects in "The Cost of a War" is

Louis XIV, responsible for leading the French army against the Palatinate in a devastating campaign. The father in the story gives unsparing details of siege warfare and the inevitable destruction of innocent lives, including a graphic description of "a woman with a new-born infant sunk perishing on the snow, while her husband hung over them in all the horror of despair" (5:59). In reply to his son Oswald's final question—Can war be prevented?—the father is both realistic and reformist: "Alas! I fear mankind have been too long accustomed to it, and it is too agreeable to their bad passions, easily to be laid aside, whatever miseries it may bring upon them. But in the mean time let us correct our own ideas of the matter, and no longer lavish admiration upon such a pest of the human race as a Conqueror, how brilliant soever his qualities may be; nor ever think that a profession which binds a man to be the servile instrument of cruelty and injustice, is an honourable calling" (63).

Antimilitarists have often been labeled idealistic and naive, but Aikin's and Barbauld's efforts are a practical and realistic attempt to shape the child's value system through revised definitions of greatness and heroism. Four more stories in *Evenings at Home* relate to this theme of the traditional military hero: in each case Aikin uses substitution as well as deconstruction as he introduces readers to the new heroes that he wishes them to emulate.

The first story, aptly named "True Heroism," begins by citing three heroes of the traditional military mold: Achilles, Alexander, and Charles of Sweden. Aikin's desire to examine the true meaning of language, to teach broad experience rather than narrowly conceived words, is clearly stated: "The world calls these men heroes; but before we give them that noble appellation, let us consider what were the motives which animated them to act and suffer as they did" (5:85). His conclusion is that their motives were without exception selfish, and "a selfish man can never be a hero" (86). The aim of "True Heroism" is to substitute for these false heroes two contemporary true heroes: the prison reformer Robert Howard and an unknown working-class boy named Tom. Aikin's choice of Howard is not surprising, for the two were friends and Aikin eventually became Howard's first biographer after his untimely death in 1792.[15] In a letter to his sister in 1777, Aikin talked of Howard as "the best man . . . in England," and his daughter, Lucy Aikin, spoke of Howard as a man "whom [her father] loved and honoured during his life, and whose memory he celebrated and protected after his death" (1:42). "True Heroism" is part of this celebration of a man who had traveled Europe investigating and improving prison conditions and who had eventually died of a fever contracted while visiting the sick. In Aikin's eyes, he was "as great a hero in preserving mankind, as some of the false heroes above mentioned were in destroying them" (5:88). Aikin's treatment of Howard is the first of many eulogies for a man who became one of a number of heroes in the new vein.

The second part of "True Heroism" tells the tale of Tom and his drunken bricklayer father. Exemplum rather than history, it too portrays heroism as a moral rather than a military quality, as classless rather than aristocratic, as independent of physical prowess and intellectual achievement, as egalitarian and altruistic, and, above all, as achievable. Christ rather than Caesar embodies heroism for Aikin, though, as a sound rational dissenter, he does not verbalize the religious parallel.

"The Colonists," the last of Aikin's revisionist tales, admits William Penn into this pantheon of philanthropic and antimilitarist heroes. The story opens with a description of a queue of professional men waiting to be assessed for their usefulness in a new colony. The soldier's skills are seen as redundant since "we are peacable [*sic*] people, and I hope shall have no occasion to fight" (5:98). It is at that point that Aikin introduces Penn, his third representative of the new heroism. His chief qualities are his justice and his pacifism. As a result of his fair dealings with the Indians, "when [they] were at war with all the other European settlers, a person in a quaker's habit might pass through all their most ferocious tribes without the least injury" (98–99).

The Aikins' criticism of the militarist system of their day, with its contrast between appearance and reality, was a new element in children's literature. The original and outspoken nature of that criticism is suggested by the modern children's literature critic Gillian Avery, who noted that Barbauld's pacifism was startling (22–23). Sarah Trimmer expressed a rather more negative view. Her *Guardian of Education,* a useful gauge of conservative Anglican evangelical opinion, represented a belief in the unregenerate nature of man, which precluded any sympathy with the perfectibilist convictions of the rational dissenters. In volume 2 (January–August 1803), Trimmer reviewed the Aikins' book in detail. She included a critical commentary on more than thirty of the stories (nearly a third), claiming that each of them was in some way exceptionable.

The stories that excited Trimmer's lengthiest criticism were precisely those that dealt with war. She devoted an entire page to "Things by Their Right Name," the first antiwar story in the collection. Her main criticism centered on Barbauld's parallel between war and murder. Trimmer condemned this unreservedly since such a correlation could lead to civil and, what was worse, spiritual disobedience: for even though God clearly condemned murder, he actively encouraged the Israelites to make war against "idolatrous nations."

Trimmer also revealed a millennialist belief that no peace was possible on earth before "the second advent of the Prince of Peace" (2:309). Her views contrasted starkly with the Aikins' perfectibilist philosophy, which encouraged ameliorative action and saw peace as a tangible hope. This fundamental distinction between qualities of peace—as a spiritual and as a temporal reality—clearly separated the evangelicals from the dissenting radicals and characterized the discourse of each. Trimmer briefly dismissed "The Two Robbers" as containing a bad lesson for children. She clearly believed that many of the Aikins' moral concerns were beyond the comprehension of children and would disturb them with irrelevant questions. Her lengthy comments on "The Price of a Victory" support this view. For her, the issue was simple: war was a reality, it was controlled by Providence, and those who suffered would eventually be rewarded. Characters like Walter should not be regarded as typical because enlistment often saved them from lives of vice, and the price of a victory, or of a defeat, to such persons was "everlasting bliss" (2:346). Her criticism of "The Cost of a War" is a fine example of evangelical jingoism: Why, she asked, was a story about a French king being told to British children? It also reflects evangelical conservatism as it comments that the only appropriate use of a monarch in a children's story would be to encourage "loyalty to their lawful Sovereign," not to offer criticism of his behavior (2:350). In all her reviews Trimmer subordinated the Aikins' rationalist philosophy to her own Bible-based religion. Trimmer's criticism of the Aikins' antiwar stories is a firm reminder that their opinions were radical and unacceptable; for her, and for many of her readers, war was both "lawful and necessary" (2:345).

Despite Trimmer's critical response, the Aikins' work appears to have influenced later peace writing. For instance, the Peace Society's journal, the *Herald of Peace*, established in 1819, contains several acknowledgments of their existence as peace writers: in a letter printed in April 1819, Barbauld's *Evenings at Home* is commended for its ability to modify the current war spirit (1:106), and in November 1820, "The Cost of a War" and "The Price of a Victory" were both quoted in full, with the comment that they are "admirable specimens of the description of writing we so much wish to recommend" (2:334). As late as

1868, the Peace Society republished "The Cost of a War" and "The Price of a Victory" in their *Illustrated Series of Peace Tracts,* though anonymously. Nevertheless, these were infrequent and often obscure references, and in the developing and widespread peace education debate of the last three decades of the century, the Aikins' work was effectively effaced, probably owing more to lack of sympathy with the ponderously didactic style of their writing or ignorance of its very existence than to any disagreement with their argument. The modern reader of *Evenings at Home,* however, cannot escape the conclusion that the child who read the antiwar stories among its many pages had indeed been exposed to the radical beginnings of what was to become a vigorous tradition of peace education.

Notes

1. See Barbauld, "The Negro Woman," in *Prose Hymns* 60; Opie, "The Negro Boy's Tale," in *Poems* 53–69; Taylor and O'Keefe, "The Little Negro," in *Rhymes for the Nursery* 317.

2. See Cutt, chapter 1.

3. See Richardson and Hofkosh, *Romanticism, Race, and Imperial Culture* on issues relating to imperialism, slavery, and gender in Romantic literature.

4. Ernest Regehr, *Militarism and the World Military Order,* quoted in Harris, *Peace Education* 9.

5. For reviews of the sermon, see the *Critical Review,* which comments on "the intrinsic merit of the composition" (207); the *Monthly Review,* which claims that if such a sermon cannot penetrate the national conscience, then "its keeper . . . has either guarded it with impenetrable locks and bars, or has 'seared it with a hot iron' " (240); and the *Analytical Review,* which classes it "in the first order of merit" (186). For an account of the reviews of "Eighteen Hundred and Eleven," see McCarthy and Kraft, *The Poems of Anna Letitia Barbauld* 310. The contrast between the two sets of reviews is a reminder of the conservative backlash that was a feature of British society after the mid-1790s.

6. Emsley, *British Society and the French Wars 1793–1815,* 2.

7. Cookson, *The Friends of Peace* 6.

8. See Wakefield's *Leisure Hours, Mental Improvement,* and *A Brief Memoir of the Life of William Penn,* Hack's *English Stories,* and Morrell's *Studies in History.*

9. Anna Barbauld's political rhetoric was outspokenly antiwar in the 1790s: see, e.g., her sermons "Sins of Government, Sins of the Nation" and "Reasons for National Penitence." John Aikin also held strong antiwar opinions, well illustrated in his correspondence with William Roscoe. See Lucy Aikin's *Memoir of Dr. John Aikin* for examples.

10. See *The Collected Essays, Journalism, and Letters of George Orwell* iv, 127–40.

11. Smollett, *Roderick Random* (1748), Johnson, "Thoughts on the Late Transactions Respecting Falkland's Islands" (1770), and Cowper, *The Task* (1785). See David McNeil, *The Grotesque Depiction of War and the Military in Eighteenth-Century Fiction.*

12. There are many examples of this type of writing in the *Olive Leaf,* a peace periodical produced for children between 1844 and 1857: for instance, "The Little Bulgarians" spares no detail in its account of the murders of Bulgarian peasant parents and the wounding of their two children in an attempt to make its young readers "hate war more than ever" (300).

13. It is interesting to speculate on Aikin's reasons for choosing this name. Butler reminds us that Oswald was the name of the subversive leading character in Wordsworth's

The Borderers (1796) and was chosen because it was "the name of a real man, an English Jacobin in Paris while Wordsworth was there in 1792" (Butler 64). Was Aikin being deliberately contentious in his choice of the name?

14. This journal was the official organ of the Peace Society and was published from 1819 to 1937.

15. The background to the biography is discussed by Lucy Aikin in her *Memoir,* i, 137–39. The biography was titled *A View of the Character and Public Service of the Late Robert Howard Esq. LLD. FRS.*

Works Cited

Aikin, John, and Anna Barbauld. *Evenings at Home.* 6 vols. London: Johnson, 1792–96.
Aikin, Lucy. *Memoir of Dr. John Aikin.* 2 vols. London: Baldwin, Cradock and Joy, 1823.
Avery, Gillian. *Nineteenth-Century Children.* London: Hodder and Stoughton, 1965.
Barbauld, Anna. *Prose Hymns.* 7th ed. London, 1798.
———. "Reasons for National Penitence." London: Robinson, 1794.
———. "Sins of Government, Sins of the Nation." London: Johnson, 1793.
Bogue, David. "Discourses on the Millennium." *Herald of Peace* 1 (1819): 107–11.
Butler, Marilyn. *Romantics, Rebels and Reactionaries.* Oxford: Oxford University Press, 1981.
Cookson, J. E. *The Friends of Peace: Anti-War Liberalism in England, 1793–1815.* Cambridge: Cambridge University Press, 1982.
Cutt, Margaret. *Ministering Angels: A Study of Nineteenth-Century Evangelical Writing for Children.* Wormley, Herts.: Five Owls Press, 1979.
Emsley, Clive. *British Society and the French Wars 1793–1815.* London and Basingstoke: Macmillan, 1979.
Hack, Maria. *English Stories.* London: Harvey and Darton, 1820.
Harris, Ian M. *Peace Education.* Jefferson, N.C., and London: McFarland, 1988.
McCarthy, William, and Elizabeth Kraft, eds. *The Poems of Anna Letitia Barbauld.* Athens: University of Georgia Press, 1994.
McNeil, David. *The Grotesque Depiction of War and the Military in Eighteenth-Century Fiction.* Newark: University of Delaware Press; London: Associated University Presses, 1990.
Meyers, Ruth. "Peace Education: Problems and Promises." *Women's Studies Quarterly* 12, no. 2 (1984): 21–23.
Morrell, Thomas. *Studies in History.* London: Holdsworth, 1827.
Opie, Amelia. *Poems.* 6th ed. London, 1811.
Orwell, George. *The Collected Essays, Journalism, and Letters of George Orwell.* London: Seeker and Warburg, 1968.
Richardson, Alan, and Sonia Hofkosh. *Romanticism, Race, and Imperial Culture.* Bloomington and Indiana: Indiana University Press, 1996.
Summerfield, Geoffrey. *Fantasy and Reason: Children's Literature in the Eighteenth Century.* London: Methuen, 1984.
Taylor, Jane, and Anne Taylor. *Rhymes for the Nursery.* Centenary ed. London: Wells, Gardner, Darton and Co., 1903.
Trimmer, Sarah. "Examination of Book for Children." *Guardian of Education* 2 (1803): 304–11, 343–53.
Wakefield, Priscilla. *Leisure Hours.* London: Harvey and Darton, 1821.
———. *Mental Improvement.* Dublin, 1799.
———. *A Brief Memoir of the Life of William Penn.* New York: Mahlon Day, 1821.

The Lion and the Lamb: Imagining and Creating Peace Through the Arts

Phyllis Bixler

It's unfortunate that Francelia Butler and Elizabeth Hostetler never met. Libby would have applauded Francelia's "peace games," and Francelia would have appreciated the fact that Libby's Lion and Lamb Peace Arts Center began as a children's literature collection. Further conversation would have revealed them to be kindred spirits—both being energetic visionaries able to enlist others in projects that initially might seem eccentric or too ambitious, both being able to release leadership of established projects to others as they themselves moved on to new pioneering adventures.

I learned about the Lion and Lamb Peace Arts Center because it resides on the campus of my Ohio alma mater, Bluffton College, an affiliate of the Mennonite church, which has historically held pacifism as one of its defining commitments; spending part of my 1998–99 sabbatical as a visiting scholar at Bluffton College, I heard the story of how the Peace Arts Center began and observed it in action.

In 1985 at Bluffton, where she was professor of education, Libby heard Dartmouth professor and peace activist Elise Boulding declare that "we cannot be peace makers unless we have a vision of peace." In response, Libby tried to clarify her own vision of peace and thought about what had shaped it. Then, she began to wonder how current and future generations of children will find their visions of peace and be motivated to become peacemakers. To answer that question, she began collecting children's literature and other relevant printed material; soon, she added musical and visual art.

Not limiting herself to that which could be called "antiwar," Libby sought anything that encourages the more difficult but also more rewarding task of imagining and creating peace—art that elicits an appreciation for human diversity and for the environment, for example, as well as that which suggests nonviolent ways for dealing with conflict. Not surprisingly, the collection soon moved beyond personal preoccupation to become something that obviously needed to be shared. And

Children's Literature 28, eds. Elizabeth Lennox Keyser and Julie Pfeiffer (Yale University Press, © 2000 Hollins University).

Libby wanted it to be the impetus for multifaceted peace-making; she wanted not just a museum and lending library but also a launching pad.

In the early, shaping stage of her vision, Libby had the help of two quite different but longtime friends. The first was Herman Parent, a Bluffton graduate from Lima, Ohio. Once a foster child, Herman was now a successful businessman devoted to helping other children have better lives by finding jobs for their homeless parents, funding their camp experience, and building an ark-shaped activity center for them to use after school. In memory of his wife, Herman provided a generous start-up fund and title for Libby's vision. He chose "The Lion and the Lamb" because it combines strength with gentleness and recalls the vision of the peaceable kingdom found in Isaiah 11:6–9.

Libby's other friend and early supporter was the children's biographer and autobiographer Jean Fritz. Libby had met Jean at a conference about ten years earlier, just after returning from two years of teaching in Taiwan; having spent most of her childhood in China, Jean was an eager audience for "homesick" Libby's stories about Taiwan. Their friendship had deepened as Libby wrote a critical biography of Jean for her 1981 Ph.D. dissertation while Jean was working on her childhood memoir *Homesick: My Own Story* (1982). Now, in the fall of 1986, Jean made a list of children's authors and illustrators Libby might ask to serve as children's literature associates on her board of directors.

The first to be asked was Katherine Paterson, who later recalled meeting this "soft-spoken, but obviously passionate young woman with a dream—a dream of a center where through the arts and literature a vision of peace could be shared with children. I remember trying hard to listen politely, while at the back of my head the ever present skeptic was busily chalking up all the reasons why such a dream had little hope of realization. But what harm if she tried? Surely a little room where some resources could be collected would be nice. Besides, she was a Mennonite and the Mennonites were in for the long haul. They'd been working for peace longer than anybody and they didn't discourage easily."

Katherine did accept, of course, for reasons she explained in a speech given during the 1992 celebration of the Peace Arts Center's first five years: "I've been writing for children for about twenty-eight years now. I got involved in working for peace because it seemed to me that if I cared about children, then I must try to make sure that they had a world to grow up in—a world worth growing up in."

These sentiments were apparently shared by other children's writers and illustrators, for acceptances soon came also from Eleanor Coerr, Leonard Everett Fisher, Jean Fritz, Milton Meltzer, Eve Merriam, Barbara Smucker, and Yoko Kawashima Watkins; these charter members were later joined by Stephen Kellogg, Jean Little, and Stephanie Tolan. The Lion and the Lamb Peace Arts Center received monetary as well as moral support from some of these and other children's authors and illustrators who donated their work for Dutton's *Big Book for Peace* (1991) and designated their share of the royalties to The Lion and the Lamb and four other peace-related organizations.

Being self-supporting except for housing, which is provided by Bluffton College, The Lion and the Lamb has sought financial assistance from industry and arts councils as well. A three-year grant from Honda Corporation funded expansion of the art collection and creation of an outdoor sculpture gallery. Grants from the Ohio Arts and Humanities Councils supported more outdoor sculpture and allowed the Peace Center to commission and produce a musical play based on the life of a former Bluffton College professor, artist, and peace activist who had emigrated from Russia in 1922.

As suggested by this brief history, The Lion and the Lamb Peace Arts Center has become the hub for a variety of activities. Available for lending are more than four thousand books for children and another one thousand reference books for adults, as well as seventy-five videos. Local teachers use the collection to augment what's available in their school libraries; teachers farther away send in topics and grade levels and receive by mail boxes of materials specially selected for them. Persons coming to the center may check out most of the more than 130 pieces of art, which include a significant number of original prints or drawings made for children's illustrated books.

The center also receives many visitors. Children come individually, with their families, and in other groups for a variety of formal and informal activities. Especially popular is the Peace Wall and Moon Gate, which frames one side of the sculpture gallery (figure 1). Here, Ohio artist Jon Barlow Hudson has replicated the Berlin Wall and connected it to prison, stockade, and memorial walls inscribed with the names of people who have devoted their lives and sometimes died in the cause of justice and peace.

Children make rubbings of names and hear the stories of their chosen peacemakers. They are invited to pass through the circular moon gate to express their refusal to allow walls to separate them from others. The entrance of the moon gate has shelves for visitors

Figure 1. Having passed through the Moon Gate to express their refusal to allow walls to separate them from others, Libby Hostetler and Jason Burt examine the tiles designed by Lima, Ohio, high school students for part of the Peace Wall at the Lion and the Lamb Peace Arts Center.

to leave objects symbolic of what they want to leave behind as they pass through. Groups of children are invited to the center for a variety of other peace-related activities as well, such as making art, singing, storytelling, and learning about different nations and cultures (figure 2).

The Peace Arts Center itself travels in the person of its director and, sometimes, one of her student assistants or interns—typically a Bluffton College graduate or a visitor from another country. Ideas and materials related to peace-making are presented at workshops for teachers; conflict-resolution skills are demonstrated in schoolrooms. In addition, Libby is often asked to speak in other countries about her work with children.

Promoting a global perspective has always been central to Libby's vision of peace. Since teaching in Taiwan after college, she has taken every opportunity to visit other countries, typically bringing back items and ideas for the Peace Arts Center. Sometimes she has answered invitations to speak and lead workshops, for example, in Serbia, China, and South Africa. In addition, visitors from all over the

Figure 2. Libby tells stories to children in front of Oscar Velazquez's mural "A World of Youth, Hope, and Peace," commissioned by the Lion and the Lamb Peace Arts Center.

world have come to observe the Peace Arts Center's collections and activities, a recent example being four representatives from the World Friendship Center of Hiroshima and Nagasaki Foundation for Peace.

The Lion and the Lamb has received several honors, including the American Library Association Social Responsibilities Roundtable Peace Award. Libby Hostetler welcomes such recognition because she hopes that the center will inspire others to give body to their own visions of peace. She herself has recently moved on to new ways of serving children and making way for peace. In March 1999, she became principal of Edison Elementary School in Lima, Ohio, her application having been solicited by teachers who considered her uniquely qualified to help them face the educational and social challenges of their school.

The Lion and the Lamb Peace Arts Center continues under new leadership and welcomes inquiries, contributions, and suggestions. The Lion and the Lamb Peace Arts Center, Bluffton College, 280 West College Avenue, Bluffton, Ohio 45817. Phone 419 358-3207. Fax 419 358-3232. E-mail *lionlamb@bluffton.edu.*

In Memoriam

In Memoriam: Francelia Butler, 1913–1998

R. H. W. Dillard

Francelia McWilliams Butler, founding editor of this journal and my friend of forty years, died on September 17, 1998. I was not only deeply saddened by the news but also deeply shocked, because Francelia was a battler and a survivor of such energy and courage that it seemed as though she could never lose a fight, not even one with death itself. I knew that Francelia was eighty-five years old and had been at war with cancer with every weapon at her disposal (including her great determination) for years, but I was surprised anyway. Some people seem to be born, to use Hemingway's phrase, to live life all the way up, and Francelia was certainly one of them. And what an interesting life it was.

Francelia McWilliams was born in Cleveland on April 25, 1913, but grew up in Elyria, Ohio. She was graduated from Oberlin College in 1934 and carried the liberal attitudes and beliefs she had gained there with her to Washington, D.C. There she lost one job writing a pamphlet titled "The Brotherhood of Man" for an education association because she dared to criticize Hitler, and she lost another at one of the best Washington hotels because she arranged an Oberlin banquet meeting that black alumni attended. She soon went off to Paris, where she married foreign correspondent Jerome Butler on July 4, 1939. She worked for her husband's paper, the *International Herald Tribune,* occupying several positions including that of drama critic. She met the literary lights of the day (among them, I recall, the novelist and professional Parisian Elliot Paul, with whom she was not at all impressed) as well as the members of the journalistic community. She actually was offered a job by CBS News as an on-air reporter to work with Edward R. Murrow, but, at the urging of her husband, she turned down the job,

Children's Literature 28, eds. Elizabeth Lennox Keyser and Julie Pfeiffer (Yale University Press, © 2000 Hollins University).

which Eric Sevareid took instead. One of my favorite photographs of Francelia shows her holding Walter Cronkite's attention at the *International Herald Tribune* Centennial Banquet at the Palais de Chaillot in Paris in 1987. The Butlers were among the last Americans to leave Paris before it fell to the Germans in 1940.

Francelia did not lose all her connections to the literary world after leaving Paris. For example, she took dictation and typed the manuscript for Stuart Gilbert's translation of Albert Camus's *L'Etranger;* she remembered that he was under a tight deadline and translated at top speed, pacing nervously back and forth across the room, seldom even pausing for a moment's reflection. That translation, published by Knopf in 1946, remained, of course, the standard English version of the novel for half a century. The birth of her daughter Annie, along with the terminal illness of her husband, soon turned her attention completely to home and family, however.

Jerome Butler died of cancer in 1949, and Francelia, while raising her daughter as a single mother, began her career in earnest as a scholar, writer, and crusader—and, of course, continued her life as an irrepressible character. As a memorial to her husband, she wrote and published a history of cancer and cancer treatment, *Cancer Through the Ages: The Evolution of Hope* (1955); it was during research for the book that she startled (and enraged) the curator of the medical museum of the New York Academy of Medicine by being unable to resist the urge to bounce the rubber dental prosthesis used by Grover Cleveland after his secret cancer surgery in 1893 on the museum floor. At this time, she also wrote the first draft of a novel based on her own abusive childhood, *The Lucky Piece,* which was not to be published until 1984 (but then with considerable success, going quickly into a mass-market paperback edition).

Once Annie was old enough, Francelia began her formal graduate study of English literature. She took her master's degree at Georgetown University in 1959 and continued her studies at the University of Virginia, where I, also a graduate student, first met her in the fall of 1959. Francelia did not allow her medical research to go to waste at Virginia. I remember that one paper she wrote, asserting that American Transcendentalism was the direct result of the New England diet of codfish and beans, was rejected by an unimpressed professor. But I also remember that another paper, which amused her condescending fellow graduate students mightily, on smells in Milton, was eventually published in *PMLA*. She received her Ph.D. in Renaissance literature from the university in 1963, and the Iowa State University Press published her dissertation, *The Strange Critical Fortunes of Shakespeare's Timon of Athens,* which was directed by Fredson Bowers, in 1966.

The rest of her story is probably more familiar to readers of this journal. After teaching two years at the University of Tennessee at Knoxville, she took a position in 1966 at the University of Connecticut that she held until her retirement in 1992. There she taught her famously popular children's literature course and, in 1972, paying the editorial costs out of her own pocket, founded this journal, *Children's Literature.* Francelia also helped to create the children's literature division of the Modern Language Association and was a founding director of the Children's Literature Association. She had earlier published a small collection of skip rope rhymes illustrated by her neighbor in Charlottesville, Gail E. Haley. *The Skip Rope Book* (1963) was, of course, followed twenty-six years later by her important study *Skipping Around the World: The Ritual Nature of Skip Rope Rhymes.* It was during the research for *Skipping Around the World* that a *New York Times* reporter found her walking down the middle of a street in war-torn Belfast at the height of the Troubles; skip ropes dangling over her arm, she was chanting "Acka-bacca-soda-cracker," hoping to lure Irish children out of their homes to repeat their rhymes for her. That book is but one of her many articles and books asserting the importance of the serious study of children's literature (and, for that matter, of children themselves). Her anthology *Sharing Literature with Children* (1977), a Book-of-the-Month selection, carried the message far beyond the groves of academe. As college courses in children's literature proliferate, the results of her efforts become clearer every day.

This brief sketch of Francelia's life is woefully inadequate, and I hope that some day someone will write the full biography that she deserves. It would be the story of a woman of intelligence and great energy who devoted her life despite great resistance to causes that she truly believed to be just. She was always embattled, it seems, one way or the other, but she never gave up and almost always prevailed. Her commitment to improving the lives of children as well as the understanding of their lives led her to fight not only for the serious study of children's literature: she also established the annual International Peace Games Festival in 1990 to encourage the creation of games for children based on the model of conflict resolution rather than war, and in 1993, she found permanent homes for the festival at Harvard and Yale universities, and in 1994, at Columbia. During her last battle with cancer, she was working to establish a program called Pigeons for Peace to allow children at different schools to send messages of peace to one another by carrier pigeon. All of her major ideas were idealistic, all were concerned with bettering the lives of children, all of them seemed flaky to her colleagues at first, and all of them worked.

Francelia tended when describing her antagonists to lump them together under a single category: The Men. "The Men," she would say scornfully, "scoffed at my course in children's literature and said that it covered material that should have been learned at the students' mothers' knees." Or, "The Men think that peace games have no place in an academic environment." She was no sexist nor an ideological feminist, but she was clear-eyed enough to notice that, although not exclusively the case, her major opposition came from a mostly male and mostly conservative academic establishment. Certainly at the University of Virginia in the early sixties, women graduate students and especially older women graduate students were in a very small minority and had to deal with an unspoken and usually unrecognized bias against them that pervaded academia at the time. I remember the very well-meant warnings I received from some of my fellow graduate students (and not all of them male either) that I should not write a dissertation on Ellen Glasgow for no other reason than "she's a woman." Francelia faced that bias all her life, from childhood throughout her career as a journalist and her academic career, and she never backed down once. She held her ground, fought the good fight, and changed the institutions that opposed her. It should have come as no surprise to anyone who knew her that, when she was pressured by the University of Connecticut to retire in 1983, she founded the Connecticut League Against Age Discrimination and won her own case as well as that of other elderly workers in the state. "I have met the enemy," she could honestly say, "and won them over."

I don't want to leave the impression, however, that Francelia was one of those embittered and unpleasant battlers for large causes whom we all admire so much but would rather not see very often. On the contrary. Francelia lived the ideals she taught. Her warmth, her charm, her exuberance, her willingness to laugh at herself and with those around her, and her boundless generosity are all legendary (and legend grounded in fact). She loved nothing better than to feed her guests extravagantly, either in her own home (most famously in the overwhelmingly elaborate eighteenth-century dinners she gave at both Virginia and Tennessee) or at the best restaurants in the area. When she was a visiting scholar at the University of Kraków, she invited

Karol Cardinal Wojtyla to dinner. He graciously accepted and showed up in his cardinal's robes. Francelia presented him with a Virginia fairy stone cross, which, I'm willing to bet, he still has. In my acquaintance, only Francelia would have both the nerve and the foresight to manage to have the future pope to dinner.

At Virginia, impoverished graduate students always knew that Francelia would give them a meal day or night—and a very good meal, for she had studied cooking at the Cordon Bleu when she was in Paris and was a very good student there, too. What we did not know was that she was often as impoverished as we were and scrimped on her own needs in order to take care of those around her. Every one of her friends and acquaintances has at least one Francelia story, usually a funny one, always one told with great affection. Here's one of mine: I remember how on my birthday in 1962 she "gave" me what turned out to be a lifelong friendship with a very attractive young philosophy graduate student named Kelly Cherry (whom Francelia had never met) by inviting us both to lunch in order to introduce us. I also recall that she had prepared a very tasty tuna casserole for the event. I offer this story as evidence not only of Francelia's generosity but also of her skill as a cook and, more important, of her need to be absolutely honest about everything sooner or later. When she came to Hollins to receive an honorary doctorate in 1992, she pulled me aside and told me that she simply had to confess that when she gave us that luncheon thirty years earlier, she had been very strapped for cash and that, in her desperation, she had used cat food for the casserole! I told her that, cat food or not, it was delicious and apparently did us no harm, since both Kelly and I were alive and well. We both had a good laugh, as we always did, but she still looked a little guilty over the "crime" that was still on her conscience after three decades.

I shall miss Francelia very much, the pleasure of hearing her distinctively warm voice with its unchanged Ohio accent on the phone (usually while I was still blinking the sleep from my eyes at dawn), the pleasure of seeing her face light up when she saw an old friend or spoke of one, her generosity, her unwavering loyalty (Francelia, like the elephant, never forgot), her absolute integrity, her commitment to doing the good and to never stop doing the good, her courage, her tenacity, her very real capacity for living life all the way up. I shall miss her very much, as will all of her friends, and all of us as well who are committed to the continuing serious study of children's literature, for truly she was the mother of us all at whose knee we learned to see and say.

In Mansfield Hollow

For Francelia
John Cech

It is six in the morning and the phone is
shaking our house awake with urgency.
It always used to be you calling, Francelia,
your voice as flat and true as a row of Ohio corn
with some ruminative Yankee drawl
and a wisp of Virginia—the Balls, no doubt,
Washington's mother's people,
from whom you thought you had descended.
For almost a decade, the calls were brimming
with the Peace Games, and then only last year
your dawn began with pigeons, carrier pigeons
(you knew the man who trained the birds
that flew through the fiery smoke of D-Day)
and how the children of Connecticut, and
soon the world, would be linked by flocks of birds
flashing across our skies,
carrying words from other souls, far away,
from other hearts who beat like yours against
loneliness and indifference and silence.
I am groggy, half in an old dream, half in a new one,
swept into your visionary calculus,
and I know you are sitting high up on your bunk
in the tiny ship's cabin where you sleep off the living room,
your address books spread like tarot across the quilt,
sending messages into the morning: exhortations,
pleas, gossip, lamentations, crises, triumphs, plans,
and somewhere around the corner of things,
there is the aching heart, from an unloving mother
and a broken father, of racism and fascism in Washington
which you had opposed and lost and left

Children's Literature 28, eds. Elizabeth Lennox Keyser and Julie Pfeiffer (Yale University Press, © 2000 Hollins University).

to find hatred in Germany, penury in Paris
and, finally, those few years of bliss with Jerry,
a *danse jolie* before the dust from Hitler's armies
rose in a cloud east of the city to choke that fragile happiness,
and still you found a story to rescue from that heart-stopping chaos,
wrapped in a rug with a crate of the Windsors' breakfast china,
presented to you by a merchant on the Champs-Elysées,
and the painting the gallery owner had let you choose
so the Nazis wouldn't get it—you had wanted the small Matisse,
Jerry insisted on the Nobody—a fortune slipped through
your fingers (one of many), and you dragged it all
to the train, onto the boat, and back to the States,
your ship's picture on the front page of every paper
here because the Germans had nearly sunk it.
The Duke and Dutchess's cups and saucers sat in your cellar
in Mansfield Hollow, where they aged like wine,
like myth, our deepest rememberings,
that are never depleted unless we
forget to tell our sufferings and our joys,
to tell how we got through.

The tears were not over when the ship docked for you.
Soon the cancer caught up to Jerry,
long years after he was gassed at Ypres,
and the struggles after that to raise your daughter, Annie,
to find some other way, a widow's way,
in a world of guarded powers and clubby privilege.
A new Ph.D., late in your forties,
they gave you "kiddie lit" instead of Shakespeare,
gave you the short end of the stick,
which you took as a scepter and with it
made lemonade—delicious, satisfying, from scratch.
What else was there to do but show them how it's done?
You knew the recipes of delight and determination by heart.
And soon there were accolades everywhere;
adoring students, admiring apprentices sought you out.
Falcons flew in your classroom;
there was laughter, song, ropes spun,
a Wampanoag princess chanted mysteries,
the maker of Wild Things blessed your rumpus,

the master of Chelm offered wry wisdom.
You talked, soul to soul, with the soul of George and Martha.
Even the Wicked Witch of the West
fell under your spell, utterly,
while some colleagues upstairs
grumbled about your popularity,
cut at you, set more hurdles higher,
farther than any of them could reach,
and still you persisted, spinning straw to gold,
sleeplessly, selflessly creating—
a field of amazements and possibilities.

Tomorrow it will be the gardener calling at seven
about the shrubs that need spraying.
Not you, Francelia, to tell me about
the wonders that ask to be brought
by each of us into this world.
"It's not that hard," you told me:
commend your soul to Heaven every morning,
then call the pope, the president,
the prime minister—whoever can help.
"Remind them," you said, "that they used to be children."
Your house in the Hollow was haunted,
and you delighted in telling the story
of how it had been exorcised before you bought it
of the murderous spirit that had committed
an atrocity more than a century ago
in the cellar where the china now stood.
A blue light hung over the house,
neighbors said, on certain nights.
You had never seen the creature,
and believed it gone from the place.
But others had, in the new wing you had added,
for visitors, that had not been purged of the ghost.
It tore at the joists and window frames,
rotted the sills, disturbed the sleep of your guests
and even attacked them.
No one told you this, for fear it would have upset you,
especially in those last months when
you drifted, made the same call twice,

forgot names and dates, which you never had before,
and in the end could not call at all.

But your guests would have added
that angels, too, were seen in the house,
guarding you and them, then and always,
from uneasy sleep: in that hollow, near the crossroads
where blankets are made of strong, feathered wings
and there is peace at last, dear friend,
peace at last.

Francelia's Dream

Eric Dawson

Pablo Casals once performed an oratorio on peace in Southern France, where two thousand years earlier, world leaders met to declare a permanent end to war. But wars are still going on. We all know they should stop. . . . Now, when children see conflicts on TV, they will think, "How can these conflicts be made into games?" They will become participants in the process of conflict resolution instead of passive observers of destruction. Perhaps, by the beginning of the twenty-first century, we will see the beginning of the ending of conflict for all time.

—Francelia Butler

Francelia Butler was a dreamer. She dreamed of a world where children would not be passive recipients of peace education but powerful agents of change. She dreamed of a time when children could apply lessons of peace and cooperation, learned through game-playing, to solve real-world problems. Francelia was also a doer. Not only was she a pioneer in the field of children's literature, she worked tirelessly toward the day when peace education would hold a prominent place in every school's curriculum. She realized that peace is not calm and quiet; instead it is laughter, shouting, righteous anger, and action.

In the late 1980s Francelia brought together two powerful convictions. First, she believed that adults had had their turn to make the world a more peaceful place, and they had failed. She believed that children deserved the opportunity and had the power to be catalysts for peace. Second, she realized that game-playing was a natural way for children to learn the skills of peace-making. It is through games that we first understand concepts of justice, fairness, and cooperation. In order to realize her vision, Francelia organized three annual festivals that brought together thousands of children from Connecticut to share their visions and plans for creating a peaceful world. Peace Games was born.

I first met Francelia in the fall of 1992. I was a freshman at Harvard College and Francelia had just asked the Phillips Brooks House As-

Children's Literature 28, eds. Elizabeth Lennox Keyser and Julie Pfeiffer (Yale University Press, © 2000 Hollins University).

sociation, Harvard's community service center, to carry on the Peace Games Festival. Here was an eighty-year-old woman in black leather pants, with a passion for Big Bird, Maurice Sendak, and Elvis Presley. That meeting began six years of 7:00 A.M. phone calls, letter writing, and sharing. Having planned to volunteer for Peace Games for just one semester, here I am, almost seven years later, still following Francelia's vision. Her dream is contagious.

Francelia's dream is one of hope, but she also acknowledged the weight of violence that children face today. According to a 1995 report by the Centers for Disease Control, 15 children are shot and killed every day with a handgun, 312 children are arrested for committing violent crimes, and 270,000 guns go into our public schools. Before finishing elementary school, a child will view approximately 8,000 murders and another 100,000 violent acts on television. Children remember the violence they see and experience.

Violence silences and inhibits physical, intellectual, and spiritual development. Children cannot learn in schools where they do not feel safe. According to *The Metropolitan Life Survey of the American Teacher, 1994,* one-quarter of elementary students say that they are very worried about their safety when going to and from school, 44 percent of public school students have had personal experiences with angry scenes or confrontations, and 48 percent of students say that their schools do not have any sort of violence prevention program. In Boston, 49 percent of students participating in Peace Games reported seeing or knowing someone who had been shot, killed, or stabbed, and 32 percent knew someone who had brought a gun or knife into their school.

As a result of the violence they witness, children learn to hate, fight, and kill. Francelia believed that just as violent behavior can be learned, so can the skills of peace-making. As a society we model violence through the media, our institutions, and our everyday actions. Through the development of skills, relationships, and knowledge we can, and must, model a new ethos of peace-making. This is Francelia's dream. This is the mission of Peace Games.

Peace Games is a catalyst for peaceful and just school communities. Just as classroom teachers instruct in reading, social studies, and science, Peace Games trains hundreds of college volunteers to teach a multiyear curriculum through which students learn how to be peacemakers. Students receive Peace Games lessons every week, every year from the beginning of kindergarten until graduation from fifth or eighth grade. Although the Peace Games curriculum is connected to other disciplines, it is taught through games, role-playing, small-group discussions, and storytelling. Families are supported in integrating the lessons into the entire life of a child through weekly activities, workshops, and parent events.

Peace Games is preparing a new generation of educators and activists. Francelia believed that young people could change the world. Peace Games is equipping them with the tools to do it. Through Peace Games, all students in a school design service projects that involve teaching others what they have learned. More than a thousand college students have volunteered to teach Peace Games. When young people are engaged in service activities they—along with the broader community—see and utilize their power as peacemakers. By training and supporting both college and elementary school students, we are developing two new generations of teachers, activists, and community leaders.

Finally, Peace Games is changing the way this country thinks about young people and violence. Children are often disciplined, medicated, and evaluated but rarely given roles of authentic leadership. Francelia believed that young people are problem-solvers, not problems. She believed that young people like myself could change the world.

In dealing with the more visible problems of physical and emotional violence, Peace Games also acknowledges and challenges institutional violence, such as economic exploitation, classism, racism, sexism, and homophobia. Our approach moves beyond violence prevention to promote peace and justice. Violence is more than what we can see and touch. When we talk about gang violence as a problem, we also need to talk about economic justice and racism. When we worry about teenage girls having children, we also need to worry about sexism and misogyny and ask why many women are still making seventy-five cents for every dollar a man makes. When we hear about teenage suicide we need to think about homophobia and ask why such a high percentage of gay, lesbian, bisexual, and transgendered youth kill themselves. We need to see the connections between how we vote, spend our money, and chose to live and the very real violence that many people face every day. Francelia believed, as Gandhi did, that we must be the change we seek in the world.

Francelia's vision continues to grow. Her dream has inspired programs not only in Massachusetts and Connecticut but in New York,

Canada, Russia, India, South Africa, and Thailand (just to name a few). Locally, Peace Games continues to grow too—deepening our commitment to elementary schools, reaching out to more communities. The problem of violence in the world is tremendous. And so is the power of Francelia's dream.

Francelia Butler was a peacemaker. She was brave enough to challenge U.S. supporters of Hitler, the old boys' network of the University of Connecticut, mandatory retirement age, and people's cynicism about peace. She believed that young people had the power to create a better, more peaceful world, and she became a strong ally of youth through her creation of Peace Games. She was crazy and loving and stubborn and creative. Above all she had hope and faith in the fundamental goodness of people.

I will miss her weekly phone calls with a new idea for Peace Games (she wanted to open the annual Peace Games Festival with thousands of doves flying through the auditorium). I will miss her warm hospitality. I will miss her tireless energy and passion for justice. I will miss her sense of humor. And I will miss her stories of the famous people she had met. (How many people are friends with both the Pope and Margaret Hamilton, who played the Wicked Witch of the West?) The world is a brighter and warmer place because of her efforts and passion. She was one of my greatest mentors and I will miss her.

Reviews

"Still so much work to be done": Taking up the Challenge of Children's Poetry

Anita Tarr

From the Garden to the Street: An Introduction to 300 Years of Poetry for Children, by Morag Styles. London: Cassell, 1998.

Children's poetry, it seems, is finally being acknowledged as a suitable venue for academic scholarship. Even within the field of children's literature, poetry for children has suffered unaccountably. Scholarly interest typically ends with nursery rhymes; only occasional articles and even fewer full-length studies such as Myra Cohn Livingston's *The Child as Poet: Myth or Reality?* have challenged the gimmick-ridden pieces that populate elementary school teacher-oriented magazines.

Morag Styles has produced a masterly piece of scholarship, a work that is so much needed in children's literature that we hardly knew how bereft we were, how much of a gap there has been, until we read it. *From the Garden to the Street* will function as the guidepost for other works to follow, because of its broad scope, its enviable grasp of so many poets, and its documentation of the Great Shift from idealized childhood to a supposedly more realistic view. The book's title is an apt one because the chapters move generally from the poetry depicting the child as part of nature, as free and untainted, to the grittier, more "realistic" poetry of the last quarter-century. Styles basically takes us from the era when the gates were being constructed around the idyllic garden to the present time, in which the gates are tumbling down.

Styles divides the poets and poetry according to genre and time period, devoting occasional chapters to specific authors. The introduction is quite useful, giving an overview of the traditional view of

Children's Literature 28, eds. Elizabeth Lennox Keyser and Julie Pfeiffer (Yale University Press, © 2000 Hollins University).

childhood derived from the Romantics and the problem of defining
children's poetry. Chapter 1 addresses the historical construction of
childhood, which in Puritan times mandated devotional verse for children. Styles takes us from the expected Bunyan and Watts up to the
much more recent Charles Causley, and she champions Anna Barbauld as a female writer unfairly maligned by male critics and unjustly
lumped with lesser poets. Chapter 2, "Romantic Visions," focuses on
the shift from devotional poetry to that of the Romantics; Scott, Keats,
Wordsworth, Burns, and John Clare are studied, though Blake receives the most emphasis. Further chapters analyze nineteenth-
century nature poetry; nursery rhymes, old and new; comic poetry;
narrative poetry; poetry that reflects a vanishing image of childhood;
poetry of the street; and Caribbean poetry. Chapters on individual
poets include one discussing the nonsense verse (and troubled lives)
of Edward Lear and Lewis Carroll; one to promote Christina Rossetti;
one to revitalize the reputation of Robert Louis Stevenson; and one on
Charles Causeley and Ted Hughes as representing the twin peaks of
children's poetry. Chapter 9 analyzes anthologies of children's poetry
published during the past two centuries. This chapter, arguably the
most important, points to two problems: the relative absence of female
poets, and the propensity for editors to marginalize the poets who
actually wrote for children.

Styles states that her intention was to "consider most of the poets
who have written for children up to the end of the 1980s, including
those who wrote for adults but whose poetry was or is regularly an-
thologized for the young" (xxvii). This is an expansive proposal difficult to argue against. Her position is altogether much more defen-
sible than Neil Philip's decision to confine his selection of poems for
The New Oxford Book of Children's Verse to those designated by the poet
as being for children (thus he includes only the three Emily Dickinson poems actually sent to children but also one poem by the novelist
Peter Dickinson that was culled from *City of Gold*). Styles avoids trying to define children's poetry, perhaps because she is attempting to
broaden its boundaries. Nevertheless, Styles's scrutiny of two hundred
years' worth of anthologies of children's poetry is eye-opening. Many
editors of anthologies have adopted unquestioningly the assumption
that the main purpose of reading children's poetry is preparation for
the reading of "great" poetry, that is, poetry written for adults. As she
declares in " 'From the Best Poets'? How the Canon of Poetry for Children Is Constructed" (chapter 9), "One of the motivations for writing

this book is to challenge these assumptions, take children's poetry out of its ghetto, and to declare loudly that *this is good poetry for everyone"* (187, emphasis in original). From her examination of (British) poetry anthologies for children from 1801 to 1995, she concludes that "Poets writing for children are half as likely to be included in anthologies as those writing for adults" (192), because a tradition was established early on that clearly preferred poets writing for adults to those writing for children, and especially *male* poets writing for adults (195). It seems we critics are our own worst enemy: by marginalizing poetry written for children, we are in essence marginalizing children's literature. I believe chapter 9 to be the crux of Styles's book; it is a powerful piece of writing that reveals her excellent use of research.

In her introduction, Styles explains that a previous draft of the book read "like an encyclopedia" (xxvii). The discussion apparently was limited to facts and descriptions. Fortunately, she was advised to add her own judgments, which, although biased owing to her childhood experiences, make the book much more valuable. Among Styles's value judgments are her obvious intent to champion female poets and her argument for them as a focus of critical study. The book would have been much leaner and less useful without her conscious efforts to decide value, in spite of her avowed attempts to define poetry broadly (xxv), to take into account children's preferences (xxv), and to break from traditional notions of idealized childhood.

The analysis of the poems assumes an easy knowledge about poetry. There are no technical, line-by-line scannings. Styles's search for meaning and value seems to rest on whether the poem accurately describes childhood in its egotism, penchant for creating idiosyncratic worlds, and sense of wonder and appreciation of humor. She offers a solid defense of Stevenson's place as a pre-eminent poet for children, despite his white middle-class view of childhood, because his descriptions of imaginary play are still valid. She emphasizes the mother-child relationship, which is not surprising since many of the most intimate poems are written by or about mothers and their children. If any construction of childhood is privileged by Styles, it is this one. In fact, the highest compliment Styles can give to Blake is that (because of his tenderness and ability to write a "gentle lullaby") some of his work could have been written by a woman "and, indeed, foreshadows what women were about to publish for children" (48).

Styles's work is particularly valuable for its feminist criticism, which is manifest in three ways: resuscitating the reputation of some lesser-known female poets, reevaluating Christina Rosetti's poems, and arguing that the provenance of many nursery rhymes has been deliberately obscured because the poets were women. Three poets among many who have been neglected are Ann Taylor, Jane Taylor, and Charlotte Smith, all of whom were publishing in the early 1800s. These women's representative poems are studied alongside the private works of other female poets, showing that the kindness and concern for children was a hallmark, even for the maligned Barbauld. Styles's chapter on nursery rhymes is telling: of its twenty-two pages of text, eight rehearse the publishing history of the rhymes, six focus on female poets' contributions, six describe more recent rhymes, and two are on non-British or American rhymes. In other words, almost a third of Morag's discussion of nursery rhymes centers on female poets' contributions, especially those now authored by "anonymous." These include Jane Taylor's "Twinkle, Twinkle, Little Star," Mary Howitt's "The Spider and the Fly," Eliza Bollen's "The Three Little Kittens," and Sarah Martin's "Old Mother Hubbard," which was probably not wholly created but certainly presented in its memorable form by Martin. Styles tries to be fair, acknowledging that the attribution of women's poems to oral tradition was probably not deliberate and could even be construed as a kind of compliment. Nonetheless, "poems credited to the oral tradition [as Anonymous] mean invisibility for their authors who were often likely to be less privileged people including, of course, women" (96).

Chapter 7 is devoted almost entirely to Christina Rossetti in an attempt to counter the oft-repeated claim that Rossetti did not work at her poems and that, as spontaneous creations, they were not real poetry. I came away from this chapter with a renewed appreciation for Rossetti's poems, not just those in *Sing-Song* but those for older readers as well. Styles's analysis of several of her poems shows Rossetti's sensuousness and her use of imagery, her craftsmanship, and her care. Rossetti is often included and credited in poetry anthologies, one of the very few women so honored, and yet her subject matter and form were used by other female poets, too. She was presumably a token female poet whose very presence excluded others.

For all my excitement about *From the Garden to the Street*, I find it has its limitations. The biggest problem is the British dominance of her study. For an American scholar, it is disappointing to say the least that such stellar poets as Emily Dickinson are afforded very little consideration. Robert Frost is only mentioned, and Langston Hughes rates quotation of one poem, as does David McCord. Although only Mc-Cord wrote deliberately and exclusively for children, Dickinson, Frost, and Hughes are widely read by American schoolchildren. Chapter 11, which mentions the Americans but focuses on de la Mare and Milne, characterizes all of these as poets "who mostly write about a world that has gone" (244). Perhaps this statement applies to de la Mare and Milne (and McCord), but to group Dickinson, Frost, and Hughes with them gives the misleading impression that American poets are even less relevant or that Styles is not cognizant of the continued critical interest in and popular appeal of these three. The second sentence of Styles's introduction prepares us for her nationalistic intentions: she intends the book to be "an informative account of the history of poetry written for children in Britain and, to a lesser extent, America in the last three centuries" (xv). I am prompted to suggest that she should have completely omitted American poets, stating up front that the book discusses British poets only, rather than slight American writers and imply that British poets are superior. Styles seems to have depended on Neil Philip's judgment of which American poets to consider rather than on Donald Hall's *The Oxford Book of Children's Verse in America*. American poets receive the most scrutiny in chapter 5, on comic poetry, which includes brief nods to Laura Richards, Ogden Nash, and Shel Silverstein, who is lauded for his "crazy, contorted, irrepressible energy" (118). Styles offers a list of British and American poets whose work is adult-directed but often included in anthologies, poets whom she has no space to discuss; the Americans include E. E. Cummings, Vachel Lindsay, Theodore Roethke, Randall Jarrell, John Updike, Myra Cohn Livingston, and William Carlos Williams (241). This list precedes the nondiscussion of Dickinson, Frost, and Hughes. Another list including Eloise Greenfield, Eve Merriam, and Jack Prelutsky is placed in a small section titled "Contemporary American Verse" (278), a subheading in the penultimate chapter, which discusses "street" poetry.

Even though the title *From the Garden to the Street* prepares readers to be led from earlier cultures and times up to the present day, I find chapter 13 the least compelling, and even the least convincing. Several of the other chapters appear to be full studies, especially the single-author chapters. The penultimate one, however, really does seem to be an introduction. Because of Styles's professed intention to take into account children's preferences and to broaden the boundaries of children's poetry, we expect her to examine how children's poetry has changed in the last few decades. But one chapter is hardly enough, even to draw connections between now and back then. Styles refers to recent children's poetry, using John Townsend's term, as "urchin verse" and praises its appeal to the reluctant reader. I read recent children's poetry and admire a lot of it. But as an older reader, not having grown up with these poems, and as an American, not being as familiar as the author is with her representative poets, I still am not convinced that just because it is accessible it is automatically good or needed or welcomed; easy accessibility neither assures nor negates its value. Because Styles's discriminating judgment, so reliable in other chapters, does not come into play as much here, this chapter will be for many readers the most controversial. Perhaps it is asking too much to expect a discussion of recent poetry to equal that of Rossetti's. In the United States, there is not the resurgence of poetry among teachers and children that Styles attributes to Great Britain. As Gregory Denman argues, in our schools it is likely that poetry, if taught at all, is included grudgingly and sparingly, and the most widely taught poet is Shel Silverstein, whose books "hardly have to be taught . . . [for] they teach themselves" (xvii). It is thus imperative that recent poetry for children be studied assiduously. Even Styles admits that "we must encourage publishing houses, in their rush to get new titles out [that is, to make money off of unsuspecting parents and teachers], to be able to recognize which of their current collections and backlist need to be truly valued and kept in print" (280). In a free-market economy, anything that sells is good. Although critics do not have to envision themselves as gatekeepers to the garden of children's poetry, we do need to be more vigilant and learn more about what is being marketed, read, and taught, and how and why these poems are being read by children and taught by teachers, often at the exclusion of all other types of poetry.

In her introduction, Styles laments that her book is not finished, never could be finished. "The challenges are endless and there is still so much work to be done in this field. I hope others will take up the debates and carry on the scholarship in this deeply fascinating area of study. If this book helps anyone to embark on that journey, I will be satisfied" (xxviii). We've been given the challenge. Now we have to journey onward.

Works Cited

Denman, Gregory A. *When You've Made It Your Own . . . Teaching Poetry to Young People.* Portsmouth, N.H.: Heinemann, 1988.

Hall, Donald, ed. *The Oxford Book of Children's Verse in America.* New York: Oxford University Press, 1985.

Livingston, Myra Cohn. *The Child as Poet: Myth or Reality?* Boston: Horn Book, 1984.

Philip, Neil, ed. *The New Oxford Book of Children's Verse.* 1996. Oxford: Oxford University Press, 1998.

A Fuzzy Genre: Two Views of Fantasy

Gillian Adams

Strategies of Fantasy, by Brian Attebery. Bloomington: Indiana University Press, 1992. *The Natural History of Make-Believe: A Guide to the Principal Works of Britain, Europe, and America,* by John Goldthwaite. New York and Oxford: Oxford University Press, 1996.

It is an indication of how easily books significant to the field of children's literature can escape critical notice that Brian Attebery's *Strategies of Fantasy* has been unreviewed to date in the standard children's literature journals. And yet Attebery's earlier work, *The Fantasy Tradition in American Literature: From Irving to Le Guin* (1980), is one of the important early works of fantasy scholarship, and most, dare I say almost all, of those who work with children's literature end up teaching and even writing about fantasy in some guise or other. They should welcome Attebery's latest contribution to fantasy scholarship for a number of reasons.

Perhaps the most important one is that in his discussion of fantasy and "science fantasy" Attebery includes a number of children's books, giving them equal status with adult works in terms of complexity and sophistication. As he remarks of Diana Wynne Jones's *Fire and Hemlock,*

> This fantasy, so intricately constructed as to defy summary; so full of metafictional devices; so Proustian, one might say, in its transformations of sequence, order, and duration . . . was published for young readers. If such readers are sufficiently well read to recognize its use of the fairy tale structure of quest and qualified happy ending, they should have no trouble in either following the tale to its conclusion or in absorbing its lessons in narrative art. Like Tolkien, Jones is educating her audience. (64)

Attebery is able to bypass much of what troubles those who struggle with the definition of children's literature or canonical questions such as that raised by Peter Hunt when he talks about books that were for children versus books that are for children. That is because Attebery

Children's Literature 28, eds. Elizabeth Lennox Keyser and Julie Pfeiffer (Yale University Press, © 2000 Hollins University).

views genre in general, and the fantasy genre (and its subgenres) in particular, as "fuzzy sets, meaning that they are defined not by boundaries but by a center . . . a book on the fringes may be considered as belonging or not, depending on one's interests. . . . Furthermore, there may be no single quality that links an entire set" (12–13). And children's literature critics who are engaged in the defense of children's literature both as a legitimate academic subject and as a genre that has produced works that deserve inclusion in the canon of great literature can find further arguments for their cause in Attebery's critically sophisticated introduction and first chapter. His defense of fantasy as a genre that deserves serious consideration is based not only on the direction in which recent fantasy seems headed but on theoretical discussions of narrative such as "Gérard Genette's analysis of time, Seymour Chatman's redefinition of character, Bakhtin's . . . theory of the dialogic nature of the novel, Hirsch and Abel's identification of primarily feminine patterns of narrative development, [and] structural and post-structural modes of analysis" (viii).

Attebery's first two chapters appear to be the only ones that have not been reworked from earlier talks and articles, and it is in them that he is at his most theoretical. In the first, "Fantasy as Mode, Genre, Formula," he works at pinning down and defining fantasy both as an evolving fuzzy genre and as a storytelling formula. In the second, "Is Fantasy Literature? Tolkien and the Theorists," Attebery addresses as the fantasy "prototype," the center, or at least the original center, from which fantasy radiates, backwards and forwards in time as well as outward, J. R. R. Tolkien's *The Hobbit* and *The Lord of the Rings*. Here he looks at critical treatments of the works, positive and negative and representing different schools of thought, such as Rosemary Jackson's *Fantasy: The Literature of Subversion* (1981), Christine Brooke-Rose's *A Rhetoric of the Unreal* (1981), Thomas Shippey's *The Road to Middle Earth* (1983), and Don D. Elgin's "ecological reading" (32), *The Comedy of the Fantastic* (1985).

Although it is not directly concerned with children's literature and takes as its central text for discussion John Crowley's *Little, Big* (1981), the third chapter, "Fantasy and Postmodernism," still proves useful for the distinction it makes between Postmodernism and Modernism. The latter omits fantasy as exemplified by Tolkien from its canonical texts because fantasy does not meet its critical expectations and because it so differs from the dominant texts exemplified by those of Pound, Eliot, and Joyce. Postmodernists, on the other hand, such as

Fredric Jameson, have broken down the distinctions between high-modernist culture and popular forms, resulting in "aesthetic populism" and works that are both popular and literary successes by such writers as Umberto Eco, Italo Calvino, and Gabriel García Márquez. In such works, "story, not meaning, is primary" (50), as is true, arguably, in much recent children's literature that is not primarily didactic.

It makes sense, then, for Attebery to take as the exemplary texts in his next chapter, "Fantasy and Narrative Conventions: Story," the children's literature of E. Nesbit, Ursula K. Le Guin, and especially Diana Wynne Jones, Tolkien's student at Oxford and the author of an important article on his work, "The Shape of the Narrative in *The Lord of the Rings*" (1983). Here Attebery examines how fantasy redefines story and the fictional representation of time, often by assuming "the pose of innocence," a "seeming simplicity" (67), producing texts that seem "readable" but are ultimately "writable," "that must be constructed, rewritten, assembled into meaningful order by the reader." Such texts place questions of "memory and fate, cause and effect, invention and experience at the level of story," by operating "at the level of narrative code" (68) rather than at the level of a narrator and narrative stance.

Fantasy, and children's literature, are often slighted by older critics on the grounds of their lack of character development, discussed here as the difference between "realistic" *(acteur)* and "archetypal" *(actant)*. In his fifth chapter, "Fantasy and Narrative Conventions: Character," Attebury returns to Tolkien and to Jones and ends with the progressive development of character in Alan Garner's novels. Attebery argues that in *The Owl Service* the characters are dialogic, operating on two planes simultaneously, and that every scene "advances both conceptions at once" (84). This mixed parentage, maternal fairy tale and paternal realism, is the key to "stories that combine literary greatness with popular appeal . . . characters are both determiners of and subservient to the action" (86).

Continuing his examination of character, in the sixth chapter, "Women and Coming of Age in Fantasy," Attebery explores the claim that "fantasy [has] a unique ability to investigate the twofold process of constructing a self" (86) by looking at the problem of portraying a heroine who comes of age in a genre whose models for coming of age ("the inherited story") seem to be exclusively male. In the past, realistic fiction has had similar problems (ending, for the heroine, in marriage or death), and although there are fairy tales with independent heroines winning their way to adulthood, they are not well known. Attebery begins with Jean Ingelow's *Mopsa the Fairy* (1869) as an early example of reversal of expected character roles, taking up Carolyn Heilbrun's suggestion that "the male who acts as catalyst for the female's transformation is also, in a sense, herself" (98). He then, among other texts, looks at Patricia Wrightson's *The Dark Bright Water* (1979) and ends with Suzette Haden Elgin's Ozark Trilogy (1981), which portrays a society run by women. There are, of course, many coming-of-age fantasies by women writers, but I miss particularly in this chapter any discussion of the work of Jane Yolen and her different, challenging solutions to the problem of female coming of age as recently detailed by Tina Hanlon.

The penultimate chapter, "Science Fantasy," deals with the initial differences between science fiction (also a fuzzy set) and fantasy familiar to most readers and discusses the difficulties in attempting to combine the two genres, an attempt, according to Attebery, that often results in "cheating" on the science or on the fantasy. Nevertheless the combination of the two can be effective, whether in humorous or parodic works or in serious ones that combine or juxtapose the mythic and the scientific. In the latter case, returning to something like his claim for the effectiveness of the dual characterization in Garner's *The Owl Service*, Attebery argues that "when two forms of discourse are given approximately equal weight, a third level of meaning develops as the voices of science fiction and fantasy are perceived by the reader to interact with and comment on one another" (111).

Attebery's last chapter, "Recapturing the Modern World for the Imagination," is an expansion of a 1988 guest of honor speech to the Mythopoeic Society. Here he argues that the center of gravity of the fantasy fuzzy set has shifted from the kind of fantasy represented by Tolkien to what is variously called "low," "real world," or "modern urban fantasies," "characterized by the avoidance of the enclosed fantasy worlds predominant in earlier fantasies" (126). Attebery suggests instead the term "indigenous fantasy," fantasy "that is, like an indigenous species, adapted to and reflective of its native environment" (129). These fantasies have existed from at least F. Anstey and Nesbit but recently have come under the influence of magic realism. Such fantasy (as well as magic realism) rests on two incompatible assertions: that the story takes place in the ordinary world of the reader's senses and that "contrary to all sensory evidence and experience [there are] magical beings, supernatural forces, and a balancing principle that makes fairy tale endings not only possible but obligatory" (129). But readers "must do a lot of hard work . . . to fill in fictional space" (132), because they can no longer rely on the long European fairy tale and romance tradition to do so. Referring in passing to some works for children by such writers as Orson Scott Card and Nancy Willard, Attebery concentrates on Megan Lindholm's *Wizard of the Pigeons* (1986), set in Seattle, and *Little, Big* again (set in the New York City area). Whereas traditional fantasy emphasizes the difference between fiction and life, "indigenous fantasy shows that fiction and life are not only separate but complementary. . . . Those eccentric viewpoints sought by fantasists . . . are enabling mechanisms, ways of evading the rational censor, so that our own tribal storytellers can resume their proper function, reclaim their unique discourse, and recapture the modern world for the imagination" (141).

Every critical work must have its disappointments for some readers, and I felt that the last three chapters, in spite of much of value, did not completely live up to the promise of the earlier ones. The last chapter in particular seemed only to touch on what could be the subject of a whole new book, and much more could be done with the complicated relation of "indigenous fantasy" to "magic realism," which has even invaded the realm of the *New Yorker* story (see, for example, Louise Erdrich's "Naked Woman Playing Chopin"). But it is to Attebery's credit that no matter how dense his argument, his writing is always succinct and clear, and there is no jargon or academic-speak. His scholarship and wide reading sit lightly—although there is a six-page, single-spaced *Works Cited,* there are no footnotes. And Attebery's is the kind of book that makes you want to go out and read the works he talks about that you haven't read yet—the best kind of criticism, to my mind.

Unlike *Strategies of Fantasy,* John Goldthwaite's *The Natural History of Make-Believe* has received a good deal of attention and, for reasons mysterious to me, even two awards: it is listed as an honor book for the 1996 Children's Literature Association Book Award and shares the Harvey Darton Award for 1996–1997. I wish that I could be more positive about this book, given the high regard bestowed on it by Brian Alderson and by Margaret Meek, whose long, thoughtful discussion of the book stands as a counterweight to this review. Nevertheless I must agree with the negatives of Donna White's evaluation (although she does conclude that the book is worth reading)—I too am put off by Goldthwaite's inflated prose, fuzzy and overjudgmental conclusions, and anglocentrism, not to mention the largely inadequate research, lack of critical sophistication, and promotion of a rather unique Christian agenda.

We know Goldthwaite is in trouble right away at the second sentence of his preface: "To my knowledge, this guide is the first such history of the world's imaginative literature for children" (vii). For Goldthwaite, for some reason, mimetic or realistic children's literature, works by such writers as Louisa May Alcott and Frances Hodgson Burnett, are neither "make-believe" nor "imaginative," in spite of their interest in and use of the imagination. Goldthwaite needs here, as elsewhere, to work with more accurate terminology. And he has certainly not written a world history. Goldthwaite's "world" of children's literature is English (not Australian or Canadian), with the inclusion of some U.S. writers and a few works by Europeans (Perrault, Andersen, Grimm, Collodi, de Brunhoff) whose English translations had an impact on the development of English children's literature.

The introduction is a further indicator of trouble ahead. There Goldthwaite comes up with the idea that the biblical Book of Proverbs is "the world's oldest surviving children's book." It is quite true that wisdom literature, of which Proverbs is a comparatively late example probably influenced by ancient Egyptian wisdom literature (see Pritchard 412–25), is, along with beast fables and school stories, part of the corpus of early children's literature (see Adams). But what does Goldthwaite mean by "surviving"? The other early material survives as well, primarily, like wisdom literature, as part of the sea of stories, the stuff of fable and folk tales. But no child now reads the originals (and, I wager, not that many adults), not even the Book of Proverbs (but see Meek 103).

In fact, Goldthwaite has a particular reason for focusing on Proverbs that has more to do with his agenda than any real claim, I suspect, that it really is the oldest surviving children's book. For one thing, there is no indication that Goldthwaite bothered to do any research on wisdom literature, and one becomes increasingly aware from the footnotes, such as they are, that extensive research is not his strong point (there is no "Works Cited"). With a very few exceptions, the works mentioned in the footnotes are outdated, and Goldthwaite seems almost entirely unaware of the periodical literature on the subjects he addresses. Particularly shocking is his citation of the second, 1958, edition of Harvey Darton's *Children's Books in England* instead of the third, a readily available, extensive, and authoritative revision by Brian Alderson.

I could rip apart this book page by page (the margins of my copy are crowded with Xs, "scarcelys," "support??," !!!, yuks, and ughs), but space restricts mention to the major high and low points. Repeating the usual outdated platitudes about the seventeenth-century discovery of childhood (without actually citing Ariès), Goldthwaite sees Charles Perrault's 1696–97 fairy tale collection, *Histoires ou Comtes du temps passé*, as "the first true children's book" (6). Since it seems that Goldthwaite is not intellectually comfortable outside of English and American literature of the second half of the nineteenth and first half of the twentieth century, one can't expect him to know about ancient, medieval, and Renaissance children's books nor the conclusions of professional historians regarding the concept of the child in the earlier periods. And even if he had taken a careful look at the first few chapters of the third edition of Darton for earlier works, one suspects that his agenda would continue to dictate the primacy of Perrault, in spite of the fact that, given their jokes and innuendos, his fairy tales must have been aimed at a sophisticated, informed, and aristocratic readership (see, for example, Gellert).

In any case, Goldthwaite divides "make-believe" authors into two groups: sentimentalists (bad) and realists (good). He further divides make-believe into three parent classes: nursery rhyme, which develops into nonsense; fairy tale, which develops into the narrative romance or muse fantasy; and beast fable, which develops into animal stories and place fantasy (11). The actual word for "development" he uses in his title chapters, however, is "descent." I had initially presumed he meant "descent" in terms of lineage, but Goldthwaite is one of the critics who tends to see the glass as half full rather than half empty, and one suspects that there is also a negative connotation to the word.

It is in his first chapter, "The Descent of Nursery Rhyme," covering "Mother Goose" through Robert Louis Stevenson, Eugene Field, Edward Lear, and Dr. Seuss, that Goldthwaite in his discussion of *A Child's Garden of Verses*, which he condemns for its sentimentality, reveals himself for the first time as an inexpert reader. He just doesn't get what is going on in this complicated collection of poems. And it is in his more extended discussion of Edward Lear that Goldthwaite first undertakes one of the two approaches to literature that he uses in this book, the biographical, here largely dependent on the 1969 biography by Vivien Noakes. I find it remarkable that although Goldthwaite almost always refers to Lear as "Queerie Learie" (34 and *passim*) and mentions the importance of his cat, Foss, he brackets entirely Lear's contested relationships with Frank Lushington and Hubert Congreve.

If he is not going to discuss the subject of Lear's sexual preferences, why use the epithet? Or is Goldthwaite just naive? He will later do the same bracketing for the controversial question of Carroll's feelings for his little girl friends and portrait subjects, in spite of continuing to use the biographical approach.

Chapter 2 broaches the subject of fairy tales, and I find it remarkable for the way it ignores the work of such authorities as Propp, Stith-Thompson, Lüthi, Bottigheimer, Tatar, and Zipes, to name a few of the scholars in the field. Some acquaintance with their work would have made a more reliable and better-supported chapter; he cites (once) only the unreliable Bettelheim. Goldthwaite's major claim here is that Perrault is the one who gave us the two muses who are still with us today, Mother Goose and the fairy godmother (55). Of course, the figure of the fairy godmother, the good mother-replacement with magic, even divine, powers who intervenes on behalf of the protagonist, in the West goes back at least as far as Greek and Roman literature (*The Odyssey, Cupid and Psyche, The Golden Ass*), as well as to medieval and Renaissance tales, and is found, as well, in many other cultures. Perrault was working with an ancient tradition well known to his contemporaries, but whether Goldthwaite is ignorant of that tradition or simply chooses to ignore it in favor of his Christian agenda is unclear.

This second chapter is followed by the longest chapter in the book, "A Tutor Recants: The Unwriting of *Alice in Wonderland*" (74–169). Here Goldthwaite employs, besides the biographical approach, his other critical strategy, the sub- or countertext, what he calls "how books beget books." Attention to countertexts, once called influence studies, has regained critical popularity since the work of Bakhtin became well known, although Goldthwaite seems unaware of Bakhtinian dialogics. In the case of Carroll's and some later works, the book is Charles Kingsley's *The Water Babies,* with which Goldthwaite has dealt at some length at the end of the previous chapter. I am no believer in always omitting the author, whatever his intentions may be, from critical studies, and certainly there have been other critics who have read the Alice books as a roman à clef, but none, I believe, have done so to the extent that Goldthwaite does. For Goldthwaite, every character and every incident can be explained either by some facet of Charles Dodgson's relationship with the Liddells or with the poet laureate Alfred Lord Tennyson, who Dodgson believed had slighted him, or by the desire to get back at and surpass *The Water Babies,* which was being serialized in *Macmillan's* at the time that the first version of *Alice's*

Adventures was being written down (1863). Both the relativist, unloving Dodgson (the Cheshire Cat) and the sentimental Dodgson (the Knave of Hearts) are present in the work, and the final version, *The Nursery Alice,* written years later, is an attempt by Carroll to atone for his earlier paganism, moral relativism, and "blasphemous" and "unholy" thoughts (165). Goldthwaite admits that his theories are speculative, and I have my doubts about his interpretation, but at least in this chapter he seems to be on home territory and has built his case from a careful examination of the texts and of primary sources such as letters and what remains of Carroll's diaries. My problem with the chapter, then, is not its content but that it is too long, repetitive (Kingsley is with us constantly), and disorganized. A good editor (does Oxford have one for children's literature?) would have cut it to a third its size and spared the reader much tedium.

Space does not permit a detailed look at the next two chapters, which cover fantasies from works by George MacDonald and Carlo Collodi through *Where the Wild Things Are* (Selma Lanes is the only reference for Sendak). It is here, in his discussion of Collodi's *Pinocchio,* that the religious component of Goldthwaite's view of make-believe, already apparent in his interpretation of the Alice books, Kingsley, and MacDonald, reaches its most explicit expression. We are all familiar with Tolkien's idea of the *eucatastrophe,* that moment that Attebery terms "wonder" and that is usually deemed characteristic of much of the fairy tale-fantasy genre. Readers have very different responses to such a moment: for some readers like myself, for example, Kenneth Grahame's Piper at the gates of dawn always brings tears to the eyes, whereas for others it is sentimental claptrap—Goldthwaite finds the chapter "intrusive" and "a pantheistic tract" (320). For the *eucatastrophe* to be legitimate, in Goldthwaite's reading, it must correspond to his rather narrow Christian critical conception—J. R. R. Tolkien and C. S. Lewis do not make the grade. MacDonald's grandmothers and Northwind, and particularly Collodi's Blue Fairy, are, on the other hand, "grace taking form to bestow grace.... I would even propose that what we have here, addressed to the understanding of children, is all of it a literature of the Holy Ghost" (199). Perhaps I am wrong to think that were Collodi to learn that his Blue Fairy (a tough customer in her way) is a figure of the Holy Ghost, he would be very surprised.

Not that I would deny that there is a strong religious element in much children's literature, or that it is important both aesthetically and ethically, but I do have trouble with Goldthwaite's intolerance of alternative religious experiences ("new agism") and with his idea that the presence or absence of divinity and the way it is formulated has something to do with whether literature is good or bad. Thus it is a relief to arrive at his final and third category of make-believe, beast fable that becomes animal fantasy, on which he is less inclined to impose his religious expectations. The two strongest chapters of Goldthwaite's history, in my opinion, are the chapters on *Uncle Remus* (6) and Beatrix Potter (7), perhaps because they originally appeared in the British journal *Signal* and had the benefit of the expert editorial hand of Nancy Chambers. Here the writing is more straightforward, the content better organized, the research a little more substantial, and there are some observations of value. In his chapter on Uncle Remus, for example, Goldthwaite claims, I think rightly, that the great impact of these stories on subsequent animal fiction in Britain and North America has been scanted, and I agree with his reading of "Miss Meadows and the gals." But Goldthwaite confines himself to a discussion (with much plot summary) of the tales themselves; although he divides the tales into categories, he seems unaware that some of the tales (those about the fox, the bear, and the wolf) are found in the beast literature of the northern European Middle Ages and probably came originally from India (perhaps slaves picked them up from their owners). Others are certainly from Africa, and others perhaps originated in the antebellum South. Given these diverse antecedents, it is misleading to talk about the tales all lumped together as characteristic creations of the slave situation; some are, no doubt, and others are not. What is more significant is the way the tales are presented and juxtaposed, and how they are framed. But Goldthwaite omits entirely any consideration of what has interested a number of critics about *Uncle Remus:* the complex narratorial situation in which a white author, Joel Chandler Harris, uses a crafty black slave narrator to tell the tales to a white boy who is the son of his owners and whom he means to influence. There is no discussion of the multiple agendas here, where it is most important.

Although Goldthwaite, in his chapter on Potter, takes as his usual tactic reading the works in terms of the life, his close attention to her journal, letters, and unpublished illustrations for *Uncle Remus* bears fruit in his discussion of Potter's fear of being caught "copying" and in her use of the *Uncle Remus* tales and other sources. The wild suppositions in which he tends to engage have been cut to a minimum (see 317 top). He could, however, have used Potter's groundbreaking studies of mushrooms to further his points.

In his eighth and final chapter, "The Green Pastures: The Descent of the Fable," Goldthwaite disposes of *The Wind in the Willows* (see above), Kipling—"flung the language too handsomely to serve the tales [*Just So Stories*] well" (325)—and A. A. Milne ("beautifully crafted" [330] and also owing much to *Uncle Remus*). Goldthwaite is to be complimented for calling attention to Howard Garis's tremendously popular *Uncle Wiggly* books (omitted from Gillian Avery's *Behold the Child*, for example) and Thornton Burgess's *Old Mother West Wind* series. With a complex work such as *Charlotte's Web* he is out of his depth again ("as a beast fable . . . a compromised specimen" [342], "a partial failure as make-believe" [343]), and he is only a little more positive about the Babar books—"the picture book as slide presentation" (343). The page on Tove Jansson's Moomintroll books is more positive: "the canniest author-illustrator since Potter" (147). The interesting final section on *Pogo*, an important part of the culture of the late 1940s and early 1950s, is, I believe, original work and could form the basis of a longer, more detailed study.

Goldthwaite begins his "Afterword: Wisdom Justified of All Her Children," with a caveat: "make-believe can be an education in the fullness of reality or a schooling in intellectual fraud" (351). For Goldthwaite the latter includes pantheism, "primitive animism smartened up for an audience too skeptical for dogma" (351), "the golden calf of self-expression" as exemplified by Keats, Carroll, and Joyce (353), and the movies and television. "Literary paganism and that great failure of the imagination before reality, sentimentalism, tell us nothing valid about life and so can convey nothing real to us nor ever awaken a meaning worth living for" (358). Here Goldthwaite loses even Meek —she comments: "this is too hard for me" (113). The "higher purpose" of make-believe is to bestow grace through the figure of the fairy godmother, a tutorial muse associated with the Holy Ghost, whom Goldthwaite sees as "feminine in character" (354). This figure, in turn, Goldthwaite identifies with the female personification of Wisdom in the Book of Proverbs, and he quotes verses 8:23–32 in support. "Lady Wisdom's existence is to be accepted as actual and as stated. . . . Her reappearance [although in fact she never disappeared] in the seventeenth and nineteenth centuries may therefore be read, literally, as the Spirit of God bridging two millennia of literature to step into the pages of some of our most famous children's books" (355). And so on for four more pages. Although I share Goldthwaite's belief that didactic literature is not necessarily bad literature and that all children's literature is in some sense value-laden and has an agenda, a much better, and certainly more critically sophisticated, case is made for the importance of literature's ethical stance by Wayne Booth in *The Company We Keep.*

It is as well that Goldthwaite ends his *History* at midcentury. I am not convinced that he has the interest or the training to address more modern children's literature. If one combines Attebery's idea of fantasy as a fuzzy set with Hunt's idea that there are books that are for children and books that were for children, Goldthwaite's *History* is about books that were for children, and he addresses those books in terms that were once for critics and are no longer. I suspect that if Goldthwaite recognizes that the center of the fuzzy set of children's literature and its criticism has shifted several times since the mid-1950s, he wants no part of the new ways. In my opinion, there would have been some excuse for this book twenty or thirty years ago, but not now. Thus, I don't know to whom I might recommend it. I would be embarrassed to give it to the younger scholars I know who work with children's literature—no matter how religious they personally may be, Goldthwaite's narrow-minded and judgmental criticism would seem alien. Given its tedious long-windedness, I certainly wouldn't inflict it on students, except perhaps as an example of how not to do it—you don't want to encourage the idea that biography and one subtext, particularly *The Water Babies* or *Uncle Remus,* will explain everything. The third edition of Darton, and Avery, although neither is perfect, offer a more reliable historical basis for the exploration of children's literature—an exploration that, at the turn of our century, should make use of recent articles and books such as Attebery's that address the issues raised by the shifting center of the fuzzy set of children's literature.

Works Cited

Adams, Gillian. "The First Children's Literature? The Case for Sumer." *Children's Literature* 14 (1986): 1–30.

Alderson, Brian. Review of *Natural History of Make-Believe. Children's Books History Society Newsletter* April 1997. Qtd. in *Signal* 86 (May 1998): 146.

Avery, Gillian. *Behold the Child; American Children and Their Books 1621–1922.* Baltimore: John Hopkins University Press, 1994.

Booth, Wayne. *The Company We Keep: An Ethics of Fiction.* Berkeley: University of California Press, 1988.

Darton, Harvey, F. J. *Children's Books in England.* 1932. 3d ed. Rev. Brian Alderson. Cambridge: Cambridge University Press, 1982.

Erdrich, Louise. "Naked Woman Playing Chopin." *The New Yorker* 27 July 1998: 62–67.

Gellert, James. "The Fairy Tales of Charles Perrault: Acute Logic and Gallic Wit." In *Touchstones: Reflections on the Best in Children's Literature.* Vol 2: *Fairy Tales, Fables, Myths,*

Legends, and Poetry. West Lafayette, Ind.: Children's Literature Association, 1987. Pp. 201–12.

Hanlon, Tina L. " 'To Sleep, Perchance to Dream': Sleeping Beauties and Wide-Awake Plain Janes in the Stories of Jane Yolen." *Children's Literature* 26 (1998): 140–67.

Hunt, Peter. "Passing on the Past: The Problem of Books That Are for Children and That Were for Children." *Children's Literature Association Quarterly* 21, no. 4 (winter 1996–97): 200–2.

Meek, Margaret. "In Two Minds: Topics & Themes in *The Natural History of Make-Believe.*" *Signal* 83 (May 1997): 101–14.

Pritchard, James B., ed. *Ancient Near Eastern Texts Relating to the Old Testament.* 1950. 2d rev. ed. Princeton: Princeton University Press, 1955.

White, Donna. "Searching for Grace in Children's Fantasy." *The Lion and the Unicorn* 21, no. 2 (April 1997): 288–90.

Crosswriting the School Story

Kenneth Kidd

Regendering the School Story: Sassy Sissies and Tattling Tomboys, by Beverly
Lyon Clark. New York: Garland, 1996.

Forget Thomas Hughes's *Tom Brown's School Days* (1857). Better yet,
remember it differently, as the hypercanonical school story that, although still underappreciated, "warped not just the earlier but also
the later history of the genre" (12). That larger history is Clark's subject, and she pursues an interesting line of inquiry that sets her project
quite apart from earlier studies such as Isabel Quigly's *The Heirs of Tom
Brown* and P. W. Musgrave's *From Brown to Bunter.* Noting the traditional
inattention to both girls' stories and gender itself, Clark explores less
canonical "crossgendered" school stories, written for boys by women
and for girls by men. Authors of such stories, she argues, are doubly
removed by age and gender from the conventions of the genre and are
more likely to stray from them. Although crossgendering takes center stage, Clark also shows how school stories are written along and
across generational, national, religious, class, and racial lines. Divided
into three major sections, Clark's investigation of authorial identification and remove is quite engaging, as much a contribution to gender
studies and literary historiography as a reassessment of this misunderstood genre.

The introduction situates Hughes's *Tom Brown* as both a "watershed"
(11) and an unfortunate primal scene. What *Huck Finn* is to the American boy book, *Tom Brown* is to the British boys' school story, and although Clark doesn't quite make this claim, I suspect that critical accounts of the school story also tend to imitate *Tom Brown* itself, just
as early scholarship on *Huck Finn* echoes as much as analyzes Twain's
literary strategies. In any case, the five chapters in part 1 defamil-
iarize the Hughes legacy by examining crossgendered school stories
predating *Tom Brown* penned by British and American writers alike,
among them Richard Johnson, Charles Lamb, Jacob Abbott, Dorothy
Kilner, Maria Edgeworth, Emily J. May, and Mary Martha Sherwood.

Children's Literature 28, eds. Elizabeth Lennox Keyser and Julie Pfeiffer (Yale University
Press, © 2000 Hollins University).

At the same time, Clark shows that overcanonization can be a form of scholarly neglect. Clark alternates chapters that survey a posse of writers with chapters devoted to a few representative figures. She draws from an impressive range of texts, and her local readings are as fascinating as her larger revisionist claims.

I found chapter 3 particularly instructive, a reading of Dorothy Kilner's *First Going to School; or, The Story of Tom Brown, and His Sisters* (1804); this was the first tale of Tom Brown, at once playful and didactic. Only "precariously a school story," Kilner's novel is less preoccupied with gender-bending than with animal-human "interface" (53). Young Tom is likened to a "stuck pig," a "little lamb," and a horse. Tom's father composes animal fables starring the family's calf, sow, and rabbits, and at the book's end, cousin Peter describes a prank featuring a sow and her pigs cross-dressed as a headmaster and his boys. Clark links this "cross-species crossdressing" (55) with the aims and anxieties of education and other civilizing projects.

In the fourth chapter Clark elaborates on one of her central emphases, the trope of "talebearing"—telling and not telling tales—in both crossgendered fiction and crossgendered commentary like her own. Typically, talebearing has taken a critical back seat to those other master tropes of schoolboy fiction, insurrection and fagging. She discovers that some women writers are less likely to condemn tattling than their male counterparts, "calling into question the cosmetic unities of subsequent male authors" and even hinting "at the deviousness of all authors who tell tales about telling tales" (84). As she remarks in the introduction, school stories foreground both peer codes of loyalty and the teacher-student struggle, offering a useful glimpse into "the intersections of literature and pedagogy and the politics of schooling" (10).

The five chapters in part 2 attend to tales that appeared during the "heyday of the canonical story" but are hardly *Tom Brown* clones. In this cluster Clark outlines how women writers in particular revised the school story by crossing gender with race and ethnicity (chapters 6 and 7) and by combining it with other genres (chapters 8 and 9). Many of these authors—notably Anna Bartlett Warner (Susan Warner's neglected sister), Elizabeth Eiloart, Louisa May Alcott, and Ellen Wood —identified with marginalized groups and accorded them some degree of sentimental power. She finds Alcott's *Little Men* (1871) a curious blend of family story and school story, at once progressive and custodial. Alcott's major "discursive field is not a playing or a battle field but a horticultural one" (190); the child botanical cultivates moral and intellectual virtues with the guidance of master gardeners Jo and Professor Bhaer.

Part 3 (chapters 11 and 12) escorts us into the twentieth century and its darker incarnations of the genre. Although some stories remained faithful to tradition and targeted children, others were decidedly adult, "more critical of school, more cynical, sardonic, subverse—also, in a sense, returning to the didactic as they criticized schooling" (231). In the context of these changes, British men returned to the crossgendering fold, in some cases impersonating and mocking crossgendered women. Desmond Coke, for instance, published *The Chaps of Harton: A Tale of Frolic, Sport and Mystery at Public School* (1913) under the pseudonym Belinda Blinders, parodying the woman author writing about boys. Homosexual possibility also became more overt. Gerald Lord Berners's *The Girls of Radclyffe Hall* (1937)—a book about girls written under the pseudonym Adela Quebec—obviously alludes to the lesbian novelist Radclyffe Hall and to a degree normalizes lesbianism (Clark adds that the copy she read had belonged to Gertrude Stein and was a gift from Berners). As Clark reports in the final chapter, the 1930s and 1950s witnessed the last major phase of crossgendered stories by British women, notably D. Wynne Wilson, the gifted modernist author of *Early Closing* (1931), who died a year after its publication.

Clark's title describes her own agenda more than the texts under review. Since both the canonical school story and early scholarly studies presume the exclusion of females, Clark is regendering the school story through her inventive attention to crossgendering. I'm not, however, persuaded that crossgendered writers enjoy "greater distance" from or are less likely to have "fully internalized" the genre (2)—quite the contrary, as some of her examples show—nor am I sure that "gender" should be so uniformly linked to biological sex (either in solidarity or transgression). It's of course hard to address gender without recourse to the usual binary and hegemonic-subversive analytic model, and although crossgendering as a critical category presumes significant difference between the sexes, Clark's readings rarely indulge in what she dubs "a new essentialism" (2).

The book's subtitle is more troubling, for sassy sissies and tattling tomboys don't actually get much attention, and I don't think Clark is asking us to reconsider the sissy and the tomboy as gendered figures. For Clark they are proof of crossgendering at the level of character, but I suspect they have a richer (and more vexed) life than she acknowledges and could be studied separately or across a wider array of texts. Might not their gender ambiguity be as significant as the sex or gender of their authors? What might we say about the sissies (sassy or otherwise) of male writers? Furthermore, talebearing occurs primarily among boys (even in books written by women); doesn't she mean tattling sissies? If this is not a major focus, then the subtitle seems misleading. If it is, then the discussion could benefit from recent work in this area, such as Eve Sedgwick's essay on the war on sissy boys and Sally Mitchell's tomboy chapter in *The New Girl* (which, in fairness, appeared only a year earlier).

In terms of the child-adult relation, I'm not entirely convinced that "adults endorse what least endorses them" (14). Clark's example is the disdain for school in nineteenth-century U.S. genres such as the bad-boy book and the family story. But as these genres make clear, resistance to school is one of school's most seductive and successful tropes, and the rhetoric of youthful rebellion is central to America's republican self-image. Authority works in mysterious ways, but I bet that more often than not, adults endorse what most endorses them.

Otherwise Clark's book is persuasive and compelling. She invites us to think twice about gender, genre, and the "peculiarly marginal institution" (7) of school. Clark has long urged scholars of all persuasions to take children's literature seriously, and certainly her own work is exemplary. The third in Garland's Literature and Culture series (edited by Jack Zipes), *Regendering the School Story* is a bold new portrait of the school story that speaks to and about the status of children's literature more generally. Don't leave home without it.

Works Cited

Mitchell, Sally. *The New Girl: Girl's Culture in England, 1880–1915*. New York: Columbia University Press, 1995.
Musgrave, P. W. *From Brown to Bunter: The Life and Death of the School Story*. London: Routledge, 1985.
Quigly, Isabel. *The Heirs of Tom Brown: The English School Story*. London: Chatto, 1982.
Sedgwick, Eve Kosofsky. "How to Bring Your Kids up Gay: The War on Effeminate Boys." *Social Text 29* (1991): 18–27. Reprinted in Sedgwick, *Tendencies*. Durham: Duke University Press, 1993. Pp. 154–64.

A New Salvo in the Literary Battle of the Sexes

Raymond E. Jones

Ventures into Childland: Victorians, Fairy Tales, and Femininity, by U. C. Knoepflmacher. Chicago: University of Chicago Press, 1998.

In one of the most famous volleys in the war over the fairies—the literary battle over whether fairy tales and fantasy were proper fare for children—Charles Lamb called the books of female didactic writers "nonsense" that was dangerous to the imaginative development of children, and then he fired this denunciation: "Damn them! I mean the cursed Barbauld Crew, those Blights and Blasts of all that is Human in man and child" (1:326). Lamb's explosive curse succeeded. In *Fantasy and Reason: Children's Literature in the Eighteenth Century* (1984), for example, Geoffrey Summerfield dismisses female didacticists as "morally shrill women" (188), saying that, "fortunately for the deeper health of young readers and listeners," the "Wordsworthian view" of reality will always have "the energy and the will to challenge" the empiricists' view (305). Most critics have credited Lewis Carroll's *Alice's Adventures in Wonderland* (1865) as the shot that made victorious this Romantic vision of childhood. Percy Muir, in *English Children's Books, 1600–1900* (1954), thus approvingly notes that *Alice* "did not kill off all the namby-pamby writers. . . . But the mortality rate was high" (149). For Muir and like-minded critics, *Alice* altered literary history for the better by establishing the hegemony of a male tradition of fantasy. Later Victorian female authors, they believe, were little more than sentimentalists reproducing an outmoded, ineffective, and imaginatively debilitating didactic tradition.

Because criticism itself has become a literary battlefield where theorists launch mortars at every redoubt of conventional interpretation, it is startling that few critics have reassessed a history of children's literature that debases the efforts of women, who have traditionally been assigned the role of educating the young. *Ventures into Childland,* U. C. Knoepflmacher's "refiguring of literary history" (430), is therefore a welcome challenge to dominant opinions about the Golden Age

Children's Literature 28, eds. Elizabeth Lennox Keyser and Julie Pfeiffer (Yale University Press, © 2000 Hollins University).

of children's literature. (In providing a critical overview for his history, Knoepflmacher quotes from Lamb's 23 October 1802 letter to Coleridge [20], including part of the sentence I cite above; he also includes part of the second of my two quotations from Summerfield [23]). Examining the work of four male and three female Victorians, this overlong volume blends literary history, biography, psychology, and close textual and graphical analysis to reassess literary battles that involved the very definition of childhood. Knoepflmacher argues that after *Alice in Wonderland* "completed the erosion of a didactic and empirical tradition of children's literature that had been dominated by female authors for over a century" (xi), female writers became subversive. In order to contest "male idealizations of a feminized innocence" (xii) that was passive, desexualized, and static, they wrote "fantasies that were covertly anti-fantastic" because they emphasized the "child's orderly progression towards maturity within a temporal world marked by boundaries and limits" (xi–xii).

Knoepflmacher begins with an introductory overview. This chapter and the brief epilogue are vital because of the complexity, abundant detail, and meandering method that he admits, in an amusing understatement, is "a bit circuitous" (xi). Essentially, he positions his book in opposition to James Kincaid's controversial *Child-Loving: The Erotic Child and Victorian Culture* (1992). He therefore argues that gender influenced Victorian representations of childhood. Male writers, he asserts, "turned to the child in order to find compensations for a middle-class culture's division of the sexes into separate spheres" (9). Customarily removed from their mothers and sent away to school, males identified the nursery with a "sustaining female imagination" (9) that they longed to recover. By representing "childland" as the realm of the prepubescent female, writers such as John Ruskin and Lewis Carroll could "resist the gender division that comes with sexual maturation" (11). At the same time, however, such males felt ambivalent about mothers. Longing for restoration of a lost union, but resenting the mother who expelled them from the undifferentiated Eden of childhood, male writers expressed their anger by representing matriarchal figures as powerful and cruel.

In contrast, Knoepflmacher argues, female writers, who did not endure the male's anxieties of separation from the mother, tended "to insist on the reality of gender binaries" (25). Instead of creating fantasies reflecting a return to a presexual childhood and a merger with the mother or a mother surrogate, women writers sought to reclaim the fairy tale as a form of female discourse. In doing so, they tried to revitalize a tradition of female authority that had been usurped by the Romantic poets and others who had projected male desires onto females. Respecting the didactic and empirical tradition that Lamb denigrated, female authors approached fantasy more cautiously than males. They also made the central female presence the "mentoria," a tutor specializing in folk wisdom, pragmatic advice, and moral instruction. According to Knoepflmacher, then, the fantasies of Victorian female writers are not, as critics have generally read them to be, feeble imitations of male fantasies. They are actually deliberate challenges to male texts, especially Carroll's *Alice* books. By detailing these challenges, Knoepflmacher calls for a new examination of both literary history and attitudes toward the representation of women and children.

Knoepflmacher's intertextual study offers incomplete coverage of the period from 1851, when John Ruskin published *The King of the Golden River,* to 1874, when Christina Rossetti issued *Speaking Likenesses.* For reasons that he does not make clear, Knoepflmacher ignores Charles Kingsley's *The Water Babies* (1863), a popular fantasy whose representations of female innocence in the figure of Ellie and of matriarchal "mentoriae" (Mrs. Doasyouwouldbedoneby, Mrs. Bedonebyasyoudid, Mother Carey, and, perhaps, Mrs. Grimes) could have provided insightful intertextual points. He also ignores relevant major fantasies by authors he discusses. Thus, he does not analyze George MacDonald's *The Princess and the Goblin,* which received book publication in the same year as *At the Back of North Wind* (1871), the focus of his seventh chapter. This omission is suspect because the *Princess* books directly challenge his claim that MacDonald reverses the insistence on growth and development displayed earlier in "The Light Princess," center of discussion in the fourth chapter. Perhaps the Grandmother, the deified maternal presence in the *Princess* books, is as morally and emotionally ambiguous as North Wind, and perhaps Curdie and Irene, because they remain childless, do not enter fully into the world of adult procreation, but Knoepflmacher's failure to consider such issues makes his thesis seem blinkered and contrived.

Knoepflmacher's ten analytical chapters set up both an opposition between male and female writers and a progression of "two distinct movements" (xii). The first movement consists of Ruskin's *The King of the Golden River,* Thackeray's *The Rose and the Ring* (1855), MacDonald's "The Light Princess" (1864), and Carroll's *Alice* books (from the first hand-produced copy of "Alice's Adventures Under Ground" of 1864 to *Through the Looking-Glass,* published in 1871, with brief discussion of the 1890 issue of *The Nursery Alice).* This movement begins with Ruskin's representation of a static, feminized nature in which the hero evades growth and concludes with Carroll's acceptance of Alice's passage into adulthood. The second movement progresses toward a reassertion of female ideas about literature and life, but it begins with MacDonald's *At the Back of the North Wind.* This novel, Knoepflmacher asserts, is like Ruskin's tale in resisting maturation, but it expresses a more positive attitude toward female power than did Ruskin or Carroll. In exploring this second movement, however, Knoepflmacher refers to Carroll's *Alice* books so frequently that in practice both the *Alice* books and *At the Back of the North Wind* appear in opposition to texts by three females: Jean Ingelow's *Mopsa the Fairy* (1869); Christina Rossetti's "Goblin Market" (1862), *Sing-Song* (1872), and *Speaking Likenesses;* and Julia Horatia Ewing's tales, especially "Amelia and the Dwarfs" (1870). Knoepflmacher again discusses maturation, the major point of contention in the first movement, but he concentrates his analysis of the second movement on the issue of female authority. He argues that MacDonald's book enabled women writers to enter into their covert debate with male writers. To illustrate, he draws parallels between the texts of the male and female writers, noting how the females repeatedly insist on the existence of limits, the necessity of growth in the real world, and the utility of a female vision of life. This movement concludes with what Knoepflmacher declares is the unappreciated artistic triumph of Ewing, who was able "to realign the fairy tale with earlier literary and cultural forms" (xii) and therefore to reassert the value of a female didactic tradition.

These weakly defined movements are more creative than convincing because the supporting analyses are too diffuse: a perceptive and knowledgeable reader, Knoepflmacher includes almost every insight and textual parallel that occurs to him. Consequently, the welter of details sometimes blurs his thesis. Nevertheless, he is an interesting guide because he combines biographical and psychological observations with scene-by-scene readings notable for their thoroughness. He is also impressive in revealing the significance of details, both textual and graphic, and in connecting details to those in other titles. These connections are his strongest support for the claim that texts by female Victorians critically interrogate those of their male predecessors.

The individual readings insist on "a rather old-fashioned relation between texts and authorial selves" (379), providing biographical background, a literary and cultural context for the publication of each work, and ample psychological speculation about motives. The readings of the male writers who form the "first movement" show them to be far from homogeneous in representing females and children. Whereas Ruskin, for example, figured his desire for childhood's "purity" (Knoepflmacher repeatedly encloses the word in quotation marks) through an effeminate hero who is restored to a sexless life in the feminine space of a new Eden, Thackeray injected "frictions and impurities" (111) into *The Rose and the Ring*. Consequently, Thackeray's ironic fairy tale reanimated the form, giving later female writers a model for combining didactic and fantastic elements. The highlight of this movement is, however, the readings of Carroll. Admittedly, Knoepflmacher belabors Carroll's internal battles between his feminine and masculine characteristics and between his desire to arrest his dream-child's growth and his knowledge that she has already grown beyond him. Nevertheless, the intensive examination of the framing verses and the exploration of Carroll's surrogates within the tales are interesting forays into a crowded field.

For most readers, however, Knoepflmacher's claims for the female writers are likely to be the major interest. In fact, the extent and depth of his critiques suggest that these writers merit further study. The reading of *Mopsa the Fairy* as a rejection of Carroll's mode of fantasy and MacDonald's ideology, for example, may cause reconsideration of a text most historians dismiss as a forgettable imitation of *Alice*. Still, his claims about *Mopsa* are troublesome. It is difficult to believe that Ingelow's 1869 novel consciously contests MacDonald's *At the Back of the North Wind*, which was serialized in 1868 and 1869. In fact, it seems likely that Ingelow, especially in creating Mother Fate as "deified motherhood" (310), was creating her own version of Kingsley's Mother Carey. Furthermore, Knoepflmacher's claim that Ingelow "engages Carroll in ways that are often so oblique that they can easily be missed" (281) is open to the rebuttal that Ingelow is so inept that it is possible to redeem her work only by considering it an awkward attack on Carroll. A similar reservation arises in response to Knoepflmacher's assertion that the "drab little story" (376) that Rossetti included in the middle of *Speaking Likenesses* is actually "the most consummate hoax in English children's literature" (374). It is possible to see the book as a challenge to Carroll, MacDonald, and even Ingelow because it rejects the wild improbabilities offered in their fantasylands. To insist that the narrator's repetitious denial of her own originality led to a situation in which the other two tales are "misread as lesser copies rather than as burlesques" (376) of Carroll cleverly suggests that Knoepflmacher alone, blessed with an intuition of authorial intention, knows how to receive texts correctly. Such claims are often necessary as part of a publishable thesis, but they also advance an ironic counterclaim that Knoepflmacher may be loathe to accept: by insisting that Ingelow and Rossetti cannot be understood properly except in the context of their arguments with males, Knoepflmacher asserts that these women needed and still need men if they are to articulate their own identities.

No similar ironic concession is necessary for Julia Horatia Ewing. As Knoepflmacher points out, Ewing, the daughter of a writer, was conscious of the female tradition of storytelling. By making the maturation process a "steady leitmotif" (382) and by trying to realign fantasy with the mundane female domestic realm, she was, he contends, implicitly in opposition to Carroll and other males who idealized arrested development. He also insists that the transmission of authority is central to these tales. Here, as throughout his book, however, his habit of making texts analogues or allegories of cultural or biographical situations hangs the argument on the thinnest of threads. The first habit is evident in Knoepflmacher's claim that in "The Magic Jar" the protagonist's choice of a plain jar for a gift "matches Ewing's belief in the value of restoring an unadorned tradition of oral tales told by *vieilles* or *Märchenfrauen*" (393). The second is apparent in his comment that in "Timothy's Shoes" a boy's "repeated attempts to rid himself of shoes he had inherited from his eight older brothers can almost be read as an allegory about the transmission of authority and, hence, of fairy tales as a vehicle for that very process of transmission" (415). Knoepflmacher doesn't insist on the allegory, nor does he indicate what kind of critical common sense prevents such transference of meaning, but the mere mention of this claim is likely to leave readers admiring his cleverness while questioning the solidity of his arguments.

Although *Ventures into Childland* is "hardly all-inclusive," as he readily admits, Knoepflmacher obviously considers it a major book. He thus pats himself on the back, saying he may well have produced "the most comprehensive history (literary and cultural) yet written about the so-called golden age of children's literature" (xiii). Perhaps he has, but this history is not an unalloyed triumph. Repetitive, over-insistent in his analyses and undisciplined in communicating major theses, Knoepflmacher not only ignores significant texts, but, in spite of occasional nods to "dual audiences" of adults and children, he also neglects the issue of reception that his introductory anecdote about the different ways in which he and his son watched Disney's *Dumbo* seems to promise. Nevertheless, *Ventures into Childland* is interesting and insightful criticism. Knoepflmacher may be using buckshot instead of cannon balls, but he has fired the opening salvo in what promises to be a renewed literary battle of the sexes.

Works Cited

Lamb, Charles. *The Letters of Charles Lamb.* 3 vols. Ed. E. V. Lucas. London: Dent, 1935.

Muir, Percy. *English Children's Books, 1600–1900.* New York: Praeger, 1954.

Summerfield, Geoffrey. *Fantasy and Reason: Children's Literature in the Eighteenth Century.* Athens: University of Georgia Press, 1984.

From Wonderland to the Marketplace: Alice's Progeny

Stephen Canham

Alternative Alices: Visions and Revisions of Lewis Carroll's Alice Books, ed. Carolyn Sigler. Lexington: University Press of Kentucky, 1997.

In *Alternative Alices: Visions and Revisions of Lewis Carroll's Alice Books,* Carolyn Sigler brings together twenty selections from nineteenth- and early twentieth-century texts that in various ways derive from Lewis Carroll's two *Alice* books. While some of the authors collected here will be familiar (for example, Jean Ingelow, Juliana Horatia Ewing, C. Rossetti, Frances Hodgson Burnett, E. Nesbit), others will most likely be known only to specialists (for example, Alice Corkan, John Rae, Caroline Lewis); this blend makes for an interesting mix of stories that have more or less "survived" and others that, although probably popular in their day, have faded out of common sight. The mix also helps support Sigler's assertion of the immediate and immense effects of the *Alice* books, effects that were not limited to mere imitation in the hope of cashing in on the lucrative "*Alice* industry" that began developing almost as the ink was drying on first editions (Carroll himself, of course, did much to impel this industry). The anthology classifies the stories into four parts: "Subverting Wonderland," "The Didactic Looking Glass," "Sentimental Re-Creations," and "Political Parodies." Although Sigler does not provide notes or glosses for the primary texts, she does offer a brief biographical sketch and analysis for each story; most of her primary texts are excerpted from longer works. In a nice touch, black and white illustrations from their original editions are reproduced well. Overall, this is a handsomely designed volume, although here and there one will find a typographical error that should have been caught (for example, note 26, p. xxiii).

Sigler's introduction surveys various historical and contemporary critical studies of the *Alice* books and notes a number of recent texts that also use *Alice* as a point of departure, but her primary interest lies in the nineteenth and early twentieth centuries' appropriation of the stories by both female and male writers in order to challenge and

Children's Literature 28, eds. Elizabeth Lennox Keyser and Julie Pfeiffer (Yale University Press, © 2000 Hollins University).

deconstruct the very concept of Alice (from the cultural right as well as from the left). Sigler asserts that the *Alice* revisions by Victorian women "illustrate the transition—especially important in the emergence of women writers—from private to public discourse: the transformation of private occasional writing for a particular child to a public text for popular consumption" (xviii) and that many of these texts subvert "the original texts' conservative images of Victorian girlhood and domestic ideology and present Alice-like heroines who demonstrate power and authority over their fantasy adventures" (xix). Curiously, this movement from private to public text is precisely that of the *Alice* books themselves, which, as the legend has it, began as an oral tale on a drowsy afternoon, matured into the gift book *Alice Underground* for the Liddell children, and ultimately evolved into the full-blown texts we know today. Part 1, "Subverting Wonderland," collects six texts that Sigler believes consciously attempt to undermine "the conventions of the Victorian fairy tale and domestic fiction [and] the gender conventions that inform them" (50). Sigler does not claim that all six stem directly from the *Alice* texts as imitations or retellings but rather that, in various ways, they all *react* to and against the *Alice* narratives and thereby expand the imaginative possibilities for their protagonists. Included in part 1 are selections from Ingelow, Ewing, C. Rossetti, Burnett, Maggie Browne, Anna M. Richards, and E. Nesbit. Sigler restricts the writers of part 1 to women—otherwise, George MacDonald (especially the "Princess" stories) might well have been included here.

In part 2, "The Didactic Looking Glass," Sigler presents three tales that "attempt to counter praise that focused on the novels' lack of moralizing" (xix). In "Naughty Children Land" from Alice Corkan's *Down the Snow Stairs* (1887), we are shown a rather Dantesque place where children practice setting the world on fire and "love to kill flies and butterflies and see them wiggle" (230); in the evangelically correct end, "two severe-looking dames, carrying birch rods . . . pounce" on the "horrid" children (232). Part 2, then, presents essentially conservative, reactionary responses to the apparent (if contingent) freedom and disorder of much of *Alice*'s Wonderland.

Part 3, "Sentimental Re-creations," contains four selections that "are concerned more with escape and laughter than with lessons or criticism" (xx). That they were often dedicated to a specific child may imply that they were intended more as diversions than as serious cultural or critical commentary. Even the titles included here, such as *The*

Wallypug of Why or *Uncle Wiggly in Wonderland* (Uncle Wiggly meets the March Hare or the White Rabbit?), suggest a certain lightness or playfulness certainly not found in, say, *Mopsa the Fairy* or *Speaking Likenesses* in part 1.

The final section, "Political Parodies," consists of five early twentieth-century stories that appropriate "the *Alice* books for adult audiences and concerns" and which "anticipate the gradual decline of the *Alice* imitation phenomenon in the early 1920s, as the *Alice* books were taken out of the literary public domain by virtue of their re-classification as serious objects of scholarship" (xx). The titles again reveal the content: *The Westminster Alice* (by Saki), *Alice in Blunderland, Alice in the Delighted States.* I question, however, the statement that the *Alice* books somehow left the "literary public domain"—although Freudian, post-Freudian, and other critics of course glommed onto *Alice* in the first half of the century, children (and, I presume, adults) continue to read and enjoy *Alice* without the immediate aid of an annotated version or of having to take Alice to Woolf's lighthouse.

In her introduction, Sigler suggests that the enduring popularity of *Alice* "responds to readers' desires . . . to possess not only the books, but the mythos surrounding the books' heroine" (xiii). Unfortunately, like most of the critics she surveys, Sigler cannot pin down just what this "mythos" consists of, except to say that the books' lasting "power and appeal may well lie in the fact that, like dreams, they *can* mean whatever readers *need* them to mean" (xiv, emphasis in original). If that is the case, do we all just climb up on the wall with Humpty Dumpty and declare words to be no more than arbitrary signs, or do we align with the White Knight and let meaning be our own invention? Although such protean, amorphic possibilities have a familiar postmodern ring, they nevertheless skirt the enduring metanarrativity of the *Alice* books. Although Sigler ably collects and sorts various types of spinoffs, *Alice* itself remains at the center, the hub of all this "industry," an overarching textual presence that reaches even into our own millennial time. It would have been interesting to have had more speculation from Sigler on the generative power of *Alice,* on the possibilities for liberation as well as constriction that it offers, or on its capacities for the anarchic, the carnivalesque.

Some thoughts on *Alternative Alices* and *Alice* itself: As Sigler points out, *Alice* is indirectly or directly responsible for all of the texts she collects; so, too, is *Alice* responsible for *Alternative Alices.* This may not be as simplistic as it sounds; like a grandchild who knows the grandparents only at a distance or from photographs, so too is *Alternative Alices* closer to the second generation than to the first. Readers will find much of interest in the various pieces that are compiled here, but they will not find much about their progenitor. Again, it might have been helpful to have more on the potential sources of *Alice's* enduring influence, on the enabling "why" of an anthology such as this. In the end, *Alternative Alices* is a fun book to browse around in: the selections are short, Sigler's categories make sense, and her introduction is useful. The anthology provides a nice intermediary between the full texts, many of which only a rather esoterically inclined reader might wish to confront, and the various *Alice* checklists, which codify but provide no textual samples (for a listing of these, see notes 3 and 21, pp. xxi–xxii, and Charles Lovett's *Alice on Stage*). Although *Alternative Alices* does not strike me as a book that one could readily *teach*, it is certainly a book in which one can enjoy encountering some of the less accessible descendants of the *Alice* books.

Work Cited

Lovett, Charles C. *Alice on Stage: A History of the Early Theatrical Productions of* Alice in Wonderland *Together with a Checklist of Dramatic Adaptations of Charles Dodgson's Works.* Westport, Conn.: Meckler, 1990.

Dealing with Victorian Fairies

Jan Susina

Victorian Fairy Painting, ed. Jane Martineau. London: Merrell Holberton, 1997.

Strange and Secret Peoples: Fairies and Victorian Consciousness, by Carol G. Silver. New York: Oxford University Press, 1999.

These two volumes explore the fascination and multiple meanings that fairies had for the Victorians. Although Rose Fyleman's 1917 poem "Fairies" begins with the line "There are fairies at the bottom of our garden!" (1), during the Victorian period, it seems, fairies could be found everywhere. One might say that the Victorians were obsessed with fairies. They frequently appear in art, music, and literature—for children and adults—as well as in the decorative arts. Charlotte Gere reports that when Queen Victoria visited the Great Exhibition of 1851, she suggested that the Crystal Palace had "quite the effect of fairyland" (64). Benjamin Disraeli privately referred to Queen Victoria as "the Faery," an ironic allusion to Edmund Spenser's *Faerie Queene.* More publicly, Gilbert and Sullivan's 1885 operetta *Iolanthe,* which was advertised as a "New and Original Fairy Opera," featured Iolanthe the Fairy Queen, who was widely assumed by the public to be a portrait of Queen Victoria.

Victorian Fairy Painting is focused on the visual interpretation of fairies—artwork, book illustration, and theatrical representation. It is the exhibition catalogue for the impressive "Victorian Fairy Painting," organized by Pamela White Tripe of the University of Iowa's Museum of Art in collaboration with the Royal Academy of Arts, London. Consequently, its primary strength lies in its beautiful full-color reproduction of seventy-six images by thirty-five artists. *Victorian Fairy Painting* stands on its own, however, as an extremely helpful visual companion to Carol Silver's *Strange and Secret Peoples,* which is a broader study of fairies emphasizing the use of folklore in Victorian culture. *Victorian Fairy Painting* is a valuable reference work since much of the artwork is in such fragile condition that it was only included in the London

Children's Literature 28, eds. Elizabeth Lennox Keyser and Julie Pfeiffer (Yale University Press, © 2000 Hollins University).

exhibition. Thus, the catalogue is more comprehensive than the impressive but select show that toured the United States and Canada. In addition to the stunning illustrations, *Victorian Fairy Painting* contains seven short critical essays. The most significant are "Victorian Fairy Painting" by Jeremy Maas, the art historian most responsible for promoting and elevating the status of Victorian art, and "Fairies on the Stage" by Lionel Lambourne, who notes that although literature provided the inspiration for fairy paintings, much of the visualization of fairies was drawn from the theater, opera, and ballet, and especially from pantomime produced for children.

Maas suggests that the Golden Age of fairy painting extended from 1840 to 1870, three decades that correspond with the Golden Age of children's literature. Although fairies have been a part of English and Irish folklore since the fourteenth century, most fairy pictures are based on literary sources. The most common literary references are to William Shakespeare's *A Midsummer's Night's Dream, The Tempest,* and the "Queen Mab" speech from *Romeo and Juliet.* Fairy tales became appropriate reading for children in England due to the success of Edgar Taylor's English translations of Jacob and Wilhelm Grimm's *German Popular Stories* (1823 and 1826). The Grimms' collection of traditional folktales was part of the Romantic movement in Germany, which helped establish fairy tales and fairy painting as a significant part of mid-Victorian culture. But it was also Wilhelm von Schlegel and Christoph Martin Wieland's translations of Shakespeare into German that helped initiate the Romantic movement in Germany. It is significant that the first English editions of *German Popular Stories* were illustrated by George Cruikshank, whose comic drawings helped make the tales accessible to children. Critics such as William Makepeace Thackeray and John Ruskin widely praised Cruikshank's imaginative book illustrations. Cruikshank would later illustrate his own *Fairy Library,* begun in 1853; his former friend and collaborator, Charles Dickens, doomed the series with his scathing attack "Frauds on the Fairies" in *Household Words* (1859), in which he took Cruikshank to task for rewriting traditional fairy tales.

Fairy paintings provided an alternative to the popular genre painting of scenes of ordinary life produced by artists such as William Frith and Augustus Egg. In contrast, fairy paintings create a mysterious glimpse into an unknown and forbidden world. Henry Fuseli's paintings clearly make the erotic an aspect of the fairy world, in contrast to the codes of Victorian respectability. Some may think that fairy paintings were just a ruse to paint and exhibit nudes by simply adding wings. But other artists, including William Blake, use fairies as part of a personal mythology or to express a longing for a more simple and elemental world.

In his essay Lambourne warns, "The politics of fairyland are never correct" (47). This evaluation is supported by the obsessive images and violent lives of some of the most prominent Victorian fairy painters. Maas suggests that fairy painting, more than most visual genres, was intimately linked to the exploration of the subconscious, which accounts for the numerous images of dreaming figures. This genre allowed the artists to explore opposing elements of the Victorian psyche including new attitudes toward sex, a curiosity about the unknown and forbidden, and a desire to escape respectability.

A minor but productive fairy painter, John Aster Fitzgerald, who earned the nickname "Fairy Fitzgerald," adds narcotics to the list of desires; several of his paintings include tell-tale medicine bottles of opium or steaming punches of the opium derivative, laudanum, clearly featured in works such as "The Artist's Dream" (1857). Maas argues that Fitzgerald's intense colors were the direct result of his opium use, and his paintings, such as "The Artist's Dream," certainly have a hallucinatory feel to them (19). Fitzgerald's use of dramatic lighting, however, is more inspired by the contemporary development of gaslight and limelight in theaters.

Although he only painted a dozen fairy paintings, most of which were only exhibited after his death, Richard Dadd is considered by Maas to be the "quintessential fairy painter" (14). He exhibited several fairy paintings at the Royal Academy in the 1840s, but it was only after his internment at the Bethlem Royal Hospital for murdering his father that he produced his two masterpieces, *Contradiction: Oberon and Titania* (1854–58) and *The Fairy Feller's Master Stroke* (1855–64). Dadd's obsession with detail results in congested and troubling designs that resemble medieval tapestries. The volume includes a disturbing photograph of Dadd in the act of painting *Contradiction* in the lunatic asylum. Mental illness also affected another fairy painter, John Altamont Doyle, the less successful brother of Richard Doyle. John Doyle voluntarily entered a lunatic asylum that he ironically referred to as "Sunnyside"; the sketchbooks of watercolors that he produced there reveal a vivid fairy world that provides an unsettling counterpart to the more public illustrations produced by his more successful brother. John's son, Arthur Conan Doyle, the author of the Sherlock Holmes stories, was influenced by his own beliefs in spiritualism and would write *The Coming of the Fairies* (1921), an emotional defense of the Cottingley fairy photographs.

Richard "Dickie" Doyle designed in 1843 the long-running cover for *Punch* magazine that included a number of fairies. He also illustrated John Ruskin's literary fairy tale *The King of the Golden River* (1851). Ruskin himself was no stranger to madness. But Richard Doyle's chief contributions to fairy painting are his thirty-six magnificent illustrations for *In Fairyland, Or Pictures from the Elf World* (1870), printed by Edmund Evans, which is often considered the masterpiece of Victorian book illustration. Doyle's comic illustrations of fairies far surpass William Allingham's poem "The Fairies," which they are meant to illustrate. Allingham's poem was first published in *The Music Master* (1855), where it was illustrated by Arthur Hughes—who would later illustrate George MacDonald's *Dealing with the Faeries* (1867)—and Dante Gabriel Rossetti—who would go on to illustrate his sister Christina's *Goblin Market and Other Poems* (1862). Andrew Lang, the compiler of the twelve-volume Color Fairy Book series, was so impressed with Doyle's illustrations that he rearranged them to create the literary fairy tale *Princess Nobody* (1884). As impressive as Doyle's book illustrations for *In Fairyland* are, and I believe it to be the greatest fairy book ever designed, even more impressive are the two large watercolors "The Enchanted Fairy Tree" (1845) and "The Fairy Tree" (undated) included in *Victorian Fairy Painting*. In my opinion, these two drawings surpass the works of Richard Dadd that are considered the most outstanding fairy paintings; Doyle's watercolors embody the comic genius of George Cruikshank while avoiding the overt eroticism that mars the work of Henry Fuseli and Joseph Noël Paton.

Paton's fairy paintings caught the eye of Lewis Carroll, who asked the artist to illustrate *Through the Looking-Glass* (1872), but Paton declined, insisting that John Tenniel was the man for the job. Carroll viewed Paton's "The Quarrel of Oberon and Titania" (1846–47) at the Scottish National Gallery in 1857 and, being a precise mathematician with a strong fascination with fairies, counted 156 of the creatures in the large painting.

Maas suggests that the Golden Age of fairy painting ended with the publication of *In Fairyland,* although the genre never completely died. The last great fairy art was produced by Arthur Rackham for J. M. Barrie's *Peter Pan in Kensington Garden* (1906), the major triumph of the artist's distinguished career. Walt Disney contacted Rackham and

hoped to have him develop some of the artwork for his first full-length
cartoon, *Snow White and the Seven Dwarves* (1937). *Victorian Fairy Painting*
gathers together the usual artists and illustrators who are associated
with the genre, but what is unusual is that it also includes artists who
are not normally associated with fairy painting. Edwin Landseer, John
Everett Millais, and J. M. W. Turner each produced at least one major
fairy painting during his career, suggesting the popularity of the genre
with Victorians. *Victorian Fairy Painting* is a fascinating study of the Victorian iconography of fairies, which blurred the distinctions between
high and low art and left a lasting mark on Victorian culture.

Whereas *Victorian Fairy Painting* is concerned with the visual and literary images of fairies, Silver's *Strange and Secret Peoples: Fairies and Victorian Consciousness* deals with the folkloristic aspect of fairies and how
the Victorian study of folklore from 1840 to 1870 functioned as a way
to reinscribe "the dominant ideas and the concealed anxieties of the
era" (57). Silver argues that the rise of science and social science in
the second half of the nineteenth century helped promote the serious
study of supernatural creatures such as fairies. Ironically Darwin, or
perhaps more accurately, social Darwinism, was used to justify the belief in fairies. Silver convincingly argues that it was the rise of Darwinism in the 1870s that made speculation on the existence of fairies re-
spectable. Who would have imagined Darwin on the side of the fairies?
Certainly not Charles Kingsley, who poked fun at the theory of evolution in his literary fairy tale *The Water Babies* (1863).

Folklore developed as an academic discipline in the nineteenth century along with other new fields of knowledge such as anthropology
and archeology. Folklore was dominated by amateur scholars, anti-
quarians, and field collectors. Much of Silver's study owes a great deal
to Richard Dorson's *The British Folklorists: A History* (1968) and its companion, the two-volume *Peasant Customs and Savage Myths* (1968). With
their interest in origins, many Victorians believed that the reality of
fairies would eventually be proved by scientific means.

Many folklorists, such as Thomas Croker and Thomas Keightley,
understood folk beliefs in fairies to be remnants of ancient Aryan religious thinking. Jacob and Wilhelm Grimm argued for a similar link
between German folk tales and mythology and proposed a similar
Aryan origin back in ancient India. Max Mueller, the Sanskrit scholar
at Oxford University, argues that fairies were part of folk beliefs that
were aspects of early mythopoeic thinking. Edward Burnet Tylor, the
founder of anthropology, maintained that all cultures went through

the same three-step evolutionary process of social development and that folk beliefs were survivals from an earlier, more savage period. Tylor made the study of fairies a significant aspect to the study of comparative anthropology and, according to his doctrine of survivals, folk tales were not just stories but embodiments of the earlier beliefs and customs.

Later David MacRitchie popularized the so-called pygmy theory in *The Testimony of Tradition* (1890), which associated fairy lore with archeology and suggested that underground mounds were evidence of an ancient, dwarflike, non-Aryan race in Britain (48). George Schweinfurth's discovery of African Pygmies in 1870 was used by some folklorists to support the pygmy theory of fairy origins and the existence of a race of fairies in Britain in a distant past. Silver notes that the Pygmies were constantly compared to goblins, gnomes, and brownies in the popular press. The discovery of Pygmies made fairies real; at the same time, their existence, coupled with the theory of cultural evolution that placed dark-skinned people at the bottom of the three stages of cultural evolution and white skinned people at the top, served to confirm the racial superiority of the English.

In a slightly different fashion, Victorian spiritualists, including William Butler Yeats and Arthur Conan Doyle, developed the concept of spiritual evolution, which linked scientific evidence to the existence of fairies. For the spiritualists, Darwin did not empty the world of nature but, as Silver writes, "peopled it with other invisible species" (56). The way folklorists and spiritualists used science and social science to support their beliefs in fairies is the process by which the demythified is remythified (129).

Silver then examines the process by which the fairies of existing folk beliefs were appropriated by educated Victorians and reconstructed via social Darwinism as monstrous symbols of the other. Concepts like that of the changeling—a child stolen by fairies for breeding purposes and replaced with a false child—were a way for educated Victorians to displace their fears of the lower classes and concerns about social mixing. The changeling was a folk explanation for disabled or diseased children, so that almost any abnormal child could be considered a changeling. This explanation for disease and deformity quickly found its way into Victorian literature, especially the novels of Dickens. The changeling theory then enabled middle-class Victorians to view the rural poor as another less culturally evolved group, like other colonized subjects of the British Empire. In a similar fashion, Silver shows how the folklorist's and the Victorian public's fascination with tales of fairy brides coincided, in the 1880s and 1890s, with the public debate on issues pertaining to women—the concept of the new woman, women's rights to property, and the marriage question.

Whereas *Victorian Fairy Painting* emphasizes the erotic elements that are to be found in fairies, Silver also observes what she calls fairy sadism (157) and the strong strand of violence and other antisocial behavior on their part. Fairies are shown to be compassionless and cruel and frequently at war with each other or with other creatures. They are generally characterized as an angry mob, wild and uncivilized. This brutal characterization of fairies allowed middle-class Victorians to feel pride in their own cultural evolution and maintain their racial superiority to other races and social groups. Silver emphasizes that this folk version of fairies is at odds with the fairy tales created for children, which promote a false set of sentimentalized assumptions. Such tales make fairies small and cute, little angels of nature who either entertain or protect children. She points out that such petite fairies are much more literary than folkloristic in origin. Fairies of folklore are a rather unpleasant, crude lot, creatures at best to be avoided, if not feared. With the gradual passing of folk beliefs and the increasing number of literary fairies, however, the creatures became domesticated and trivialized, so that the connections between children and fairies, children and fairy tales, was forged. This romanticizing and sentimentalization of fairies was still another way for the urban middle class to neutralize a once powerful social source of rural and lower-class power in Victorian culture. After reading Silver's remarkable study of Victorian folklore and the folk construction of the fairies, one no longer will be able to look at the charming images of Victorian fairy painting with such an innocent eye. Beneath those diminutive features may lurk a hostile attitude.

Those interested in nineteenth-century children's literature and fairy tales in particular will find both *Victorian Fairy Painting* and *Strange and Secret Peoples* fascinating cultural history and necessary reading. Using differing critical lenses, both volumes provide an extremely rich and ambiguous cultural context for Victorian fairies.

Works Cited

Dorson, Richard M. *The British Folklorists: A History*. Chicago: University of Chicago Press, 1968.

————, ed. *Peasant Customs and Savage Myths: Selections from the British Folklorists.* 2 vols. Chicago: University of Chicago Press, 1968.

Fyleman, Rose. "Fairies." In *The Rose Fyleman Fairy Book.* New York: Doran, 1923. Pp. 1–2.

Gere, Charlotte. "In Fairyland." In *Victorian Fairy Painting.* Ed. Jane Martineau. London: Merrell Holberton, 1997. Pp. 63–72.

Lambourne, Lionel. "Fairies and the Stage." In *Victorian Fairy Painting.* Ed. Jane Martineau. London: Merrell Holberton, 1997. Pp. 46–53.

Maas, Jeremy. "Victorian Fairy Painting." In *Victorian Fairy Painting.* Ed. Jane Martineau. London: Merrell Holberton, 1997. Pp. 10–21.

Silver, Carole G. *Strange and Secret Peoples: Fairies and Victorian Consciousness.* New York: Oxford University Press, 1999.

Reading a Feminist Romance: Literary Critics and Little Women

Gregory Eiselein

Little Women: *A Family Romance,* by Elizabeth Lennox Keyser. New York: Twayne, 1999.

Little Women *and the Feminist Imagination: Criticism, Controversy, Personal Essays,* ed. Janice M. Alberghene and Beverly Lyon Clark. New York and London: Garland, 1999.

Prior to 1940, as Alberghene and Clark explain in their introduction and as Aiko Moro-oka and Clark and Linnea Hendrickson document in the volume's bibliographies, Louisa May Alcott's work was never discussed in professional literary journals. Beginning with Madeleine Stern's and Leona Rostenberg's work in the 1940s and especially since the mid-70s, academic attention to Alcott has expanded exponentially. The major reason for this transformation in critical attitudes has been feminism. Earlier in the century critics were accustomed to seeing this popular girls' book as "beyond the reach of criticism" (qtd. in Alberghene and Clark xxix). Alcott's later, feminist critics disagreed, and their analysis discovered a significant cultural phenomenon and a resonant work of art.

It is perhaps also true that feminist critics needed *Little Women.* It was an opportunity to consider the construction of gender; the value of women's and girls' experience, intellect, and creativity; the importance of women's and girls' relationships with other women and girls; the role of identification and affect in reading; and the question of women's power (what constitutes rebellion, resistance, subversion, submission? how do you tell the difference?). These are the issues that animate Little Women: *A Family Romance* and Little Women *and the Feminist Imagination,* though the treatment of these characteristically feminist concerns is often surprising.

Divided into two sections, "Literary and Historical Context" (chapters 1–3) and "A Reading" of the novel and its sequels (chapters 4–9), Little Women: *A Family Romance* does not explicitly announce itself

Children's Literature 28, eds. Elizabeth Lennox Keyser and Julie Pfeiffer (Yale University Press, © 2000 Hollins University).

as feminist in the way the Alberghene and Clark volume does, but its feminist perspective is salient. The opening chapter, "Historical and Biographical Context," highlights the well-known biographical connections between the novel and Alcott's life as well as the formative influence of the women's movement on Alcott. Chapter 2, "The Importance of the Work," examines not only the novel's influence on the female bildungsroman but also "the role that *Little Women* has played in the lives of countless women and girls" (13). Keyser's account of the novel's critical reception (chapter 3) devotes most of its attention to feminist examinations of the novel, though such an emphasis perhaps reflects the history of Alcott's critical treatment within the academy as much as Keyser's own theoretical orientation.

As her subtitle suggests, Keyser's reading of *Little Women* turns partly around the Freudian notion of "family romances," the daydreams in which subjects imagine for themselves new relations with their family members. Such fantasies (for instance, imagining oneself born of aristocrats, though living with a set of imposter parents) are part of developmental processes whereby subjects liberate themselves from parental authority to establish an identity. Keyser uses the Freudian concept to shed light, for example, on Jo's dream of becoming a writer. Freud tells us that such daydreams "have two principal aims, erotic and ambitious" (qtd. on 33), and Keyser demonstrates the concept's relevance to *Little Women* by showing how Jo's own conflicted family romance involves her ambitious desire for fame and her erotic wish to win her family's approval.

Yet Keyser's deployment of the family romance formulation is not simply an application of Freudian theory. Indeed her departures from Freud are as interesting as her uses of his work. Although she is extraordinarily attentive to the dark, aggressive aspects of Alcott's writing (as she demonstrates in her dazzling *Whispers in the Dark* [1993]), Keyser's family romance theory does not always take up Freud's emphasis on hostility, retaliation, and devaluation of parents. Instead she highlights the idealizing and romanticizing of family members as a means of distancing subjects from their parents. Moreover, Keyser has seized the notion of "family romances" not merely for its developmental psychology but also for its allusion to Hawthorne's romances, its association with popular romance heroines, and its relevance to the erotic nature of the relations within the March family.

In chapters 5–8, Keyser provides a tour de force of interpretation of *Little Women* from opening scene to final tableau. Certain themes reappear in the course of her reading: the development of individual identity, the sometimes fluid, sometimes ambiguous treatment of gender and sexuality, the intensity of the relations among the March sisters and Marmee. But Keyser's analysis is not polemical. She prefers to reveal the ambiguities and conflicts that shape the story and avoids assigning absolute meanings. For example, her treatment of Jo's marriage (a topic that generates strong positions among readers and critics) is actually a series of questions, a laying out of possibilities and complications: "Is *Little Women* a romantic story, encouraging us, rightly or wrongly, to believe that romance is both attainable and sustainable? Or does Alcott, especially by having Jo marry Professor Bhaer, deflate romance in favor of a more prosaic but ultimately more satisfying version of reality? Or does she despair of either?" (87). Such an approach is ideal for a volume intended for a broad audience that will include general readers wondering what to make of a classic, college students, teachers, and scholars. Students who turn to this book, when writing a term paper or simply wanting a better grasp on the novel, will not find a plot summary and explanation of its "deeper" meaning. Instead they'll find Keyser's expert delineation of the questions and contradictions that make *Little Women* a memorable novel. Teachers and critics will notice that because the analysis rejects easy answers in favor of open-ended inquiry, Little Women: *A Family Romance* is valuable pedagogically and critically. (There are also a useful chronology and a bibliography; "Appendix: Approaches to Teaching" offers teachers various ways to encourage critical thinking and in-class exchange about the novel.)

Like feminist critics before her, Keyser opens up aspects of the novel that some readers might quickly pass over or dismiss. For instance, always identifying with Jo, I never paid much attention to Amy—except as that awful little girl who burns Jo's book and gets everything Jo doesn't (a trip to Europe, Laurie, sunshine). I disliked Amy and tended to ignore her. Keyser's analysis—here and in "'The Most Beautiful Things in All the World'? Families in *Little Women*" (reprinted in Little Women *and the Feminist Imagination*)—compels one to rethink such a perception. Whereas many readers find Amy selfish, Keyser sees also a "sturdy independence" (39). Beneath Amy's "outer conformity," Keyser detects a "strong sense of self" (78). Although the narrator moralizes about Amy's selfishness and vanity, the novel may also subvert that moralizing. "After all, it is Amy's *amour propre* and vitality that are rewarded" (45). Lest one start to think such subversion an anomalous mistake, Keyser clarifies this "distinguishing feature of *Little Women*": "some of the most thought-provoking and potentially subversive passages are those in which the narrator appears to be preaching. Readers who skip or skim over these passages to avoid a sermon miss their subversiveness as well" (45). Such insights are as helpful to professors as they are to students.

Alberghene and Clark's Little Women *and the Feminist Imagination* also guides readers to subversive and overlooked aspects of Alcott's art. Yet where Keyser's slim volume offers a distinguished critic's nuanced reading, Alberghene and Clark assemble a nearly five-hundred-page archive of feminist scholarship. Their introduction explains the project, previews the contributions, and narrates with lavish documentation a history of *Little Women* in the popular and critical imagination. The twenty contributions that follow provide a marvelously diverse view of *Little Women* as a feminist text and as a text read by feminists.

Alberghene and Clark devote about 20 percent of Little Women *and the Feminist Imagination* to previously published pieces. These include the best from the late-70s feminist interest in Alcott (Nina Auerbach's "Waiting Together: Alcott on Matriarchy" and Judith Fetterley's "*Little Women:* Alcott's Civil War") and a pair of more recent essays (Keyser's piece on families and Catharine R. Stimpson's wonderful "Reading for Love: Canons, Paracanons, and Whistling Jo March"). To indicate that scholarly books and journals are not the only venues for feminist interpretations of Alcott, the editors reprint Ann Douglas's introduction to a 1983 paperback edition of *Little Women,* Victoria Roberts's 1988 cartoon from *Ms.,* "Meg, Amy, Beth, Jo, and Marmee Face Life in the '80s," and a 1995 *New York Times* article on the Hollywood versions of *Little Women,* Anne Hollander's "Portraying *Little Women* Through the Ages."

Perhaps the most exciting part of Little Women *and the Feminist Imagination* is the wealth of brilliant new critical essays. The most impressive and informative of these treat *Little Women* in relation to a specific historical or cultural context. In "A Greater Happiness: Searching for Feminist Utopia in *Little Women,*" an essay well suited to this collection, Kathryn Manson Tomasek explores the novel as "a site of feminist utopian thought" (237), linking the novel to nineteenth-century utopian reformers and their acceptance, rejection, and revision of nineteenth-century gender ideology. Susan R. Gannon's "Getting Cozy with a Classic: Visualizing *Little Women* (1868–1995)" examines the relation between the novel and the history of its visual representations, from

May Alcott's first-edition illustrations to twentieth-century covers, films, and posters. Gannon illustrates convincingly that popularizing visualizations have ignored the novel's complexity and its darker or unconventional implications and scenes. In "'A Power in the House': *Little Women* and the Architecture of Individual Expression," a splendid interdisciplinary essay that draws from detailed knowledge of the Alcott family homes and mid-nineteenth-century thinking about domestic architecture, David H. Watters takes a close look at the architecture and decor of the various residences in *Little Women*. Designed to foster self-expression, the styles of these homes mirror the architectural theory and practice of the era as well as the novel's thematic concern with the March girls' individual development.

Other critics in this collection contextualize Alcott within a transatlantic literary history. In "The Prophets and the Martyrs: Pilgrims and Missionaries in *Little Women* and *Jack and Jill*," a persuasive and even-handed essay on the misunderstood significance of *Pilgrim's Progress* to Alcott's work, Anne K. Phillips shows how Bunyan's worldview provided Alcott's pilgrims with a kind of liberation from societal constraints of the nineteenth century, countering the supposition that the novel's Bunyanesque elements restrain and subordinate the girls. If one wants to see lessons in conformity and submission, Phillips suggests, don't look at the happy, feminist protagonists of *Little Women;* look instead at the dreadfully conventional and self-denying missionaries in Alcott's second-to-last novel, *Jack and Jill*. Christine Doyle's "Transatlantic Translations: Communities of Education in Alcott and Brontë" also examines *Little Women*'s literary influences. By examining Brontë's impact on Alcott's work and comparing their representations of educational communities, Doyle distinguishes Alcott as a specifically American writer who transformed a pessimistically Brontëan attitude toward educational institutions (as in *Little Women*) into her own more hopeful vision of family-based schooling (as depicted in *Jo's Boys*).

In "Learning from Marmee's Teaching: Alcott's Response to Girls' Miseducation," Susan Laird takes up Doyle's interest in Alcott as educational thinker and writer. Laird considers the significance and limitations of Alcott's feminist pedagogy and the ways her ideas might inform contemporary efforts to contest the miseducation of girls. One of the limitations she identifies is Alcott's evasion of the difficult questions of race in America, something Alberghene likewise notes in "Autobiography and the Boundaries of Interpretation: On Reading *Little*

Women and *The Living Is Easy.*" Using personal memoir and a comparative critical analysis of Dorothy West's *The Living Is Easy* as a response to *Little Women,* Alberghene asks "what difference race might make in reading *Little Women*" (347). West's (and Alberghene's) critique of Alcott's "privileging of whiteness" (347) is trenchant, and the reading of *The Living Is Easy* reveals West's powerful, complex, and often ironic treatment of race, class, gender, and identity.

Like Alberghene, Sue Standing and Jan Susina also offer autobiographical responses to *Little Women,* a novel that seems to encourage subjective readings. Standing's "In Jo's Garret: *Little Women* and the Space of Imagination" turns to personal narrative and textual fragments from various authors to meditate on the notion of space in *Little Women* and in her own life. In "Men and *Little Women:* Notes of a Resisting (Male) Reader," Jan Susina uses a personal voice to suggest that "Alcott systematically limits participation by male readers in the novel" (169), and he asks an important question: "Why don't more male readers read *Little Women?*" (161). His answer may seem disappointing, however, as it emphasizes Alcott's women-centered focus and the supposed inadequacy of her male characters while avoiding a discussion of, say, the sexual politics of education and the canon or the systematic cultural devaluation of women and girls.

Personally, I never felt excluded by the novel, and Alcott's thinking about men, women, gender, and sexuality strikes me as remarkably progressive. As critics have long understood, Jo's (and Laurie's) gender identity hardly conforms to essentialist ideas about sex. Before Simone de Beauvoir (a devoted reader of *Little Women*), Alcott understood that one is not born, but rather becomes, a little woman. Representing that perspective in this volume, Roberta Seelinger Trites's " 'Queer Performances': Lesbian Politics in *Little Women*" sees Jo's refusal to conform to socially prescribed gender roles as not only a dissent from essentialist notions of femininity but also "a critique of heterosexuality that can be read as a strong affirmation of lesbian politics" (139). Because "the destruction of the independent, energetic, and endearing Jo" in *Good Wives* is also "the destruction of the lesbian Jo" (155), Trites sees the novel's ending as "tragic," a lesson about how "patriarchy ultimately divides and conquers the women who empower each other through their love" (156). In an equally innovative essay, "Songs to Aging Children: Louisa May Alcott's March Trilogy," Michelle A. Massé sees Jo's development from narcissistic teenage tomboy to rather maternal adult woman as far less tragic. In the course of the trilogy, Jo learns to balance her own autonomy with connection to others; hence, according to Massé, "the older Jo is no sham stand-in for the younger but, instead, the result of a genuine maturation" (332).

Taken together, Trites's and Massé's essays exemplify what I most admire about Little Women: *A Family Romance* and Little Women *and the Feminist Imagination:* they offer up conversations, dialogues, dilemmas, questions. They invite in seasoned academics as well as readers new to *Little Women*. They encourage scholarly, subjective, critical, and self-critical responses to the novel. In other words, these volumes are ideal examples of how discerning feminist criticism can open up and make surprising again a text as culturally familiar as *Little Women*. They are also models of feminist pedagogy in action.

The Wizard of Oz *in the Twentieth Century: Studying Baum's Masterwork*

Anne K. Phillips

The Wizard of Oz: Shaping an Imaginary World, by Suzanne Rahn. New York: Twayne, 1998.

In time for the centenary of L. Frank Baum's *The Wizard of Oz* (1900), Twayne has published Suzanne Rahn's *The Wizard of Oz: Shaping an Imaginary World* as a selection in its Masterwork Studies series. The volume includes a detailed chronology, three short background chapters, "The Historical Context," "The Importance of *The Wizard of Oz*," and "The Critical Reception," and four chapters presumably organized around Rahn's own reading of the novel: "The Road to the Emerald City," "Dorothy Opens the Door: The Inner Landscape of Oz," "'Now We Can Cross the Shifting Sands': The Outer Landscape of Oz," and "'Toto, I've a Feeling We're Not in Kansas Anymore': The Movie's Oz." Rahn's book includes a striking frontispiece of Baum, representative illustrations by W. W. Denslow and John R. Neill, and maps of portions of Oz and the surrounding countries. Nonetheless, the text itself suffers from a lack of organization and an unclear conception of its audience that undermine its substance and usefulness.

Problems with organization, particularly with unnecessary duplication and repetition of material, plague the volume. There are no different contexts or circumstances justifying the repetition; instead, such examples convey the impression that the book was hastily written or not carefully edited. For instance, Rahn uses the same quotation from *The Wizard of Oz,* "Everyone seemed happy and contented and prosperous," on page 34 and again on page 36, with no apparent recognition in the latter instance that she has previously addressed it. In chapter 4, she refers in only slightly greater detail to the scholarship of Henry M. Littlefield, which she has already summarized in chapter 3. She introduces and returns to very similar descriptions of Rose Lawn, Baum's childhood home, in chapters 4 and 6. The same quotation from C. Warren Hollister, "Where is the theme? The theme is Oz,"

Children's Literature 28, eds. Elizabeth Lennox Keyser and Julie Pfeiffer (Yale University Press, © 2000 Hollins University).

appears on pages 27 and 79, and Rahn's summary of the movie's popularity (touching on exactly the same details) can be found on page 9 and page 109. In none of these cases does the second reference significantly expand on the subject matter. The repetition also gives the volume a curiously circular approach that undermines its effect. These duplicated materials suggest that the chapter organization developed for this volume has not served its content as it should, or that Rahn needed to reconceptualize the content of the early chapters in particular.

The volume's sense of its audience is equally unfocused. Is it intended for teachers, as the appendix, "Approaches to Teaching *The Wizard of Oz*," would suggest? If so, the ideas contained here, including map-drawing and celebrating the author's birthday, are not especially challenging, even for elementary school students. Although Rahn includes a list of other fantasy novels that might serve as related reading, there is no substance to her comparisons, no guideline for teachers to consider or follow in studying fantasy. Rahn's potentially useful suggestion in this section that teachers introduce their students to the kinds of discussion generated by enthusiasts and scholars through such groups as the International Wizard of Oz Club or "any of several Oz discussion groups on the Internet" (133) would be more valuable if she included the addresses for these groups in the appendix or elsewhere in the volume.

If the volume isn't well-designed for teachers, might it be effective for students, as the promotional material printed on the back cover of the dust jacket would suggest? We are told that the Masterworks series provides "[a] necessary addition to collections serving high school and university students." If so, the overview of critical commentaries on the novel and other sections need to be developed to be comprehensible to this audience. For instance, in chapter 3, "The Critical Reception," Rahn provides no more than one- or two-sentence references to the critical analyses of Baum's book; she doesn't provide enough context for students at any level to comprehend or apply them. Referring to Marius Bewley's 1970 essay "The Land of Oz: America's Great Good Place," Rahn provides a one-sentence summary: "The tension between pastoralism and technology, he argues, is one of the main themes of American literature, and in Oz that tension is successfully resolved" (19). Providing even a brief explanation of pastoralism, for instance, might make this a much more useful, meaningful reference for student audiences—a concept they might practice applying to Baum's novel even without finding and reading Bewley's article. (Such a brief description is also not likely to inspire them to seek out Bewley's essay.) Also in chapter 3, summarizing what is known about Anne Carroll Moore's and other librarians' blacklisting of the Oz books, Rahn includes a note directing readers to Angelica Shirley Carpenter and Jean Shirley's *L. Frank Baum: Royal Historian of Oz* (1992) for further information about recent censorship of the novel. Wouldn't it have been more useful preparation for classroom discussion or writing assignments to include at least a paragraph within the text about the various reasons behind contemporary attempts to censor Baum's work? For a student audience, more specifics and more context would make Rahn's discussion far more significant and compelling.

Is this volume, then, for scholars of children's or American literature? If so, it remains a frustrating reading experience because it relies so heavily on Michael Patrick Hearn's Critical Heritage edition (1983), which incorporates the 1900 text, other short, relevant writings by Baum, and key critical commentaries from the 1920s to the 1980s by such figures as Edward Wagenknecht, Ray Bradbury, and Gore Vidal. Scholars already familiar with that volume will find little in this one that is new and significant; although Rahn discusses the characters, setting, theme, and other literary elements in some detail, her approach is descriptive rather than analytic. Similarly, readers familiar with Aljean Harmetz's *The Making of* The Wizard of Oz or Noel Langley, Florence Yerson, and Edgar Allan Woolf's The Wizard of Oz: *The Screenplay* (with its extensive introduction by Hearn) may find it difficult to discover what is new and original in Rahn's discussion of the 1939 film adaptation in chapter 7.

This would have been a splendid opportunity to trace in greater detail the work that has been done in the fifteen years since Hearn's edition appeared, or to discuss the recent contributions of scholars in areas other than what Rahn identifies as the most common approaches to Baum's novel: "the literary historical, the sociopolitical . . . , the spiritual, and the psychological" (19). New Historicism, for instance, has brought Stuart Culver, David Westbrook, and others to new discoveries about Oz. But other than references to the titles of some of these works in the notes and the bibliography, very little of that recent work has been incorporated or considered here.

This is a pity, because Rahn can be a fine scholar. Her argument in chapter 4 that Frank Stockton (as much as Carroll or Andersen) is an important influence on Baum (inspired perhaps by her work on Stockton for a chapter in her earlier book, *Rediscoveries in Children's Literature* [1995]), has merit in its specific comparison of Stockton's and Baum's fiction and, perhaps more important, in its contribution to our development of a distinctly American tradition in children's literature. In addition, her extensive analysis in the same chapter of the probable influence of the 1893 Chicago World's Fair on Baum's vision of the Emerald City is the most well-developed, specific, and compelling sequence in the volume.

Rahn does incorporate some recent work: on a relatively minor point, for instance, she draws on a 1996 article in the *Baum Bugle* in her discussion of the possible influence on Baum of the death of his wife's niece—a four-month-old girl named Dorothy. It is quite probable that the Dorothy Gale of Baum's masterpiece could have been a tribute and memorial to the Dorothy Gage who is buried in Indiana. And it's exciting to see Rahn argue against previously published (and commonly accepted) interpretations of the text and the film—for instance, she suggests that Salman Rushdie's British Film Institute publication on the film version of *The Wizard of Oz* doesn't accurately interpret the landscape of the film Oz. This is only a brief reference, however; more development of this idea and more specific refutation of earlier critics throughout the book might have made Rahn's own argument seem more concrete and original. At the very least, she should have more carefully distinguished the ways in which her work contributes to the tradition of commentary on *The Wizard of Oz*—to provide a capstone to the work that has been done on Oz throughout the twentieth century and to prepare the way for twenty-first-century scholars who will continue to study Baum's classic American novel.

"Where the Girls Are"—and Aren't

June Cummins

Delinquents and Debutantes: Twentieth-Century American Girls' Cultures, ed. Sherrie A. Inness. New York: New York University Press, 1998.

With this absorbing and compelling collection of essays concerned with the lives, habits, and attitudes of American girls throughout the twentieth century, Sherrie Inness aims to correct what she sees as the hegemonic view that "girls are inconsequential" (1). To this end, Inness assembles essays providing fresh perspectives on the ways in which American girls have reflected as well as shaped social attitudes toward girlhood throughout the century. Often working within a system that forces them into molds and inhibits exceptional or individual claims and practices, but also at times actively challenging those forces and breaking out of those molds, girls have found ways to both accommodate and resist. Through essays that look closely at what may seem to be very narrow swaths of girls' culture, this collection establishes that girls as a unit have significant, growing power and are themselves forces to be reckoned with. As a whole, this collection is highly informative and inspiring about the roles of girls in American culture. At the same time, it is somewhat weakened by a curious distancing effect. Although girls' culture is discussed in detail, girls themselves often seem to be hovering on the edges of several of these essays rather than being their primary focus. This is an interesting tension in a book that argues that girls and their culture have been marginalized and not been adequately studied (1).

Perhaps one reason for this distancing effect is that the book is deeply invested in historical analyses of girls' culture. Seven of the thirteen essays provide interpretations of cultural events, movements, and artifacts occurring before the 1960s. A minority of the essays (five) are concerned with girls' lives in the 1990s, and it happens that a few of these essays are among the thinnest in the collection, although it should also be said that one of the strongest essays, "Producing Girls: Rethinking the Study of Female Youth Culture," focuses on this time period. Generally speaking, however, and especially because the es-

Children's Literature 28, eds. Elizabeth Lennox Keyser and Julie Pfeiffer (Yale University Press, © 2000 Hollins University).

says tend to deal with the material aspects of girls' culture rather than girls themselves, the contemporary girl is somehow absent, her experiences less accounted for and probed. In and of itself, this relative absence is not problematic, but in a book attempting to cultivate interest in girls and their culture, it seems that the contemporary girl should have been more rather than less present.

That said, some of the historical essays are excellent. In particular, Rhona Justice-Malloy's "Little Girls Bound: Costume and Coming of Age in the 'Sears Catalog' 1906–1927" is a compelling analysis of how the Sears Catalog not only mirrored but propagated changing ideas of women's fashions during this period. After establishing the dominance of the Sears Catalog for many segments of society throughout this period, Justice-Malloy sensitively and closely examines how seemingly small changes in women's clothing reflected changing attitudes toward women and their roles in society. For example, the "Gibson Girl" look, popular from 1906 to 1909, forced the female form into the unnatural position of a greatly extended, forward-thrusting bust and large, backward-thrusting bottom, pushing the body into an S shape. Intelligently using kinetic theory, which focuses on the meanings of how bodies move in space, Justice-Malloy demonstrates how girls and women's bodies were unbalanced, restricted, and idealized with this enforced S shape. In later years, female clothing became much less restrictive, allowing girls and women more freedom of movement and access to physical activities, such as sports, previously considered the domain of men and boys. Yet even the columnar "flapper" look enforced an unnatural coercion of the female body as it attempted to deny breasts and hips, literally through squelching them with corsets and binding brassieres. Fascinatingly, Justice-Malloy connects this cylindrical look with increased social attention to the machine and other industrial developments: the ideal female form mimicked the piston that drove the modern machine. With such observations, Justice-Malloy connects girls' and women's culture to the general society, proving the significance and depth of its role.

Another historical essay that also provides important contextual information is Rachel Devlin's "Female Juvenile Delinquency and the Problem of Sexual Authority in America, 1945–1965." Devlin analyzes the rise in female juvenile delinquency during this time period, noting that such behavior could range from "immorality" and "ungovernability," which were not criminal activities in and of themselves, to

theft, assault, and other activities that clearly were. Linking these behaviors to economic and social conditions after the war, Devlin concentrates especially on the reconfiguration and significance of the
father-daughter relationship. The teenage girl "became a site for the
expression of cultural anxiety about the authority of the family generally and of fathers specifically" (84). Devlin's examination of the treatment of female juvenile delinquency in the popular and academic
media reveals that many commentators saw the problem in psychoana-
lytic terms, especially those of the Oedipal complex, demonstrating
both the growth of the delinquency and the prevalence of the psycho-
analytic approach to explaining social changes. Devlin also incorporates class analysis in her insightful study of the changing relations
between fathers and daughters as well as the implications of female
juvenile delinquency in the Cold War era.

Similarly, Mary C. McComb's essay, "Rate Your Date: Young Women
and the Commodification of Depression Era Courtship," analyzes the
dating attitudes and practices of college men and women during the
Depression from an economic perspective. Although most college-
aged people were not enrolled in college at this time, those who were
received a lot of attention in the form of media directed to them, particularly advice books that gave lessons on social behavior, attracting
a mate, and marriage. McComb's analysis exposes how the writers of
these books advocated a kind of courtship marketplace that overtly
viewed women as commodity objects. The goal of a young woman,
then, was to increase her market value as much as possible. These
books and manuals provided extensive, detailed advice as to how
to achieve this increased value, ranging from encouraging college
women to send themselves flowers so it will appear that they are being
courted by more than one man to dissuading bright, achievement-
oriented women from developing intellectually. For example, one
manual describes a woman "who wishes to pursue a career in science
as someone who wishes to compete with men rather than as a person
who desires a rewarding vocation" (57). McComb does an excellent
job explaining why the hard economic realities of the Depression era
motivated these advice writers to "reinforc[e] male dominance in gender relations [so as to] bring about an end to the crisis of masculinity
and help to mediate the larger economic crisis faced by the nation"
(44). Although McComb might have explained in more detail the origins and effects of this crisis of masculinity and its connection to view-

ing the dating and mating process as an economic exchange, she very successfully describes and analyzes the impact of that crisis on the culture of young women.

Other historically based essays lack these contextual examinations or do not take opportunities to explore the ramifications of the cultural movements or changes they describe. For example, Laureen Tedesco's essay on the beginnings of the scouting movement, "Making a Girl a Scout: Americanizing Scouting for Girls," provides an interesting historical overview of how this organization was started in the United States at the beginning of the twentieth century, focusing especially on how it separated itself both from its British counterpart and from the Boy Scouts of America. Tedesco sees these processes of separation as modes of resistance, an intriguing argument. But she does not follow through with what this sort of resistance might mean for developing girls. In fact, her potentially most intriguing points are formed as projects for future researchers, including this one: "How all of this affected twentieth-century American womanhood, however, requires more study" (35). Tedesco's essay ultimately seems more descriptive than analytical when she does not fit her ideas into the general purported goals of the book.

Other essays that are removed in time and thus do not incorporate the voices or experiences of girls living in the second half of the century but that are nonetheless thoughtful and revelatory include "Truculent and Tractable: The Gendering of Babysitting in Postwar America," by Miriam Formanek-Brunell, and "The Flapper and the Chaperone: Cultural Constructions of Identity and Heterosexual Politics Among Adolescent Mexican American Women, 1920–1950," by Vicki L. Ruiz. Formanek-Brunell discusses the surprising politicization of babysitting by the babysitters themselves and by the adults trying to control this emerging employment category; Ruiz provides insight into generational, cultural, and gendered conflict in an immigrant community that has not yet received much attention.

It is important to note that one reason why girls may seem relatively silent in this collection is that most of the essays deal with adolescents. In fact, only one essay deals directly with material aimed at girls younger than twelve years of age, Sherrie Inness's " 'Anti-Barbies': The American Girls Collection and Political Ideologies." Even the essay by Jennifer Scanlon about board games, which would seem to be about grade-school girls, is not, as its title demonstrates: "Boys-R-Us: Board Games and the Socialization of Young Adolescent Girls." The almost total absence of the younger girl in these essays is indicative of a problem larger than this book alone—the erasure of preadolescent girlhood. Girls at younger and younger ages are pushed to grow up faster and faster, as illustrated by the clothes, media, and entertainment choices marketed to them, and their childhoods are almost completely obviated. In this regard, *Delinquents and Debutantes* obtains a certain sad veracity in its omission of the elementary-school-aged girl.

Finally, another reason why actual girls participating in contemporary culture seem somewhat elided in this collection is that several of the essays deal with very small groups of people, thus making it difficult to generalize from them to the wider culture of girlhood. For example, Angela E. Hubler's "Can Anne Shirley Help 'Revive Ophelia'?: Listening to Girl Readers" is concerned with how girls' "views of femininity [are] influenced by reading" (268). Hubler talked with forty-two girls, but her essay is based "primarily" on the interviews with six individual girls (269). Her conclusions are intelligent and interesting, but they are limited by this small sample size.

It may not be a coincidence, then, that some of the most successful essays concern mass media that reach many girls across the country. In addition to Justice-Malloy's essay on the Sears catalog, two different essays discuss the role of magazines. " 'Teena Means Business': Teenage Girls' Culture and *Seventeen* Magazine, 1944–1950," by Kelly Schrum, provides a sensitive examination of the genesis and evolution of the first hugely successful periodical marketed to teenage girls. Debuting in 1944, *Seventeen* was able to declare that it was being read by more than half of American teenage girls by 1947 (139). Schrum focuses specifically on how the magazine, in developing a readership, was also developing a market. As they created a readership for the magazine, the editors were also creating consumers, and these two roles became inseparably intertwined in the teenager. Delving deeply into economic, political, and social analyses of the editorial content of the magazine, the advertising, and the communication between the readers and the editors, Shrum very convincingly proves her assertion that *Seventeen* "articulated a complex, multifaceted set of identities of the teenage girl as consumer and citizen" (159).

One of the strongest essays in the collection, Mary Celeste Kearney's "Producing Girls: Rethinking the Study of Female Youth Culture," also examines the role of teen magazines (including *Seventeen*) in girls' culture and views the contemporary girl as both one who is produced ideologically by society and one who herself produces the culture she

inhabits. An excellent companion piece to " 'Teena Means Business,' "
Kearney's essay continues the investigation of the evolution of teen
magazines and girls' responses to them. Providing a useful overview
of previous studies of female youth culture, which were mostly concerned with girls as consumers, Kearney broadens the investigation of
this cohort to view girls as actively responding to and shaping their
worlds, not just passively consuming what is proffered to them.
Through activities such as writing letters to the editors of national
magazines and producing "zines" that are disseminated on paper or
through the Internet, contemporary girls seem much more resistant
to dominant discursive modes and able to criticize and circumvent
their ideologies. Kearney includes the sad story of *Sassy* magazine, a
breakthrough periodical that consciously departed from magazines
like *Seventeen* through addressing taboo topics such as sexuality and
eating disorders, publishing overtly politicized editorial copy, and pos-
iting their young readers as intelligent, active producers as well as consumers of society. Unfortunately, when *Sassy* was sold to Petersen Publishing, it was forced to do an about-face, and it quickly became no
different from the mainstream fashion-and-beauty-soaked magazines
already on the market. Kearney quotes extensively from girl-produced
zines; in her essay the teenage girl is perhaps more present than she is
anywhere else in the collection. Her voice is clearly heard.

With this last essay, Inness fully reaches the goal that in her introduction she sets out to accomplish: making real and viable the American teenage girl who has so often been slighted as a subject worthy
of academic and sociological inquiry. Interestingly, the cover of the
paperback edition is indirectly a comment on the tension between absence and presence this book straddles. An extreme closeup of the
face of a teenage girl, her face literally "in your face," the cover photograph displays a wide-open mouth with two tongue piercings, a nose
with a nose ring through the septum, and two eyes darkened with mas-
cara. The picture is disconcerting, even frightening (my young children insisted I turn the book over when they were in the room, claiming that the cover was "scary and ugly") and inarguably off-putting. On
one hand, the picture seems oddly chosen if the goal of the collection
is to draw people to a segment of our culture that has been discounted
and neglected. On the other, this is the girl who is reading if not producing zines and who seems to have done the resisting and challenging of her culture that the book has advocated all along. Perhaps this
tension is inevitable; like children's literature, which is written *for* chil-

dren but almost never written *by* them, studies of girls will necessarily inadvertently silence them because they are not the ones conducting them. But Inness has compiled a collection of voices that very eloquently, intelligently, and convincingly argue for the study of this underrepresented and important group and speak for its constituents.

Letters from the Editor: The Making of Modern Children's Literature

Deborah Stevenson

Dear Genius: The Letters of Ursula Nordstrom, ed. and comp. Leonard
  Marcus. New York: HarperCollins, 1998.

The face of modern children's literature would have been unimagin-
ably different without the legendary Ursula Nordstrom, director of
Harper's Department of Books for Boys and Girls from 1940 to 1973.
Her editorial contributions include some of the most significant and
best-known works of the century: *Goodnight Moon* (1947), *Charlotte's Web*
(1952), *Where the Wild Things Are* (1963), *Harriet the Spy* (1964). She over-
saw Russell Hoban's *Bedtime for Frances* (1960) from back when it was
titled *Who's Afraid?,* changed from initial doubt to wholehearted support for Crockett Johnson's *Harold and the Purple Crayon* (1955), and
worked around the bedroom-scene problems entailed by the mother-
daughter switch in Mary Rodgers's *Freaky Friday* (1972). She enabled
groundbreaking mention of menstruation in Louise Fitzhugh's *The
Long Secret* (1965) and groundbreaking mention of homosexuality in
John Donovan's *I'll Get There. It Better Be Worth the Trip* (1969), and she
sent Mickey "STAKE NARKID" (282) into the world in *In the Night
Kitchen* (1970).

  Leonard Marcus, whose previous work includes other investigations
of publishing and publishing history as well as *Margaret Wise Brown:
Awakened by the Moon* (1992), has selected from "many tens of thousands of letters" written by Nordstrom several hundred; although it's
always difficult to know how much of such a collection's shape comes
from the source and how much from the selection, Nordstrom's tone
and approach are sufficiently consistent to suggest fair sampling rather
than editorial topiary. The book doesn't just opt for latitudinal representation, however; instead it effectively follows particular examples
of talent development and of changing editorial relationships, of
booktalk and of industry illumination. Significant strains include
Nordstrom's grooming of Maurice Sendak, her thorny relationship

Children's Literature 28, eds. Elizabeth Lennox Keyser and Julie Pfeiffer (Yale University
Press, © 2000 Hollins University).

with Meindert DeJong, the evolution of her friendship with Mary Stolz, and her struggles to support a young, suspicious, and elusive John Steptoe (Nordstrom resorts, after failure to reach Steptoe himself, to writing his mother in an attempt to find him).

Her epistolary persona is witty, engaged, and dramatic, with a stylish *New Yorker*esque breeziness; it's easy to see why people, including Nordstrom herself, relish telling Nordstrom stories. Shrewdly noting that her exaggerated claims of her failings and self-doubts undercut their believability, Marcus states, "Her letters were her stage" (xxxiv), and indeed they bespeak Ursula Nordstrom performing "Ursula Nordstrom" and doing so very well indeed. The eternal editor, she relentlessly edits herself as she writes ("That doesn't look as funny written down" is a repeated refrain), providing an earnest token of editorial integrity to recipients of her missives. She's unable to resist editorial suggestions for her correspondents' correspondence—after nearly thirty years' friendship, she observes to Mary Stolz that "you never really write as though you'd heard from me" and models some samples of more desirable responses, attempting, not entirely convincingly, to pass her guidance off as a joke (377). Marcus doesn't limit his scope to her tours de force, however; the collection encompasses less assured and dashing productions as well. A 1953 letter to the elderly Laura Ingalls Wilder, though warmly polite, suggests in its contrast to the tone of other letters that Nordstrom really had very little to say to the revered author. And though Nordstrom's responses to letters of complaint are individually thoughtful and effective, their smoothness collectively starts looking somewhat slick and practiced, especially in conjunction with her witty private parody of such objections.

Nordstrom's company is a pleasure in its own right, but it's as a window into the making of literature that this collection really excels. The compilation provides intriguing insight into Nordstrom's editorial approach, including several instances of her painstaking and detailed analyses. There is a near-microscopic examination of Garth Williams's illustrations of Charlotte the spider—"I think that if the nose dots were made larger . . . and the line he has put in for a mouth were omitted, she would be still attractive but more of a spider" (45)—and she devotes seven pages to fine-toothed-comb work on Syd Hoff's *Danny and the Dinosaur* (1958). In a letter to eighteen-year-old John Steptoe she covers both the technical, carefully explaining how to make a dummy for *Stevie* (1969), and the conceptual, compellingly arguing the importance of his book; there are examples galore of her entreating, urging, admonishing, and sometimes funding the authors and artists she worked with into creativity and completion. Her relentless search, practically panhandling, for new talent was unflagging: a casual thank-you note to the writer-producer Susan Harris includes an invitation to do a children's book, she mentions trying to talk several others including Marlo Thomas and Herb Gardner into authorship, and she insists that the phone be answered because it "might be the next Mark Twain" (xxxi). She seemed eternally haunted by the idea of great children's books lying trapped in people's heads for want of a Nordstrom to free them and consequently made it her mission to leave as few of them orphaned as possible. It was presumably this same sense of mission that prompted her vicarious selfishness on behalf of her authors and artists; her fierce protectiveness of their precious creative time led her, despite amiable wishes sent to her correspondents' family members, to write "I love children. . . . But any children or indeed any relatives—husbands, mothers, fathers, brothers, sisters, who are connected in any way with 'my' authors are MY ENEMIES"—and one suspects that decorum alone forced those quotation marks around the word *my* (191).

Yet Nordstrom was well aware that it took more than artistic creativity to get books into the hands of children, and she never lost sight of the post-publication work required for success. She maintained an enduring friendship with Frances Chrystie, book buyer for F.A.O. Schwarz (who connected Nordstrom up with the young Maurice Sendak); on their trip abroad, Nordstrom tested out the acoustics in a Greek amphitheater with the exhortation "Buy Harper books," to which Chrystie responded, "At the proper discount I will" (xxxiii). Marcus never uses the word *politician,* but it's relevant: juggling demands from all directions, the editor treats compromises as glorious victories. She writes to a Harper sales representative, sympathizing with his struggle, jollying him along, coaxing him into support of a controversial title that she apparently fully supports—and a footnote reveals that Nordstrom notes, on her carbon copy of the letter, that she herself had tried to convince the author to remove the offending passage. In a preemptive strike against criticism, she enlists Dr. Frances Ilg, head of the Gesell Institute at Yale University, to provide a prepublication quotation attesting to the value of *I'll Get There. It Better Be Worth the Trip;* in another vein, she attempts to walk the line between restricting its author, John Donovan, and leaving the book open to more criticism than it might be able to overcome: "If I still flinch over his calling his mother a ball-buster it is because for your sake and ours we want to secure the widest possible acceptance for this book" (260).

"Widest possible" also describes Nordstrom's acquaintanceship: the gallery of who's who starts with the acknowledgments, and the names continue to flow throughout. There are authors and illustrators, of course, starting with Laura Ingalls Wilder and finishing with Mary Stolz (or Charlotte Zolotow, depending on whether you're classifying her as editor or author). Also addressed or mentioned in dispatches, however, are more than a century's worth of luminaries in children's literature and out. Even mere office correspondence is aglitter, since Harper's editorial department graduated the likes of Charlotte Zolotow, Susan Hirschman, and Phyllis Fogelman (not to mention Margaret Warner, now a correspondent on PBS's *Newshour with Jim Lehrer*); competitor Margaret McElderry's literary productions at Harcourt get an approving mention as well. Nordstrom views the end of an era with the passing of pioneer editor May Massee, comments on interesting work done at the University of Connecticut by "a woman there named Butler" (319), and arranges to have material sent to an inquiring "woman in Winnipeg," identified in a footnote as Perry Nodelman, whose gender had been misconstrued (383). The response to novelist Henry Miller seems to have been a one-off, but Virginia Haviland of the Library of Congress and Zena Sutherland of the University of Chicago are graced with what are clearly representative letters from more continuous correspondence.

Between Marcus's introduction and Nordstrom's letters, we see the trajectory of an amazing career that spanned more than four decades. Demonstrating that her stated preference for children's books was no empty boast, she rejected Harper's offer to "promote" her to the editing of adult books and continued to produce her "good books for bad children," thereby achieving unprecedented success. She became the first woman to sit on Harper's board of directors and later that publisher's first female vice-president; she was the first woman and the first children's publisher to win the Curtis Benjamin Award (yet she was still, in a 1973 telephone call, being asked "Whose secretary are you?"). Some things did change during that period: several of Nordstrom's letters address complaints about racist imagery or phraseology, sometimes promising (and at least in the instance of Wilder's *Little House on the Prairie,* delivering) changes in future editions. Some things have since changed even further: with its focus on Jesse Jackson's books from the 1940s, her proud 1963 listing of the six Harper books "in which Negro characters appear" looks woefully deficient now (169); the great breaker of taboos is also rather shocked to find the word *shitty* in a manuscript (282). Eventually, in fact, Nordstrom begins to look back rather than looking forward, finishing the collection with a retrospective tone as she takes her professional leave from longtime correspondents and contemplates all that has been.

We don't see that "all," of course, and one can't help but wonder about what's not included. The lengthy correspondence with Sendak addresses moral questions, creative dilemmas, and family matters, but there's no elaboration on the artistic evolution of *Wild Things* or *In the Night Kitchen;* selected letters to Louise Fitzhugh explore details about *The Long Secret,* but there's no hashing through of *Harriet the Spy.* Did these landmarks emerge without epistolary coaching, or were those letters less memorable, or less effective, than those Marcus included? Did she never commit to paper anything stronger about Anne Carroll Moore's magisterial condemnation of *Stuart Little* (1945) than these few wry references? Are there things missing that we don't even know to miss? Even within selected letters Marcus occasionally draws a veil over matters with tantalizing mid-letter ellipses; they probably suggest more significant omissions than really took place, but they do serve as a reminder that not everything said is being heard here.

Marcus fills in the picture somewhat with a prefatory chronology and detailed introduction, which provides a biographical précis and a taste of what's to come as well as explaining Marcus's formatting and selection. The letters are diligently if somewhat unevenly footnoted: Marcus carefully explains who Holden Caulfield is but rarely satisfies reader curiosity about the result of Nordstrom's editorial suggestions, so you'll have to dig out your own copy of *Danny and the Dinosaur* to see if Danny still looks like an "adenoidal dumbbell" (108). The book's index of titles and names will make you pull your hair out in frustration, as several important correspondents and a multitude of references go missing (Anne Carroll Moore's omission may simply be Nordstrom's getting the last word, but what happened to Ethel Heins, Susan Hirschman, and Zena Sutherland?)—so take your notes as you read.

Though the collection can't, of course, be the Compleat Nordstrom, it is consistent and vital enough to be clearly True Nordstrom, thereby providing a portrait of one of the figures most important to this century's American children's literature, the world in which she worked, and the genre she shaped. It's an affectionate rather than an incisive portrait, with little here in the way of shocking revelation or startling

Letters from the Editor

261

iconoclasm; the worst sin of which Marcus accuses his subject is a ne-glect of nonfiction literature (and it is tempting to contemplate what the effect might have been had she taken an interest). In some ways this is the Nordstroming of Nordstrom: Marcus does for UN what she had done for so many, editing her without diluting her, leaving enough rough edges to make things inviting while letting the strength and the complications of the voice shine through. His introduction argues that Nordstrom was the force that "propel[led] American chil-dren's literature headlong into the modern age" (xviii); though it took more than Nordstrom alone to do that, she was indeed one of the chief architects of that literary progression. This compilation offers a look at that progression as it happens and from the inside, providing an unorthodox, individual, and extremely entertaining chronicle of the world of children's literature.

Dangerous Images: The Pictorial Construction of Childhood

Hamida Bosmajian

Pictures of Innocence: The History and Crisis of Ideal Childhood, by Anne Higonnet. New York and London: Thames and Hudson, 1998.

Not since Martha Banta's *Imaging American Women* (1987) have I experienced the kind of intellectual excitement over reading a study about images that I felt while reading Anne Higonnet's *Pictures of Innocence.* On one level, Higonnet's findings are even more challenging than Banta's, for *Pictures of Innocence* has the courage to rise against a dangerous and politically empowered point of view in late twentieth-century America. It is a point of view that raised "misreading" to the level of legally constituted public policies. The misreading in question is that any photograph of a child's body, clothed or unclothed, is suspect because it could lead some perceivers to engage in pornographic fantasies and even act out such fantasies through criminal behavior against children. As Higonnet puts it: "Recent child pornography laws cast shame on the child's body" (180). How we got there and what we can do about it is a primary concern in Anne Higonnet's *Pictures of Innocence.*

The nine chapters of her study divide into two parts: "The Invention of Innocence" and "An Ideal in Crisis." The first part subdivides into "Pictures' Imagination," the creation of the Romantic child in a golden age of innocence; part 2, "Photography's Truth," shows how the ideal and conventions of innocence began to be challenged with the advent of photography at points of vulnerability that could and did unravel the ideal. With its claim to representational truth, photography confuses the boundary between the imitation of an image or action and the lived experience that the photograph ostensibly records. At the same time, the traditional conventions of a "golden age of innocence" either persist in the new medium or are altered through an ironic mode to the extent that at times the archetype of innocence becomes an inversion of its former self.

Children's Literature 28, eds. Elizabeth Lennox Keyser and Julie Pfeiffer (Yale University Press, © 2000 Hollins University).

The negation of innocence, either in the image itself or in the perception of the beholder, has raised the social and legal specter of child pornography. It is this issue that provides both text and subtext, academic investigation and personal motivation for Anne Higonnet. As a parent, she feels the threat of even the remote possibility of a child being exploited and abused sexually; as an academic, she is anxious that she might become suspect because she analyzes and interprets the sacred conventions of childhood innocence. Moreover, her field, child studies, is still dismissed by the academy as trivial and sentimental, appropriate for women and second-rate minds (13). Writers and scholars of children's literature will find in Anne Higonnet a kindred spirit. We know all too well the attitudes of the "literary establishment" to children's literature and we, too, must remain alert to the attacks and actions of those who would censor children's literature. It may well be that one of the reasons for the academy's continued resistance to studies (other than psychology) of children and their world is precisely the assumption that children are pictures of innocence, untouched by the complexities of human existence, even though the individual academic may silently admit that his or her neurosis had its origin in childhood. Moreover, culturally, politically, and legally the binary child-sexuality, a persistent topic in Higonnet's study, retains its rigidly defined separation along with conventionalized denotations and connotations as to the meanings of *child* and *sexuality.*

Ironically, it is not, as some envision, the legions of child pornographers nor artists such as the photographers Sally Mann or Robert Mapplethorpe who threaten the binary division; rather, it is the commercialism of a consumer society that has conventionalized the child as object of desire. That advertisers are conscious of the ambivalences constructed into their images is made glaringly evident by the fact that Higonnet was not granted permission to reproduce even one contemporary advertisement that includes a child. Higonnet must, therefore, rely on description, as she does in her introduction, where she describes the Estée Lauder advertisement (1997) for the fragrance *Pleasures for Men,* which, in the convention of the family snapshot, depicts a man and boy in a hammock. But the image did not become a father-son idyll until the original was withdrawn and reissued with the image of the man wearing a wedding band, "a tiny but densely symbolic detail" (7–8). Interpretation and analysis are indeed a formidable threat when the subtexts of images used for commerce and profit might be exposed!

In her discussion of the evolution of images of childhood, Higonnet points out that before the middle of the eighteenth century the representation of actual children depicted their bodies as similar to adult bodies (17). In contrast, Higonnet notes, the countless images of cherubs and cupids "in art before the eighteenth century witness or even incite bodily acts that are the diametric opposite of what we in the twentieth century would call innocent" (18). Because in Carravaggio's raunchy *Cupid* (1598–99) the boy becomes an "other" because he has wings, the image is acceptable, whereas Robert Mapplethorpe's *Jessie McBride* (1976), in which a naked boy is poised chastely in classically simplified lines on the back of a dark chair in a kitchen, has been labeled "pornographic" (166–68). Furthermore, traditional imaging projected the Christ child's flesh, its penis "at the center of most Madonna and Child images, whether exposed outright or covered," acting as the compositional fulcrum, even in Raphael's *Sistine Madonna* (19). Aside from the centering of the Christ Child's genitalia, the divine infant "is hardly innocent." Higonnet reminds us that "Madonna and Child images were intended to show that Christ, though humanly infant, already omnisciently knows his divine fate" (19).

The Madonna and Child conventions powerfully influenced all mother and child representations, which, in turn, generated their own ambivalences. A case in point is the influence on and restructuring by Benjamin West of Raphael's *Madonna della Sedia* (1514) in his *Mrs. West and her son Raphael* (c. 1770). Gone is the centering of the child's body for theological purposes; instead, as Higonnet notes, pleasure and desire, legitimized as maternal desire, dominate West's portrait of his family. Higonnet does not go so far as to note that if Mrs. West, who looks at the viewer rather suggestively, would turn her head towards her son, their lips would meet. At the same time little Raphael is depicted with wide-eyed and open-mouthed innocence as if he has just rushed into his mother's arms. This early imaging of domestic innocence has a rich subtext that prepares for the potential and eventual deconstruction of innocence that began in the nineteenth century.

Middle-class values and the technologies of image reproduction contributed immensely to the fixing of archetypes and stereotypes in the golden age of childhood innocence. Joshua Reynolds's very popular and gently ironic *Penelope Boothby* (1788), cocooned in her somewhat "too-big-for-her-age" clothing, is, almost a hundred years later, sentimentalized and cutesified in Millais's suggestively titled *Cherry Ripe* (1879), a widely reproduced posturing of innocence where the upward glance of the little girl's down-tilted face and the pubic delta, defined by her dark-laced half-gloves, undermine innocence. In short, Lewis Carroll's photographic reconstruction of Alice Liddell as a beggar girl (a very private work of art) is not the first expression of childhood innocence with a subtext of adult desire. Even a producer of such "darling children" as Kate Greenaway contributed to the undermining of the ideal through the commercialization of the image of the child. Higonnet points out that her first greeting card (1873), ironically a Valentine, sold 25,000 copies within a few weeks (52). Her images look childlike, but they sold the child to the adult consumer.

My one criticism of Higonnet's discussion is that she could, at times, have gone further in exploring the subtexts of these conventionalized images instead of privileging their official message. A case in point might have been a comparison of Van Dyck's portraits of George Villiers, Second Duke of Buckingham, and Lord Francis Villiers (16), both painted as boys in 1635, with Gainsborough's historically costumed and immensely popular *Blue Boy* (c. 1770), a romanticized image of the aristocratic child. The "blue boy" appears provocative with his knowing smile and his sassy posture of precocious masculinity, whereas Van Dyck's boys establish an invisible barrier between themselves and the viewer through their reserved aristocratic demeanor. Higonnet's restraint in exploring subtexts in such conventional paintings is most likely motivated by her focus on how tradition influenced the commercialization of innocence in the transition from painting to photography. The photographing of a child for commercial purposes may raise controversy, as did the famous Calvin Klein jeans advertisement with Brooke Shields, but a child photographed by an artist such as Mapplethorpe may lead to public demonstrations and antipornography legislation. Art is more dangerous than commerce!

Higonnet's discussions of Betsy Cameron, Dorothea Lange, and Edward Weston enable the reader to understand the evolution of child imaging toward an ever greater complexity. With Mapplethorpe and, to a lesser extent, with Sally Mann, the child's consent as a photographic subject has become an issue because the child, powerless in relation to adults, is considered incapable of giving consent (168). Even family situations are problematized here, for "some would argue that the only person to whom a child can give consent is a parent, while others would retort that a parent is the last person from whom a child would be able to withhold consent" (169).

Before she turns to the restructuring of the "innocent child" into the "knowing child," her final chapter, Higonnet turns to "Photographs Against the Law," a chapter that is most enlightening and useful to any reader interested in First Amendment rights and censorship. She summarizes here the escalation of antipornographic laws and their effects. In full acknowledgment of the evil of the well-documented sexual exploitation and abuse of children on a global scale, she urges a clear distinction between image and action. Child pornography in which children are depicted in sexually abusive situations does indeed exist and must be prosecuted because it records illegal acts. On the other hand, when we consider that the famous Coppertone commercial (192), where a small dog pulls the bathing suit off a little girl's well-tanned back side and reveals her white bottom, has functioned as a stimulus for child molesters, we have to acknowledge that in one way or another any image, public or private, of a child's body can be interpreted sexually. A child's imaged body becomes then a dangerous site.

After summarizing the legal history of antipornography laws, Higonnet turns to *Knox v. the United States* (1993), which "treated all photographs of children as actions" (184) and involved the entire U.S. government in discussion and debate leading to the Child Pornography Prevention Act of 1996. Higonnet lauds many of the concerns of the debate as they relate to children but faults the oversimplifications that led to *child pornography* meaning "any image of any child's body" (185). We have focused, she argues, on a relatively small issue as the main cause of the suffering of children: In 1995–96 the U.S. Justice Department convicted around sixty child pornographers, but "of 3 million children whose abuse or neglect was reported in 1993, 1,300 died, 300,000 were sexually abused. . . . The United States devotes more and more resources to eradicate child pornography while social funding that would protect real children is slashed" (188–89). She becomes impassioned, rightly so, when she says: "We live in a society that is willing to pay for FBI agents and DA offices to launch massive legal investigations based on photographs of naked children that might or might not be interpreted by some person as possibly showing lascivious intent, but not willing to pay for social workers who deal every day with already documented abuse of, rape and murder of children" (189).

To protect children she advocates laws that target actions. Our antipornography laws must be worded in such a way that they protect children *and* the constitutional right to free expression. Moreover, we must understand how and why we image the child as we do, and that may well involve a change of our perception of the child, either as an ideal of innocence or as a dangerous site.

Her discussion of "the knowing child," which focuses on the photographs of Sally Mann, Nicholas Nixon, and others, reveals to the reader the child as a complex human being who is neither sacralized nor demonized by the perceiver. Some of these images, such as Mann's *Jessie at Five* or *The New Mothers,* may disturb the perceiver, but if they do, it is not because children in such poses cannot be found in "real life"; it is because these images run counter to conventions of childhood imaging by adults. Anyone, however, who has observed children in the contexts of human situations knows that children are not always darling and cute; their expressions and behaviors can be sulky and sullen, angry or depressed, apathetic or ecstatic, provocative and flirtatious. The photographic image freezes one moment; we choose that moment and through it stereotype the child. Only when our gaze directs itself to the child's range and acknowledges that range does the child become part of our human world. The new photographs, Higonnet argues, are "emotionally ambitious, free-ranging in their moods, intelligent, beautifully composed, and finely crafted." We have to admit to ourselves that "childhood has the power to threaten as well as to delight, to repel as well as to rivet" (225). The artist challenges us, as always, to examine our deepest desires and fears. Unfortunately, it is adults who want to be protected from such an examining and, I fear, in spite of Higonnet's provocative and intelligent exploration, they will continue to transfer the anxiety to the image of the child under the guise of doing the right thing.

Work Cited

Banta, Martha. *Imaging American Women: Ideas and Ideals in Cultural History.* New York: Columbia University Press, 1987.

The Transactional School of Children's Literature Criticism

Roberta Seelinger Trites

Signs of Childness in Children's Books, by Peter Hollindale. Stroud, Gloucs.: Thimble, 1997. *Reading Otherways,* by Lissa Paul. Stroud: Thimble, 1997.

Thimble Press has long held a leadership role in negotiating the gap between what Peter Hollindale in a 1988 article called the "book people" and the "child people" (5). In *Signs of Childness in Children's Books,* he defines the divide as existing between those who "prioritiz[e] either the children or the literature" in the study of children's literature (8). He advocates instead a study of children's literature as a "reading event" (30) in a strategy that allows both the child and the text to have a place. Lissa Paul's *Reading Otherways* has a similar orientation: she rejects the validity of hermeneutic readings and demonstrates how much the reader can gain by understanding a text's contextuality. Hollindale and Paul—and a number of critics including Peter Hunt, Jill May, Maria Nikolajeva, Perry Nodelman, and John Stephens—have become core members of a type of literary criticism that could be called "transactional criticism" for the way that these people acknowledge the importance of the child's multiple interpretations as a critical component of the fluid complexity involved in reading children's texts. These critics' position is one that relies on reader response theory to mediate between the extremes of aesthetic criticism and pedagogical criticism in children's literature, although transactional critics still tend to treat child readers in the abstract as a theoretical construct rather than as an empirical group of beings whose needs can actually be quantitatively or qualitatively tested. Nevertheless, the willingness of the transactional school to grapple with the complexity of childhood as a social construct and with textuality as a literary construct is perhaps the most significant contribution that poststructural theorists have made to the study of children's literature.

At first glance, Paul's *Reading Otherways* seems to be the much-

Children's Literature 28, eds. Elizabeth Lennox Keyser and Julie Pfeiffer (Yale University Press, © 2000 Hollins University).

needed introduction to feminist reading that those of us teaching children's literature at the college level have sought for the past ten years. *Reading Otherways* is certainly that—it will be an essential work of feminist criticism in children's literature for many years to come—but it also has an even broader usefulness. *Reading Otherways* challenges the reader to learn new ways of reading. And since the reader is quite likely to be a pre-service teacher, by extension, the book challenges teachers to teach children new ways of reading. By *reading* Paul means "literary interpretation"; her work is a relatively jargon-free tour de force of demonstrating how to read poststructurally. Written with a casual stylistic felicity that feels as comfortable as chatting with an old friend on the phone, *Reading Otherways* makes poststructuralism accessible to even the most wary of theory-phobes.

Paul bases her argument on the principle that readers need to interrogate texts in order to gain multiple interpretations. She shows how asking simple questions can change our interpretations of such texts as "Blue Beard" and *Little Women*. She suggests that readers learn to ask the following questions routinely:

—whose story is this?
—who is the reader?
—when and where was the reading produced? . . .
—how are value systems determined? (16)

These questions may have originated in Paul's feminism, but they also serve any number of purposes, all of which empower the reader by engaging her critical acumen. Paul argues that readers who understand when and where and why a text was produced will understand more of the story than they otherwise would, so these questions validate historical study (both of the traditional kind and the so-called New Historicism). She asks that we look at oppression of all forms, so she engages multiculturalism and Marxism. She wants us to know who the reader is supposed to be, so she employs the reader response theories that are the hallmark of the transactional critics. And as she explores how meanings can compete with one another in a text, she shows how deconstruction creates interpretive richness for the reader. The net result is not only a course in learning to read poststructurally, but it is also a course in the history of literary criticism, for Paul provides practical commentary on how these theories have evolved.

I do, however, have one complaint with this text: at eighty-three pages, it is far too short. I found myself frustrated more than once when Paul says words to the effect of "but I have gone on too long," to which I mentally responded, "But no! You haven't." I would have enjoyed knowing more about the relationship Paul sees between the female characters in "Hansel and Gretel," more about the passivity of the little mermaid, more about the significance of the names in Nina Bawden's *Carrie's War,* more about the language of the nursery in *Teletubbies.* I suppose my yearning for "More More More" (Paul unpacks a picture book by that name for the reader) is a stirring testimony to how *Reading Otherways* has engaged me as a reader. But in being so brief, the book may prove problematic for beginning scholars who require more scaffolding if they are to understand literary intricacies and problematic for advanced scholars seeking greater explication. I suspect that this book will have its greatest usefulness with upper-division students who already know some of the rudiments of literary study but who seek to know more about the feminist study of children's literature.

Hollindale's *Signs of Childness in Children's Books* offers yet another perspective for the study of children's literature because it is "an exercise in definition" (7). While engaged in this exercise, Hollindale both identifies the issues that inform the field of children's literature and proposes new ways of studying books for children and adolescents. Some of the major issues Hollindale explores include the many definitions of *childhood* and whether it is a developmental preface to adulthood or an autonomous stage of life; the fact that children's literature is not a peer-written literature; the social and literary construction of childhood; and definitions of *children's literature.* He concludes that it is most adequately described as "a body of texts with certain common features of imaginative interest, which is activated as children's literature by a reading event: that of being read by a child. A child is someone who believes on good grounds that his or her condition of childhood is not yet over" (30). Two aspects of this definition prove especially crucial to the framework of the rest of his argument: the idea of imagination and the idea of the reading event. Hollindale structures his theory that children's books exist as individual reading events that are redefined each time a child reads a book on a belief that he expands at some length: children need multiple imaginative stimuli in order to mature into creative and aware adults. "If childhood is indeed an imaginative construct for the child, children need to come across a variegated imaginary world of childhood, a multiplicity of childhood possibilities, which will enrich and diversify their sense of what it can mean to be a child, both in itself and as a stage en route to being something else" (14–15). In his earnest and sometimes Romantic belief that children's literature has the potential to save the world, Hollindale's premise parallels the conclusion of Perry Nodelman's *Words About Pictures* (1988): "Good picture books, then, offer us what all good art offers us: greater consciousness—the opportunity, in other words, to be more human" (285).

Because Hollindale feels limited by existing terms, he reifies several words that have fallen out of contemporary usage. For example, objecting to the pejorative *childish* and the condescending *childlike*, Hollindale opts for the more positive connotations of the terms *childly* and *childness*—a Shakespearean coinage—to describe that which makes the transaction between child and book successful. In Hollindale's economy, *childness* is "the quality of being a child—dynamic, imaginative, experimental, interactive and unstable" (46). The thesis of Hollindale's book depends on our understanding this term: "I wish to argue here that childness is the distinguishing property of a text in children's literature, setting it apart from other literature as a genre, and it is also the property that the child brings to the reading of a text. At its best the encounter is a dynamic one. The childness of the text can change the childness of the child, and vice versa" (47). In an intricate chapter that forms the heart of his theory, Hollindale looks for childness in a text by asking such questions as "Who is the implied reader?" and "Is the implied reader consistently a child?" and "Does the authorial voice place the reader in an intermediate relationship with characters?" and "What is the linguistic relationship between dialogue and narrative prose?" and "What is expected (shown as normative) of children in the text, and what is expected (demanded) of the child reader?" (94–95). Many of these questions owe much to Aidan Chambers's application of Wolfgang Iser's theories to children's literature, but Hollindale takes them even further so that they can be applied broadly to any number of books. In Hollindale's paradigm, evaluating childness is assessing at once both the verisimilitude of the depiction of child characters and whether the text connects with that which is unique to childhood. The best type of childness "invites the child to explore himself through exploring the story" (105).

Hollindale identifies the presence of childly characters with a strong narrative line that he finds essential to good children's books. He believes that the author's use of memory in constructing such plot lines can be invaluable, not so much for the purposes of fabulation as for the sake of creating language and a style that accommodate children. One can extrapolate from his argument that fiction such as the *Nancy Drew* books, with their absent authors—in negative capability even more clear-cut than Shakespeare's—succeed with children because the writers have enough memory to employ language in a swift narrative line that children enjoy. Hollindale distinguishes "child-being" from "child-becoming," privileging, perhaps, books that challenge the child over those that acknowledge children's need for complacency, but he admits, "We need our Blytons and our Dahls, just as slightly later we need Sweet Valley High" (118).

The third term Hollindale asks the field to reemploy is *youth*, as in "literature for youth." Noting that *adolescence* seems to limit readers to teenage years although full maturity and entry into adult life happens for many people well into their twenties, Hollindale advocates the nineteenth-century concept of youth, with its greater flexibility, as a way of supporting those who are going through the later stages of adolescence. In a chapter devoted solely to the evaluation of literature for youth, Hollindale investigates the importance of the epiphany in adolescent literature. He finds epiphanies, in fact, the sine qua non of the genre because they "are essential to effective growth" (120). He fears for current Western culture because it does not offer youth more powerful rites of passage than rebelling against authority figures; he sees in literature for youth one potential salvation for an errant culture.

Having just read *Reading Otherways,* I do have one concern about Hollindale's chapter on adolescent literature. He directly states that most of the examples he provides will be about boy protagonists because he perceives males to be at greater risk in our society than girls: "On the whole it is not girls who carry knives, commit assaults, steal cars and crash them. Boys rather than girls resort to negative demonstrations of self worth" (121). I agree that boys more often than girls display antisocial behavior that is other-directed, but I share the same level of concern for girls who resort to negative demonstrations of self-worth with eating disorders, self-mutilation, and suicide. I object to the implied corollary of his assertion: if, as he maintains, books can improve the culture, and if boys need books with male protagonists more than girls need female protagonists, then boys' books and their reading necessarily become more important to the culture than girls' books and their reading. Balderdash. I wish that instead of falling into the age-old trap of "boys only read books about boys," Hollindale's otherwise visionary gaze had been able to perceive a possibility of training male readers to expand their imaginations by enjoying the childness of female characters. Girls, after all, have been expected to be cross-readers for centuries. If Hollindale's argument is that the more imaginative worlds we offer children, the more possibilities they can engage in as adults, then surely we should also include the possibility of gender inclusion rather than gender exclusion. Hollindale is particularly weak on this score in the chapter in which he analyzes childness at work in a number of adult novels. In a work that professes in its title to be about children's books, this chapter seems oddly out of place, but the number of male-dominated texts in both this chapter and the chapter on adolescent literature seems at times quite exclusionary for someone who several times reminds his reader to be aware of the gender issues surrounding childness.

The other trap that Hollindale's paradigm runs the risk of falling into is the subjectivity of the term *childness*. On occasion, Hollindale's praise for something's childness seems quite arbitrary, as when he praises Beatrix Potter's Latinate diction for inviting child readers to ally themselves with her in viewing adulthood satirically. One could also criticize Potter's diction for alienating children and thus being unchildly—the very rationale for some of the horrid revisions of Potter's books that now proliferate. On the other hand, the concept of childness works best when Hollindale offers it as a means of assessing both verisimilitude and the reader's ability to connect imaginatively with the language of a narrative. The term is useful enough that I suspect it will eventually take a well-deserved place in the critical lexicon of children's literature.

Childness also proves useful as a term of cultural critique, as a way of addressing a larger culture than the world of children's literary criticism. Hollindale makes a convincing case that what is at stake is the fate of childhood in our culture: if we do not learn to recognize and value childhood, we stand to impoverish ourselves as a culture. What Hollindale and Paul thus share with most of the transactional critics is a reformer's zeal to improve the world for children. I can only hope that the institutional discourses best prepared to make the changes they suggest—most notably the discourse of education, at all levels—will be able to take heed of what they have to offer.

274

ROBERTA SEELINGER TRITES

Works Cited

Chambers, Aidan. "All of a Tremble to See His Danger." *Signal* 51 (Sept. 1986): 193–212.
Hollindale, Peter. "The Adolescent Novel of Ideas." *Children's Literature in Education* 26 (1995): 83–95.
Nodelman, Perry. *Words About Pictures.* Athens: University of Georgia Press, 1988.

Dissertations of Note

Compiled and Annotated by Elizabeth Mayfield and Rachel Fordyce

Applebaum, Susan Rae. "Mentor Mothers and Female Adolescent Protagonists: Rethinking Children's Theatre History Through Burnett's *The Little Princess* (1903), Chorpenning's *Cinderella* (1940), and Zeder's *Mother Hicks* (1983)." Ph.D. diss. Northwestern University, 1998. 253 pp. DAI 59:1401A.

This study uses theories of feminist dramatic criticism, semiotics, and women's psychological development to examine the intersection of children's theater history and changing theories of the mother-daughter relation. Applebaum argues that theatrical representation of female adolescent protagonists and their relationships with mothers both deny and affirm twentieth-century theories of female adolescent development. Analysis of the three representative works reveals ambivalences toward gendered stereotypes of their day, and these resulted in alternative readings. "Resistant representations in the turn-of-the-century work of Burnett and the mid-century work of Chorpenning, and a revisionist representation by Zeder after the women's movement of the seventies, offer a genealogy for the 'mentor mother' paradigm of mother-daughter relationships. This model gives subjectivity to both the maternal figure and the adolescent girl, extends the view of mother beyond the biological, and allows for autonomy without sacrificing emotional connection."

Benson, Linda Gayle. "The Constructed Child: Femininity in Beverly Cleary's Ramona Series." Ph.D. diss. Illinois State University, 1997. 247 pp. DAI 58:3116A.

After examining the way feminine roles may be constructed and replicated, and how these dynamics play out in the seven Ramona novels, Benson reveals the conflicts between explicit and implicit gender ideologies that extend through the depiction of female relationships, parental roles, and the discourse community represented by Ramona's school experiences. Benson concludes with a discussion of constructivist composition theory that suggests "pedagogical strategies by which students may question ideological constructs which position them as constructs within the dominate hegemony." She suggests that applying the concept of interrogation to reading and writing practices in college-level children's literature classes "allows students to develop an awareness of how texts inculcate on explicit and implicit levels particular subject positions."

Black, Kathleen Alison. "The Use of Children's Literature to Promote Anti-Bias Education: A Transactional Study of Teachers' Use and Student Response." Ph.D. diss. Syracuse University, 1997. 425 pp. DAI 58:4598A.

Black's qualitative study explores the "transactions that occur among teachers, students, and children's literature when that literature is used to promote anti-bias education." Based on the concept of literary transactions discussed by Rosenblatt and the concept of anti-bias education (Derman-Sparks and the A. B. C. Task Force), the methodology developed for this study is a transactional ethnography, a research strategy that examines specific routine events through the transactions that comprise such events. Findings suggest that transaction is embedded in the notion of the classroom community affecting and being affected by a teacher's specific use of literature, including book selection and teaching.

Children's Literature 28, eds. Elizabeth Lennox Keyser and Julie Pfeiffer (Yale University Press, © 2000 Hollins University).

Bloem, Patricia Lynn. "A Case Study of American Young Adult Response to International Literature." Ph.D. diss. Kent State University, 1997. 223 pp. DAI 58:4537A.

Bloem's study tests the metaphor of the bridge to describe how international literature links readers to another country or culture by examining the ways six eighth-grade American students read international literature. Based on reader response theory nested in the broader context of multiculturalism and literacy studies, her data analysis reveals that students make meaning personally and passionately, experience the books visually and through their senses, identify with characters, and enter imaginatively into settings in the books. Students expressed considerable metacognitive awareness and were amazed at the similarities that humans share throughout the world, although their responses suggest that the bridge metaphor is "more complex than it first appears" and that "each reader's bridge is a unique structure."

Bowles-Reyer, Amy Grace. "Our Secret Garden: American Popular Young Adult Literature in the 1970s and the Transmission of Sexual and Gender Ideology to Adolescent Girls." Ph.D. diss. George Washington University, 1998. 335 pp. DAI 58:4649A.

This dissertation analyzes young adult literature for girls written in the 1970s to demonstrate the influence of the contemporary women's movement on this literature. Focusing specifically on sexual identity, Bowles-Reyer argues that these feminist-influenced young adult books offer the possibility of a new sexual identity to adolescent female readers. She argues that popular young adult literature, informed by the women's movement, empowers girls by providing them with a language to express their sexuality, as in Judy Blume's *Forever* (1975) and *Are You There God? It's Me, Margaret* (1970), although readers were often unaware of the political significance of their attitudes.

Brown, Jeffrey A. "New Heroes: Gender, Race, Fans and Comic Book Superheroes." Ph.D. diss. University of Toronto, 1997. 351 pp. DAI 59:1818A.

"This study focuses on the African American comic books published by Milestone Media, and how fans relate to the stories and the new Black heroes according to six fundamentally connected principles and points of comparison." The superheroes are a focal point for interpreting revisionist notions of African American characters, and they facilitate a progressive interpretation of black masculinity that incorporates intelligence with physicality. The study argues that the reading of comic books is interpreted according to the ideological encodings of the producers and the social position of the audience.

Chandler, Kelly. "Jumpstarting the Reader: Considering the Instructional Implications of Adolescents' Responses to Fiction by Stephen King." Ed.D. diss. University of Maine, 1998. 212 pp. DAI 59:1492A.

This collective case study of twelve high school juniors examines the different students' responses to fiction by Stephen King, as well as the social contexts—home and school—in which those texts are read. Students saw little relation between required school reading and the reading they pursued out of school, and this study advocates an active role for teachers in scaffolding students' more reflective reading of popular literature.

Cirella, Anne Violette. "Avant-Gardism in Children's Theatre: The Use of Absurdist Techniques by Anglophone Children's Playwrights." Ph.D. diss. University of Texas, Austin, 1998. 245 pp. DAI 59:2007A.

This study posits that the "historical intersection of adult drama with children's theatre is the point of departure for the reconsideration of the neglected field of children's theatre as high theatre, and not as a sub-theatre." Cirella argues that the first step in this rehabilitation is to claim that there is an avant-garde children's theater and that both movements intersect historically and aesthetically while diverging in their socio-critical goals. The French playwright Alfred Jarry's use of the puppet theater, especially Punch and Judy, in his play *Ubu roi* (1896) and the American playwright Aurand Harris's use of the same tradition in *Punch and Judy* (1970) underscore how both authors continue a single tradition of social critical drama. The French playwright Eugene Ionesco's *Les chaises* (1952) and the British children's playwright Mary Melwood's *The Tingalary Bird* (1964) both make use of the farce, all of which leads Cirella to conclude that theater historians interested in audience reaction should extend their study of avant-garde theater to include children's theater.

Coats, Karen S. "Performing the Subject of Children's Literature." Ph.D. diss. George Washington University, 1998. 201 pp. DAI 59:1157A.

Coats uses a close reading of children's books and Lacanian theory to show how children's texts become vehicles through which the child performs his or her subjectivity. She argues that certain postmodern trends in literature for children undermine the movement toward closure, present in earlier children's texts that are based on modernist subjectivity, and therefore have the possibility to radically alter subjectivity as we currently understand it.

Comer, Melissa Jean Reese. "A National Survey to Determine the Status of the Design and Teaching Techniques of Young Adult Literature Courses at the College or University Level." Ed.D. diss. University of Tennessee, 1997. 130 pp. DAI 59:71A.

Comer's statistical analysis reveals that young adult literature courses are intended to do one or two things: familiarize students with young adult literature and serve as teaching methods courses. The five core novels most often used by these classes are *The Giver* by Lois Lowry, *The Chocolate War* by Robert Cormier, *Jacob I Have Loved* by Katherine Paterson, *The Outsiders* by S. E. Hinton, and *Fallen Angel* by Walter Dean Myers; the most common textbook is *Literature for Today's Young Adults* by Donelson and Nilsen. The topic most often addressed in these courses is censorship, but the classes also stress that students need to become familiar with adolescent literature journals and organizations.

Cook, Bonnie Sue. "Teaching *Adventures of Huckleberry Finn* at the Turn of the Twenty-First Century." Ph.D. diss. University of North Carolina, Greensboro, 1997. 128 pp. DAI 58:4538A.

This dissertation looks at the controversy surrounding Mark Twain's *Adventures of Huckleberry Finn* since its first publication in 1885. Cook notes that the controversy has shifted in focus from the tale's use of vernacular language and questionable central protagonist to its depiction of African Americans through the character of Jim. She examines the influences from Twain's life apparent in the content of the story, how the novel became part of the English curriculum, and how the controversy has escalated as she reflects on the novel's themes and its present-day significance with emphasis on what the novel has to say about parenting, race and friendship, and living in a moral society.

Cumbo, Kathryn Blash. "The Meaning of Books and Reading in a Preschool Classroom: A Focus on Peer Contexts." Ph.D. diss. University of Colorado, Boulder, 1998. 355 pp. DAI 59:1902A.

Cumbo examines the use of books in a preschool classroom from a sociocultural perspective and identifies the lack of study regarding role books and how they affect the peer world of preschool children. Focusing on child-governed reading (as opposed to teacher-governed reading), she notes that reading for young children involves a "participatory intersubjectivity—a process of coming to shared understanding through challenges and dispute."

Dobson, Warick. "Truth in Dialogue: A Knowledge-Centered Approach to Drama in Education." D.Phil. diss. University of Sussex, 1997. 302 pp. DAI 58:322A.

Dobson determines that there are three discernible approaches to drama in education: state-centered, child-centered, and knowledge-centered, and he evaluates how effectively these approaches fulfill the claim that drama in education is a radical pedagogy. Dobson concludes that only one, the knowledge-centered approach, fulfills this claim.

Eisenberg, Erica Speiser. "Flying-Frog Tales and the Theory of the Listener: The Impact of the *Other* on Children's Storytelling." Ph.D. diss. Long Island University, The Brooklyn Center, 1997. 143 pp. DAI 58:1563B.

Eisenberg compares children's storytelling in a variety of interpersonal contexts. After previewing a picture book, forty-five second- and third-grade children were asked to produce narratives for three different listeners: an adult, a peer, or a younger child (a kindergartner). The choice of listener is found to have a significant effect on the variability of story length, density, and cohesiveness. "In general, there is more variability in measures when the listeners differed in age from the storyteller . . . evidence for the child having developed different concepts about the expectations of different listeners, a 'theory of the listener' which guides narrative performance . . . conceived of as a product of socially-mediated activity."

Englund, Sheryl Ann. " 'An Excellent Likeness of the Author': Gender and Personality in the Nineteenth-Century Literary Marketplace." Ph.D. diss. University of Texas, Austin, 1997. 268 pp. DAI 59:487A.

Englund demonstrates that the images of American authors during the first half of the nineteenth century were products of the publication process. Examining the writings of Margaret Fuller, Louisa May Alcott, and Marion Harland in comparison to the visual portrayals of these authors, she posits that "the sale of a single publication could be sufficient to shape a widely-held and recognized image of the work's author, an image that later came to dominate these women writers' literary celebrity."

Fisher, Susan Rosa. "The Genre for Our Times: The Menippean Satires of Russell Hoban and Murakami Haruki." Ph.D. diss. University of British Columbia, 1997. 295 pp. DAI 59:161A.

After carefully examining the novels of the Anglo-American author Russell Hoban and the Japanese author Murakami Haruki as Menippean satire, Fisher suggests that this form of satire—or a postmodernist form with notable affinities to Menippean satire—has reemerged as a genre and that this form is particularly appropriate for the fictional treatment of life in the postmodern world.

Flores Duenas, Leila. "Second Language Reading: Mexican American Student Voices on Reading Mexican American Literature." University of Texas, Austin, 1997. 239 pp. DAI 59:398A.

The results of a study in which Mexican American bilingual students responded to selected literature from Mexican American and non-Mexican American authors reveal that students better understood the major themes and events of the Mexican American stories. Flores Duenas concludes that this study supports using culturally familiar literature in the classroom.

Ginsberg, Lesley Ellen. "The Romance of Dependency: Childhood and the Ideology of Love in American Literature, 1825–1870." Ph.D. diss. Stanford University, 1998. 357 pp. DAI 59:2023A.

Studying the dynamics of dependency and enslavement in literature for children, as well as similar products aimed at adults, Ginsberg explores "how representation of childhood and/or dependency in the fictions of Poe, Hawthorne, Stowe and Alcott both reify and challenge the period's dominant ideologies of love."

Gwinn, Carolyn Beth. "The Effect of Multicultural Literature on the Attitudes of Second Grade Students." Ph.D. diss. University of Minnesota, 1998. 230 pp. DAI 59:407A.

Gwinn's purpose is to "determine the influence of multicultural literature, coupled with reader response, on the attitudes of second grade students." The study consisted of forty-one participants from a large, racially homogeneous elementary school; two research methods, quantitative and qualitative, were used in this study. "Quantitative data analysis did not reveal significant differences between the experimental and control groups. However, qualitative data analysis revealed that children linked events from the literature to their personal lives, verbalized acceptance of and identification with a minority character, and enjoyed the multicultural literature." Gwinn asserts that these results support the call to integrate multicultural literature across the curriculum.

Hinten, Marvin Duane. "Allusions and Parallels in C.S. Lewis's Narnian Chronicles." Ph.D. diss. Bowling Green State University, 1997. 233 pp. DAI 59:182A.

Hinten attempts to show how C. S. Lewis's reading affected his composing of *The Chronicles of Narnia*. Lewis was a voluminous reader, and Hinten states that this trait, along with Lewis's extraordinary memory and inclination toward imitation of his medieval studies, led him to write in an allusive manner.

Johnson, Holly Anne. "Reading the Personal and the Political: Exploring Female Representation in Realistic Fiction with Adolescent Girls." Ph.D. diss. University of Arizona, 1997. 597 pp. DAI 58:4212A.

Working with adolescent girls aged twelve to fourteen from diverse ethnic, racial, class, and religious backgrounds, Johnson studies their responses to female literary characters in realistic adolescent fiction. She applies feminist methodology, with a focus on consciousness-raising, in her questions about female roles and representation in realistic novels, class and race representation as it intersects with female representation, and the girls' own connections to the situations and female characters in the novels. She concludes that the girls perceive narrow limitations of normality for female roles and that their challenging of this norm requires further study.

Kohl, Robin J. "Literary Responses of Ludic Adolescent Readers to Two Short Stories." Ed.D. diss. Northern Illinois University, 1997. 150 pp. DAI 58:3064A.

Extending previous reader-response research on stance and complexity of response, Kohl studies written literary response of ludic adolescent readers to two short stories, one assigned and one chosen by the participants. Fifty-four students in grades 6–8 engaged in the study, and their responses are analyzed for predominant stance (efferent or aesthetic), complexity of aesthetic response, complexity of literary response, and content of response. For the assigned story, Kohl observes that "a moderate positive relationship exists between aesthetic complexity and grade level," with the complexity level of responses increasing as grade level increases. A relation is also found between stance and gender, males responding with a predominantly efferent stance and females with a predominantly aesthetic stance.

Koning, Kim Coghlan. "Victorian Palimpsests: Feminist Editorial Readings of Elizabeth Barrett Browning, Charlotte Brontë, Christina Rossetti, and Lewis Carroll." Ph.D. diss. University of Michigan, 1997. 298 pp. DAI 58:1723A.

"The layers of composition and revision underlying published works constitute a palimpsest, the hidden layers of which illuminate the final product." In this dissertation Koning analyzes the manuscript versions of major works by Elizabeth Barrett Browning, Charlotte Brontë, Christina Rossetti, and Lewis Carroll to show "how the patterns of composition and revision reveal the author's shifting perspectives on gender and sex." She concludes in each case that the analysis illuminates the gendered aspects of the authors' development and of their published works and that the readings "point toward a feminist editorial theory."

Lee-Harris, Stephanie. "Every Family Has a Story: An Overview of Early Childhood Children's Literature on Contemporary Families." Ph.D. diss. Union Institute, 1998. 246 pp. DAI 59:720A.

Lee-Harris's study supports the idea that "providing young children with literature that depicts their own world is beneficial to their social and emotional development. . . . It helps those who have trouble expressing themselves to be able to do so through reading, opens communication and dialogue between adults and children on topics that might be subject to censorship by parents, church, or school, and promotes an on-going appreciation and respect for books." She concludes that using picture books as a teaching tool in early childhood curricula enables young children to construct meaning from life around them and that they can acquire an understanding of others, explore their own feelings, and develop self-esteem by seeing their world reflected in both the written world and in illustrations.

Le Roux, Marlene. "Ernst Wiechert's Literary Fairy Tales in Comparison to the Folk Tales of the Grimm Brothers." D.Litt., University of Pretoria, 1997. N.p. DAI 58: 4287A. In German.

  Le Roux compares the two hundred folk fairy tales collected by the Grimm brothers and the forty literary tales of Ernst Weichert. Weichert's fairy tales show that his choice of title, theme, motif, content, stylistic elements, and composition clearly correspond to the folktale. Le Roux also demonstrates how Weichert deviates from and develops the traditional folktale significantly in his treatment of main characters' use of realistic detail and the importance of the hero's pure heart, and by his use of personal symbols and miracles.

Liu, Fiona Feng-Hsin. "Images of Chinese-Americans and Images of Child-Readers in Three of Laurence Yep's Fictions." Ph.D. diss. Pennsylvania State University, 1998. 113 pp. DAI 59:1950A.

  Liu examines how the author Laurence Yep, as an image-maker for Chinese American children's books, creates cultural and ethnic images of Chinese Americans in his three novels, *Child of the Owl, The Star Fisher,* and *Ribbons,* and how, as an adult writer, he constructs the images of child-readers in these three novels. Grounded in the theoretical framework of writers as image-makers, this study closely examines how Yep's social, ethnic, and cultural experience influences his image-making process as well as his role as an image-maker, and how Yep's perception of the child as reader and the child as narrator is reflected in his role as image-maker. Liu suggests that exploring these two aspects of a literary text helps the reader understand the kinds of images that a writer makes and how the writer reflects his assumptions about different ethnic groups or different readers through those images.

Madura, Sandra L. "Transitional Readers and Writers Respond to Literature Through Discussion, Writing, and Art." Ph.D. diss. University of Nevada, Reno, 1998. 438 pp. DAI 59:1494A.

  This multiple case study traces the oral, written, and art production responses of four transitional readers to the picture books of Patricia Polacco and Gerald McDermott. Using a modified art criticism model that includes description, interpretation, evaluation, and thematic trends, Madura compares the children's interpretative comments in regard to both of the artists as well as their own artworks. She concludes that this study "supports classroom instruction that considers the picture book as a complete aesthetic object worthy of intense study that encourages children to engage in art criticism that expands their thinking of how art education plays an active role in their literacy learning."

McCrary, William. "The Fairy Tale Operas of Seymour Barab." D.A. diss. University of Northern Colorado, 1997. 215 pp. DAI 58:1146A.

  McCrary stylistically examines Barab's five fairy tale operas: *Little Red Riding Hood, Who Am I* (based on the Grimm Brothers' *The Goose Girl*), *The Maker of Illusion* (based on Hans Christian Andersen's *The Snow Queen*), *Snow White and the Seven Dwarves,* and *Sleeping Beauty.* Chapter 6 presents McCrary's conclusions concerning Barab's adaptations of the classic fairy tales, his compositional style with regard to these five operas for child audiences, and his importance to American classical music.

Nauman, April Diana. "Reading Boys, Reading Girls: How Sixth Graders Understand and Are Influenced by Fictional Characters." Ph.D. diss. University of Illinois, Chicago, 1997. 219 pp. DAI 58:1234A.

Nauman explores children's interpretations of the negative, patriarchal view of women in children's and canonized literature. She discovers that students relate best to fictional characters who share their life experience, values, key personality traits, and gender, and that most children want to read books about characters of their own sex. She concludes that children's books can be an important enculturating mechanism by which boys and girls learn the traditional gender roles of relationship-tenders and adventurers. She emphasizes that after choosing children's books critically, educators should encourage children to find ways of relating to characters who seem unlike them.

Neemann, Harold Peter. "Piercing the Magic Veil: Toward a Theory of the *Conte*." Ph.D. diss. University of Colorado, Boulder, 1998. 272 pp. DAI 59:840A.

Neemann proposes a "multidisciplinary theoretical approach to the complex phenomenon of the *conte merveilleux*, both as a seventeenth century narrative genre and as a subject of twentieth century international scholarship." His study examines the ways in which the seventeenth-century *mondain* authors of literary fairy tales have shaped the subsequent definition and reception of the genre, and he concludes that "the complexity of the *conte* poses many theoretical and methodological problems, which require (re)defining the genre in all its ramifications."

Pustz, Matthew John. "Fanboys and True Believers: Comic Book Reading Communities and the Creation of Culture." Ph.D. diss. University of Iowa, 1998. 558 pp. DAI 59:1636A.

This dissertation analyzes the variety of reading communities for American comic books, demonstrating that they function not just as separate entities but also as a broad culture. Pustz explains the worlds of these readers and examines how the comic books contribute to the construction of fan cultures. Beginning with an introduction to comic book culture and continuing through the history of the publishing format, Pustz includes a description of historical and contemporary reading communities and those centering on both mainstream and alternative comic books. The comic books themselves are analyzed, with special attention to how they work to define and limit their own audiences through "comics literacy: the deep knowledge of the medium, its history, and its genres that is needed to appreciate many of the stories."

Rappoport, Phillippa Ellen. "Doll Folktales of the East Slavs: Invocations of Women from the Boundary of Space and Time." Ph.D. diss. University of Virginia, 1998. 299 pp. DAI 59:509A.

Rappoport interprets doll folktales and their origins and places them within a cultural context using "data from life-cycle and agrarian ritual, as well as related artifacts, such as traditional icons, ritual embroideries, and nesting dolls." She hypothesizes that the doll tales are related to narratives from agrarian rituals held between the winter and summer solstices. On another level the tales also articulate the submersion and subversion of pagan traditions under the influence of Orthodox Christianity in the tenth century.

Rifkind, Bryna Beth. "The Palo Alto Children's Theatre (1932–1997): Theatre by and for Children." Ph.D. diss. New York University, 1998. 528 pp. DAI 59:1403A.

Rifkind charts the history of the Palo Alto Children's Theatre from its inception in 1932 to 1997, focusing on its artistic, social, and educational programs. Included in the study are profiles of the leaders, their philosophies, descriptions of the programs, and the role of the community in supporting this institution. Rifkind identifies three major components that have contributed to the longevity and success of the Palo Alto Children's Theatre: community support, stability in leadership, and high-quality programs and productions. She also includes an extensive appendix including reproductions of organizational documents, financial statements, production photographs, theater brochures, program flyers, facility sketches, outreach guides, letters, and news articles.

Robinson, Laura Mae. "Educating the Reader: Negotiation in Nineteenth-Century Popular Girls' Stories." Ph.D. diss. Queen's University of Kingston (Canada), 1998. 219 pp. DAI 59:2040A.

Coming from a cultural studies and feminist perspective that suggests that texts do not simply reflect but also construct reality, Robinson argues that Charlotte M. Yonge, Louisa May Alcott, and L. M. Montgomery educate their readers about the valuable skill of negotiation in their novels *The Daisy Chain, Little Women,* and *Anne of Green Gables,* respectively. She explores the authors' agency in negotiating the cultural scripts they have inherited, examines the contradictions inherent in their heroine's family lives, and traces the heroine's clever negotiations of contradictory gender identity in each of these works. She concludes with an examination of the sequels to these works to show that, "even while the heroine seems to retreat from the action of the stories, her agency continues to be underscored."

Rogers, Mark Christiancy. "Beyond Bang Pow Zap: Genre and the Evolution of the American Comic Book Industry." Ph.D. diss. University of Michigan, 1997. 212 pp. DAI 58:1783A.

Rogers proposes that comic books in America are produced in a particular environment that has been shaped by three factors: the evolution of the industry as a system of production, the changing culture of readers of comics, and the generic conventions of the comics themselves. He concludes that "the evolution of the comic book industry has been shaped by both social and material factors" and that "continuing dominance of the superhero genre, its centrality to the culture of comic book fans, and even the enduring structures of genre are all inter-related products of the social economic factors that have molded the industry."

Sagan, Alex Philip. " 'I Want to Go on Living Even After My Death': The Popularization of Anne Frank and the Limits of Historical Consciousness." Ph.D. diss. Harvard University, 1998. 388 pp. DAI 59:1730A.

Sagan chronicles and analyzes Anne Frank's private and public "history" up to 1960, examining events during her life and since her death. He focuses on the process by which the diary of Anne Frank, and the play and film based on it, were created and became "uniquely popular accounts of the experience of Jews under Nazism." He pays particular attention to "the development of public memory or historical awareness regarding the Holocaust in the United States, Germany, and the Netherlands." He shows that Frank's popularization "depended on limiting the depiction of her persecution (a notion that has been suggested by various critics but never demonstrated empirically)" and concludes that Frank's influence on historical consciousness is, therefore, "simultaneously substantial and ambiguous."

Sharpless, Geoffrey Parvin. "The Erotics of Culture: Masculinity and the Victorian Public School." Ph.D. diss. University of Pennsylvania, 1997. 205 pp. DAI 58:4283A.

Sharpless tests a pair of related premises: "The first . . . that the literary work of a group of prominent British writers, especially Thomas Hughes, Matthew Arnold, A. H. Clough, Lewis Carroll, and Anthony Burgess, owes an insufficiently appreciated debt to nineteenth century public school developmental narratives, especially those of Dr. Thomas Arnold's *Rugby.* Secondly, that when expressed as a function of Arnoldian pedagogy, this prosopography illuminates a significant map of masculine erotics in canonical western literature." He traces the formation of Arnoldian masculinity and how it is interpreted and developed by these authors, who experienced a shared school experience, and he concludes by demonstrating that Thomas Arnold fulfilled his desire to "write his pedagogy across the face of the modern world."

Silliman, Betty. "Four Girls Respond to Young Adult Horror Fiction." Ph.D. diss. University of North Dakota, 1997. 256 pp. DAI 58:3461A.

In this qualitative study, Silliman's analysis and interpretation of data focuses on the appeal of texts and the sociological implications of the reading experience. Four categories—race, social class, gender, and sexuality—are examined. Silliman concludes that both the texts and the responses of the readers did reflect the ideologies of the dominant group, the white middle class, whose members display gender and sexually appropriate behaviors. Evidence of ideological socialization as a result of the textual experience did not materialize in the data, however.

Silver, Anna Krugovoy. "Waisted Women: The Anorexic Logic of Victorian Literature." Ph.D. diss. Emory University, 1997. 207 pp. DAI 58:888A.

Silver argues that Victorian literature employs "the physical signs of the female body—hunger, appetite, fat and slenderness—to construct cultural ideals of womanhood and girlhood." She demonstrates that the widespread discourse concerned with the regulation of hunger in women reveals an "anorexic logic that makes discipline over the body and its appetites symbolic of femininity." She analyzes the treatment of women's bodies in the conduct books, beauty manuals, and other nonfiction of the period to show that slenderness was a sign of the "incorporeal and regulated female body." In evaluating the fictional works of Charlotte Brontë, Christina Rossetti, Lewis Carroll, Kate Greenaway, John Ruskin, and Charles Dickens, Silver explores how this view of women's bodies functions in Victorian novels, poetry, and prose. She argues that "one must not read literature as merely symptomatic of a 'diseased' culture": the literary works discussed here "not only reflect but helped shape Victorian ideology about gender and the body."

Smith, Stacia Ann. "The Exploration of Middle School Students' Interests in and Attractions to the Writings of R. L. Stine." Ph.D. diss. Ohio State University, 1998. 186 pp. DAI 59:1511A.

Smith's analysis of the nineteen novels of R. L. Stine's Fear Street novel series identifies elements found in young-adult literature: youthful protagonists, fast-paced plot action, adolescent viewpoints, absence of adult interferences, coming-of-age concerns, and pop culture trends. She finds that there are benefits for middle-school students who became avid Stine readers: adolescents' interest in the mystery genre and teen pop culture interactions helped in building their reading fluency.

Spiker, Thecla Marie Wagner. "Dick and Jane Go to Church: A History of the Cathedral Basic Readers." Ed.D. diss. University of Pittsburgh, 1998. 542 pp. DAI 59:1967A.

The purpose of this study is to trace the historical development of the Cathedral Basic Reader series (Dick and Jane), a special edition used to teach reading in the Catholic schools of North America. Spiker traces the development of the Basic Reader series and the Cathedral editions of these texts to answer questions concerning (1) the creation, development, and discontinuance of the Catholic Basic reader series, (2) the differences between the Basic and the Cathedral Readers, and (3) the changes to the Basic and the Cathedral Readers series within and across time periods—from the 1920s through the late 1960s.

Tarbox, Gwen Athene. "The Clubwomen's Daughters: The Collectivist Impulse in Progressive Era Girls' Fiction, 1890–1940." Ph.D. diss. Purdue University, 1997. 208 pp. DAI 58:4658A.

Tarbox traces the development and aims of the clubwomen's movement and includes an analysis of the movement based on issues of race and class. She describes the economic factors that led "culturally conservative book publishers to put aside their personal beliefs concerning women's rights in order to cash in on the lucrative girls' fiction market" and analyzes the way young girls used their purchasing power to "demand fiction that mirrored their desires for peer interaction and for success in the public realm." Authors discussed include Christina Catrevis, Jessie Graham Flower (pseudonym of Josephine Chase), Frances E. W. Harper, Emma Dunham Kelley, Irene Elliot Benson, Laura Lee Hope (pseudonym of Lilian Garis), Carolyn Keene (pseudonym of Mildred Wirt Benson), and Margaret Sutton.

Tolson, Nancy Deborah. "Black Children's Literature Got the Blues: The Aesthetic Creativity of Black Writers and Illustrators of Black Children's Literature." Ph.D. diss. University of Iowa, 1998. 177 pp. DAI 59:1576A.

Tolson examines black children's literature from the perspective of the blues aesthetic. After providing a general overview, she addresses specific areas of black children's literature, including its history, the scholars who have defined the blues aesthetic found within black culture, the blues aesthetic as it is displayed in the artwork for black children's literature, and blues poetry, including the work of Tom Feelings, that has been dedicated to black children. She argues that the blues aesthetic can provide a "powerful lens for seeing the value of Black children's literature and for tracing its connections to the roots of Black literature and Black culture" and concludes that "Black children's literature, too long overlooked, can assist children in their understanding of cultural differences and cultural similarities."

Torres, Mychelle Marie. "Understanding the Multiracial Experience Through Children's Literature: A Protocol." Psy.D. diss. California School of Professional Psychology, Berkeley-Alameda, 1998. 149 pp. DAI 59:3126B.

Torres addresses the lack of recognition of multiracial people in research, in media, and in discussions of race and ethnicity in schools. She examines common psychological dynamics that have been established in research literature and uses them to develop a children's book that conveys the intricacies of being multiracial. "The book is intended to help teachers, psychologists, parents, and children to generate conversations that examine the questions of race and ethnicity."

Vogele, Yvonne Alice. "The Reluctant Witches in Benedikte Naubert's *Neue Volksmaehrchen der Deutschen (1789–1792).* Ph.D. diss. University of Washington, 1998. 217 pp. DAI 59:2044A.

Vogele argues that Benedikte Naubert makes a personal statement regarding women's place in society in her fairy tales. She argues that Naubert, without openly attacking the status quo, challenges the sixteenth- and seventeenth-century view that unless a woman is a submissive, saintly wife and mother, she is an inherently evil, rebellious witch. She states that Naubert presents alternatives to traditional female roles through her reluctant witches' untraditional behavior and that Naubert saw "new hope and possibilities for women in the message of the Enlightenment and for that reason her fairy tales are a contribution to women's issues."

Ward, Annalee Ruth. "Unearthing a Disney World View: The Rhetorical Dimensions of Disney Morality in *The Lion King, Pocahontas,* and *Disney's The Hunchback of Notre Dame.*" Ph.D. diss. Regent University, 1997. 244 pp. DAI 58:3343A.

Ward asks, "What Disney version(s) of morality is (are) portrayed in the last three animated feature films, *The Lion King, Pocahontas,* and *Disney's The Hunchback of Notre Dame,* and what Disney worldview is consequently being revealed?" After examining each film using rhetorical criticism, he concludes, "Taken together, the moral messages reveal a postmodern world view and, because of their frequent contradictions, demonstrate a need for critical awareness."

Washick, James Stewart. "He Who Fears to Doubt: Doubt and Faith in George MacDonald's Major Verse." Ph.D. diss. University of South Carolina, 1997. 159 pp. DAI 58:889A.

This dissertation examines the value that George MacDonald placed on intellectual and spiritual doubt in the development of the Christian's faith. Focusing on MacDonald's poetry, Washick proposes that "MacDonald's beliefs about the nature of God, love, and faith are intertwined with his views on doubt, that the biographical events in his life had an effect upon how he viewed religion and how he presented these views during these periods, and that by looking at his poetry we can understand more about MacDonald and the Victorian society of faith which surrounded him." He includes an overview of influences on MacDonald's writings and discusses MacDonald's role as a literary figure, looking at the influence he has had on subsequent writers such as C. S. Lewis and J. R. R. Tolkien.

Weinstein, Paul Barry. "The Practice and Ideals of Education as Portrayed in American Films, 1939–1989." Ph.D. diss. Ohio University, 1998. 274 pp. DAI 59:1315A.

Weinstein's analysis of seventeen significant commercial films provides insight into American social history during the pivotal period 1939–89 and is guided by four dichotomies: individual vs. community, community vs. society, nature vs. culture, and change vs. stability. The study groups the films into three historical periods: 1939–45, when the teacher and school are portrayed as helping to build the new order of opportunity and class harmony; the 1950s and 1960s, when schools in films prepared youth for the Cold War and the strategies of counterinsurgency; and the 1970s and 1980s, which began with rebellion against Cold War consensus and concluded with a restatement of traditional values against a political background of resurgent conservatism. Weinstein concludes that "filmmakers have used the setting of the school and the characters of educators to explore stresses as the nation grappled with its new international power and . . . as society dealt with problem areas such as race, gender, and youth."

Westerlund, Blake Richard. "The Construction of British Masculinity in Adventure Fiction, 1883–1890: G. A. Henty, H. Rider Haggard, and Rudyard Kipling." Ph.D. diss. University of Tulsa, 1998. 266 pp. DAI 59:1587A.

Westerlund argues that adventure novels from the 1800s examined here "imprint a masculine paradigm on [their] readers." He investigates the role of an all-male hegemony (known as the dominant fiction) and how it flourished in the literature, art, and history of the era. "These novels of the 1800s rely on Thomas Hughes' *Tom Brown's Schooldays* (1857) as a masculine ideal to follow." The scope of the research is twofold: it explores current masculinity theory to see how particular men in the narrative are constructed, and it provides numerous readings of a wide range of texts, supported by historical research, to demonstrate the theories presented. He concludes with a chapter recording the impact of the novels of the 1880s on early twentieth-century constructions of masculinity.

Williams, Amanda Jane. "Providers' Perceptions of Public Library Storytime: A Naturalistic Inquiry." Ph.D. diss. University of Texas, Austin, 1998. 342 pp. DAI 59:1818A.

Williams examines how individuals who provide storytime in public libraries perceive what happens during storytime. Cross-analysis compares and contrasts the data from the individual case reports to experts' storytime models and situates the research findings in a broader framework—the theory of emergent literacy from a Vygotskian perspective. Data indicate that "storytime providers find pleasure in providing storytime and recognize that storytime is an important social experience for young children that facilitates learning." She concludes by conceptualizing a preschool storytime model for large groups and includes suggestions for further research.

Young, Debra Bailey. "'A Woman's Pen Presents You with a Play': The Influence of Drama and the Theatre on the Life of Louisa May Alcott." Ph.D. diss. Indiana University of Pennsylvania, 1997. 244 pp. DAI 58:4275A.

Young focuses on the fictional and dramatic adaptations of Louisa May Alcott and suggests that theater and drama, aspects glossed over by previous critics, comprise one of the greatest areas of influence on the life and writing of Alcott and create a motif that Alcott used to characterize her work. The dissertation includes Alcott's use of theater and drama in her juvenile stories, in her sensational stories, and in her adult fiction. Alcott is examined in terms of her historical setting, in terms of the theatrical history of 1830–1890, and in her search for self-expression through the use of theatrical terminology. Young argues that Alcott "consistently incorporates the elements of theater and drama in constructing her stories" and that by examining Alcott's work "we can see their importance in her writing and to her personally."

Also of Note

Al-Jafar, Ali Ashour. " 'Not Like Now': The Dialogic Narrative in the Educational Act." Ph.D. diss. Indiana University, 1998. 202 pp. DAI 59:1441A. Al-Jafar presents a study of Kuwaiti folklore.

Black, Kathleen Alison. "The Use of Children's Literature to Promote Anti-Bias Education: A Transactional Study of Teachers' Use and Student Response." Ph.D. diss. Syracuse University, 1997. 425 pp. DAI 58:4598A.

Bookout, Nannette Marie. "An Analysis of Children's Written Responses to Selected Literature." Ed.D. diss. Texas Woman's University, 1997. 150 pp. DAI 58:4599A.
    First, second, and third graders respond to forty-seven books from the Children's Choices list for 1993–94.

Broughton, Mary Ariail. "Early Adolescent Girls and Their Reading Practices: Reflection and Transformation of Subjectivities Through Experiences with Literature." Ph.D. diss. University of Georgia, 1998. 216 pp. DAI 59:1948A.
    Broughton examines reader response to a text about Hispanic characters and culture.

Cary, Stephen. "The Effectiveness of a Contextualized Storytelling Approach for Second Language Acquisition." Ed.D. diss. University of San Francisco, 1998. 208 pp. DAI 59:758A.
    Cary analyzes positive effects of a contextualized storytelling approach (CSA) on second language acquisition.

Chen, Ren-Fu. "Knowledge, Experience, and Perspectives of Teachers Toward Implementing Creative Drama in Taiwanese Kindergartens." Ph.D. diss. Pennsylvania State University, 1997. 186 pp. DAI 58:2466A.

Church, Gladdys Westbrook. "The Significance of Louise Rosenblatt on the Field of Teaching Literature." Ph.D. diss. State University of New York, Buffalo, 1998. 523 pp. DAI 59:110A.
    Church presents a bibliographic analysis of the work of Rosenblatt.

Colaresi, Judith McColl. "A Case Study of a High School Theatre Teacher: Planning, Teaching, and Reflecting." Ph.D. diss. University of Maryland, College Park, 1997. 270 pp. DAI 58:2047A.
    Colaresi uses the techniques of Stanislavski and Viola Spolin.

Daleas, Bryan Charles. "Children in the Roman World: Status and the Growth of Identity." Ph.D. diss. Indiana University, 1998. 214 pp. DAI 59:1557A.

De Cecco, Daniela Pamela. "Entre femmes et jeunes filles: Le roman pour adolescentes en France et au Quebec." [Between Women and Young Girls: Novels for Adolescents in France and Quebec.] Ph.D. diss. University of British Columbia, 1998. 264 pp. DAI 59:1561A. In French.
    De Cecco discusses novels and series written between 1930 and 1995.

Dougherty, Pamela S. "Reading Informational Tradebooks Aloud to Inner City Intermediate Fourth- and Sixth-Grade Students: A Comparison of Two Styles." Ph.D. diss. University of North Texas, 1997. 127 pp. DAI 58:4220A.

Ellington, William Ferrell. "A Serendipity of the Feminine: A Comparative Psychological Study of C. G. Jung and C. S. Lewis in Their Spiritual Quests." Ph.D. diss. Pacifica Graduate Institute, 1998. 187 pp. DAI 59:3055B.

   Ellington explores the possibility of concurrently sustaining Christian Orthodoxy and an awareness of psychological theories while examining the juxtaposition of these qualities in Jung and Lewis. He concludes that occasional convergences of theology and psychology are possible.

Fernadez, Melanie Catherine. "Emergent Readers' Responses to Read Aloud Stories and Stories Presented by a Computer." Ph.D. diss. University of South Florida, 1997. 200 pp. DAI 58:800A.

Fitzgerald, Robin. "Childhood Home and School Factors Related to the Development of the Reading Habits, Attitudes, Preferences, and Future Plans of Adult Avid Leisure Readers and Literate Non-Readers." Ph.D. diss. University of Alabama, 1997. 135 pp. DAI 58:2137A.

   Fitzgerald deals with the interaction of children, parents, teachers, librarians, and higher education.

Flint, Amy Seely. "Building Sand Castles and Why Ralph and Keith Are Friends: The Influences of Stance, Intertextuality, and Interpretive Authority on Meaning Construction." Ph.D. diss. University of California, Berkeley, 1997. 219 pp. DAI 59:771A.

   Flint discusses the use of "authentic literature" in the classroom.

Ford, Karen Sue. "An Analysis of Young Children's Attitudes Toward African-Americans Before and After Exposure to Literature About African-Americans." Ph.D. diss. Ohio University, 1997. 236 pp. DAI 59:727A.

   Ford examines the effects of reading literature about African Americans on primary-age children's attitudes toward African Americans. Conflicting results between the pretest-posttest and the students' journal responses lead Ford to suggest techniques to improve similar future studies.

Fuller, Mary Christine. "The Reactions of Young Adult Women to Negative Portrayals of Females in Film." Ph.D. diss. Fordham University, 1998. 199 pp. DAI 59:1391A.

   "High egalitarian attitudes were related to high comprehension . . . [and] frequent movie-viewing was related to low . . . comprehension."

Gioia, Barbara Emma. "Once Upon a Time . . . : A Collaborative Study of the Storybook Experiences of Three Deaf Preschoolers." Ph.D. diss. State University of New York, Albany, 1997. 238 pp. DAI 58:1640A.

Hansen, Cory Cooper. "Getting the Picture: Talk About Story in a Kindergarten Classroom." Ph.D. diss. Arizona State University, 1998. 260 pp. DAI 59:719A.

Kotapish, Sharon Ruth. "Native Culture Influence in Reader Response to Translated Literature." Ph.D. diss. Indiana University of Pennsylvania, 1997. 832 pp. DAI 58:3493A.

   Kotapish compares responses to translated literature in the United States, Bahrain, and two areas of Nepal.

Land, Lillian. "The Role of Talk in Kindergarten Children's Construction of Story." Ph.D. diss. Auburn University, 1998. 246 pp. DAI 59:78A.

Madura, Sandra L. "Transitional Readers and Writers Respond to Literature Through Discussion, Writing, and Art." Ph.D. diss. University of Nevada, Reno, 1998. 438 pp. DAI 59:1494A.

   Madura presents a multiple-case study that deals with the picture books of Patricia Polacco and Gerald McDermott.

Maguire, Maureen Reidy. "Uncovering the Hidden Curriculum in High School English: How Teachers' Questions of Moral Values Inform Classroom Discussion of Literature." Ph.D. diss. New York University, 1997. 248 pp. DAI 58:2056A.

Marchant, Jamie Laree. "Novel Resolutions: Revising the Romance Plot, the Woman's Movement and American Women Novelists, 1870–1930." Ph.D. diss. Claremont Graduate University, 1998. 232 pp. DAI 59:172A.

Marchant includes discussions of Louisa May Alcott, among others.

Martin, Jean Ann McNeil. "Teachers as Readers: The Relationship Between TAR Participation and the Use of Trade Books in the Classroom." Ed.D. diss. Wilmington College, 1997. 57 pp. DAI 58:415A.

Medows, Pamela L. "Effects of Reading Aloud on the Book Selections and Attitudes Toward Science of Third Grade Students." Ed.D. diss. Ball State University, 1997. 124 pp. DAI 58:3839A.

Medows reports positive effects.

Morefield, Kenneth Robert. "Why Christian Fiction? Expressing Universal Truth in a Relative World." Ph.D. diss. Northern Illinois University, 1998. 165 pp. DAI 59:1567A.

Morefield deals with the works of George MacDonald and C. S. Lewis, among others.

Mrazek, Jan. "Phenomenology of a Puppet Theatre: Contemplations on the Performance Technique of Contemporary Javanese Wayang Kulit." Ph.D. diss. Cornell University, 1998. 973 pp. DAI 58:4476A.

Pearlman, Joan P. "Teaching and Assessing Skills in a Fifth Grade Literature-Based Literacy Program." Ed.D. diss. Rutgers The State University of New Jersey, New Brunswick, 1998. 121 pp. DAI 59:123A.

Pearlman reaffirms the value of using literary, as opposed to basal, reading programs.

Rice, Peggy Sue. "Texts and Talk: A Close Look at Gender in Literature Discussion Groups." Ph.D. diss. Louisiana State University and Agricultural and Mechanical College, 1998. 184 pp. DAI 59:1893A.

Rice demonstrates the different responses to literature by girls and boys in same-sex and mixed-sex discussion groups.

Siddal, Jeffrey Lee. "Fifth Graders' Social Construction of Meaning in Response to Literature: Case Study Research." Ed.D. diss. National-Louis University, 1998. 178 pp. DAI 59:760A.

Smith, Sally Anne. "Texts, Transactions and Talk: Early Adolescent Girls' Construction of Meaning in a Literature Discussion." Ph.D. diss. New York University, 1998. 297 pp. DAI 59:1495A.

Discussing literature helps girls "to resist confirming gender expectations."

Voorhees, Susan C. "An Investigation of Children's Re-Enactments During Episodes of Storybook Reading as a Reflection of Parents' Mediating Styles." Ed.D. diss. Hofstra University, 1998. 159 pp. DAI 59:1511A.

Westbrook, Matthew David. "Invisible Countries: The Poetics of the American Information Community, 1891–1919." Ph.D. diss. University of Michigan, 1997. 319 pp. DAI 58:459A.

Westbrook deals with mass communication, comic strips, William Dean Howells, and L. Frank Baum.

Young, Shannon Elaine. "The Narcissism of the Imperial Encounter in the Works of H. Rider Haggard." Ph.D. diss. Claremont Graduate University, 1997. 186 pp. DAI 58:890A.

"The communities [Haggard] creates in remotest Africa are veiled opportunities to dramatize his concerns relating to the ills of English society."

Contributors and Editors

GILLIAN ADAMS is the former editor of *Children's Literature Abstracts* and the *Children's Literature Association Quarterly*. She plans to devote her retirement to further research on ancient and medieval children's literature.

PHYLLIS BIXLER, professor of English at Southwest Missouri State University, has published two books on Frances Hodgson Burnett and won the ChLA article award twice, for 1979 and 1994 articles in *Children's Literature.*

HAMIDA BOSMAJIAN is a professor of English at Seattle University. She has published widely about children, Nazism, and the Holocaust and is currently finishing a book-length study, *Sparing the Child: Young Readers' Literature About Nazism and the Holocaust: A Study in Grief.*

STEPHEN CANHAM directs the Undergraduate English Program at the University of Hawaii at Manoa, where he teaches children's literature, among other subjects.

JOHN CECH is the author of numerous books for children and, most recently, the novel *A Rush of Dreamers.* He is the director of the University of Florida's Center for the Study of Children's Literature and Media.

JUNE CUMMINS is an assistant professor in the Department of English and Comparative Literature at San Diego State University, where she specializes in children's literature. She has published essays on *Beauty and the Beast, Curious George,* Laura Ingalls Wilder, and Virginia Woolf. She is currently working on a book about children's literature and American national identity.

ERIC DAWSON is the co-founder and executive director of Peace Games, Boston. Using cooperative games, role-playing, and community service projects, Peace Games helps young people to become peacemakers in their own schools and communities. He has authored six curricula and teaching guides and dozens of evaluation reports, and he holds a M.Ed. in risk and prevention from the Harvard Graduate School of Education.

R. H. W. DILLARD is professor of English and chair of the creative writing program at Hollins University. The author of several scholarly books, he is also a novelist and a poet. His new verse translation of Aristophanes' *Ecclesiazusae* is included in the *Aristophanes,* 2 volume of the Penn Drama Series.

CHRISTINE DOYLE is an associate professor of English at Central Connecticut State University, where she teaches courses in children's literature, American literature, and women writers. She co-edited *Children's Literature* 21 and is the author of *Transatlantic Translations: Louisa May Alcott and Charlotte Brontë,* forthcoming from the University of Tennessee Press.

GREGORY EISELEIN is associate professor and director of graduate studies in English at Kansas State University, where he teaches American literature and cultural studies. He is the author of *Literature and Humanitarian Reform in the Civil War Era* and co-editor of the forthcoming *Louisa May Alcott Encyclopedia.*

RACHEL FORDYCE is a professor of English and dean of the College of Humanities and Social Sciences at Montclair State University and is the former executive secretary of the Children's Literature Association. She is the author of five books, on late Renaissance literature, children's theater, creative dramatics, and Lewis Carroll.

MARGARET R. HIGONNET, who teaches English and comparative literature at the University of Connecticut, co-edited *Children's Literature* for several years. With Beverly Lyon Clark she has co-edited a study of gender in children's literature and culture,

Girls, Boys, Books, Toys (1999). Her other interests include romantic women writers, nineteenth-century poetry, and the literature of World War I.

PETER HOLLINDALE is a reader in English and educational studies at the University of York. His many publications on children's literature include editions of J. M. Barrie's *Peter and Wendy* and *Peter Pan and Other Plays.* He is currently producing a series of essays on Beatrix Potter as naturalist and on environmental issues in the modern animal story.

ANDREA IMMEL is curator of the Cotsen Children's Library at the Princeton University Library. She has published notes, essays, and reviews on various aspects of eighteenth-century children's books. Currently she is overseeing the compilation of the three-volume printed catalogue of the Cotsen collection: the first volume, which comprises twentieth-century imprints A–L, appeared in 1999.

RAYMOND E. JONES teaches children's literature at the University of Alberta. He has published on such authors as Maurice Sendak, Philippa Pearce, Monica Hughes, and Peter Dickinson. He is co-author of *Canadian Books for Children* (1988) and author of *Characters in Children's Literature* (1997).

ELIZABETH LENNOX KEYSER teaches American and children's literature at Hollins University. Since 1994 she has edited *Children's Literature.* She is also the author of *Whispers in the Dark: The Fiction of Louisa May Alcott* (1993) and *Little Women: A Family Romance* (1999).

KENNETH KIDD is assistant professor of English at the University of Florida, where he teaches children's literature, American literature, and gender studies. This essay is part of a book in progress about boyology and its discontents.

PENNY MAHON is head of the humanities department at Newbold College, Berkshire, England. Her Ph.D. dissertation at Reading University (1998) was titled " 'Toward a Peaceable Kingdom': Women Writing Against War 1790–1825." She has an article forthcoming for the journal *Women's Writing* on a comparison between the antimilitarist rhetorical strategies of Anna Barbauld and Amelia Opie. She is working on an article on the role of women writers in the early nineteenth-century Peace Society journal, the *Herald of Peace.*

ELIZABETH MAYFIELD teaches in the Department of English at Montclair State University in New Jersey and is a collector of American, British, and German children's books. Her current research focuses on Lord Byron and his treatment of the Bluestocking Circle, as well as Native American fiction and mythology.

RODERICK MCGILLIS teaches in the English Department at the University of Calgary. He is the editor of *Voices of the Other* (1999).

PERRY NODELMAN is the author of a hundred or so articles and chapters in books about children's literature and of two books on this subject: *Words About Pictures: The Narrative Art of Children's Picture Books* and *The Pleasures of Children's Literature.* His latest novels for young adults are *Behaving Bradley* and, in collaboration with Carol Matas, *A Meeting of Minds.*

MARILYNN OLSON, editor of the *Children's Literature Association Quarterly* from 1996 to 2000, teaches at Southwest Texas State University.

JULIE PFEIFFER is assistant professor of English at Hollins University, where she teaches courses in children's and British literature, Milton, and women's studies. She is currently writing on gender theory and children's literature, and is delighted to be editing *Children's Literature.*

ANNE K. PHILLIPS is an associate professor of English at Kansas State University. Her research focuses on nineteenth- and twentieth-century American children's literature. She is the co-editor of *Children's Literature* 21 and *The Louisa May Alcott Encyclopedia.*

JOSEPH STANTON, an associate professor of arts and humanities at the University of Hawai'i at Manoa whose Ph.D. is from New York University, is working on a study of picture-book traditions in American culture. His recent articles include pieces on

Chris Van Allsburg, Margaret Wise Brown, Arnold Lobel, Barbara Cooney, Edward Hopper, and Winslow Homer. His most recent book is *Imaginary Museum,* a collection of poems.

DEBORAH STEVENSON is the associate editor of the *Bulletin of the Center for Children's Books* at the Graduate School of Library and Information Science, University of Illinois, Urbana-Champaign, where she also teaches children's literature. She has published articles on various aspects of contemporary children's literature.

JAN SUSINA is an associate professor of English at Illinois State University, where he teaches courses in children's literature.

ANITA TARR is an assistant professor of English at Illinois State University, where she teaches courses in adolescent literature and children's literature, including children's poetry. She has published articles on Esther Forbes, Marjorie Kinnan Rawlings, and Scott O'Dell and is working on a study of the children's *Künstlerroman.*

THOMAS TRAVISANO, professor of English at Hartwick College, is the author of *Elizabeth Bishop: Her Artistic Development* (1988) and *Midcentury Quartet: Bishop, Lowell, Jarrell, Berryman and the Making of a Postmodern Aesthetic* (1999) and the co-editor of *Gendered Modernisms: American Women Poets and Their Readers* (1996).

ROBERTA SEELINGER TRITES is associate dean of the College of Arts and Sciences and associate professor of English at Illinois State University, where she teaches children's and adolescent literature. She is the author of *Waking Sleeping Beauty: Feminist Voices in Children's Books.*

Award Applications

The Children's Literature Association (ChLA) is a nonprofit organization devoted to promoting serious scholarship and high standards of criticism in children's literature. To encourage these goals, the Association offers various awards and fellowships annually.

ChLA Research Fellowships and Scholarships have a combined fund of $1,000 per year, and individual awards may range from $250 to $1,000, based on the number and needs of the winning applicants. The fellowships are awarded for proposals dealing with criticism or original scholarship with the expectation that the undertaking will lead to publication and significantly contribute to the field of children's literature. In honor of the achievement and dedication of Dr. Margaret P. Esmonde, proposals that deal with critical or original work in the areas of fantasy or science fiction for children or adolescents will be awarded the Margaret P. Esmonde Memorial Scholarship. The awards may be used only for research-related expenses, such as travel to special collections or materials and supplies. The annual deadline for applications is February 1. For further information and application guidelines, contact the Scholarship Chair (see address below).

In addition to fellowships and scholarships, ChLA recognizes outstanding works in children's literature annually through the following awards. The ChLA Article Award is presented for an article deemed the most noteworthy literary criticism article published in English on the topic of children's literature within a given year. The ChLA Book Award is presented for the most outstanding book of criticism, history, or scholarship in the field of children's literature in a given year.

The Phoenix Award is given to the author, or estate of the author, of a book for children published twenty years earlier that did not win a major award at the time of publication, but that, from the perspective of time, is deemed worthy of special recognition for its high literary quality.

The Carol Gay Award is presented for the best undergraduate paper written about some aspect of children's literature. The annual deadline for applications is January 20.

For further information or to send nominations for any of the awards, contact the Children's Literature Association, P.O. Box 138, Battle Creek, MI 49016-0138, phone 616 965-8180; fax 616 965-3568; or by e-mail chla@mlc.lib.mi.us. This information is also at our web site, address http://ebbs.english.vt.edu/chla.

Order Form   Yale University Press
P.O. Box 209040, New Haven, CT 06520-9040
Phone orders 1-800-YUP-READ (U.S. and Canada)

Customers in the United States and Canada may photocopy this form and use it for ordering all volumes of **Children's Literature** available from Yale University Press. Individuals are asked to pay in advance. All payments must be made in U.S. dollars. We honor both MasterCard and VISA. Checks should be made payable to Yale University Press.

Prices given are 2000 list prices for the United States and are subject to change without notice. A shipping charge of $3.50 for the U.S. and $5.00 for Canada is to be added to each order, and Connecticut residents must pay a sales tax of 6 percent.

Qty.	Volume	Price	Total amount	Qty.	Volume	Price	Total amount
____	10 (cloth)	$50.00	_____	____	21 (cloth)	$50.00	_____
____	11 (cloth)	$50.00	_____	____	21 (paper)	$18.00	_____
____	12 (cloth)	$50.00	_____	____	22 (cloth)	$50.00	_____
____	13 (cloth)	$50.00	_____	____	22 (paper)	$18.00	_____
____	14 (cloth)	$50.00	_____	____	23 (cloth)	$50.00	_____
____	15 (cloth)	$50.00	_____	____	23 (paper)	$18.00	_____
____	15 (paper)	$18.00	_____	____	24 (cloth)	$50.00	_____
____	16 (paper)	$18.00	_____	____	24 (paper)	$18.00	_____
____	17 (cloth)	$50.00	_____	____	25 (cloth)	$50.00	_____
____	17 (paper)	$18.00	_____	____	25 (paper)	$18.00	_____
____	18 (cloth)	$50.00	_____	____	26 (cloth)	$50.00	_____
____	18 (paper)	$18.00	_____	____	26 (paper)	$18.00	_____
____	19 (cloth)	$50.00	_____	____	27 (cloth)	$50.00	_____
____	19 (paper)	$18.00	_____	____	27 (paper)	$18.00	_____
____	20 (cloth)	$50.00	_____	____	28 (cloth)	$50.00	_____
____	20 (paper)	$18.00	_____	____	28 (paper)	$18.00	_____

Payment of $_____ is enclosed (including sales tax if applicable).

MasterCard no. _____

4-digit bank no. _____ Expiration date _____

VISA no. _____ Expiration date _____

Signature _____

SHIP TO: _____

_____

_____

See the next page for ordering issues from Yale University Press, London. Volumes out of stock in New Haven may be available from the London office.

Volumes 1–7 of **Children's Literature** can be obtained directly from John C. Wandell, The Children's Literature Foundation, P.O. Box 370, Windham Center, Conn. 06280.

Order Form   Yale University Press, 23 Pond Street, Hampstead, London NW3 2PN, England

Customers in the United Kingdom, Europe, and the British Commonwealth may photocopy this form and use it for ordering all volumes of **Children's Literature** available from Yale University Press. Individuals are asked to pay in advance. We honour Access, VISA, and American Express accounts. Cheques should be made payable to Yale University Press.

The prices given are 2000 list prices for the United Kingdom and are subject to change. A post and packing charge of £1.95 is to be added to each order.

Qty.	Volume	Price	Total amount	Qty.	Volume	Price	Total amount
___	8 (cloth)	£40.00	_____	___	18 (paper)	£14.95	_____
___	8 (paper)	£14.95	_____	___	19 (cloth)	£40.00	_____
___	9 (cloth)	£40.00	_____	___	19 (paper)	£14.95	_____
___	9 (paper)	£14.95	_____	___	20 (paper)	£14.95	_____
___	10 (cloth)	£40.00	_____	___	21 (paper)	£14.95	_____
___	11 (cloth)	£40.00	_____	___	22 (cloth)	£40.00	_____
___	11 (paper)	£14.95	_____	___	22 (paper)	£14.95	_____
___	12 (cloth)	£40.00	_____	___	23 (cloth)	£40.00	_____
___	12 (paper)	£14.95	_____	___	23 (paper)	£14.95	_____
___	13 (cloth)	£40.00	_____	___	24 (cloth)	£40.00	_____
___	13 (paper)	£14.95	_____	___	24 (paper)	£14.95	_____
___	14 (cloth)	£40.00	_____	___	25 (cloth)	£40.00	_____
___	14 (paper)	£14.95	_____	___	25 (paper)	£14.95	_____
___	15 (cloth)	£40.00	_____	___	26 (cloth)	£40.00	_____
___	15 (paper)	£14.95	_____	___	26 (paper)	£14.95	_____
___	16 (paper)	£14.95	_____	___	27 (cloth)	£40.00	_____
___	17 (cloth)	£40.00	_____	___	27 (paper)	£14.95	_____
___	17 (paper)	£14.95	_____	___	28 (cloth)	£40.00	_____
___	18 (cloth)	£40.00	_____	___	28 (paper)	£14.95	_____

Payment of £ _____ is enclosed.

Please debit my Access/VISA/American Express account no. _____

Expiry date _____

Signature _____ Name _____

Address _____

See the previous page for ordering issues from Yale University Press, New Haven.

Volumes 1–7 of **Children's Literature** can be obtained directly from John C. Wandell, The Children's Literature Foundation, Box 370, Windham Center, Conn. 06280.